gen circ

D0815054

Geological Survey of Canada
Miscellaneous Report 48

ROCKS AND MINERALS

FOR THE COLLECTOR:

Ottawa to North Bay and Huntsville, Ontario; Gatineau (Hull) to Waltham and Témiscaming, Quebec

Ann P. Sabina

2007

BOOK SOLD
NO LONGER R.H.P.L.
PROPERTY

©Her Majesty the Queen in Right of Canada 2007

Catalogue No. M41-8/48E
ISBN 0-660-19556-9

Available in Canada from the Geological Survey of Canada Bookstore
(see inside front cover for details)

A copy of this publication is also available for reference by depository
libraries across Canada through access to the Depository Services Program's
Web site at http://dsp-psd.pwgsc.gc.ca

A free digital download of this publication is available from GeoPub:

http://geopub.nrcan.gc.ca/index_e.php
Click on "Free Download".

Cette publication est aussi disponible en français.

Cover illustration

Pendant: almandine garnet cabochon set in silver. Cut and set by Jim Robertson, New
Liskeard, Ontario. The cabochon measures 12 mm by 10 mm. The garnet is from River
Valley, Ontario. Photograph by R.K. Herd, Geological Survey of Canada. GSC 2005-244

Almandine garnet crystal from Laniel, Quebec. Collected by Philip Anderson, Deep
River, Ontario. The crystal measures 38 mm from left to right. Photograph by R.K. Herd,
Geological Survey of Canada. GSC 2005-245

Author's address
Geological Survey of Canada
601 Booth Street
Ottawa, Ontario
K1A 0E8

**All requests for permission to reproduce this work, in whole or in part, for
purposes of commercial use, resale, or redistribution shall be addressed to: Earth
Sciences Sector Information Division, Room 402, 601 Booth Street, Ottawa,
Ontario K1A 0E8.**

Frontispiece: Justin Purdy, discoverer of the Purdy muscovite deposit, holding a muscovite sheet from the largest crystal he found in the main dyke, Purdy mine, 1942. Photograph by N.B. Davis, courtesy of the Canadian Institute of Mining, Metallurgy and Petroleum.

CONTENTS

Table

Figure

Maps

Plates

Abstract

Occurrences of minerals, rocks, and fossils are described from about 200 easily accessible localities on either side of the Ottawa River from Ottawa–Gatineau (Hull) to North Bay. They are reached by following Highway 17 in Ontario and Highway 148 in Quebec.

Most of the collecting localities are in Renfrew County, Ontario. A wide variety of minerals are found in this area, and some localities are known for the museum-type specimens collected from them. The earliest mines were the apatite and iron mines that were operated in the 1880s. Other deposits were subsequently worked for corundum, molybdenite, zinc, celestine, garnet, pyrite, beryl, marble, limestone, feldspar, rare-element minerals, and dolomite.

Numerous former feldspar mines as well as deposits of kyanite, garnet, muscovite, niobium, and brucite occur in the Nipissing District. Some of these deposits are accessible only by boat.

The region north of the Ottawa River between Gatineau (Hull) and Waltham was formerly mined for iron, mica, feldspar, apatite, uranium, molybdenum, lead-zinc, and limestone. A dolomite deposit is currently (2005) being operated. Occurrences of brucite, pyroaurite, szaibelyite, cordierite, scapolite, and asbestos are also known. Farther west, in the Témiscaming–Kipawa area, a wide variety of minerals include garnet, kyanite, and amazonite, and the rare-mineral suite of the Kipawa complex. In recent years, the Témiscaming area has been the scene of exploration for diamonds, and some diamonds have been reported from a location south of Lake Beauchêne.

Minerals and/or rocks that could be used for lapidary purposes include feldspar (peristerite, sunstone), rose quartz, graphic granite, and corundum from Renfrew County; feldspar (peristerite, amazonite), jaspilite, and graphic granite from the North Bay area; peristerite and cordierite from the Quebec side of the Ottawa River. Ordovician fossils may be collected from numerous roadcuts, rock outcrops, and quarries in the Ottawa–Pembroke and Aylmer areas.

Résumé

Le présent rapport décrit les venues de minéraux, de roches et de fossiles que l'on retrouve dans 200 sites faciles d'accès, situés des deux côtés de la rivière des Outaouais, depuis Ottawa-Gatineau (Hull) jusqu'à North Bay. On peut s'y rendre par la route 17 en Ontario et par la route 148 au Québec.

La plupart des sites de cueillette sont dans le comté de Renfrew, en Ontario. Cette région recèle une grande variété de minéraux; certains emplacements sont d'ailleurs reconnus pour la qualité des échantillons qu'on y a prélevés, qui est digne d'une collection de musée. Les plus anciennes mines sont celles où on extrayait de l'apatite et du fer : elles datent des années 1880. Des gisements de corindon, de molybdénite, de zinc, de célestine, de grenat, de pyrite, de béryl, de marbre, de calcaire, de feldspath, de lanthanides et de dolomite ont été exploités par la suite.

Le district de Nipissing compte beaucoup de vieilles mines de feldspath, de même que des gisements de kyanite, de grenat, de muscovite, de niobium et de brucite. Certains sites ne sont accessibles que par bateau.

On a jadis exploité le fer, le mica, le feldspath, l'apatite, l'uranium, la molybdénite, le plomb-zinc et le calcaire dans la région qui s'étend au nord de la rivière des Outaouais, entre Gatineau (Hull) et Waltham. Un gisement de dolomite y est actuellement (2005) en exploitation. Il existe également des venues de brucite, de pyroaurite, de szaibelyite, de cordiérite, de scapolite et d'amiante. La région de Témiscaming-Kipawa à l'ouest renferme un large éventail de minéraux, dont le grenat, la kyanite, l'amazonite et les minéraux des terres rares qu'on retrouve dans le complexe de Kipawa. La région de Témiscaming a en outre fait l'objet récemment de travaux de prospection à la recherche de diamants, lesquels ont d'ailleurs conduit à la découverte d'une venue au sud du lac Beauchêne.

Parmi les roches et les minéraux utilisables à des fins lapidaires, on compte le feldspath (péristérite et pierre de soleil), le quartz rose, le granite graphique et le corindon du comté de Renfrew; le feldspath (péristérite, amazonite), la jaspilite et le granite graphique de la région de North Bay; et enfin, la péristérite et la cordiérite du côté québécois de la rivière des Outaouais. Par ailleurs, un grand nombre de tranchées de route, d'affleurements rocheux et de carrières dans la région d'Ottawa-Pembroke et dans la région d'Aylmer se prêtent à la cueillette de fossiles ordoviciens.

ROCKS AND MINERALS FOR THE COLLECTOR: OTTAWA TO NORTH BAY AND HUNTSVILLE, ONTARIO; GATINEAU (HULL) TO WALTHAM AND TÉMISCAMING, QUEBEC

INTRODUCTION

This guidebook describes mineral, rock, and fossil occurrences from Ottawa to North Bay and Huntsville, Ontario, and from Gatineau (Hull) to Waltham and Témiscaming, Quebec. It is a revision of Geological Survey of Canada Paper 70-50 published in 1971. Occurrences in adjacent parts of Ontario and Quebec are described in the Geological Survey of Canada guidebook series of Rocks and Minerals for the Collector covering the following areas: Bancroft–Parry Sound area and southern Ontario (GSC Miscellaneous Report 39), Gatineau (Hull)–Maniwaki, Quebec and Ottawa– Peterborough, Ontario (GSC Miscellaneous Report 41); Sudbury–Winnipeg, Ontario and Manitoba (GSC Miscellaneous Report 49); Cobalt–Belleterre–Timmins, Ontario and Quebec (GSC Miscellaneous Report 57); Kirkland Lake–Rouyn-Noranda–Val d'Or, Ontario and Quebec (GSC Miscellaneous Report 77).

Most occurrences are accessible by automobile from the main highways and from secondary roads branching from them. A short hike and/or boat trip are needed to reach some localities. Directions to each occurrence are designed for use with official provincial road maps. Thirty mineral occurrence maps provide more information by showing the locations of many of the occurrences. Additional details can be obtained from the appropriate topographic and geological maps indicated for each occurrence. These maps are available from the agencies listed on p. 168.

Most inactive mines have not been operated for many years. Entering shafts, adits, and other workings is dangerous and should be avoided. Collecting in operating mines is at the discretion of the operator and may not be permitted; these mines are included in the guidebook as points of interest to collectors and students. Most occurrences are on private property or are held by claims; this guidebook does not authorize access nor imply permission to visit them. Permission must be obtained from the owner and the rights of property owners must be respected at all times.

The collecting localities were originally investigated in 1969 by the author ably assisted by Louise Bevington. Further investigations were made by the author in 1988, 1989, 1992, 1994, and 1995. The field investigation was facilitated by information received from M.R. Dence, Dominion Observatory; D.D. Hogarth, University of Ottawa; L. Moyd, G.W. Robinson, and T.S. Ercit, Canadian Museum of Nature; H.G. Ansell and R.K. Herd, Geological Survey of Canada; Bruce Campbell, Scarborough; Court Saunders, Brampton; Jurgis Urbaitis, Campbell's Bay; Adolf Vogg, Arnprior; and Adolph Zimmerling, Otter Lake. The identification of minerals by X-ray diffraction was done by M. Bonardi, A.C. Roberts, and R.N. Delabio, and microprobe analyses by J. Sterling, A. Tsai, L. Radburn, and D.C. Harris, all of the Geological Survey of Canada. Specimens shown in the photographs are from the National Mineral Collection. This assistance is gratefully acknowledged.

COLLECTING ALONG THE ROUTE

The main collecting route is from Ottawa to North Bay, Ontario, along Highway 17, and from Gatineau (Hull) to Waltham, Quebec, along Highway 148.

Side trips lead to the following collecting areas: Calabogie, Renfrew, Renfrew–McArthurs Mills, Renfrew–Madawaska, Eganville–Quadeville–Combermere, North Bay–Huntsville, Ontario; Shawville–Otter Lake and Témiscaming, Quebec.

Kilometre distances along the road logs for the main route and for the side trips are shown in bold print. The main collecting route and side trips are shown in Figure 1.

Information on each locality is listed systematically as follows: name of the mine, quarry, or occurrence; minerals and/or rocks found (shown in capital letters); mode of occurrence; brief description of the minerals or rocks, mining history, and special features of interest to collectors; location and access; publication references (indicated by a number listed in the 'References' section; references to maps of the National Topographic System (T) and to geological maps (G) of the Geological Survey of Canada (GSC), the Ontario Geological Survey (OGS), and Quebec's ministère des Ressources naturelles (MRNQ).

UNITS OF MEASUREMENT

Units of measurement obtained from publications referred to in the text have been converted from the Imperial system to the International System (SI). The following conversion factors were used:

1 inch = 2.54 cm	1 ounce (Troy) = 31.103 g
1 foot = 0.305 m	1 ton (short) = 0.907 t
1 mile = 1.609 km	1 pound (avoirdupois) = 0.453 kg
1 acre = 0.40469 ha	1 oz (Troy)/ton (short) = 34.285 g/t

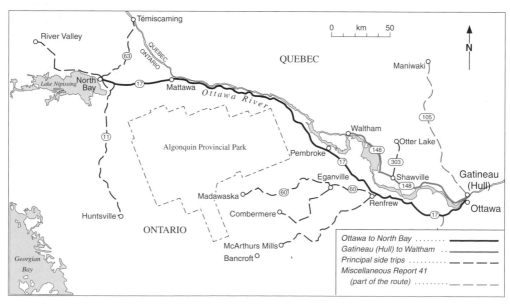

Figure 1. Map showing the collecting routes.

A BRIEF GEOLOGICAL HISTORY

Most of the collecting area is within the geological region known as the Canadian Shield — an immense shield-shaped body of Precambrian rocks occupying over half of Canada and part of the northeastern United States. Another geological province — the St. Lawrence Lowland — is represented in the region between Ottawa and Arnprior. This is an area of unfolded Paleozoic sedimentary rocks south of the Canadian Shield and north of Lake Ontario and Lake Erie.

During Precambrian time, repeated cycles of inundation, sedimentation, mountain-building, intrusion, and erosion produced a variety of igneous, metamorphic, and volcanic rocks. The rocks on both sides of the Ottawa Valley from Arnprior westward were formed during this time. The Precambrian rock formations contain deposits of feldspar, mica, apatite, molybdenite, pyrite, uranium, garnet, iron, gold, celestine, and brucite.

At the close of the Precambrian Era, a long period of erosion reduced the shield to a nearly featureless plain and set the stage for uplift, inundation, and deposition that took place during the long Paleozoic Era that followed. Paleozoic seas deposited great thicknesses of sediments over much of the shield, particularly along its margins including the St. Lawrence Lowland. These accumulated sediments, about 700 m thick, formed the existing sandstone and limestone deposits between Ottawa and Pembroke, and in the Aylmer (Quebec) area.

In more recent times — during the Pleistocene Period — great ice sheets spread southward across the shield and lowland areas, moulding the landscape as we know it today and leaving behind deposits of sand, gravel, and till. As the ice withdrew, marine waters flooded the Ottawa Valley and formed the Champlain Sea, which extended as far north as the Eardley Escarpment. Upon its retreat, the sea left unconsolidated deposits of clay and sand over the flat-lying Paleozoic strata. Other deposits of recent times include beach sands and stream detritus. The Bonnechère Caves are an example of an erosional feature of recent times.

The geological history with examples of rocks formed is summarized in Table 1.

OTTAWA TO NORTH BAY, ONTARIO

Collecting localities between Ottawa and North Bay are described following the road log. A page reference is indicated in parentheses following the names of each mine or occurrence.

The main road log is along Highway 17 in Ontario. It begins at the junction of highways 417/17 and 7, about 30 km west of the Parliament Buildings in Ottawa, proceeds west along Highway 17, and ends in North Bay. Along the route, several occurrences in the Calabogie and North Bay (Ontario) and Témiscaming (Quebec) areas are described as well as three major side trips to the Renfrew–McArthurs Mills, Renfrew–Madawaska, and North Bay–Huntsville areas. The Highway 17 road log is given in two segments: Ottawa to Renfrew (beginning below) and Renfrew to North Bay (p. 74). The kilometre distances along Highway 417/17 are shown in bold type.

Ottawa to Renfrew area – Highway 17 road log

| km | 0 | Ottawa, Highway 417/17 at the Highway 7 exit; the road log to North Bay proceeds west along Highway 417/17. Road logs to South March feldspar mine (p. 6) and March mica mine (p. 6) start 1.2 km east of this junction. |

Table 1. Rock formations referred to in text.

AGE (millions of years)	ERA	PERIOD	ROCKS FORMED	WHERE TO SEE THEM
65.5	Cenozoic	Quaternary	Gravel, sand Clay Peat	Lake and river shores and gravel pits throughout the area. Renfrew, Arnprior, Pembroke, North Bay pits. Meath and Westmeath bogs.
251	Mesozoic		Not represented	
		Permian Pennsylvanian Mississippian Devonian Silurian	Not represented	
	Paleozoic	Ordovician	Limestone	Highway 17 roadcuts between Ottawa and Pembroke; Bonnéchere Caves and nearby quarries; Deschênes, Lavigne, Pembroke, Pakenham quarries; Deux Rivières, Mattawa outliers.
		Ordovician or Cambrian	Sandstone	MacMillan quarry, Highway 17 outcrops near South March.
542			Granite pegmatite	Feldspar quarries at South March, Madawaska, Caribou Lake, Cecebe Lake, Waltham; Quadeville beryl, rose quartz mines; Hunt mine; Sairs Lake occurrence.
			Crystalline limestone	Highway 132 roadcuts; Bryson roadcuts; Jamieson, Biederman, Carswell, Foresters Falls quarries; Virgin Lake celestine occurrence; Renprior, Hunt mines.
			Dolomitic crystalline limestone	Portage-du-Fort, Legendre, Dominion Magnesium quarries. Hunt, Spain, Squaw Lake mines.
			Pyroxenite	Bluff Point, Radnor, Sunset, Ruby mines; River Valley garnet occurrence; Narco kyanite mine.
			Biotite gneiss	Renfrew quarry; Buckhorn mine.
	Proterozoic		Hornblende gneiss	Crocan Lake kyanite occurrence.
			Feldspar gneiss	Caldwell mine.
			Hornblende schist	River Valley garnet occurrence; Laniel garnet occurrence.
			Biotite schist	Moss mine.
			Syenite	Lount copper-garnet occurrence: New Calumet mine.
			Amphibolite	Craig mine; Jewellville, Gutz occurrences; Kipawa occurrence.
			Syenite gneiss	Craig, Burgess mines.
			Syenite pegmatite	Nipissing Black Granite quarry.
			Anorthosite	Golden Rose (Afton) mine.
2500			Iron-formation	

Precambrian

4

km	**8.5**	Junction, Highway 44/County Road 49 (March Road) to Humphreys feldspar mine (p. 7).
km	**19.6**	Junction, Breezy Heights Road to Currie barite occurrence (p. 8).
km	**23.8**	Junction, Lanark County Road 20 (at Antrim) to Pakenham quarry (p. 8) and Cedar Hill soapstone occurrence (p. 9).
km	**30.0**	Junction, Galetta Side Road (Carleton County Road 22) to Galetta celestine occurrence (p. 10), Kingdon (Fitzroy, Galetta) mine (p. 11), and Stanton lead occurrence (p. 12).
km	**35.5**	Junction, Highway 15 to Pakenham.
km	**38.1**	Junction, White Lake Road (Renfrew County Road 2) to Bell's mine (p. 13).
km	**40.0**	*Roadcuts* expose crystalline limestone containing finely disscminated amber mica and graphite. Cavities measuring up to 3 cm long are lined with microcrystals of quartz and calcite. Serpentine occurs as a dull green alteration of clinopyroxene. The crystalline limestone is cut by veins of pink to white calcite that fluoresces pink when exposed to ultraviolet light.
km	**41.4**	Junction, Campbell Drive.
km	**41.5–42.9**	*Roadcuts* expose grey crystalline limestone containing disseminations of amber mica, pyrite, and graphite. Grains of orange-brown tourmaline and white talc occur with light green prismatic aggregates of tremolite--actinolite and greyish-green clinopyroxene in coarse crystalline limestone containing lenses of pink calcite.
km	**49.5**	Junction, Highway 508 to collecting localities in the Calabogie area: Bluff Point mine (p. 14), Calabogie iron mine (p. 14), Blithfield (Caldwell) mine (p. 16), Clyde Forks mine (p. 17), Radenhurst and Caldwell mine (p. 18), Virgin (Dempseys) Lake celestine mine (p. 19), Tatlock Angelstone quarry (p. 21), Tatlock Omega quarry (p. 21), and Black Donald mine (p. 22).
km	**49.6–55.2**	*Roadcuts* expose biotite granite containing grains of titanite, magnetite, and pyrite.
km	**55.6**	Junction, Goshen Road.
km	**57.6**	*Roadcuts* expose crystalline limestone containing disseminated grains and aggregates of phlogopite, graphite, titanite, pyrite, hematite, magnetite, chlorite, talc, serpentine, white barite, yellow tourmaline, and blue anatase. The limestone encloses a vertical zone of white cleavable calcite containing light bluish-green massive clinopyroxene, serpentine, phlogopite, and pyrite. Large brown tourmaline (dravite) crystals up to 4 cm in diameter and pink apatite crystals up to 3 mm in diameter occur in this zone.
km	**62.1**	Junction, O'Brien Road (Highway 60) to occurrences in the Renfrew area (Jamieson Lime quarry (p. 24), Renprior mine (p. 25), Zenith (Phoenix) mine (p. 27), and Buckhorn mine, (p. 28)) and the Renfrew–McArthurs Mills (p. 29) and Renfrew–Madawaska (p. 42) areas.

The Highway 17 road log from Renfrew to North Bay continues on p. 74.

South March feldspar mine

MICROCLINE, QUARTZ, BIOTITE, TOURMALINE, CHLORITE, HEMATITE, PYRITE, MAGNETITE, URANINITE, CALCITE, FLUORITE, GOETHITE, GRAPHIC GRANITE

In granite pegmatite

Pink to orange-red microcline occurs with white quartz and biotite in pegmatite. Accessory minerals include black tourmaline, dark green chlorite, hematite, pyrite, magnetite, uraninite, calcite, and fluorite. Uraninite occurs as black nodules up to 1 cm in diameter. Goethite occurs as rusty yellow coatings on feldspar. Pink graphic granite is also present.

The deposit has been known since 1897. O'Brien and Fowler of Ottawa worked the mine for feldspar from 1919 to 1921. About 2700 t of feldspar for use as stucco was produced from a pit 40 m by 9 m and 9 m deep. Another pit, 15 m by 9 m and 6 m deep, was opened on the same dyke, about 500 m to the northeast. The pits were filled in 2002 and the dumps bulldozed. The mine is included in this guidebook for historic interest.

The mine is in Kanata.

Road log from Highway 417 at the Carp Road exit, 1.2 km east of the junction of highways 417/17 and 7 at **km 0** (*see* Highway 17 road log on p. 3):

km 0 Proceed onto the Carp Road North exit from Highway 417.

1.7 Junction; turn right (northeast) onto Richardson Side Road.

6.5 Junction, Goulbourn Forced Road; continue on Richardson Side Road.

6.55 South March feldspar mine, on left, at the northeast corner of the junction.

Refs.: 45 p. 238; 92 p. 220–221; 188 p. 36; 192 p. 165; 219 p. 20–22.

Maps (T): 31 G/5 Ottawa
(G): 414A Ottawa sheet (west half), Carleton and Hull counties, Ontario and Quebec (GSC, 1:63 360)
789 Parts of counties of Renfrew, Lanark, Lennox and Addington, Frontenac and Carleton (Perth sheet, No. 119), Ontario (GSC, 1:253 440)

March mica mine

PHLOGOPITE, CLINOPYROXENE, CLINOAMPHIBOLE, TITANITE, TOURMALINE

In pyroxenite

Phlogopite occurs as dark greenish-amber to almost black books in a pyroxenite vein in granite gneiss. The pyroxenite is composed mainly of greyish-green massive clinopyroxene. Green prismatic crystal aggregates of clinopyroxene, green prismatic clinoamphibole, and brown titanite grains also occur in the pyroxenite. Black prismatic aggregates of tourmaline occur in quartz-feldspar veinlets.

The mine was worked by A.G. Martin of Ottawa in 1923–1924. About 635 t of scrap mica were removed from an open cut 3 m wide and 4.5 m deep on the north side of the Carp Ridge. It is about 6 km east of Carp.

Road log from Highway 417 at the Carp Road exit, 1.2 km east of the junction of highways 417/17 and 7 at **km 0** (*see* Highway 17 road log on p. 3):

km	0	Proceed onto the Carp Road North exit from Highway 417.
	1.7	Junction; turn right (northeast) onto Richardson Side Road.
	4.4	Junction; turn left (northwest) onto Huntmar Road.
	7.0	Bridge over Carp River.
	7.3	Railway underpass. On the east side of the railway a path leads north to the Carp Ridge. Follow this path to the base of the ridge where an old road branches to the right (east); continue straight ahead along the path along the west side of the ridge, then along the north side of the ridge. The March mica mine is on the slope of the ridge near the base. The distance from the Huntmar Road is about 350 m.

Refs.:   187 p. 74; 192 p. 82.

Maps   (T):   31 F/8 Arnprior
         (G):   414A Ottawa sheet (west half), Carleton and Hull counties, Ontario and Quebec (GSC, 1:63 360)
         789 Parts of counties of Renfrew, Lanark, Lennox and Addington, Frontenac and Carleton (Perth sheet, No. 119), Ontario (GSC, 1:253 440)

Humphreys feldspar mine

MICROCLINE, ALBITE, BIOTITE, TOURMALINE, PYRITE, HEMATITE

In granite pegmatite

White to greyish-white and brownish-white microcline and colourless quartz are the main constituents of the pegmatite. The microcline is intergrown with albite producing a perthitic texture. Tiny colourless crystals of albite occur in small cavities in microcline. Biotite, black tourmaline, pyrite, and hematite are also present.

The deposit was worked for feldspar in about 1897. The feldspar was shipped to pottery works in Ottawa. Mr. Charles Humphreys was the owner of the property at that time. The mine is on the Carp Ridge in Carp on the property of C. Saunders.

Road log from Highway 417/17 at **km 8.5** (*see* Highway 17 road log on p. 5):

km	0	Junction, Highway 44 and Carleton County Road 49 (March Road); proceed onto County Road 49 leading northeast.
	3.5	Junction; turn left (northwest) onto Carp Road (Carleton County Road 5).
	4.9	Carp, at the junction of Donald B. Munro Road; continue straight ahead along Carp Road.
	7.2	Saunders property on the right (northeast) side of the road. The Humphreys feldspar mine is on this property.

Refs.:   92 p. 220–221; 174 p. 11; 192 p. 165.

Maps   (T):   31 F/8 Arnprior
         (G):   789 Parts of counties of Renfrew, Lanark, Lennox and Addington, Frontenac and Carleton (Perth sheet, No. 119), Ontario (GSC, 1:253 440)
         1363A Arnprior, Ontario (GSC, 1:50 000)
         P1838 Renfrew area, eastern part, southern Ontario (OGS, 1:63 360)

Currie barite occurrence

BARITE, CALCITE

In brecciated limestone

Barite occurs as white cleavable masses associated with white to greyish-white massive calcite. The barite-calcite masses cement angular fragments of brownish-grey limestone in a vein cutting Ordovician limestone.

The deposit was explored by two small pits in the 1880s. The pits are in a lightly wooded area on the west side of a ridge on the property of Terry Currie, about 18 km southeast of Arnprior.

Road log from Highway 17 at **km 19.6** (*see* Highway 17 road log on p. 5):

km		
	0	Junction of Highway 17 and Breezy Heights Road; proceed southeast onto Breezy Heights Road.
	1.1	Junction, lane leading north to the Terry Currie farmhouse and the Currie barite occurrence.

Refs.:   70 p. 26; 186 p. 49; 192 p. 19–21.

Maps   (T): 31 F/8 Arnprior
        (G): 789 Parts of counties of Renfrew, Lanark, Lennox and Addington, Frontenac and Carleton (Perth sheet, No. 119), Ontario (GSC, 1:253 440)
        1363A Arnprior, Ontario (GSC, 1:50 000)
        P2726 Arnprior-Quyon area, southern Ontario, Paleozoic geology (OGS, 1:50 000)

Pakenham quarry

FOSSILS, CALCITE, CHERT

In limestone

Fossils are abundant in Ordovician Black River limestone in this inactive quarry and in rock exposures nearby. The fossils include corals, cephalopods, trilobites, brachiopods, bryozoans, and cystoids. Chert and calcite are also present in the rock.

The quarry was in operation when William E. Logan, the first director of the GSC, examined the geology of the area in 1845. The quarry and nearby mill were then operated by Andrew Dickson. Logan reported cephalopods (orthoceratites) 45 to 60 cm long in the limestone along the Mississippi River in the vicinity of Dickson's mills, and noted that some contained yellow bituminous fluid. He described the limestone as being a clouded dark smokey or snuffy brown marble that took a good polish. Mr. Dickson set up grinding wheels driven by power from his mill to polish limestone slabs that were used locally as chimney and ornamental stone. Specimens of this brown marble were displayed at the GSC exhibit at the 1851 Grand Industrial Exhibition at the Crystal Palace in London, England.

The quarry produced limestone for road metal and for building stone. The stone was used in the construction of the five-span bridge over the Mississippi River in Pakenham. The bridge was built in 1901 and is said to be only one of its kind in North America. The largest single stone measures 2.7 m by 0.75 m square.

The Pakenham quarry is on the face of a hill at the east end of the bridge in Pakenham; it is on the east side of Lanark County Road 20 at a point 5.8 km southwest of its junction with Highway 17 at **km 23.8** (*see* p. 5).

Plate 1.

Limestone bridge over Mississippi River, Pakenham. GSC 153197

Refs.: 6 p. 83–85; 43 p. 11; 64 p. 111; 114 p. 62–63, 84–85; 115 p. 115; 216 p. 10; 217 p. 6; 218 p. 11; 219 p. 38; 221 p. 11.

Maps (T): 31 F/8 Arnprior
       (G): 789 Parts of counties of Renfrew, Lanark, Lennox and Addington, Frontenac and Carleton (Perth sheet, No. 119), Ontario (GSC, 1:253 440)
             1363A Arnprior, Ontario (GSC, 1:50 000)
             P2726 Arnprior-Quyon area, southern Ontario, Paleozoic geology (OGS, 1:50 000)

Cedar Hill soapstone occurrence

SOAPSTONE, CLINOPYROXENE, APATITE, MICA, SERPENTINE, PYRITE

In quartzite

Massive greyish- to brownish-white soapstone is associated with white dolomitic crystalline limestone. The soapstone is composed of talc with varied amounts of white to pink calcite and some colourless mica. The talc is an alteration of clinopyroxene. The prismatic form of clinopyroxene is preserved; the prisms are randomly oriented and produce attractive patterns on polished surfaces. This variety of soapstone is referred to as rensselaerite, which is slightly harder than most soapstone and takes a higher polish. Disseminated microcubes of pyrite and specks of hematite and goethite occur sparingly in the soapstone. The deposit also contains a dark greyish-brown, smooth-textured soapstone that takes a very good polish; the brown colour is due to inclusion of organic matter. The crystalline limestone associated with the soapstone contains disseminations of blue apatite, colourless mica, light green serpentine, white talc, and pyrite.

9

The deposit was opened by J. Bell of Almonte in 1937. The soapstone was to be used as a carving stone. The excavations consist of shallow pits on the farm of Ann and Carson Timmons, about 18 km south of Arnprior.

Road log from Highway 17 at **km 23.8** (*see* Highway 17 road log on p. 5):

km		
	0	Junction of Highway 17 and Lanark County Road 20; proceed southwest along Lanark County Road 20 to Pakenham.
	6.1	Pakenham, junction of Highway 15; turn left (south) onto Highway 15.
	11.7	Junction at a bend in the road; turn right onto Cedar Hill Road.
	16.1	T-junction; turn right.
	16.6	Turnoff (right) to the Timmons property and the Cedar Hill soapstone occurrence.

Refs.:   31 p. 678; 56 p. 179–182; 109 p. 174–177; 189 p. 79; 192 p. 195–196.

Maps   (T):   31 F/8 Arnprior
        (G):   789 Parts of counties of Renfrew, Lanark, Lennox and Addington, Frontenac and Carleton (Perth sheet, No. 119), Ontario (GSC, 1:253 440)
        1363A Arnprior, Ontario (GSC, 1:50 000)
        P2726 Arnprior-Quyon area, southern Ontario, Paleozoic geology (OGS, 1:50 000)

Galetta celestine occurrence

CELESTINE, CALCITE, QUARTZ CRYSTALS, SPHALERITE, MARCASITE, CHALCOPYRITE, CLINOAMPHIBOLE, PHLOGOPITE, GRAPHITE, PYRITE, HEMATITE, KAOLINITE

In crystalline limestone

Celestine occurs as small colourless to white tabular prisms and crystal aggregates in cavities in coarse white calcite. Also occurring in cavities are small scalenohedral crystals of calcite, prisms and rosettes of colourless quartz, and microcrystals of sphalerite, marcasite, and chalcopyrite. The calcite containing these crystals occurs as a vein in crystalline limestone. Grains of light yellow clinoamphibole, phlogopite, graphite, pyrite, and hematite are disseminated in calcite and in the host crystalline limestone. Kaolinite occurs as white finely granular compact patches on calcite.

The vein was explored by Claude McPhee of Arnprior in 1910. He sank a shaft to 13.7 m in an attempt to locate lead ore, which he failed to find. The old shaft and small dump are in a wooded area along the road leading to the Kingdon mine, just northeast of Galetta, and about 9 km east of Arnprior.

Road log from Highway 17 at **km 30.0** (*see* Highway 17 road log on p. 5):

km		
	0	Junction of Highway 17 and Galetta Side Road (Carleton County Road 22); proceed northeast onto Galetta Side Road.
	4.25	Junction; turn left onto Loggers Way.
	4.7	Junction, overgrown road on left. This road leads west about 10 m to the Galetta celestine occurrence.

Refs.:   186 p. 77–78; 192 p. 21; 224 p. 115–116.

Maps (T): 31 F/8 Arnprior
(G): 789 Parts of counties of Renfrew, Lanark, Lennox and Addington, Frontenac
and Carleton (Perth sheet, No. 119), Ontario (GSC, 1:253 440)
1363A Arnprior, Ontario (GSC, 1:50 000)
1739 Portions of Bristol, Onslow, McNab, Fitzroy, and Torbolton townships,
Quebec and Ontario (GSC, 1:63 360)
P1838 Renfrew area, eastern part, southern Ontario (OGS, 1:63 360)
2462 Renfrew, Precambrian geology (OGS, 1:100 000)

Kingdon (Fitzroy, Galetta) mine

GALENA, SPHALERITE, HEMATITE, MARCASITE, SELENITE, FLUORITE, BARITE,
CELESTINE

In calcite veins in crystalline limestone

This mine produced lead and zinc. Galena occurred as crystal aggregates, thin sheets, and grains
in white calcite. Brown sphalerite and hematite were associated with galena. Spectacular transparent crystals of selenite up to 30 cm long were recovered during mining operations. Fluorite,
barite, and celestine occurred with selenite. The deposit consists of two veins occupying fissures in crystalline limestone containing flakes of graphite and light amber mica. The main vein
is up to 3 m wide, over 825 m long, and was the source of all the production. The north vein is
about 0.75 m wide and about 500 m northwest of the shafts on the main vein; it was explored by
a long trench.

The deposit was found by a farmer alerted by the discovery of lead-bearing veins in eastern
Ontario in the 1860s. The original work was done in 1884–1885 by James Robertson who sank
a shaft 13.7 m deep. The galena ore was hand cobbed from the calcite matrix and shipped in
bags to Kingston for smelting. From 1914 to 1931, Kingdon Mining, Smelting and Manufacturing Company Limited mined the deposit from two new shafts 441.6 m and 68.6 m deep. A
concentrating mill began operations in 1915. In the following year, the company installed a
smelter using the newly invented Newmann hearth to refine the concentrates. This hearth
replaced the hand rabbler with a mechanical rabbler and resulted in eliminating severe muscular
labour and illness due to lead fumes and lead poisoning; it also increased the recovery of lead
from about 55 per cent to 96 per cent. The high-purity lead was poured into 27 kg moulds (pigs)
to produce pig lead for shipment. The mine produced 27 313 554 kg of pig lead valued at
$4 266 938, and 388 362 kg of zinc concentrates from 820 835 t of ore. During its period of
operation, it was virtually the only lead producer in Ontario, the only other production coming
from the cobalt-silver ores. The shafts are now filled and most of the mine dumps have been
removed. The mine is included in this guidebook for historical interest. The property belongs to
Donald C. Johnson of Arnprior; it is about 8 km east of Arnprior.

Road log from Highway 17 at **km 30.0** (*see* Highway 17 road log on p. 5):

km 0 Junction of Highway 17 and Galetta Side Road (Carlcton County Road
22); proceed northeast onto Galetta Side Road.

4.25 Junction; turn left onto Loggers Way.

6.0 Junction; turn left.

6.4 Junction, Kingdon (Fitzroy, Galetta) mine road on left. Obtain permission
from D.C. Johnson to enter the property.

Refs.: 2 p. 136–138; 21 p. 29–31; 27 p. 46; 72 p. 180–187; 186 p. 77–78; 224 p. 95–102;
225 p. 6; 226 p. 5.

Maps   (T):   31 F/8 Arnprior
        (G):   789 Parts of counties of Renfrew, Lanark, Lennox and Addington, Frontenac
                and Carleton (Perth sheet, No. 119), Ontario (GSC, 1:253 440)
                1363A Arnprior, Ontario (GSC, 1:50 000)
                1739 Portions of Bristol, Onslow, McNab, Fitzroy, and Torbolton townships,
                Quebec and Ontario (GSC, 1:63 360)
                P1838 Renfrew area, eastern part, southern Ontario (OGS, 1:63 360)
                2462 Renfrew, Precambrian geology (OGS, 1:100 000)

Stanton lead occurrence

GALENA, CALCITE, SPHALERITE, CLINOPYROXENE, SERPENTINE, TOURMALINE (UVITE), GRAPHITE, PHLOGOPITE, HEMATITE, ANATASE

In crystalline limestone

Galena occurs in calcite veins in white to grey crystalline limestone. The calcite is massive and contains some sphalerite, as well as cavities lined with calcite crystals. The crystalline limestone contains greyish-green clinopyroxene (partly altered to serpentine), orange tourmaline (uvite), graphite, phlogopite, hematite, and anatase.

This occurrence was first reported in 1847 by William E. Logan, the first director of the GSC, who examined the geology of the area in 1845. He reported that a galena-bearing calcite vein had been opened by three pits near the Galetta–Fitzroy road, about 3 km northeast of Galetta. One of the pits, on the John Marshall property, yielded 45 kg of lead ore, including fist-sized masses of galena. About 36 kg of ore were obtained by Mr. Hays and Mr. Henderson from their pits farther west on the same vein.

Further exploration on the vein was done in the 1890s. Mr. McFee and Mr. Gillies opened a pit, 7.6 m by 3 m and 3 m deep, on the deposit originally worked by John Marshall at the east end of the vein. Mr. Cowan opened two pits about 300 m farther west; one pit was 2.5 m square and 3 m deep, the other was 1.5 m square and about 1 m deep. In 1949, Stanton Lead Mines Limited did some work and drilling on the deposit. The work consisted of a shaft reported to be 21 m deep and several trenches extending over a distance of 500 m. The property belongs to Hugh Montgomery; it is about 10 km east of Arnprior.

Road log from Highway 17 at **km 30.0** (*see* Highway 17 road log on p. 5):

km   0   Junction of Highway 17 and Galetta Side Road (Carleton County Road
                    22); proceed northeast onto Galetta Side Road.

            4.25   Junction; continue straight ahead.

            5.35   Junction, turn right to the Montgomery property and the Stanton lead
                    occurrence.

Refs.:   21 p. 31–33; 43 p. 68; 114 p. 80–81; 224 p. 103; 231 p. 200–201.

Maps   (T):   31 F/8 Arnprior
        (G):   789 Parts of counties of Renfrew, Lanark, Lennox and Addington, Frontenac
                and Carleton (Perth sheet, No. 119), Ontario (GSC, 1:253 440)
                1363A Arnprior, Ontario (GSC, 1:50 000)
                1739 Portions of Bristol, Onslow, McNab, Fitzroy, and Torbolton townships,
                Quebec and Ontario (GSC, 1:63 360)
                P1838 Renfrew area, eastern part, southern Ontario (OGS, 1:63 360)
                2462 Renfrew, Precambrian geology (OGS, 1:100 000)

Bell's mine

HEMATITE, GOETHITE

In crystalline limestone

Fine-grained, compact, massive blue-black hematite occurs in brecciated crystalline limestone associated with bluish-grey to reddish dolomitic crystalline limestone. The hematite occurs in masses in a vein 1.5 to 1.8 m wide. It also occurs as pebbles, veins, and disseminated grains in tan-coloured breccia.

Hematite ore was discovered near White Lake in about 1865. James Bell of Arnprior prospected several locations on his 405 ha property on the east side of White Lake, north of Pickerel (Bennett) Bay, in the early 1870s. He made a number of openings on several veins, and these were known as Bell's mines. One of these mines is near Eggshape Bay (locally known as Egg Bay). Several pits expose the vein. The largest pit is 10.7 m by 1 to 4.6 m, and 1.8 m deep. About 12 m northeast of this pit, nine other variously sized pits are found in a zone 53 m long.

The mine is along the road to Eggshape Bay, White Lake, on the property of Duncan Stewart of Arnprior; it is about 21 km southwest of Arnprior.

Road log from Highway 17 at **km 38.1** (*see* Highway 17 road log on p. 5):

km		
	0	Junction of Highway 17 and White Lake Road (Renfrew County Road 2); proceed southwest along White Lake Road.
	12.5	White Lake village; turn left (southeast).
	21.2	Junction; turn right onto Peneshula Road.
	24.3	Junction; turn right onto Pickerel Bay Road.
	25.2	Junction; turn right.
	26.0	Overgrown road on right just south of a clearing. Walk east along the south edge of the clearing for 150 m to the Bell's mine pits in a lightly wooded area.

Refs.:   21 p. 91–92; 22 p. 129, 141–142; 43 p. 64; 51 p. 82–83; 149 p. 55–56; 150 p. 37–38; 180 p. 249.

Maps   (T):   31 F/7 Renfrew
(G):   789 Parts of counties of Renfrew, Lanark, Lennox and Addington, Frontenac and Carleton (Perth sheet, No. 119), Ontario (GSC, 1:253 440)
1046A Renfrew, Renfrew and Lanark counties, Ontario (GSC, 1:63 360)
P1838 Renfrew area, eastern part, southern Ontario (OGS, 1:63 360)
1956-4 Clarendon-Dalhousie-Darling area, counties of Frontenac and Lanark (OGS, 1:63 360)
2462 Renfrew, Precambrian geology (OGS, 1:100 000)

Calabogie area

The starting point for collecting localities in the Calabogie area is the junction of highways 17 and 508 at **km 49.5** (*see* Highway 17 road log on p. 5). The localities described are Bluff Point mine (p. 14), Calabogie iron mine (p. 14), Blithfield (Caldwell) mine (p. 16), Clyde Forks mine (p. 17), Radenhurst and Caldwell mine (p. 18), Virgin (Dempseys) Lake celestine mine (p. 19), Tatlock Angelstone quarry (p. 21), Tatlock Omega quarry (p. 21), and the Black Donald mine (p. 22).

Bluff Point mine

MAGNETITE, ACTINOLITE, CHLORITE, PYRITE, CHALCOPYRITE

At the contact of crystalline limestone and hornblende gneiss

Magnetite, the ore mineral, occurs as finely granular compact masses. It is associated with masses of silvery green foliated chlorite and dull green bladed actinolite. Pyrite, chalcopyrite, calcite, and quartz are present in small amounts.

The deposit was worked for iron intermittently from 1881 to 1901. The openings consist of four shafts and several open pits, now overgrown. The deepest shaft is 90 m deep. Algoma Ore Properties Limited did some diamond drilling on the deposit in 1952. Small dumps are adjacent to the workings.

The mine is on the north side of Grassy Bay, Calabogie Lake, about 1 km south of Calabogie. *See* Map 1 on p. 15.

Road log from Highway 17 at **km 49.5** (*see* Highway 17 road log on p. 5):

km		
	0	Junction of highways 17 and 508; proceed onto Highway 508.
	22.0	Junction, Highway 511 in Calabogie; turn south onto Highway 511.
	23.6	Bridge over the Madawaska River.
	23.8	Junction; turn right (southwest) onto a single-lane road.
	25.0	East end of causeway. A trail leads southeast 300 m to the Bluff Point mine workings on a lightly wooded bluff. The workings extend over 300 m northeast from the end of the trail.

Refs.: 21 p. 64–67; 93 p. 55–57; 113 p. 129–130; 161 p. 25; 170 p. 56–57.

Maps (T): 31 F/7 Renfrew
(G): 53b Renfrew area, Ontario (OGS, 1:126 720)
789 Parts of counties of Renfrew, Lanark, Lennox and Addington, Frontenac and Carleton (Perth sheet, No. 119), Ontario (GSC, 1:253 440)
1046A Renfrew, Renfrew and Lanark counties, Ontario (GSC, 1:63 360)
P1838 Renfrew area, eastern part, southern Ontario (OGS, 1:63 360)
2462 Renfrew, Precambrian geology (OGS, 1:100 000)
GDIF 171 Bagot Township, County of Renfrew (OGS, 1:31 680)

Calabogie iron mine

MAGNETITE, PYRITE, PYRRHOTITE, CHALCOPYRITE, GOETHITE, HEMATITE, SPHALERITE, APATITE

In hornblende gneiss and schist

The ore mineral, magnetite, occurs in disseminated and massive forms. Associated with it are minor amounts of pyrite, pyrrhotite, and chalcopyrite. Goethite and hematite occur as coatings on magnetite and on the host rock. Orange sphalerite occurs as small granular aggregates in white calcite. Small crystals of colourless to light red apatite occur in the hornblende rock.

This mine is also known as the Campbell-Caldwell deposit. It was worked by several pits and trenches between 1883 and 1901. It was originally opened by Mr. Coe of Madoc; subsequent operations were by Hamilton Steel and Iron Company, T.B. Caldwell, Kingston and Pembroke Mining Company, and Calabogie Mining Company. A total of about 13 600 t of ore were shipped.

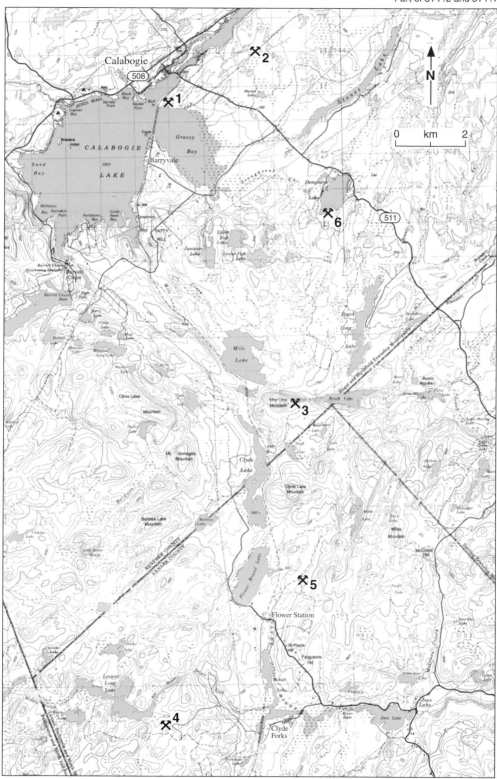

1. Bluff Point mine   2. Calabogie iron mine   3. Blithfield (Caldwell) mine   4. Clyde Forks
mine   5. Radenhurst and Caldwell mine   6. Virgin (Dempseys) Lake celestine mine

Map 1. Calabogie.

The mine is about 3 km east of Calabogie. *See* Map 1 on p. 15.

Road log from Highway 17 at **km 49.5** (*see* Highway 17 road log on p. 5):

km		
	0	Junction of highways 17 and 508; proceed onto Highway 508.
	22.0	Junction, Highway 511 in Calabogie; turn south onto Highway 511.
	23.6	Bridge over the Madawaska River.
	23.8	Junction, Bluff Point Road; continue along Highway 511.
	24.6	Junction; turn left (northeast) onto a single-lane road.
	25.5	Calabogie iron mine. There are pits on the left side of the road and additional pits extending northeastward to the northwest side of the swamp.

Refs.: 21 p. 67–69; 161 p. 30–32; 170 p. 53–54.

Maps (T): 31 F/7 Renfrew
     (G): 53b Renfrew area, Ontario (OGS, 1:126 720)
         789 Parts of counties of Renfrew, Lanark, Lennox and Addington, Frontenac and Carleton (Perth sheet, No. 119), Ontario (GSC, 1:253 440)
         1046A Renfrew, Renfrew and Lanark counties, Ontario (GSC, 1:63 360)
         P1838 Renfrew area, eastern part, southern Ontario (OGS, 1:63 360)
         2462 Renfrew, Precambrian geology (OGS, 1:100 000)
         GDIF 171 Bagot Township, County of Renfrew (OGS, 1:31 680)

Blithfield (Caldwell) mine

PYRITE, CALCITE, QUARTZ, PYRRHOTITE, ROZENITE, APATITE, TITANITE, ZOISITE

In hornblende-biotite schist

Pyrite was formerly mined from this deposit. It is massive and occurs with calcite and quartz. A small amount of pyrrhotite is associated with the ore. White powdery rozenite is found as an encrustation on specimens in the dumps. Apatite, titanite, and zoisite are also reported from the deposit.

The deposit was discovered in about 1885 by gold prospectors. It was not worked until World War I, which brought a demand for pyrite. Mr. T.B. Caldwell, the original operator, worked the deposit from 1915 until 1917 when the Grasselli Chemical Company of Hamilton took over operations until 1920. Mining ceased in that year but ore shipments were made until 1928. Canadian Pyrites Limited then acquired the property and continued shipments until 1930. The workings consist of two inclined shafts (23 m and 71 m deep) connected by a 140 m drift, and a few small pits. Specimens are available from the dumps adjoining the shafts.

The mine is about 11 km southeast of Calabogie. *See* Map 1 on p. 15.

Road log from Highway 17 at **km 49.5** (*see* Highway 17 road log on p. 5):

km		
	0	Junction of highways 17 and 508, proceed onto Highway 508 toward Calabogie.
	22.0	Junction, Highway 511 in Calabogie; turn south onto Highway 511.
	23.6	Bridge over the Madawaska River.

23.8   Junction, Bluff Point Road; continue along Highway 511.

24.6   Junction, road to Calabogie iron mine; continue along Highway 511.

26.8   Junction, road to Barryvale; turn right.

30.1   Junction; turn left.

33.3   Intersection of K & P Trail; turn left (south).

37.5–   *Roadcuts* expose amphibolite and quartz-amphibole gneiss containing
37.8   small pink almandine garnet crystals (4 mm across), pyrrhotite, and
        ilmenite.

39.9   Junction, single-lane road on left; proceed on foot along this road.

41.9   Blithfield (Caldwell) mine.

Refs: 21 p. 83–86; 170 p. 93–96; 223 p. 30–35.

Maps   (T):   31 F/2 Clyde Forks
        (G):   53b Renfrew area, Ontario (OGS, 1:126 720)
               789 Parts of counties of Renfrew, Lanark, Lennox and Addington, Frontenac
               and Carleton (Perth sheet, No. 119), Ontario (GSC, 1:253 440)
               P1838 Renfrew area, eastern part, southern Ontario (OGS, 1:63 360)
               2462 Renfrew, Precambrian geology (OGS, 1:100 000)
               P3093 Clyde Forks area, Precambrian geology (OGS, 1:50 000)
               GDIF 171 Bagot Township, County of Renfrew (OGS, 1:31 680)

Clyde Forks mine

TETRAHEDRITE, CHALCOPYRITE, PYRITE, PYRRHOTITE, GRAPHITE, HEMATITE,
AZURITE, MALACHITE, BARITE, TOURMALINE (UVITE), PYROXENE, TITANITE,
MICA, QUARTZ, PLAGIOCLASE, STIBNITE, ARSENOPYRITE, CHALCOSTIBITE,
GETCHELLITE

In crystalline limestone

Tetrahedrite occurs as finely granular masses associated with grains of chalcopyrite (also
microcrystals), pyrite, and pyrrhotite in white crystalline limestone containing amber and
colourless mica, graphite, quartz, and coarse pink calcite. Hematite occurs as an earthy alteration of pyrite, and as fine disseminations forming brown streaks in the rock. Azurite and malachite occur as irregular coatings on the ore-bearing rock. Barite is common as white masses;
small cavities in massive barite are lined with microcrystals of colourless barite. Tourmaline
(uvite) occurs as small yellow prisms and black granular aggregates in crystalline limestone.
Other minerals present include green pyroxene, titanite, and light yellow plagioclase. Stibnite,
arsenopyrite, chalcostibite, cinnabar, and getchellite have been identified in the ore.

The deposit was originally opened by T.B. Caldwell in 1918–1919; about 1 t of barite was
shipped to the United States. The deposit was investigated between 1964 and 1969 as a copper-
antimony-silver-mercury prospect by West Branch Explorations Ltd., who drove an adit about
30 m into the north side of a ridge. In 1969–1970, Carndesson Mines Limited investigated the
deposit. Specimens are available from scattered piles of rock near the adit.

The mine is about 4 km southwest of Flower Station and 18 km south of Calabogie. *See* Map 1
on p. 15.

Road log from Highway 17 at **km 49.5** (*see* Highway 17 road log on p. 5):

km		
	0	Junction of highways 17 and 508; proceed onto Highway 508 to Calabogie.
	22.0	Junction, Highway 511 in Calabogie; turn south onto Highway 511.
	26.8	Junction; turn right onto Barryvale Road.
	30.1	Junction; turn left.
	33.3	Intersection of K & P Trail; turn left (south).
	41.9	Junction, road on left to Blithfield (Caldwell) mine; continue straight ahead.
	44.8	Junction; turn left.
	45.0	Junction at Flower Station; the road on left leads north to the Radenhurst and Caldwell mine. Continue straight ahead to Clyde Forks.
	48.0	Junction; turn right. (This junction is 12.5 km west of Highway 511 at a point 19 km south of the junction of highways 508 and 511 in Calabogie.)
	49.2	Clyde Forks, at church; continue straight ahead.
	50.4	Junction; turn right.
	50.7	Junction; turn left onto Forest Access Road.
	53.9	Junction; follow main road on left.
	54.4	Junction; turn right.
	54.6	Junction at fallen shack; follow road on right.
	55.3	Clearing and single-lane road on left. Follow this road for about 400 m to the Clyde Forks mine.

Refs.: 21 p. 36–39; 33 p. 54; 147 p. 72–75, 106; 148 p. 40, 42–45.

Maps (T): 31 F/2 Clyde Forks
(G): 789 Parts of counties of Renfrew, Lanark, Lennox and Addington, Frontenac and Carleton (Perth sheet, No. 119), Ontario (GSC, 1:253 440)
1956-4 Clarendon-Dalhousie-Darling area, counties of Frontenac and Lanark (OGS, 1:63 360)
2515 Lavant area, Frontenac and Lanark counties (OGS, 1:31 680)
P2610 Precambrian geology, Lavant area, Frontenac and Lanark counties (OGS, 1:15 840)
P3093 Clyde Forks area, Precambrian geology (OGS, 1:50 000)

Radenhurst and Caldwell mine

MAGNETITE, PYRITE, JAROSITE

In hornblende gneiss and schist

Magnetite, the ore mineral, occurs with pyrite as disseminations in gneiss and schist. Jarosite occurs as yellow to rust-coloured earthy coatings on magnetite-bearing rock.

The deposit was opened sometime before 1899 by two shafts and several small pits, now over-grown. The deposit is on the Crosbie farm.

The mine is about 1.5 km northeast of Flower Station and 15 km southeast of Calabogie. *See* Map 1 on p. 15. The road log to the deposit begins at km 45.0 of the road log to the Clyde Forks mine (*see* p. 18):

km		
	0	From the junction at Flower Station (just east of the bridge over the Clyde River), proceed north along a gravel road.
	0.5	Junction; follow the road on right.
	1.0	Trail on right leads beyond a sand pit, then through a pasture to a Radenhurst and Caldwell mine shaft in a wooded area, about 90 m from the road. To reach the other shaft continue along the road.
	1.1	Junction; follow the road on right.
	1.6	Junction; follow the road on right.
	1.7	Another shaft is located to the left of the road, at a distance of about 45 m.

Refs.: 21 p. 104–106; 161 p. 47–49.

Maps (T): 31 F/2 Clyde Forks
(G): 789 Parts of counties of Renfrew, Lanark, Lennox and Addington, Frontenac and Carleton (Perth sheet, No. 119), Ontario (GSC, 1:253 440)
1956-4 Clarendon-Dalhousie-Darling area, counties of Frontenac and Lanark (OGS, 1:63 360)
P3093 Clyde Forks area, Precambrian geology (OGS, 1:50 000)

Virgin (Dempseys) Lake celestine mine

CELESTINE, DOLOMITE, CALCITE, PYRITE

In crystalline limestone

Celestine occurs as white fibrous to columnar radiating masses measuring up to 30 cm in diameter. Closely associated with the celestine is dolomite, which fluoresces yellowish white when exposed to long ultraviolet rays. Calcite and pyrite occur sparingly.

This deposit has been known since 1888. Mining from three open cuts was conducted from 1918 to 1921 and again in 1941. The openings are along the side of a small ridge and measure 1.2 m by 3 m, 21 m by 18 m, and 12 m by 3 m. A grinding plant was installed at the site during the early mining operations. The strontium ore had been intended for use in the refining of beet sugar and as a substitute for barite in the paint, paper, and rubber industries; it was found to be unsuitable for these purposes.

The occurrence is near the south end of Virgin (Dempseys) Lake, about 6 km southeast of Calabogie. *See* Map 1 on p. 15. The property belongs to Ronald and Marlene Camelon of Arnprior; obtain permission prior to visiting the occurrence.

Road log from Highway 17 at **km 49.5** (*see* Highway 17 road log on p. 5):

km		
	0	Junction of highways 17 and 508; proceed onto Highway 508 to Calabogie.
	22.0	Junction, Highway 511 in Calabogie; turn south onto Highway 511.

Plate 2.

Grinding mill at Virgin (Dempseys) Lake celestine mine, 1920. National Archives of Canada PA 13972

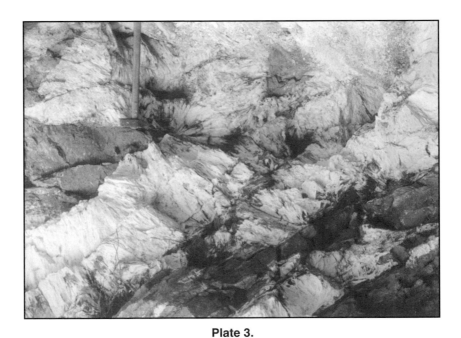

Plate 3.

Celestine in the face of a pit at Virgin (Dempseys) Lake celestine mine, 1919. GSC 46625

24.2   Junction, road to Bluff Point mine; continue straight ahead.

26.8   Junction, road to Barryvale; continue straight ahead.

29.1   Wagon road on right to the Virgin (Dempseys) Lake celestine mine.
        Proceed along the wagon road for about 1.5 km to a fork just beyond a
        small beaver dam; take the left fork and continue 35 m to the first open cut
        on right. The next and largest open cut is located 20 m farther down the
        road and a small pit is another 15 m down the road.

Refs.:   170 p. 111–113; 186 p. 80–82; 192 p. 21–24.

Maps   (T): 31 F/7 Renfrew
        (G): 53b Renfrew area, Ontario (OGS, 1:126 720)
              789 Parts of counties of Renfrew, Lanark, Lennox and Addington, Frontenac
              and Carleton (Perth sheet, No. 119), Ontario (GSC, 1:253 440)
              1046A Renfrew, Renfrew and Lanark counties, Ontario (GSC, 1:63 360)
              P1838 Renfrew area, eastern part, southern Ontario (OGS, 1:63 360)
              2462 Renfrew, Precambrian geology (OGS, 1:100 000)
              P3093 Clyde Forks area, Precambrian geology (OGS, 1:50 000)
              GDIF 171 Bagot Township, County of Renfrew (OGS, 1:31 680)

Tatlock Angelstone quarry

MARBLE

The deposit consists of white marble composed of coarsely crystalline calcite. There are small
amounts of light green and colourless tremolite, white granular diopside, quartz, and rare grains
of titanite and pyrite. The marble was sold under the trade name *Temple White* for use in interior
decoration.

The quarry was operated by Angelstone Limited from 1962 to 1971 for interior building stone.
William R. Barnes Company Limited worked the deposit for decorative marble chips and
calcium carbonate filler from 1977 to 1985. The property belongs to Steep Rock Resources Inc.

The Tatlock Angelstone quarry is on Lanark County Road 9, just west of Tatlock and 24 km
southeast of Calabogie. For access, *see* the road log to the Tatlock Omega quarry described
next.

Refs.:   80 p. 16; 91 p. 34; 191 p. 55–57.

Maps   (T): 31 F/1 Carleton Place
        (G): 1362A Geology, Carleton Place, Ontario (GSC, 1:50 000)
              1956-4 Clarendon-Dalhousie-Darling area, counties of Frontenac and Lanark
              (OGS, 1:63 360)
              P1980 Marbles of the Pembroke-Renfrew area, southern Ontario (OGS,
              1:126 720)

Tatlock Omega quarry

MARBLE

The deposit consists of marble in a belt 79 m wide between hornblende-biotite schist and
diorite-gabbro. The marble belt is zoned in several colour varieties including light blue, white to
light grey, pink, green, and light brown. Some light green tremolite and green clinopyroxene
occur in the marble.

The quarried area consists of several open cuts. The blue, white, and grey marbles were extracted from two open cuts on the western part of the marble belt; the main quarry is 20 m long, 15 m wide, and 11 m deep. Pink, green, light brown, and white marble occurs in a quarry about 25 m southeast of the main quarry. These quarries were operated by Omega Marble Tile and Terrazzo Limited from 1962 to 1971. Marble blocks weighing 10 to 15 t were extracted for use as a building stone. Since 1981 Steep Rock Resources Inc. has been quarrying the white marble and processing it at the company's plant just west of Perth. The plant produces calcium carbonate for use as fillers for the paper, floor tile, wall joint, paint, and plastic industries. It also produces aggregate and terrazo chips, stucco mix, poultry grit, and agricultural limestone.

The quarry is just north of Lanark County Road 9 west of Tatlock, and about 24 km southeast of Calabogie.

Road log from Highway 17 at **km 49.5** (*see* Highway 17 road log on p. 5):

km

	0	Junction of highways 17 and 508; proceed onto Highway 508 to Calabogie.
	22.0	Junction, Highway 511 in Calabogie; proceed south onto Highway 511.
	41.0	Junction, road to Joes Lake and Flower Station. The Clyde Forks mine and Radenhurst and Caldwell mine can be reached from this junction, which is 15.5 km from km 45.0 at Flower Station (*see* the road log to Clyde Forks mine on p. 18). The road log to the Tatlock quarries continues along Highway 511.
	50.9	Junction, turn left (east) onto Lanark County Road 9.
	52.5	Tatlock Angelstone quarry on left.
	53.3	Junction; turn left (north).
	53.5	Tatlock Omega quarry.

Refs.: 80 p. 16; 81 p. 64–68; 91 p. 34; 110 p. 374–375; 191 p. 74–76.

Maps (T): 31 F/1 Carleton Place
(G): 1362A Geology, Carleton Place, Ontario (GSC, 1:50 000)
1956-4 Clarendon-Dalhousie-Darling area, counties of Frontenac and Lanark (OGS, 1:63 360)
P1980 Marbles of the Pembroke-Renfrew area, southern Ontario (OGS, 1:126 720)

Black Donald mine

GRAPHITE, DIOPSIDE, TREMOLITE, SCAPOLITE, QUARTZ, MICA

In crystalline limestone

The graphite was greyish black, mostly compact massive with some flake variety occurring in pockets and stringers. White diopside, tremolite, scapolite, quartz, and mica occurred in crystalline limestone. The graphite ore zone formed a bed in crystalline limestone interbanded with quartzite and gneiss.

During its time of operation, the Black Donald mine was Canada's largest producer of graphite and North America's only producer of high-quality flake graphite suitable for lubricants. Graphite was discovered in 1889 on the John Moore property near the south shore of White Fish Lake (now Black Donald Lake), but it was considered to be uneconomic at that time. In 1895

Moore obtained the mining rights and prospected the deposit by opening several pits and trenches. He outlined a graphite vein 91.5 m long and 3.7 to 7.6 m wide; the northern part of the vein extended beneath the lake. Moore mined 426 t of ore, which he shipped to Ottawa to a mill built on the Ottawa River near Chaudière Falls. In 1896 the Ontario Graphite Company was formed to work the deposit. Fifteen miners worked the mine for four months in that year, recovering 571.4 t of ore that were processed at the Ottawa mill. The workings then consisted of three shafts, 24.4 m, 13.7 m, and 10.4 m deep, and three pits, 6 to 7.6 m deep. In 1902, the company sank a new shaft after a cave-in flooded the main shaft near the lakeshore, installed a mill at the mine site, and built a power plant at Mountain Chute on the Madawaska River, about 3.5 km southeast of the mine. The Black Donald Graphite Company Limited undertook operations in 1908. The company converted the main shaft to an open pit from which ore was recovered until 1916 when underground mining was resumed. A new mill was installed in 1917. In 1938 mining operations ended because the ore was thought to be depleted; graphite was recovered from the tailings for the next five years. Frobisher Limited mined the deposit from underground workings from 1944 to 1952, and from then to 1954 from an open pit. Production from 1896 to 1954 amounted to 77 243.75 t of graphite valued at $5 751 631.

The mine was located near the south shore of Black Donald Lake, about 17 km southwest of Calabogie. It was flooded when the Mountain Chute hydroelectric dam was built, and now lies beneath the lake. A plaque commemorating the mine occupies the site of the old Black Donald Mines village church.

Access is from Highway 17 at **km 49.5** (*see* Highway 17 road log on p. 5) along Highway 508 to Calabogie, then continue for 24 km along Black Donald Road to the Black Donald mine historic site.

Refs.: 17 p. 30–31; 18 p. 37–38; 24 p. 23, 46–49; 43 p. 69; 52 p. 22–25; 83 p. 45–56; 119 p. 47–48; 170 p. 43–46; 185 p. 35–38; 192 p. 55–58; 200 p. 36.

Plate 4.

Black Donald mine, 1914–1918. Harold A. Briggs/National Archives of Canada PA 94787

Maps   (T):   31 F/2 Clyde Forks
           (G):   53b Renfrew area, Ontario (OGS, 1:126 720)
                 789 Parts of counties of Renfrew, Lanark, Lennox and Addington, Frontenac and Carleton (Perth sheet, No. 119), Ontario (GSC, 1:253 440)
                 1046A Renfrew, Renfrew and Lanark counties, Ontario (GSC, 1:63 360)
                 P1838 Renfrew area, eastern part, southern Ontario (OGS, 1:63 360)
                 P3093 Clyde Forks area, Precambrian geology (OGS, 1:50 000)
                 GDIF 333 Brougham Township, Renfrew County (OGS, 1:31 680)

Renfrew area

Renfrew is the starting point for road logs to the Jamieson Lime quarry (p. 24), Renprior mine (p. 25), Zenith (Phoenix) mine (p. 27), Buckhorn mine (p. 28), and to occurrences in the Renfrew–McArthurs Mills area (p. 29) and the Renfrew–Madawaska area (p. 42).

Jamieson Lime quarry

TOURMALINE, TREMOLITE, TITANITE, SERPENTINE, PYROXENE, MICA, PYRITE, PYRRHOTITE, GRAPHITE, VESUVIANITE, FLUORITE

In crystalline limestone

Golden brown transparent tourmaline crystals measuring 2 cm in diameter are common in the limestone. They are generally too fractured to be used for lapidary purposes. Colourless, light green, and yellow tremolite crystals are also abundant. Other minerals identified from the deposit are titanite, as small dark brown grains, light green serpentine, deep green pyroxene, mica (muscovite and phlogopite), pyrite, pyrrhotite, and graphite. Vesuvianite and fluorite have also been reported. The limestone is white with grey to blue bands.

The quarry was formerly operated by Jamieson Lime Company for the production of lime. It measures 150 m by 75 m with a 10 m face. It is now partly overgrown and rock piles are scattered across the floor of the quarry. Two lime kilns were operated on the site.

The quarry is about 3 km southeast of Renfrew. *See* Map 2 on p. 26.

Road log from Renfrew:

km   0   Renfrew at the junction of Raglan and Hall streets; proceed southeast along Raglan Street. (This junction is 3.3 km from **km 62.1** on the Highway 17 road log on p. 5.)

              3.0   Junction; turn left.

              3.3   Gate to the Jamieson Lime quarry on right.

Refs.:   64 p. 169; 170 p. 103.

Maps   (T):   31 F/7 Renfrew
           (G):   53b Renfrew area, Ontario (OGS, 1:126 720)
                 1046A Renfrew, Renfrew and Lanark counties, Ontario (GSC, 1:63 360)
                 P1838 Renfrew area, eastern part, southern Ontario (OGS, 1:63 360)
                 P1980 Marbles of the Pembroke-Renfrew area, southern Ontario (OGS, 1:126 720)
                 2462 Renfrew, Precambrian geology (OGS, 1:100 000)

Plate 5.

Lime kilns, Jamieson Lime quarry, 1969. GSC 153196

Renprior mine

SPHALERITE, TREMOLITE, DIOPSIDE, PHLOGOPITE, APATITE, SERPENTINE, TALC, PYRITE, GALENA, GRAPHITE, PYRRHOTITE, HEMATITE, CHALCOPYRITE, TETRAHEDRITE, BARITE, ANHYDRITE

In crystalline limestone

Dark brown sphalerite occurs as granular aggregates in dolomitic crystalline limestone. It also occurs as brilliant crystals up to 2 cm in diameter. Bladed aggregates of light green, grey, and light brown tremolite and light green massive diopside are common. Other minerals present are phlogopite, light green apatite, light green serpentine, talc, pyrite, galena, graphite, pyrrhotite, hematite, and chalcopyrite. Tetrahedrite, barite, and purple anhydrite have also been reported.

The deposit was worked for zinc at various times since Joseph Legree discovered it in 1922. Shortly after the discovery, Legree and William Dean opened the first pit. Since then, about 50 openings have been made in an area 820 m long. Involved in the exploration were Coniagas Mines Limited (1935), Ottawa Valley Mines Limited and British Metal Corporation (1926), New Calumet Mines Limited (1947), Cadieux Mines Limited (1950), Renprior Mines Limited (1951), Novamin Resources Inc. and Eldor Resources Limited (1978–1985). The property currently (1995) is held by Breakwater Resources Limited.

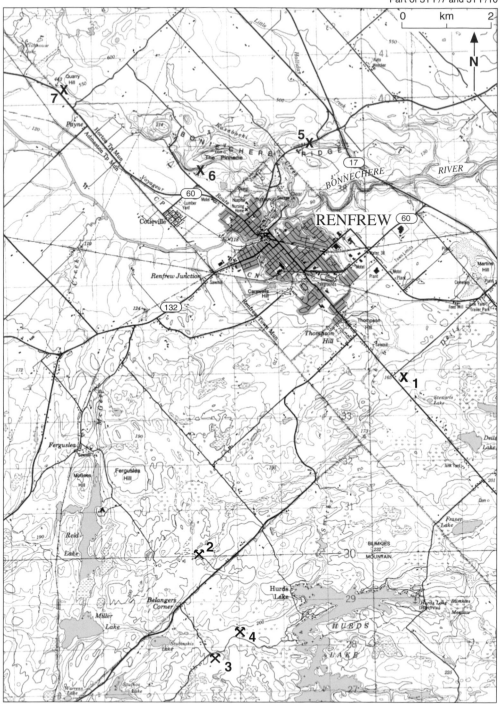

1. Jamieson Lime quarry   2. Renprior mine   3. Zenith (Phoenix) mine
4. Buckhorn mine   5. Renfrew County Road 4 (Bruce Avenue) roadcut
6. Highway 60 quarry   7. Jamieson marble quarry

Map 2. Renfrew.

The mine is about 7 km south of Renfrew. *See* Map 2 on p. 26.

Road log from Renfrew:

km	0	Renfrew at the junction of Raglan and Hall streets; proceed southeast along Raglan Street. (This junction is 3.3 km from **km 62.1** on the Highway 17 road log on p. 5.)
	1.8	Junction; turn right onto a gravel road.
	4.0	Junction; turn left.
	9.2	Junction, single-lane road; turn right.
	10.2	The Renprior pits extend in a northeasterly direction from this point.

Refs.: 2 p. 132–135; 21 p. 17; 150 p. 73–75; 170 p. 114–118; 181 p. 226; 183 p. 45–47.

Maps (T).   31 F/7 Renfrew
(G):   53b Renfrew area, Ontario (OGS, 1:126 720)
1046A Renfrew, Renfrew and Lanark counties, Ontario (GSC, 1:63 360)
P1838 Renfrew area, eastern part, southern Ontario (OGS, 1:63 360)
2462 Renfrew, Precambrian geology (OGS, 1:100 000)
GDIF 409 Admaston Township, Renfrew County (OGS, 1:31 680)

Zenith (Phoenix) mine

MOLYBDENITE, PYRITE, PYRRHOTITE, MAGNETITE, DIOPSIDE, CALCITE, BIOTITE, TITANITE, APATITE, SCAPOLITE, CHLORITE, SERPENTINE, TOURMALINE, ANHYDRITE, GARNET, MARTITE

In pyroxenite and pegmatite

Molybdenite occurs as coarse flakes measuring up to 5 cm across in pyroxenite skarn. It is closely associated with abundant pyrite and with smaller amounts of pyrrhotite and magnetite. Dark green diopside crystals (about 3 cm in diameter) occur with pink to white calcite and biotite. Less common are brown titanite (small grains), massive light green apatite, grey scapolite, chlorite, and serpentine. Black tourmaline is found in pegmatite. Anhydrite, garnet, and martite have also been reported from the orebody.

The deposit was discovered by William Warren while he was digging a well on his farm. The mineral rights were sold to Sir Henry Pellat in 1914. Between 1915 and 1917, 3500 kg of molybdenite were produced by A.W. Taylor and 60 kg by the Canadian Molybdenite Company. The Phoenix Molybdenite Corporation worked the deposit between 1934 and 1937; during this time, a two-compartment shaft was sunk to 62 m, a mill was installed, and 11 000 kg of molybdenite were produced. Subsequent operators were the Zenith Molybdenite Corporation (1938–1940) and Wartime Metals Corporation (1942–1943). In 1955, Goldyke Mines Limited examined the deposit for radioactive mineralization. The workings consist of a shaft, a pit 30 m by 5 m, and several small pits.

The mine is just west of Hurds Lake, about 8 km southeast of Renfrew. *See* Map 2 on p. 26.

Road log from Renfrew:

km	0	Renfrew at the junction of Raglan and Hall streets; proceed southeast along Raglan Street and follow the road log toward the Renprior mine. (This junction is 3.3 km from **km 62.1** on the Highway 17 road log on p. 5.)

	9.2	Junction, road to Renprior mine; continue straight ahead.
	10.3	Junction; turn left.
	11.7	Junction, single-lane road on left at bend; turn left onto this road.
	11.9	Fork; bear left.
	12.1	Zenith (Phoenix) mine.

Refs.:   21 p. 136–140; 37 p. 83–86; 52 p. 16–20; 98 p. 56; 112 p. 21–22; 126 p. 26–28; 150 p. 58–59; 170 p. 73–75.

Maps   (T):   31 F/7 Renfrew
        (G):   53b Renfrew area, Ontario (OGS, 1:126 720)
               1046A Renfrew, Renfrew and Lanark counties, Ontario (GSC, 1:63 360)
               P1838 Renfrew area, eastern part, southern Ontario (OGS, 1:63 360)
               2462 Renfrew, Precambrian geology (OGS, 1:100 000)
               GDIF 171 Bagot Township, County of Renfrew (OGS, 1:31 680)

Buckhorn mine

MOLYBDENITE, PYRITE, JAROSITE, AMPHIBOLE, TALC, GARNET, QUARTZ, SPECULARITE

In pyroxenite

Molybdenite, the ore mineral, occurs as flakes measuring up to 2 cm across. Massive pyrite is associated with it. Yellow jarosite is found as a powdery coating on ore-bearing specimens. Green massive amphibole partly altered to talc was found on the dumps. Garnet and vugs lined with alternating bands of smoky amethystine quartz, carbonate, and specularite have been reported from the deposit.

The property was worked by Buckhorn Mines Limited between 1939 and 1943. The workings consist of three pits (the largest is 7 m by 9 m and 5 m deep) and several trenches in two areas 535 m apart. The pits are water filled but specimens are available from small adjacent dumps.

The mine is about 700 m southwest of the Zenith (Phoenix) mine and about 9 km south of Renfrew. *See* Map 2 on p. 26.

Road log from Renfrew:

km	0	Renfrew at the junction of Raglan and Hall streets; proceed southeast along Raglan Street and follow the road log toward the Renprior mine. (This junction is 3.3 km from **km 62.1** on the Highway 17 road log on p. 5.)
	11.7	Junction, single-lane road on left at a bend; turn left onto this road.
	11.8	Junction; follow road on left.
	12.2	Trail on left leads to a Buckhorn pit in a lightly wooded area; continue along the trail to the main pit.
	12.7	Buckhorn mine main pit and dump to the left of the road.

Refs.:   21 p. 132; 98 p. 57; 150 p. 57; 170 p. 72–73.

Maps (T): 31 F/7 Renfrew

    (G): 53b Renfrew area, Ontario (OGS, 1:126 720)
      1046A Renfrew, Renfrew and Lanark counties, Ontario (GSC, 1:63 360)
      P1838 Renfrew area, eastern part, southern Ontario (OGS, 1:63 360)
      2462 Renfrew, Precambrian geology (OGS, 1:100 000)
      GDIF 171 Bagot Township, County of Renfrew (OGS, 1:31 680)

Renfrew–McArthurs Mills area

Collecting localities between Renfrew and McArthurs Mills are described following the road log. A page reference is indicated in parentheses following the name of each mine or occurrence. The starting point is in Renfrew, at the junction of highways 60 (Raglan Street) and 132 (Munroe Avenue). The collecting route is along highways 132, 41, and 28. Kilometre distances are shown in bold type.

Road log for collecting localities between Renfrew and McArthurs Mills

km	**0**	Renfrew, junction of highways 60 (Raglan Street) and 132 (Munroe Avenue); the road log proceeds along Highway 132.
km	**9.8**	*Roadcut* on right exposes crystalline limestone and pegmatite. Brown tourmaline, light brown amphibole, amber mica, pink calcite, graphite, pyrite, and pyrrhotite occur in limestone. Titanite, mica, and amphibole occur in pegmatite.
km	**18.8**	*Roadcuts* expose crystalline limestone with disseminated clinopyroxene, titanite, and pyrite.
km	**19.6**	Junction, Admaston Township Road 15 to Mount St. Patrick and Hunt mine (p. 30).
km	**22.4–24.6**	*Roadcuts* expose siliceous crystalline limestone containing disseminations of serpentine, titanite, clinopyroxene, graphite, pyrite, and pyrrhotite.
km	**27.8**	Dacre, junction of Mount St. Patrick Road to Dacre iron occurrence (p. 31).
km	**29.3**	*Roadcut* on left is similar to the roadcuts at **km 22.4** and **24.6**. White graphic granite is also exposed.
km	**30.4**	Junction, Highway 41. Highway 41 North leads to Keyfortmore mine (p. 32) and Radnor mine (p. 33). The road log continues along Highway 41 South.
km	**31.65**	*Roadcut* on the east side of the highway at the top of a long hill exposes crystalline limestone containing prismatic aggregates of mauve scapolite associated with light green clinopyroxene, white massive calcite, and colourless mica.
km	**34.9–39.6**	*Roadcuts* expose crystalline limestone containing graphite, amber mica, pyrite, pyrrhotite, clinopyroxene, apatite, titanite, light green to yellow and black clinoamphibole, pink calcite, and serpentine. Orange monazite grains in mica, pink zircon crystals, and black massive tourmaline occur in the roadcut at **km 39.6**.

km	40.5	Junction, road to Sunset mine (p. 34).
km	41.8	*Roadcut* on right exposes crystalline limestone containing amber mica, clinopyroxene, titanite, and reddish-orange garnet.
km	42.6	Junction, road to Spain mine (p. 34).
km	42.7	*Roadcuts* expose crystalline limestone and granite pegmatite. The pegmatite contains magnetite, pyrrhotite, amber mica, fluorite, serpentine, epidote, rutile, titanite, and hornblende. White heulandite and stilbite occur in fractures in the pegmatite. Crystalline limestone contains grains of magnetite, clinoamphibole, and pyrrhotite, and flakes of amber mica and talc.
km	52.9	Junction, in Griffith, of Hyland Creek Road to Jamieson molybdenite mine (p. 35), Easton Minerals quarry (p. 37), and Two Island Marble quarry (p. 38).
km	68.5	Junction, Highway 28. The road log proceeds along Highway 28.
km	82.2	Junction, road to Ruby mine (p. 39).
km	85.6	Junction, Bruceton Road to McCoy mine (p. 40).
km	102.4	McArthurs Mills, junction of Hartsmere Road to Mayo marble quarry (p. 41).

End of road log.

Hunt mine

MOLYBDENITE, PYRITE, PYRRHOTITE, PYROXENE, SCAPOLITE, HORNBLENDE, CALCITE, ROZENITE, SERPENTINE, DIOPSIDE, MICA, APATITE, TITANITE, OLIVINE, GRAPHITE, MAGNETITE, GRAPHIC GRANITE, STILBITE

In pyroxenite skarn at contact of crystalline limestone and pegmatite

Molybdenite occurs as coarse flakes in yellowish-green pyroxenite. Closely associated with it are pyrite, pyrrhotite, grey massive hornblende, and coarse smoky calcite. Yellowish- to smoky-green crystals of pyroxene up to 2 cm in diameter are common in pyroxenite. Rozenite occurs as a white powdery coating on rusty-weathered ore specimens. The crystalline limestone associated with the orebody contains the following minerals: charcoal-grey serpentine, pale yellow to light green diopside, amber mica, light blue apatite (uncommon), dark brown titanite, grey granular olivine, graphite, and pyrite. Magnetite occurs in pegmatite. Pink graphic granite composed of microcline and quartz is associated with pegmatite. Stilbite, as white platy aggregates, occurs with massive and crystalline pyrite.

This molybdenite deposit was discovered in about 1910 on Daniel Hunt's farm by his son Cornelius. A specimen was taken to the Black Donald mine for identification. Some time before 1914, a small amount of ore was mined from small pits. From 1915 to 1918, Renfrew Molybdenum Mines Limited operated the mine and a mill, producing 44 000 kg of concentrate, 85 per cent of which averaged 95 per cent MoS_2. The underground workings, now inaccessible, consist of an inclined adit leading to approximately 610 m of crosscuts and drifts, and two shafts. During mining operations 60 to 70 people were employed. Several open cuts extend over 18 m. Specimens may be obtained from the dumps.

The mine is about 25 km southwest of Renfrew.

Plate 6.

Hunt mine, 1919. National Archives of Canada PA 15760

Road log from Highway 132 at **km 19.6** (*see* the Renfrew–McArthurs Mills road log on p. 29):

km	0	Junction, Highway 132 and Admaston Township Road 15; proceed south on Admaston Township Road 15 toward Mount St. Patrick.
	5.3	Mount St. Patrick village, at church; continue straight ahead.
	7.1	Junction, road on right to Dacre; continue straight ahead.
	7.4	Junction; turn left.
	9.0	Junction; turn right.
	10.0	Junction; continue straight ahead (road on left leads to a fire tower).
	11.0	Hunt mine on right.

Refs.: 21 p. 144–149; 37 p. 89–94; 98 p. 58; 112 p. 24–25; 150 p. 61–62; 208 p. 146–150; 211 p. 47; 223 p. 36–41.

Maps (T): 31 F/7 Renfrew
 (G): 53b Renfrew area, Ontario (OGS, 1:126 720)
    1046A Renfrew, Renfrew and Lanark counties, Ontario (GSC, 1:63 360)
    P1838 Renfrew area, eastern part, southern Ontario (OGS, 1:63 360)
    2461 Barry's Bay, Precambrian geology (OGS, 1:100 000)
    GDIF 333 Brougham Township, Renfrew County (OGS, 1:31 680)

Dacre iron occurrence

MAGNETITE

In quartz-feldspar gneiss

Magnetite occurs as grains in quartz-feldspar gneiss. Pyrite is also present. A band of massive magnetite up to 5 cm thick has been reported.

The deposit was explored by a pit 7.6 m in diameter and about 7 m deep. The work was done by Canada Iron Furnace Company in 1901. About 50 years later, Algoma Ore Properties Limited examined the deposit (H.A. Legris, pers. comm., 1995). More recently, it was used as a garbage disposal site.

The occurrence is just south of Dacre on the property of Henry A. Legris of Renfrew.

Road log from Highway 132 at **km 27.8** (*see* the Renfrew–McArthurs Mills road log on p. 29):

km	0	Dacre, junction of Mount St. Patrick Road; proceed south onto Mount St. Patrick Road.
	0.4	Gate on right. A road leads west 45 m from the gate to the Dacre iron occurrence.

Refs.: 21 p. 87; 43 p. 64; 161 p. 35; 170 p. 89.

Maps (T): 31 F/7 Renfrew
(G): 53b Renfrew area, Ontario (OGS, 1:126 720)
789 Parts of counties of Renfrew, Lanark, Lennox and Addington, Frontenac and Carleton (Perth sheet, No. 119), Ontario (GSC, 1:253 440)
1046A Renfrew, Renfrew and Lanark counties, Ontario (GSC, 1:63 360)
P1838 Renfrew area, eastern part, southern Ontario (OGS, 1:63 360)
2462 Renfrew, Precambrian geology (OGS, 1:100 000)
GDIF 333 Brougham Township, Renfrew County (OGS, 1:31 680)

Keyfortmore mine

TOURMALINE, GRAPHIC GRANITE, MICROCLINE, PLAGIOCLASE, QUARTZ, MICA, GARNET, PYROXENE, TITANITE, ZIRCON, GYPSUM

In pegmatite

Black tourmaline crystals and pink graphic granite are abundant. The tourmaline crystals measure up to 5 cm in diameter and several centimetres in length. The graphic granite is medium textured and is suitable for lapidary purposes. Pink microcline, colourless to smoky quartz, and, less abundantly, grey plagioclase are the chief components of the pegmatite. Other minerals present include silvery to pale yellow mica, brownish-red garnet, dark green pyroxene, brown titanite, and reddish-orange zircon (prisms). Gypsum occurs as a white coating on feldspar.

The deposit was worked for feldspar in 1943 by G. Colautti of Barry's Bay. Production amounted to 1065 t. The mine consists of two open cuts (21.3 m by 4.6 m and 2.5 m deep, and 6 m by 1.2 m and 1.5 m deep) and two strippings.

The property is on the L. St. Louis farm, about 10 km northwest of Dacre.

Road log from Highway 17 at **km 30.4** (*see* the Renfrew–McArthurs Mills road log on p. 29):

km	0	Renfrew, junction of highways 17 and 132; proceed onto Highway 132.
	30.4	Junction, Highway 41; turn right.
	34.6	*Roadcut* on left exposes hornblende gneiss containing red garnet.
	35.9	*Roadcut* on left exposes crystalline limestone cut by calcite veins containing mica, titanite, pyroxene, and hornblende.

36.4	Junction, Constan Lake Road; continue straight ahead.
38.6	Turnoff (left) to the St. Louis farmhouse. Obtain permission to enter the property, then proceed along the farm road leading west. (This turnoff is 13.8 km south of the junction of highways 41 and 60.)
39.0	Clearing on left. The Keyfortmore mine is at the edge of the wooded area on the west side of the clearing and about 30 m from the road.

Refs.: 19 p. 12; 170 p. 37–38.

Maps (T): 31 F/6 Brudenell
       (G): 53b Renfrew area, Ontario (OGS, 1:126 720)
             P2357 Renfrew area, western part, southern Ontario (OGS, 1:63 360)
             2461 Barry's Bay, Precambrian geology (OGS, 1:100 000)

Radnor mine

MAGNETITE, PYRITE, JAROSITE, PYROXENE, TITANITE, ZIRCON, CHLORITE, BIOTITE

In hornblende-feldspar gneiss

Magnetite occurs as coarse granular masses and disseminations in greenish-grey gneiss. Pyrite occurs sparingly with the magnetite; specimens from the dump are coated with yellow powdery jarosite. Other minerals occurring in the gneiss are dark green pyroxene, brown titanite, turbid pink zircon (prisms about 4 mm long), chlorite, and biotite.

The deposit was worked for iron by numerous open pits that are now water filled. Extensive dumps adjoin them. The largest pits measure 50 m by 10 m and over 9 m deep, 105 m by 4 to 12 m and 12 m deep, 88.5 m by 3 to 6 m and 6 to 9 m deep, and 30 m by 7.5 m and 12 m deep. The mine was operated by Canada Iron Furnace Company from 1901 to 1907. About 17 200 t of ore grading more than 48 per cent iron were shipped to Radnor-des-Forges.

The mine is about 8 km northwest of Dacre on the property of Joe Larmond of Eganville.

Road log from Highway 132 at **km 30.4** (*see* the Renfrew–McArthurs Mills road log on p. 29):

km	0	Junction, highways 132 and 41 North; proceed onto Highway 41 North.
	8.2	Junction, lane to the Keyfortmore mine; continue along Highway 41 North.
	10.5	Junction, Perrault Road; turn right. (This junction is 11.6 km south of the junction of highways 41 and 60 in Eganville.)
	11.8	Junction, single-lane road on right; turn right.
	12.2	Fork; follow the road on right leading uphill.
	13.5	Radnor mine on right. The pits extend over 395 m.

Refs.: 43 p. 63–65; 161 p. 49–50; 170 p. 59–60; 196 p. 50–52.

Maps (T): 31 F/6 Brudenell
       (G): 53b Renfrew area, Ontario (OGS, 1:126 720)
             789 Parts of counties of Renfrew, Lanark, Lennox and Addington, Frontenac and Carleton (Perth sheet, No. 119), Ontario (GSC, 1:253 440)
             P2357 Renfrew area, western part, southern Ontario (OGS, 1:63 360)
             2461 Barry's Bay, Precambrian geology (OGS, 1:100 000)

Sunset mine

MOLYBDENITE, PYRITE, PYRRHOTITE, MOLYBDITE, SCAPOLITE, TREMOLITE, TITANITE, MICA

In pyroxenite

The orebody consisted of molybdenite, pyrite, and pyrrhotite in pyroxenite. Molybdite occurs as a yellow powder on molybdenite. Scapolite, tremolite, titanite, and mica are associated with the ore.

This deposit was worked briefly for molybdenite during World War I, first by the Legree brothers of Dacre and later by Steel Alloys Corporation, which also operated the Spain mine. The openings consist of a main pit (21.3 m by 9 m and up to 3 m deep) with a 21 m vertical shaft in the centre, a small pit on the opposite side of the road, and an open cut (30 m by 2 m) with a 3 m pit in the centre. The open cut is about 36.5 m east-northeast of the main pit. These openings and small dumps are now partly overgrown and ore-bearing specimens are not uncommon.

The mine is about 11 km northeast of Griffith. *See* Map 3 on p. 36.

Road log from Highway 41 at **km 40.5** (*see* the Renfrew–McArthurs Mills road log on p. 30):

km		
	0	Junction, Highway 41 and single-lane road leading south; proceed along this road.
	1.2	Bridge over a creek.
	1.4	Sunset mine.

Refs.: 37 p. 99–100; 145 p. 291; 170 p. 81–82; 208 p. 158–160.

Maps (T): 31 F/6 Brudenell
(G): 53b Renfrew area, Ontario (OGS, 1:126 720)
P2357 Renfrew area, western part, southern Ontario (OGS, 1:63 360)
2454 Khartum, Renfrew County (OGS, 1:31 680)
2461 Barry's Bay, Precambrian geology (OGS, 1:100 000)
GDIF 333 Brougham Township, Renfrew County (OGS, 1:31 680)

Spain mine

MOLYBDENITE, PYRITE, PYRRHOTITE, MAGNETITE, ROZENITE, PYROXENE, CHLORITE, SCAPOLITE, TITANITE, EPIDOTE, MICA, CALCITE, AMPHIBOLE, FELDSPAR, QUARTZ, AMETHYST

In pyroxenite and pegmatite

The orebody consists of molybdenite, pyrite, pyrrhotite, and magnetite. It occurs in pyroxenite at the contact of gneiss and crystalline limestone. Pegmatite dykes cutting the pyroxenite contain a small amount of molybdenite. During mining operations, molybdenite crystals up to 30 cm in diameter were found and much of the ore was hand picked. In the dumps, rozenite occurs as a white coating on rusty-weathered specimens. Crystals of pyrite are common. Other minerals found in the deposit are chlorite, light green to white scapolite, titanite, epidote, mica, pink calcite, green amphibole, feldspar, and amethystine and smoky quartz. Some scapolite is suitable for lapidary purposes.

The deposit was discovered in 1912 by Mr. Joseph Legree of Renfrew who did a small amount of surface work. From 1915 to 1917, Mr. W.J. Spain of New York operated the deposit and a mill that he installed at the mine site. The workings consisted of a pit (23 m by 37 m and 3 to 8 m deep) with a 10 m shaft at its northeastern corner, and two small pits located 30 m west and 120 m northeast of the main pit. The mill, office, and bunk houses were located north of the

Plate 7.

Molybdenite, Spain mine. The specimen is 14 cm from left
to right. GSC 201420-I

main pit. Steel Alloys Corporation took over operations from 1918 until 1919. Recent exploration work was done by North American Molybdenite Corporation Limited (1939) and by New Far North Exploration Limited (1965–1966).

The mine is about 9 km northeast of Griffith. *See* Map 3 on p. 36.

Road log from Highway 41 at **km 42.6** (*see* the Renfrew–McArthurs Mills road log on p. 30):

| km | 0 | Junction, Highway 41 and a single-lane road leading south; proceed along this road. |
| | 0.2 | Spain mine. |

Refs.: <u>37</u> p. 101; <u>98</u> p. 61; <u>145</u> p. 297; <u>170</u> p. 83; <u>197</u> p. 46–49; <u>208</u> p. 155–158; <u>223</u> p. 41–32.

Maps (T): 31 F/6 Brudenell
(G): 53b Renfrew area, Ontario (OGS, 1:126 720)
P2357 Renfrew area, western part, southern Ontario (OGS, 1:63 360)
2461 Barry's Bay, Precambrian geology (OGS, 1:100 000)
GDIF 407 Griffith Township, Renfrew County (OGS, 1:31 680)

Jamieson molybdenite mine

MOLYBDENITE, PYRITE, PYRRHOTITE, MOLYBDITE, PYROXENE, MICA, TITANITE, CALCITE, ROZENITE, JAROSITE, APATITE, SPHALERITE, GALENA, CHALCOPYRITE

In pyroxenite and pegmatite at contact of crystalline limestone and gneiss

35

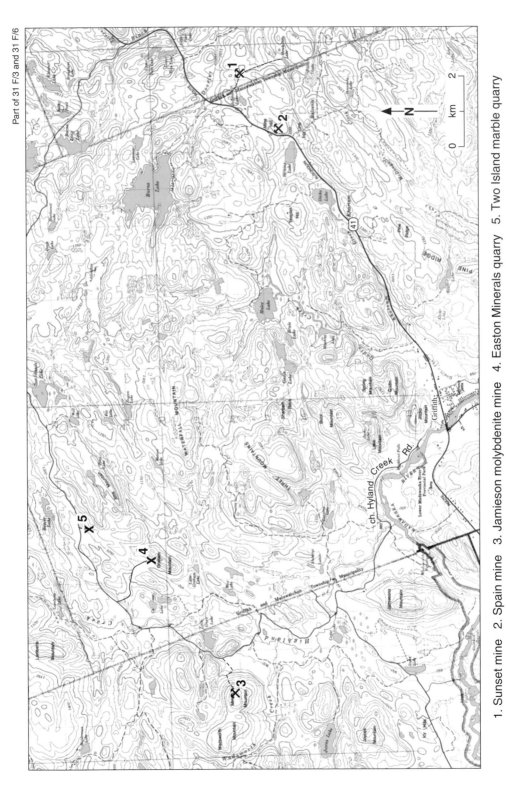

Map 3. Griffith.

1. Sunset mine   2. Spain mine   3. Jamieson molybdenite mine   4. Easton Minerals quarry   5. Two Island marble quarry

Large crystals of molybdenite were found during early mining operations. They occurred with pyrite and pyrrhotite. Green granular pyroxene, amber mica, and titanite occur in pink calcite associated with crystalline limestone. Powdery coatings of white rozenite, yellow molybdite, and yellow jarosite were noted on ore specimens in the dumps. A breccia composed of calcite and pink pegmatite fragments in a fine-grained, greenish-brown matrix and containing green apatite crystals occurs in the dumps; vugs in the breccia are lined with sphalerite, pyrite, galena, tiny quartz crystals, calcite crystals, and chalcopyrite.

The deposit was discovered by Mr. R.A. Jamieson in 1907. He extracted an estimated 1 t of molybdenite without the use of machinery and hand cobbed it. The mine was later (1915–1916) worked by the International Molybdenum Company Limited. About 5795 kg of pure molybdenite were mined from this deposit. The mine consists of two pits (14 m by 7.6 m and 18 m by 6 m) connected by a 60 m trench with a 12 m inclined shaft midpoint between the pits. Both pits are about 6 m deep; small dumps are located near the openings.

The mine is on Mining Mountain, about 14 km northwest of Griffith. *See* Map 3 on p. 36. The property belongs to Randy Wheeler of Douglas.

Road log from Highway 41 at **km 52.9** (*see* the Renfrew–McArthurs Mills road log on p. 30):

km		
	0	Junction, Highway 41 and Hyland Creek Road in Griffith; proceed north onto Hyland Creek Road.
	8.2	Junction; turn right.
	8.6	Junction; turn left.
	11.1	Junction; turn left.
	13.4	Junction, single-lane road on left; turn left (west).
	13.9	End of the road at a farmhouse. From the farmhouse proceed northwest along a partly overgrown mine road leading up a hill to a clearing at the summit. At the clearing, proceed to the right, then straight ahead for about 20 m to the Jamieson molybdenite mine in a wooded area. The distance from the farmhouse to the mine is about 800 m.

Refs.: 37 p. 103–105: 98 p. 62–63: 145 p. 303–304; 170 p. 86.

Maps (T): 31 F/6 Brudenell
(G): 53b Renfrew area, Ontario (OGS 1:126 720)
P2357 Renfrew area, western part, southern Ontario (OGS, 1:63 360)
2461 Barry's Bay, Precambrian geology (OGS, 1:100 000)
GDIF 135 Lundoch Township Renfrew County (OGS, 1:31 680)

Easton Minerals quarry

MARBLE

The deposit consists of coarse-grained dolomitic and calcitic crystalline limestone (marble). The dolomitic marble is white to buff with light green and brown bands. It contains some mica (muscovite and phlogopite), serpentine, and tremolite. The marble varies from white, grey, pink, to light green. It contains some serpentine, phlogopite, graphite, and pyrite.

A quarry was opened by Easton Minerals Limited in 1988–1989. It is on the northwest side of Graham Mountain, about 10 km northwest of Griffith. *See* Map 3 on p. 36

Road log from Highway 41 at **km 52.9** (*see* the Renfrew–McArthurs Mills road log on p. 30):

km		
	0	Junction of Highway 41 and Hyland Creek Road in Griffith; proceed north onto Hyland Creek Road.
	8.2	Junction; turn right.
	8.6	Junction; follow the road on left.
	11.1	Junction, road on left; continue straight ahead.
	14.5	Junction, road on left; continue straight ahead.
	15.3	Junction, just before the bridge over Highland Creek; turn right (east).
	16.3	Junction; turn right (south) onto the quarry road.
	18.3	Easton Minerals quarry.

Ref.:   <u>111</u> p. 67–69.

Maps   (T):   31 F/6 Brudenell
(G):   53b Renfrew area, Ontario (OGS, 1:126 720)
          2454 Khartum, Renfrew County (OGS, 1:31 680)
          2461 Barry's Bay, Precambrian geology (OGS, 1:100 000)
          GDIF 333 Brougham Township, Renfrew County (OGS, 1:31 680)

Two Island Marble quarry

MARBLE

The deposit consists of coarse-grained crystalline limestone (marble). It is white with light blue and green bands about 3 cm wide. Some serpentine, light green mica, and pink calcite veins occur in the marble.

The deposit was originally stripped and trenched in 1982–1985 by Trisar Resources. In 1988, the Two Island Marble Corporation began operations from a quarry, extracting marble blocks. The blocks are transported to a dressing plant at Dacre where polished slabs and ashlar blocks are produced. In 1991, polished marble slabs were exhibited at the 29th Annual Verona Marble and Machine Fair in Italy.

The quarry is on the west side of a ridge west of Two Islands Lake, about 11 km northwest of Griffith. *See* Map 3 on p. 36.

Road log from Highway 41 at **km 52.9** (*see* the Renfrew–McArthurs Mills road log on p. 30):

km		
	0	Junction of Highway 41 and Hyland Creek Road in Griffith; proceed north onto Hyland Creek Road.
	8.2	Junction; turn right.
	8.6	Junction; follow the road on left.
	11.1	Junction, road on left; continue straight ahead.
	14.5	Junction, road on left; continue straight ahead.
	15.3	Junction, just before the bridge over Highland Creek; turn right (east).
	19.0	Junction; turn right (south) onto the quarry road.
	19.7	Two Island Marble quarry.

Refs.:   110 p. 374; 111 p. 73; 142 p. 354.

Maps   (T): 31 F/6 Brudenell
        (G): 53b Renfrew area, Ontario (OGS, 1:126 720)
               2454 Khartum, Renfrew County (OGS, 1:31 680)
               2461 Barry's Bay, Precambrian geology (OGS, 1:100 000)
               GDIF 333 Brougham Township, Renfrew County (OGS, 1:31 680)

Ruby mine

GARNET, TITANITE

In hornblende-biotite gneiss

Pinkish-red garnet grains and crystals up to 1 cm in diameter occur in gneiss that averages 30 per cent garnet. Small grains of titanite are associated with it. Much of the hornblende in the gneiss is fibrous.

The deposit was originally staked for garnet by James Coyne and Thomas Ryan. J.J. Jewell and Company took over the claims in 1910 and did some exploratory work. From 1922 to 1924, Bancroft Mines Syndicate Limited worked the deposit from an open cut and treated the ore in a small on-site concentrator. Over 1360 t of picked ore and concentrates were shipped to the Carborundum Company in Niagara Falls, New York, for use in manufacturing abrasive sandpaper. The open cut is 12 m by 15 m with a 4.5 m face. Operations ended soon after a fire destroyed the mill.

The mine is on the northeast side of a ridge east of Snake Creek, about 5 km southeast of Hardwood Lake. *See* Map 4 on p. 40.

Road log from Highway 28 at **km 82.2** (*see* the Renfrew–McArthurs Mills road log on p. 30):

km   0   Junction, Highway 28 and a single-lane road leading south; this junction is 200 m east of the Highway 28 bridge over Snake Creek. Proceed onto the single-lane road.

          0.3   Junction; turn right, just after crossing a creek.

          0.5   Junction; turn right.

          1.2   The road bends to the left.

          1.7   Ruby mine on right.

Refs.:   39 p. 13–14; 47 p. 32–33; 170 p. 126.

Maps   (T): 31 F/3 Denbigh
        (G): 2031 Ashby Township, County of Lennox and Addington (OGS, 1:15 640)
               P2357 Renfrew area, western part, southern Ontario (OGS, 1:63 360)
               2461 Barry's Bay, Precambrian geology (OGS, 1:100 000)

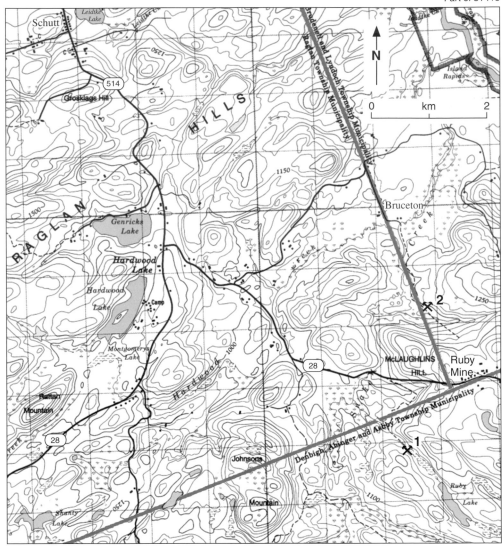

1. Ruby mine   2. McCoy mine
Map 4. Hardwood Lake.

McCoy mine

MOLYBDENITE, PYRITE, TOURMALINE

In syenite pegmatite

Molybdenite occurs as coarse flakes with pyrite and black tourmaline in hornblende-pyroxene pegmatite.

The deposit was originally worked in 1916–1917 for molybdenite from a pit and open cuts that yielded about 10 t of ore. A two-compartment shaft was sunk to a depth of 12 m in 1937–1938 by the McCoy Molybdenite Limited. The main pit is 3 m by 15 m and 1.8 to 3.7 m deep. The openings are now overgrown but some ore specimens can be found in the dumps.

The mine is about 5 km southeast of Hardwood Lake. *See* Map 4 on p. 40.

Road log from Highway 28 at **km 85.6** (*see* the Renfrew–McArthurs Mills road log on p. 30):

km		
	0	Junction, Highway 28 and Bruceton Road; proceed northeast along Bruceton Road.
	3.5	Junction; turn right (south).
	3.8	*Rock exposure* on right exposes crystalline limestone containing light green radiating tremolite, amber mica, and pink calcite.
	4.7	End of the road at a farmhouse. Proceed south along a wagon road. Several branch trails lead east from the wagon road; do not turn onto them.
	6.3	McCoy mine on left, to the east of a swampy area.

Refs.: 21 p. 167–168; 170 p. 84–85.

Maps (T): 31 F/3 Denbigh
(G): 53b Renfrew area, Ontario (OGS, 1:126 720)
1953-2 Brudenell-Raglan area, County of Renfrew (OGS, 1:63 360)
P2357 Renfrew area, western part, southern Ontario (OGS, 1:63 360)
2461 Barry's Bay, Precambrian geology (OGS, 1:100 000)
GDIF 135 Lyndoch Township, County of Renfrew (OGS, 1:31 680)

Mayo marble quarry

MARBLE

A band of dolomitic crystalline limestone (marble) 100 to 200 m wide occurs in biotite gneiss and schist. The marble is white, with some light brown bands due to the presence of phlogopite. It is fine grained with a sugary texture, and contains some tremolite and quartz.

The marble deposit is on the west side of Smith Lake. The deposit was originally worked by Rainbow Exploration and Development Syndicate in 1964, and by Rainbow Marble Company Limited in 1965. A new quarry was opened in 1991 by Upper Canada Stone Company Limited of Mississauga. The rock is crushed for use in landscaping.

The quarry is about 12 km south of McArthurs Mills.

Road log from Highway 28 at **km 102.4** (*see* the Renfrew–McArthurs Mills road log on p. 30):

km		
	0	Junction of Highway 28 and Hartsmere Road in McArthurs Mills; proceed south onto Hartsmere Road.
	4.7	Junction; continue straight ahead (south).
	12.4	Mayo marble quarry.

Refs.: 111 p. 94–97; 142 p. 351; 191 p. 72–73.

Maps (T): 31 F/4 Bancroft
(G): 1955-8 Dungannon and Mayo townships, County of Hastings, Ontario (OGS, 1:31 680)
P1980 Marbles of the Pembroke-Renfrew area, southern Ontario (OGS, 1:126 720)
GDIF 411 Mayo Township, Hastings County (OGS, 1:31 680)

Renfrew–Madawaska area

Collecting localities along Highway 60 between Renfrew and Madawaska, and along a side trip in the Eganville–Quadeville–Combermere area, are described following the road log. A page reference is indicated in parentheses following the name of each mine or occurrence. The starting point is in Renfrew, at the junction of Highway 60 (Raglan Street) and Renfrew County Road 4 (Bruce Avenue). Kilometre distances are shown in bold type.

Road log for collecting localities between Renfrew and Madawaska

km	0	Renfrew, at the junction of Highway 60 (Raglan Street) and Renfrew County Road 4 (Bruce Avenue). Bruce Avenue leads to the Renfrew County Road 4 roadcut (p. 44). The road log proceeds along Highway 60.
km	1.6	Highway 60 quarry (p. 44) on right.
km	5.0	Junction, road to Jamieson marble quarry (p. 45).
km	8.0	Junction, Renfrew County Road 61; the road log continues along Highway 60.
km	12.0	*Roadcuts* expose crystalline limestone containing massive clinopyroxene and serpentine, pink calcite, light brown tremolite, amber mica, pyrite, graphite, and small grains of light blue apatite, black tourmaline, blue anatase, and brown titanite.
km	20.8	Douglas, at the junction of Renfrew County Road 5; the road log continues along Highway 60.
km	26.7	*Roadcuts* expose crystalline limestone and pink pegmatite. The crystalline limestone contains massive pyroxene, orange-pink calcite, greyish-green clinoamphibole, amber mica, brown serpentine, yellow clinohumite, dark green spinel, apatite, chlorite, ilmenite, pyrrhotite, magnetite, and molybdenite. Red earthy hematite occurs in spaces between mica flakes. Tochilinite occurs as greasy black, smear-like patches on serpentine. White hydrotalcite coats spinel and clinohumite. Allanite, pyrite, magnetite, actinolite, mica, titanite, and clinopyroxene occur in microcline-quartz pegmatite. Some secondary minerals occur as crusts on rusty-weathered, pyrite-bearing rock; these include white botryoidal rozenite, white acicular gypsum, and yellow powdery jarosite.
km	28.3	Junction, Renfrew County Road 9; the road log continues along Highway 60.
km	30.2	*Roadcut* on right exposes syenite pegmatite containing bronze-yellow prismatic aggregates of scapolite, dark green clinopyroxene, titanite, and pyrite.
km	32.9– 34.2	*Roadcuts* expose pegmatite and gneiss. The pegmatite contains sunstone, clinopyroxene, titanite, garnet, peristerite, serpentine, biotite, calcite (fluoresces pink), and magnetite.
km	34.6	*Roadcuts* expose granite gneiss containing clinopyroxene, titanite, bronze-yellow scapolite, and magnetite.

km	**37.0**	Eganville, junction of Highway 41 to Bonnechere quarry (p. 45), Kneichel quarries (p. 46), Bonnechere Caves (p. 46), and to the Eganville–Quadeville–Combermere area (p. 47). The road log continues along highways 60/41.
km	**40.9**	Junction; Highway 41 North to the Berger amazonite occurrence (p. 64). The road log continues along Highway 60.
km	**51.0**	Golden Lake, junction of Renfrew County Road 30 (Reserve Road) to Beiderman (Germanicus) quarry (p. 65). The road log continues along Highway 60.
km	**53.2**	*Roadcut* on left exposes crystalline limestone and granite pegmatite. The crystalline limestone contains massive grey scapolite, hornblende, and calcite; grains of clinopyroxene, amber mica, orange chondrodite, brown serpentine, light blue apatite, yellow clinoamphibole, rutile, graphite, pyrite, and pyrrhotite; and aggregates of white flaky talc. Red earthy hematite occurs between flakes of mica. The rare minerals perrierite and tochilinite occur in crystalline limestone. Perrierite is sparsely distributed as black resinous to adamantine plates less than 1 mm long. Tochilinite occurs as dendritic coatings composed of thin black plates with a bronze lustre. Titanite, pyrite, and chlorite occur in pegmatite.
km	**54.7**	*Roadcut* on right exposes pink granite pegmatite containing titanite crystals to 2 cm long, massive magnetite, and dull greyish-green to tan bastnaesite.
km	**69.8**	Junction, highways 60 and 512. The road log continues along Highway 60.
		Roadcuts on Highway 512, 12.5 km south of this junction, expose granite pegmatite and crystalline limestone. The pegmatite contains light green radiating tremolite, pink zircon (cyrtolite) prisms, greyish-green to greyish-brown bastnaesite laths, loose aggregates of dark brown anatase, and some mica, titanite, hornblende, graphite, and pyrite.
		Pink and grey graphic granite occurs in pegmatite.
km	**86.1**	*Roadcut* on left exposes pink pegmatite containing massive magnetite.
km	**87.8**	*Roadcut* on left exposes biotite gneiss containing massive magnetite and taffy-brown allanite.
km	**93.4**	Barry's Bay, junction of highways 60 and 62; the road log continues along Highway 60.
		Roadcuts on Highway 62, at points 3.8 to 7.9 km and 13.7 km south of this junction, expose biotite gneiss containing red garnet crystals to 1 cm across.
km	**98.9**	Carson Lake Provincial Park on right.
km	**107.1**	Deady mine (p. 66) on right at the west end of a small lake.
km	**109.3**	Junction, Aylen Lake Road leading to Bambrick mine (p. 66) and Five Mile mine (p. 67).
km	**110.5**	Junction, Spectacle Lake Road to Spectacle Lake (Lake) mine (p. 67).
km	**111.2**	Plexman mine (p. 69), just south of the highway.
km	**116.5**	Junction, road on right leading to Davis mine (p. 69).

km	120.1	Madawaska, junction of Highway 523 and Major Lake Road leading to Madawaska River mine (p. 70), J.G. Gole (Comet) mine (p. 71), Cameron and Aleck mine (p. 72), and Cameron mine (p. 73).

End of road log.

Renfrew County Road 4 (Bruce Avenue) roadcut

TOURMALINE, TREMOLITE, TITANITE, PYROXENE, GRAPHITE, PYRITE, MICA, CALCITE

In crystalline limestone

Orange-brown granular tourmaline and colourless bladed tremolite occur with smoky brown titanite, green pyroxene, graphite, amber mica, and pink calcite in grey marble exposed in a roadcut. The road has been cut through a ridge of crystalline limestone that was originally quarried in 1922 by J.A. Jamieson for use as building, monument, and foundation stone, and for the production of lime. The Renfrew post office is built of this stone.

The quarries, now overgrown, are on the south side of the limestone ridge, just south of Renfrew County Road 4 (Bruce Avenue), at a point 2.4 km east of its junction with Highway 60 (Raglan Street) in Renfrew. A roadcut exposes the crystalline limestone. *See* Map 2 on p. 26.

Refs.: 64 p.170; 170 p. 104; 191 p. 67–68.

Maps (T): 31 F/7 Renfrew
      (G): 53b Renfrew area, Ontario (OGS, 1:126 720)
           1046A Renfrew, Renfrew and Lanark counties, Ontario (GSC, 1:63 360)
           P1838 Renfrew area, eastern part, southern Ontario (OGS, 1:63 360)
           2462 Renfrew, Precambrian geology (OGS, 1:100 000)

Highway 60 quarry

CALCITE, GRAPHITE, TITANITE

In hornblende gneiss

The quarry was opened to provide rock for road construction. White calcite veins cutting the gneiss fluoresce pink when exposed to ultraviolet rays. Crystalline limestone associated with the gneiss contains disseminations of pyrite, graphite, mica, and titanite.

The quarry, now inactive, is on the west side of a ridge facing Highway 60 at **km 1.6** (*see* Renfrew–Madawaska road log on p. 42). It is 0.5 km northeast of Highway 60 and about 2 km northwest of Renfrew. *See* Map 2 on p. 26.

Ref.: 170 p. 103.

Maps (T): 31 F/7 Renfrew
      (G): 53b Renfrew area, Ontario (OGS, 1:126 720)
           1046A Renfrew, Renfrew and Lanark counties, Ontario (GSC, 1:63 360)
           P1838 Renfrew area, eastern part, southern Ontario (OGS, 1:63 360)

Jamieson marble quarry

SERPENTINE, TREMOLITE, MICA, TITANITE, GRAPHITE, PYRITE, PYRRHOTITE, MAGNETITE, CHLORITE, TALC, TOURMALINE

In dolomitic marble

Dull green serpentine is common as masses and bands in crystalline limestone (marble). Also abundant are bladed aggregates and crystals of smoky, light brown tremolite, which also forms bands in the limestone. Other minerals in the deposit include amber and greenish-blue mica, dark brown titanite, graphite, pyrite, pyrrhotite, magnetite, chlorite, talc, and orange tourmaline.

The quarry was opened into a steep hill facing Highway 60. It is 85 m long with a 6 to 9 m face and was formerly operated by the Jamieson Lime Company.

The quarry is about 5 km northwest of Renfrew.

Access to the Jamieson marble quarry is via a 0.15 km road leading east from Highway 60 at **km 5.0** (*see* the Renfrew–Madawaska road log on p. 42). *See* Map 2 on p. 26.

Refs.:   64 p. 170; 170 p. 103; 191 p. 68–69.

Maps   (T):   31 F/7 Renfrew
        (G):   53b Renfrew area, Ontario (OGS, 1:126 720)
                1046A Renfrew, Renfrew and Lanark counties, Ontario (GSC, 1:63 360)
                P1838 Renfrew area, eastern part, southern Ontario (OGS, 1:63 360)
                2460 Cobden, Precambrian geology (OGS, 1:100 000)

Bonnechere quarry

FOSSILS, CALCITE, CHERT

In limestone

Fossils including corals, bryozoans, crinoids, brachiopods, trilobites, and pelecypods occur in Ordovician Black River limestone. White calcite crystals occur in the limestone; the crystals fluoresce yellow in ultraviolet light. Black and white chert also occurs in the rock.

Similar fossil-bearing limestone is exposed along the Bonnechere River at Jessups Rapids in Eganville, and about 8 km farther east at Fourth Chute.

The Bonnechere quarry is on top of a 30 m escarpment on the south side of the Bonnechere River. Kilns formerly used for burning lime are across the road from the quarry and are connected to it by an overhead tramway. The tops of the kilns are at the same elevation as the quarry floor. The quarry consists of two benches: the lower one is 58 m by 30 m and 9 m deep, and the upper one is 43 m by 46 m and 3 to 5.5 m deep. Quarry operators were Dominion Rock Products Limited (1928–1939), Federal Lime Company (1939–1942), Shane Lime and Charcoal Company Limited (1942–1944), and Bonnechere Lime Company Limited (1960–1965).

The Bonnechere quarry is about 7 km southeast of Eganville. The property belongs to Mary E. Tracey.

Road log from Highway 60 at **km 37.0** (*see* the Renfrew–Madawaska road log on p. 43):

km   0   Junction of highways 60 and 41 in Eganville; proceed south onto Highway 41.

            0.5   Junction; proceed straight ahead toward the Bonnechere Caves.

            7.0   Bonnechere quarry on right.

Refs.:   44 p. 69, 71; 64 p. 165–166; 114 p. 66; 170 p. 100–101; 196 p. 54; 216 p. 10; 217 p. 6; 218 p. 11; 220 p. 10.

Maps   (T):   31 F/11 Golden Lake
        (G):   53b Renfrew area, Ontario (OGS, 1:126 720)
               660 Quebec and Ontario, parts of counties of Ottawa and Pontiac, Que. and Carleton and Renfrew, Ont. (Pembroke Sheet No. 122) (GSC, 1:253 440)
               P2356 Pembroke area, eastern part, southern Ontario (OGS, 1:63 360)
               2433 Clontarf, Renfrew County (OGS, 1:31 680)
               2459 Pembroke, Precambrian geology (OGS, 1:100 000)

Kneichel quarries

FOSSILS, CALCITE

In limestone

Ordovician limestone contains fossil corals, gastropods, and crinoids. The limestone is dark grey, fine grained, and belongs to the Chazy Formation. It contains crystal aggregates of white calcite that fluoresce yellow in ultraviolet light.

The deposit was worked for lime and for use in the pulp industry. Two shallow quarries, 23 m by 345 m and 60 m by 100 m, and two wood-burning kilns were operated. Shane Lime Company Limited was the operator from 1933 to about 1944.

The Kneichel quarries are about 8 km southeast of Eganville.

Road log from Highway 60 at **km 37.0** (*see* the Renfrew–Madawaska road log on p. 43):

km   0   Junction of highways 60 and 41 in Eganville; proceed south onto Highway 41.

            0.5   Junction; proceed straight ahead toward the Bonnechere Caves.

            8.7   Junction; continue straight ahead.

            8.8   Junction quarry road; turn right.

            9.0   Kneichel quarries.

Refs.:   64 p. 165–166; 170 p. 100–101; 216 p. 10; 217 p. 6; 218 p. 11; 220 p. 10.

Maps   (T):   31 F/11 Golden Lake
        (G):   53b Renfrew area, Ontario (OGS, 1:126 720)
               660 Quebec and Ontario, parts of counties of Ottawa and Pontiac, Que. and Carleton and Renfrew, Ont. (Pembroke Sheet No. 122) (GSC, 1:253 440)
               P 2356 Pembroke area, eastern part, southern Ontario (OGS, 1:63 360)
               2459 Pembroke, Precambrian geology (OGS, 1:100 000)

Bonnechere Caves

The Bonnechere Caves have been known since 1853 and have been accessible to the public through guided tours since 1955. The cavern comprises three chambers (approximately 3 m by 6 m and 3 m high, 7.6 m by 4.6 m and 3 m high, and 4.6 m in diameter by 4.6 m high) connected by passages from 3 to 6 m high. Minor passages (0.6 to 0.9 m high) branch from the main channels. The total distance covered by the chambers and passages is about 300 m, making this the most extensive cavern in Ontario. A subterranean stream connects the caves with the Bonnechere River.

The Bonnechere Caves are about 9 km southeast of Eganville.

Road log from Highway 60 at **km 37.0** (*see* the Renfrew–Madawaska road log on p. 43):

km		
	0	Junction of highways 60 and 41 in Eganville; proceed south onto Highway 41.
	0.5	Junction; proceed straight ahead.
	8.7	Junction; turn left.
	9.2	Entrance to the Bonnechere Caves.

Ref.:   50 p. 22–25.

Maps   (T): 31 F/11 Golden Lake.
 (G): 53b Renfrew area, Ontario (OGS, 1:126 720)

Collecting localities along a side trip from Eganville to Combermere are described in the following text. The description of collecting localities along Highway 60 from Renfrew to Madawaska resumes on p. 64.

Eganville–Quadeville–Combermere area

Collecting localities in the Eganville–Quadeville–Combermere area are described following the road log. A page reference is indicated in parentheses following the name of each mine or occurrence.

The road log for this side trip begins in Eganville at the junction of highways 60 and 41; this junction is 37.0 km west of the junction of Highway 60 (Raglan Street) and Renfrew County Road 4 (Bruce Avenue) in Renfrew. The road log proceeds along highways 41, 512, and 515. Kilometre distances are shown in bold type.

Road log for collecting localities in the Eganville–Quadeville–Combermere area

km		
km	**0**	Junction of highways 60 and 41 in Eganville; the road log proceeds south along Highway 41.
km	**1.1**	Junction; the road log turns right onto Highway 512.
km	**10.6**	Junction, Lake Clear cottage road to Meany mine (p. 48) and Smart mine (p. 50).
km	**14.3**	*Roadcuts* expose mica-apatite-calcite veins cutting red syenite. Small brown titanite crystals occur in calcite and syenite. A trail on the left side of the highway leads 30 m to a small pit exposing a calcite vein containing red apatite and dark green pyroxene crystals, and brown titanite. The calcite is pale pink and it fluoresces pink when exposed to ultraviolet rays. *See* Map 5 on p. 49.
km	**14.6– 14.8**	*Roadcuts* expose pink syenite containing titanite, magnetite, and pyroxene. On the other side of the road, just beyond a house and up a slope facing the road, is a pit exposing a calcite vein in syenite. Crystals of deep red apatite, black hornblende, dark green pyroxene, and some titanite and mica occur in the calcite. The apatite crystals measure up to 5 cm in diameter. To reach the occurrence, proceed up the hill along an outcrop area for about 100 m to the pit in a lightly wooded area. *See* Map 5 on p. 49.

km	16.3	Junction, road to Lake Clear and Turners Island mine (p. 51). The road log continues on Highway 512. A small *roadcut* opposite this junction exposes green epidote veinlets in hornblende gneiss.
km	24.7	*Roadcuts* expose syenite pegmatite containing abundant maroon-red apatite in massive form and as crystals up to 4 cm in diameter. Dark brown titanite crystals (1 cm in diameter), magnetite, and large hyacinth-red zircon crystals are also present. Red sunstone, an orthoclase feldspar with gold flecks, was also observed in coarse pegmatite at the west end of the cut.
km	24.9	Junction, highways 512 and 515; the road log proceeds south along Highway 515.
km	28.3	Junction, road on left leading to A. Edgecombe property and Kuehl Lake occurrence (p. 52).
km	29.6	Rock exposure on left exposes red syenite containing small red apatite crystals, titanite, tourmaline, and pyroxene.
km	30.0	*Roadcuts* on left opposite Anderson (Yukes) Lake. Red apatite occurs in a pink calcite vein cutting red syenite. Titanite, pyroxene, mica, and greyish-pink sunstone occur in syenite.
km	42.9	Junction, Letterkenny Road in Quadeville to Quadeville East mine (p. 53). The road log continues along Highway 515.
km	44.5	*Roadcuts* expose crystalline limestone containing grains and aggregates of amber mica, graphite, green serpentine, diopside, amber tourmaline, light green amphibole, brown titanite, tan dolomite, and colourless columnar scapolite.
km	45.5	Junction, single-lane road on right to Quadeville West mine (p. 55).
km	48.1	Junction, road to Rosenthal and to Gutz corundum occurrence (p. 56) and Michaelis corundum occurrence (p. 57).
km	51.2	Junction, road to Edgemont mine (p. 58).
km	53.8	Junction, Highway 514; the road log continues along Highway 515.
km	57.5	Jewellville, at a junction on the north side of the bridge over the Madawaska River and road to Jewellville corundum occurrence (p. 59).
km	68.2	Junction, Highway 62 to Combermere and Craigmont (Craig) mine (p. 59) and Burgess mine (p. 62).

End of road log.

Meany mine

APATITE, HORNBLENDE, PYROXENE, SCAPOLITE, TITANITE, MICA, CHLORITE, CALCITE, ZIRCON

In crystalline limestone

Maroon-red apatite (massive and crystals) is associated with black hornblende, dark green pyroxene, yellowish-green scapolite, dark brown titanite, and less abundantly, with amber mica and chlorite in bright salmon-orange, coarsely crystalline calcite. During mining operations, large, well formed crystals of hyacinth-red zircon, titanite, and apatite were found.

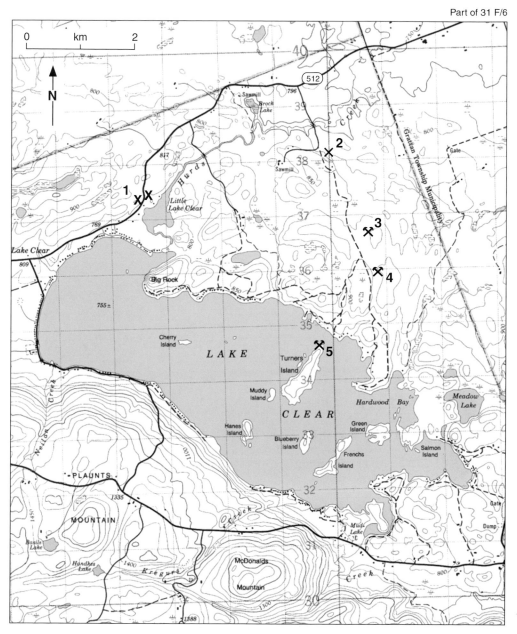

Part of 31 F/6

1, 2. Apatite pits   3. Meany mine   4. Smart mine   5. Turners Island mine

Map 5. Lake Clear.

The deposit was worked briefly for apatite from several small pits, the deepest measuring 7.5 m deep. Between 1880 and 1883, about 300 t of apatite were removed. The workings are now partly overgrown. Fairly large dumps lie adjacent to the pits.

The mine is about 9 km southwest of Eganville; it is near Lake Clear on the property of Edmond Platt of Eganville. *See* Map 5 on p. 49.

Road log from Highway 512 at **km 10.6** (*see* the road log to the Eganville–Quadeville–Combermere area on p. 47):

km		
	0	Junction, Highway 512 and Lake Clear cottage road; turn left (south) onto the Lake Clear cottage road.
	1.1	Fork; bear left.
	1.2	Junction, single-lane road on left. This road leads 30 m to a small *pit* and *dump*. Pinkish-red apatite crystals (about 15 mm in diameter) occur with dark amber mica, actinolite, chlorite, and dark green pyroxene crystals in light pink calcite.
	3.1	Junction, trail in clearing on left. Proceed along this trail. Beyond the clearing the trail is overgrown and obscure. From the clearing proceed east along the north side of a low wooded ridge (a swampy area is to the left) for about 475 m to the Meany mine.

Refs.: 184 p. 59; 196 p. 53; 214 p. 7.

Maps (T): 31 F/6 Brudenell
(G): 53b Renfrew area, Ontario (OGS, 1:126 720)
P2357 Renfrew area, western part, southern Ontario (OGS, 1:63 360)
2433 Clontarf, Renfrew County (OGS, 1:31 680)
2461 Barry's Bay, Precambrian geology (OGS, 1:100 000)
GDIF 406 Sebastopol Township, Renfrew County (OGS, 1:31 680)

Smart mine

APATITE, TITANITE, MICROCLINE, HORNBLENDE, PYROXENE, MICA, ZIRCON, CHLORITE, PYRITE, CALCITE, CROCIDOLITE

In crystalline limestone

Large crystals of maroon-red apatite, brilliant brown titanite, hyacinth-red zircon, and perthitic microcline have been removed from this deposit. The apatite crystals are similar to those occurring at the Meany mine. Dark brown titanite crystals and microcline crystals are associated with apatite in pink calcite. Hornblende and pyroxene are common. Other minerals found in the deposit include amber mica, pink zircon (crystals averaging 1 cm long), dark green chlorite, and pyrite. Silvery-green fibrous crocidolite occurs on feldspar. Crystal specimens from both the Meany and Smart mines are in the collections of major museums.

The mine was worked briefly some time before 1880 by Mr. Townsend for mineral specimens. It consists of a few small pits, now overgrown. Small dumps surround the openings, which are located along the west side of a low ridge overgrown with junipers.

The mine is about 9 km southwest of Eganville, on the property of Frank and August Miller of Eganville. It is just south of the Meany mine. *See* Map 5 on p. 49.

Road log from Highway 512 at **km 10.6** (*see* the road log to the Eganville–Quadeville–Combermere area on p. 47):

km   0   Junction of Highway 512 and Lake Clear cottage road; turn left (south) onto the Lake Clear cottage road.

              1.1   Fork; bear left.

              3.1   Junction, trail to Meany mine; continue straight ahead.

              3.7   Smart mine on left 200 m from the road. Proceed east through the woods to the mine on the ridge.

Refs.:   91 p. 45–46; 184 p. 59; 196 p. 53–54; 214 p. 7.

Maps   (T):   31 F/6 Brudenell
              (G):   53b Renfrew area, Ontario (OGS, 1:126 720)
                     P2357 Renfrew area, western part, southern Ontario (OGS 1:63 360)
                     2433 Clontarf, Renfrew County (OGS, 1:31 680)
                     2461 Barry's Bay, Precambrian geology (OGS, 1:100 000)
                     GDIF 406 Sebastopol Township, Renfrew County (OGS, 1:31 680)

Turners Island mine

APATITE, SCAPOLITE, PYROXENE, HORNBLENDE, TITANITE, MICA, CALCITE, ZIRCON

In veins cutting hornblende gneiss

Plate 8.

Twinned zircon crystal with pyroxene in calcite, Turner's Island mine.
The crystal is 32 mm by 13 mm. GSC 201420-E

51

Maroon-red to brownish-red apatite crystals up to 7.5 cm in diameter can be found in the dumps at this former apatite mine. Larger crystals are less common. Also abundant are greyish-white to yellowish-green scapolite (fluoresces pink under short ultraviolet rays) and dark green pyroxene, both as crystals and in massive form. Less common are hornblende, titanite (dark brown brilliant crystals up to 5 cm long), and dark brown mica. These minerals occur in salmon-orange to pale pink calcite. Outstanding crystals once found in this deposit include a 318 kg apatite crystal; a zircon crystal measuring 30 cm in diameter; a titanite crystal measuring over 30 cm long, now in the Harvard University collection; titanite crystals weighing 18 kg; and twinned crystals of zircon.

The mine, consisting of several pits, was worked between 1879 and 1882. In 1943, one of the pits was re-opened for rare-element minerals. The pits measure 53 m by 1 to 4.5 m and 0.5 to 3.7 m deep, 3 m by 4.6 m and 1.5 m deep, and a 12 m trench with a pit 6 m wide at one end.

The Turners Island mine is at the north end of Turners Island in Lake Clear, approximately 5 km east of the west end of the lake and 12 km southwest of Eganville. *See* Map 5 on p. 49. Access is by a road leading from Highway 512 at **km 16.3** (*see* the road log to the Eganville–Quadeville–Combermere area on p. 47) to Lake Clear shore, and then by boat.

Refs.: 67 p. 209–213; 91 p. 45–48; 128 p. 12–13; 170 p. 18–19; 196 p. 54–55; 214 p. 7.

Maps   (T):   31 F/6 Brudenell
        (G):   53b Renfrew area, Ontario (OGS, 1:126 720)
             P2357 Renfrew area, western part, southern Ontario (OGS, 1:63 360)
             2433 Clontarf, Renfrew County (OGS, 1:31 680)
             2461 Barry's Bay, Precambrian geology (OGS, 1:100 000)
             GDIF 406 Sebastopol Township, Renfrew County (OGS, 1:31 680)

Kuehl Lake occurrence

ZIRCON, APATITE, TITANITE, HORNBLENDE

In syenite pegmatite and gneiss

Large brownish-red (hyacinth-red) zircon crystals, commonly 30 cm long and 10 cm wide, were once recovered from this deposit. They occurred in yellowish-brown syenite and in lenses consisting of calcite, apatite, biotite, and hornblende in syenite gneiss. Zircon, titanite, biotite, and apatite occur in the syenite pegmatite.

The deposit was discovered in the early 1880s, and reported in 1884 by C.W. Willimott of the GSC. The locality is known for the large crystals, which are in various museum collections in North America. The zircon is generally opaque, but some gemstones have been cut from transparent portions of some crystals. Cut stones were included in the GSC mineral exhibit at the Columbian Exposition of 1892 in Chicago, and at the International Exhibition of 1900 in Paris.

The deposit is exposed by an open cut 12 m by 3 m and 1.5 m deep at the eastern end of Kuehl Lake, on the property of Allan Edgecombe at **km 28.3** on Highway 515. (*See* the road log to the Eganville–Quadeville–Combermere area on p. 47.) The Kuehl Lake occurrence is about 23 km southwest of Eganville.

Refs.:   67 p. 211; 77 p. 85–86; 146 p. 21–23; 170 p. 118–119; 192 p. 197–198; 214 p. 15; 227 p. 170–172; 228 p. 183.

Maps   (T):   31 F/6 Brudenell
        (G):   53b Renfrew area, Ontario (OGS, 1:126 720)
             1953-2 Brudenell-Raglan area, County of Renfrew (OGS, 1:63 360)

P2357 Renfrew area, western part, southern Ontario (OGS, 1:63 360)
2461 Barry's Bay, Precambrian geology (OGS, 1:100 000)
GDIF 405 Brudenell Township, Renfrew County (OGS, 1:31 680)

Quadeville East mine

BERYL, PERISTERITE, CLEAVELANDITE, AMAZONITE, BIOTITE, QUARTZ, LYNDOCHITE, ZIRCON, ALLANITE, TOURMALINE, GARNET, FLUORITE, APATITE, MAGNETITE, STRUVERITE, MONAZITE, COLUMBITE, EUXENITE

In granite pegmatite

Beryl was formerly mined from this deposit. It occurs as blue-green to green crystals generally less than 5 cm in diameter; during mining operations, crystals up to 20 cm in diameter and 90 cm long were recovered. Some faceting-grade blue beryl (aquamarine) has been found in the deposit. The beryl occurs in pegmatite consisting of white peristerite (with blue iridescence), white cleavelandite, amazonite, microcline, perthite, biotite, and smoky quartz. Accessory minerals include brilliant black lyndochite prisms to 5 cm long; disc-shaped masses of columbite in feldspar cleavages; zircon; black platy allanite; black tourmaline prisms to 15 cm across; reddish-brown garnet; violet fluorite; brown monazite; green apatite; euxenite; struverite; and magnetite.

The mine consists of an open cut 76 m long, 15 m wide, and 2 to11 m deep. The western part of the cut exposes microcline-perthite-cleavelandite-quartz pegmatite containing tourmaline. The eastern part of the cut exposes albite-perthitic microcline-quartz-biotite pegmatite. Beryl occurs in both parts.

Plate 9.

Beryl crystal in pegmatite, Quadeville East mine. The crystal is 7 cm by 2 cm. GSC 201420-U

Plate 10.

Tourmaline crystals in quartz, Quadeville East mine. The large crystal is 6 cm by 1 cm. GSC 201420-F

This deposit has been known since 1897. It was opened for beryl in 1926 by T.B. Caldwell of Perth, Ontario. An estimated 2 to 4 t of beryl crystals were recovered. In 1927, 2020 kg of beryl were mined and shipped to Germany. Canadian Beryllium Mines and Alloys Limited operated the deposit in 1939 and did most of the development. The mine is currently (2001) being worked by Richard Farmery and David Paterson. Arrangements for visiting the mine should be made at Kauffeldt's General Store in Quadeville.

The mine is on the south side of Casey Hill, about 2 km northwest of Quadeville. *See* Map 6 on p. 55.

Road log from Highway 515 at **km 42.9** (*see* the road log to the Eganville–Quadeville–Combermere area on p. 47):

km | 0 | Junction of Letterkenny Road and Highway 515 in Quadeville; proceed north along Letterkenny Road.

    1.9   Junction; turn right onto the mine road.

    2.4   Quadeville East mine.

Refs.: 45 p. 228–230; 46 p. 424; 52 p. 30; 77 p. 36–41; 85 p. 40–46; 91 p. 48–50; 126 p. 84–86; 128 p. 7–8; 134 p. 25–26; 162 p. 25; 170 p. 20–22, 97–98; 192 p. 177–180.

Maps (T): 31 F/6 Brudenell
      (G): 53b Renfrew area, Ontario (OGS, 1:126 720)
            1953-2 Brudenell-Raglan area, County of Renfrew, Ontario (OGS, 1:63 360)
            P2357 Renfrew area, western part, southern Ontario (OGS, 1:63 360)
            2461 Barry's Bay, Precambrian geology (OGS, 1:100 000)
            GDIF 135 Lyndoch Township, Renfrew County (OGS, 1:31 680)

Part of 31 F/3, 31 F/4, 31 F/5 and 31 F/6

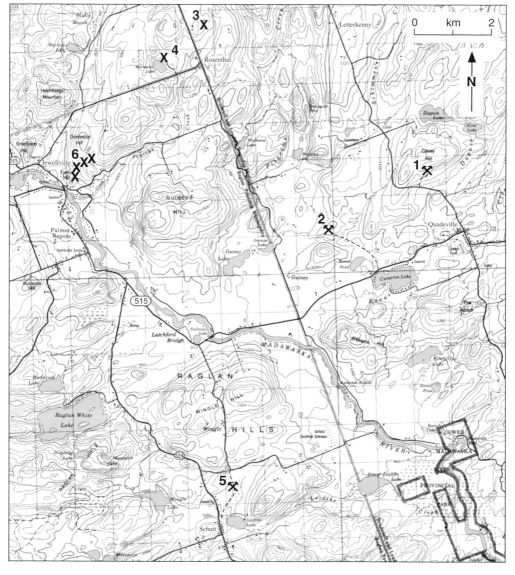

1. Quadeville East mine   2. Quadeville West mine   3. Gutz corundum occurrence
4. Michaelis corundum occurrence   5. Edgemont mine   6. Jewellville corundum occurrence
Map 6. Quadeville.

Quadeville West mine

ROSE QUARTZ, BERYL, PERISTERITE, COLUMBITE, EUXENITE, FERGUSONITE, GARNET, TOURMALINE, FLUORITE, HORNBLENDE, MICA, SPECULARITE, MAGNETITE, PYRITE, GRAPHIC GRANITE

In granite pegmatite

Massive rose quartz that exhibits the star effect (asterism) when cut en cabochon occurs in this former feldspar-beryl mine. The rose quartz has an attractive mauve tint. The principal constituents of the pegmatite are pink microcline, white, smoky, and rose quartz, pink and white peristerite, light green muscovite, and biotite. The beryl occurs as bluish-green to deep green crystals up to 20 cm in diameter. Among the rare-element minerals occurring in the deposit are columbite, as dark brown platy aggregates, dark brown to black euxenite, and fergusonite. Other minerals in the deposit include red garnet, black tourmaline, violet fluorite, black hornblende, specularite, magnetite, and pyrite. Pink graphic granite with a medium texture occurs in the pegmatite; it is suitable for lapidary purposes.

The deposit was opened for beryl in 1935 by Renfrew Minerals Limited, but results proved to be disappointing. The company, however, operated the deposit for feldspar and extracted 612 t in a two-year period. From 1948 until 1950, Canadian Beryllium Mines and Alloys Limited worked the deposit for beryl and feldspar. Rose quartz is now being extracted. The openings, extending from west to east, consist of a T-shaped cut in which the rose quartz is exposed, an open cut 40 m by 24 m, and an open cut 6 m by 23 m, from which the beryl was obtained.

The mine is 4.5 km west of Quadeville. *See* Map 6 on p. 55. The property belongs to Don McKay of Quadeville.

Road log from Highway 515 at **km 45.5** (*see* the road log to the Eganville–Quadeville–Combermere area on p. 47):

km		
	0	Junction of Highway 515 and a single-lane road; turn right (north) onto the single-lane road.
	0.5	Fork; follow the left fork.
	1.9	Quadeville West mine.

Refs.: 45 p. 230; 46 p. 424–425; 52 p. 30–31; 77 p. 42–45; 85 p. 40–46; 126 p. 84–86; 162 p. 25; 170 p. 23, 98–99; 192 p. 180–184.

Maps (T): 31 F/6 Brudenell
(G): 53b Renfrew area, Ontario (OGS, 1:126 720)
1953-2 Brudenell-Raglan area, County of Renfrew, Ontario (OGS, 1:63 360)
P2357 Renfrew area, western part, southern Ontario (OGS, 1:63 360)
2461 Barry's Bay, Precambrian geology (OGS, 1:100 000)
GDIF 135 Lyndoch Township, Renfrew County (OGS, 1:31 680)

Gutz corundum occurrence

CORUNDUM, SCAPOLITE, PYRITE, SODALITE, CANCRINITE

In syenite pegmatite

Bronze to blue-grey corundum crystals averaging 2 cm in diameter occur in white pegmatite. Crystals up to 20 cm long have been reported. Greenish-yellow turbid scapolite impregnated with pyrite crystals was found in the dump near the pit. Slender crystals of corundum occur with small patches of sodalite and cancrinite in a nepheline pegmatite outcrop 40 m north of the pit.

Plate 11.

Gutz corundum occurrence, 1969. GSC 153184

The deposit was discovered by Ontario Bureau of Mines geologists in about 1897, soon after the corundum deposits at Carlow became known. The outcrop was blasted and the rock was shipped to the Kingston School of Mining for mill tests. Further shipments were made to the mill at Palmer Rapids. Prior to the discovery of this corundum deposit, nepheline syenite was recovered from the outcrops and burned in a kiln located near the farm lane, the syenite being mistaken for crystalline limestone.

The occurrence is about 1 km north of the settlement of Rosenthal. *See* Map 6 on p. 55. The property belongs to Raymond Gutz.

Road log from Highway 515 at **km 48.1** (*see* the road log to the Eganville–Quadeville–Combermere area on p. 47):

km 0 Junction of the road to Rosenthal and Highway 515; turn right (north) onto the road to Rosenthal.

8.2 Junction, at Rosenthal church; continue straight ahead.

9.2 Junction, lane to the Gutz farm on right. The pit is on the hill facing the road and about 60 m from the road. To visit the Gutz corundum occurrence, inquire at the farmhouse.

Refs.: <u>77</u> p. 50; <u>91</u> p. 50; <u>130</u> p. 222; <u>170</u> p. 28–29.

Maps (T): 31 F/6 Brudenell
(G): 53b Renfrew area, Ontario (OGS, 1:126 720)
1953-2 Brudenell-Raglan area, County of Renfrew, Ontario (OGS, 1:63 360)
P2357 Renfrew area, western part, southern Ontario (OGS, 1:63 360)
2461 Barry's Bay, Precambrian geology (OGS, 1:100 000)
GDIF 405 Brudenell Township, Renfrew County (OGS, 1:31 680)

Michaelis corundum occurrence

CORUNDUM, MAGNETITE

In syenite gneiss

Corundum crystals occur with magnetite grains in white and red syenite. The crystals average about 1 cm in diameter and range in colour from pinkish brown to bluish and brownish grey.

The deposit has been exposed by a small pit (18 m by 4.5 m and 2 to 3 m deep) in a pasture on the farm of A. Michaelis, about 1 km west of Rosenthal. The pit is water filled and is surrounded by small piles of corundum-bearing rock. *See* Map 6 on p. 55.

Road log from km 8.2 of road log to the Gutz corundum occurrence:

km		
	0	Junction, at Rosenthal church; turn left (west).
	1.0	Junction, at school; turn right.
	1.4	End of the road at the Michaelis farmhouse. Arrangements may be made here to visit the Michaelis corundum pit located at the edge of a wooded area about 300 m north of the barn.

Refs.:   77 p. 54; 170 p. 30–31.

Maps   (T):   31 F/6 Brudenell
(G):   53b Renfrew area, Ontario (OGS, 1:126 720)
1953-2 Brudenell-Raglan area, County of Renfrew, Ontario (OGS, 1:63 360)
P2357 Renfrew area, western part, southern Ontario (OGS, 1:63 360)
2461 Barry's Bay, Precambrian geology (OGS, 1:100 000)

Edgemont mine

MOLYBDENITE, GRAPHIC GRANITE, PYRITE, MAGNETITE, PYRRHOTITE, HORNBLENDE, CALCITE, PYROXENE, TREMOLITE, MICA, APATITE

In granite pegmatite

Molybdenite occurs in pegmatite and, less commonly, in crystalline limestone. The pegmatite is composed of pink graphic granite, plagioclase, and biotite. Pyrite, pyrrhotite, magnetite, hornblende, and calcite are associated with molybdenite. Disseminated grains of pyroxene, light brown amphibole, amber mica, apatite, and molybdenite occur in crystalline limestone.

This mine, also known as the Liedtke and Windle mine, was operated for molybdenite in 1917 and between 1939 and 1942. During the latter period, Edgemont Molybdenite Mines Limited did most of the development and produced 24.5 t of 0.75 per cent molybdenite. The mine consists of two trenches (30 m and 21 m long) and a 12 m shaft extending over a distance of about 225 m in a north-south direction along the side of a lightly wooded low ridge.

The mine is about 1 km northeast of Schutt on the farm of Gordon Liedtke. *See* Map 6 on p. 55.

Road log from Highway 515 at **km 51.2** (*see* the road log to the Eganville–Quadeville–Combermere area on p. 47):

km		
	0	Junction of Highway 515 and a gravel road; turn left (south) onto the gravel road.
	3.7	Junction; turn right.

3.8   Junction, single-lane road opposite the school; turn left.

4.3   Edgemont mine on right, at a bend in the road.

4.5   Drill shed on left; a second trench is located on the slope about 30 m above the shed.

Refs.:   21 p. 171–172; 52 p. 15–16; 77 p. 76–77; 98 p. 63; 170 p. 87.

Maps   (T):   31 F/6 Brudenell
         (G):   53b Renfrew area, Ontario (OGS, 1:126 720)
              1953-2 Brudenell-Raglan area, County of Renfrew, Ontario (OGS, 1:63 360)
              P2357 Renfrew area, western part, southern Ontario (OGS, 1:63 360)
              2461 Barry's Bay, Precambrian geology (OGS, 1:100 000)
              GDIF 178 Raglan Township, County of Renfrew (OGS, 1:31 680)

Jewellville corundum occurrence

CORUNDUM

In syenite gneiss

Corundum occurs as brown grains and as bronze crystals averaging 15 mm in diameter.

Numerous pits were worked between 1901 and 1907 and between 1915 and 1918. In the latter period, Manufacturers Corundum Company operated the deposit and a nearby mill, which was transferred from Burgess Mines. The pits are on a wooded ridge northeast of the bridge at Jewellville.

The occurrence is on the south side of Donnellys Hill about 2 km north of Palmer Rapids. *See* Map 6 on p. 55.

Road log from Highway 515 at **km 57.5** (*see* the road log to the Eganville–Quadeville–Combermere area on p. 47):

km   0   Jewellville, at the north end of the bridge over the Madawaska River; turn right (east).

           0.8   Old mill site on right. Park here and proceed up the trail on the opposite side of the road. The trail leads to the Jewellville corundum pits along the crest of the ridge. The first pit is located about 325 m from the road.

Refs.:   77 p. 60–61; 170 p. 34–35.

Maps   (T):   31 F/5 Barry's Bay
         (G):   53b Renfrew area, Ontario (OGS, 1:126 720)
              1953-2 Brudenell-Raglan area, County of Renfrew, Ontario (OGS, 1:63 360)
              P2357 Renfrew area, western part, southern Ontario (OGS, 1:63 360)
              2461 Barry's Bay, Precambrian geology (OGS, 1:100 000)
              GDIF 178 Raglan Township, County of Renfrew (OGS, 1:31 680)

Craigmont (Craig) mine

CORUNDUM, SCAPOLITE, MICROCLINE, PLAGIOCLASE, HORNBLENDE, PYROXENE, GARNET, BIOTITE, MUSCOVITE, TITANITE, MAGNETITE, CHLORITE, PYRITE, MOLYBDENITE, MONAZITE, ZIRCON, APATITE, SPECULARITE, EPIDOTE, JAROSITE, EUXENITE, ALLANITE, NATROLITE, CHABAZITE, TOURMALINE, ZOISITE, ANHYDRITE, GYPSUM

In alkalic gneiss and nepheline-bearing gneiss

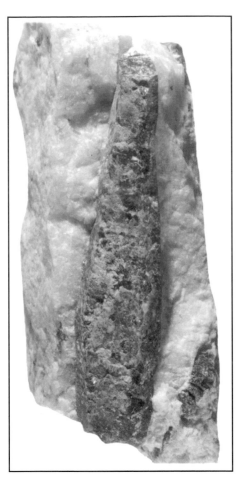

Plate 12.

Corundum crystal in nepheline syenite, Craigmont mine. The crystal is 8 cm long and 1 to 2 cm wide. GSC 201420-D

Plate 13.

Craigmont mine, Robillard Mountain, 1913. The Klondike cuts are at far left. GSC 23804

Plate 14.

Corundum mill, Craigmont mine, 1904–1910. The mill, built in 1904, was destroyed by fire in 1913. Ontario Archives Acc 13281-152

Corundum occurs as crystals several centimetres long and as grains and aggregates. Most crystals occur in nepheline-rich gneiss. The colour ranges from blue-grey, greenish grey, brownish grey to bronze, and nearly colourless to yellow and green including colour zoning. Corundum is generally associated with feldspar or light green scapolite. The largest crystal found measured 20 cm by 15 cm and is in the mineral collection of the Royal Ontario Museum in Toronto. Other minerals in the deposit include hornblende, pyroxene, microcline, plagioclase, dark red garnet (12 mm crystals and crystal aggregates), muscovite, biotite, brown titanite (small crystals), chlorite, magnetite (crystals), pyrite, and molybdenite. Monazite (yellow grains), zircon (pink prisms), apatite (light green), specularite, and epidote are less abundant. Jarosite occurs as an earthy yellow to rusty coating on the host rock. Euxenite, allanite, natrolite, chabazite, tourmaline, zoisite, anhydrite, and gypsum have also been reported from the deposit.

This deposit was discovered in about 1876 when a young girl drew the attention of her father, Henry Robillard, to some corundum crystals in an outcrop on the hill on his property. To her, the crystals resembled cruet bottle stoppers. The crystals were compared to and mistaken for the Lake Clear apatite crystals and plans were made to mine phosphate. It was not until 10 years later that the mineral was identified as corundum by a geologist, Hubert Ross Wood. A few years later, federal and provincial geologists surveyed the corundum-bearing rocks in the area and, within a few years, mining began.

The mine was the province's first producer of corundum. Mining operations were conducted in two areas about 1500 m apart on the south slope of Craigmont Hill (formerly Robillard Mountain). Mining was done by Canada Corundum Company from 1900 to 1908, and by Manufacturers Corundum Company from 1909 to 1913. At that time the deposit was regarded as the largest corundum deposit in the world. A mill was installed at the mine site in 1900. Corundum was also produced from the tailings in 1920–1921 and from 1944 to 1946. The total production amounted to 18 827 t, which accounted for 84 per cent of Canada's total corundum production. The main workings are at the eastern end of Craigmont Hill. They consist of 20 open cuts extending 150 m from the base to the top of the hill, and an adit driven north 67 m into the mountain slope. There are eleven open cuts on the upper slopes at the western end of the mountain. These

61

workings are known as the Klondike Cuts. The largest open cut is at the eastern end; it is 152 m long, up to 30 m wide, and 15 m deep. The largest of the Klondike Cuts is 98 m long, up to 30 m wide, and 18 m deep. Extensive dumps are found along the slope.

The mine is about 11 km south of Combermere. *See* Map 7 on p. 63.

Road log from Highway 515 at **km 68.2** (*see* the road log to the Eganville–Quadeville–Combermere area on p. 47):

km	0	Junction, highways 62 and 515; proceed west along Highway 62 toward Combermere.
	0.5	Junction, Highway 517 in Combermere; turn left onto Highway 517.
	9.3	Junction, single-lane road; turn left.
	10.0	The Klondike Cuts are on the hill on the left.
	10.3	Fork; bear left.
	11.4	The Craigmont (Craig) mine dumps on the south slope of Craigmont Hill are visible on left.
	11.7	Remnants of the old mill are on both sides of the road. A trail on left leads to the Craigmont mine open cuts beginning 300 m from the mill site.

Refs.: 12 p. 16–27; 20 p. 102–116; 38 p. 15–16; 45 p. 230–231; 77 p. 56–60; 89 p. 15R; 91 p. 51–53; 128 p. 18; 170 p. 11, 32–33; 192 p. 31–35.

Maps   (T): 31 F/5 Barry's Bay
(G): 53b Renfrew area, Ontario (OGS, 1:126 720)
1953-2 Brudenell-Raglan area, County of Renfrew, Ontario (OGS, 1:63 360)
P2357 Renfrew area, western part, southern Ontario (OGS, 1:63 360)
2461 Barry's Bay, Precambrian geology (OGS, 1:100 000)
GDIF 178 Raglan Township, County of Renfrew (OGS, 1:31 680)

Burgess mine

CORUNDUM, SCAPOLITE, HORNBLENDE, MAGNETITE, MUSCOVITE, BIOTITE, TITANITE, PYRITE, EPIDOTE, CHLORITE, ZIRCON, RUTILE

In syenite and pegmatite

Corundum occurs as pinkish-brown to grey crystals and as irregular masses. It is associated with feldspar, light green granular scapolite, hornblende, magnetite, muscovite, and biotite. Occurring less abundantly are titanite, pyrite, epidote, chlorite, zircon (tiny pink prisms), and tan-coloured rutile. Radioactive minerals have been reported from the deposit.

This corundum deposit was discovered in 1896 by W.F. Ferrier of the Geological Survey of Canada who investigated the occurrence after identifying some corundum specimens from the area mistakenly sold to him as pyroxene crystals. The Ontario Corundum Company began mining operations in 1902. An opening was made into the side of a cliff, a mill was installed, and the location was known as Burgess Mines. During the next ten years various companies worked the deposit, including Manufacturers Corundum Company, the last operator, who at the same time operated the Craigmont mine. The openings include two main cuts into the cliff (30 m and 23 m long) and several small cuts in the hill to the northeast.

The mine is 18 km southwest of Combermere. *See* Map 7 on p. 63.

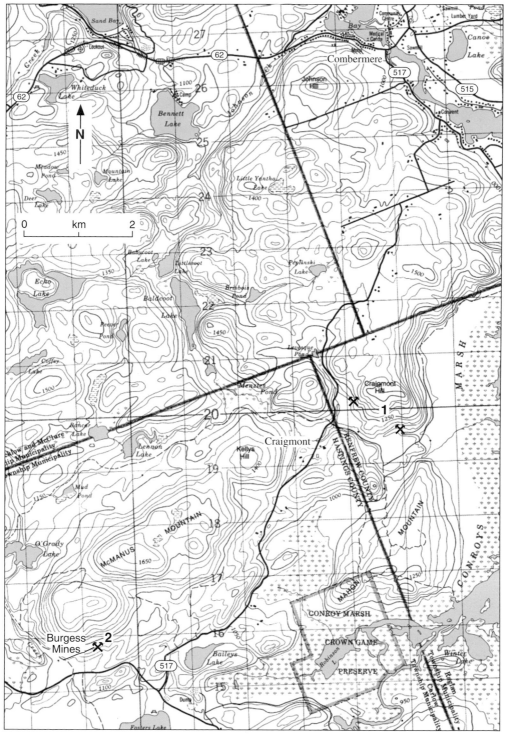

1. Craigmont (Craig) mine   2. Burgess mine

Map 7. Craigmont.

Road log from Highway 515 at **km 68.2** (*see* the road log to the Eganville–Quadeville–Combermere area on p. 48):

km 0 Junction of highways 62 and 515; proceed west along Highway 62 toward Combermere.

0.5 Combermere, at the junction of Highway 517; proceed south onto Highway 517 toward the Craigmont mine.

9.3 Junction, road to Craigmont mine; continue straight ahead.

15.9 Junction, Boulter-New Carlow Road; turn right.

17.8 Junction, single-lane road; turn right.

18.2 Fork; bear right.

18.8 Burgess mine on right.

Refs.: <u>12</u> p. 18–19, 28–30; <u>38</u> p. 14–15; <u>45</u> p. 231; <u>78</u> p. 32; <u>192</u> p. 27.

Maps (T): 31 F/5 Barry's Bay
(G): 1954-3 Monteagle and Carlow Townships, Ontario (OGS, 1:31 360)
GDIF 332 Carlow Township, Hastings County (OGS, 1:31 680)

This is the last occurrence described for the side trip to the Eganville–Quadeville–Combermere area. The description of occurrences along the Renfrew–Madawaska road log continues from **km 40.9** (*see* p. 43).

Berger amazonite occurrence

AMAZONITE, PERISTERITE, QUARTZ, MICA, GRAPHIC GRANITE, TOURMALINE, ACTINOLITE, CHLORITE, PYRITE, JAROSITE, GOETHITE

In pegmatite dyke cutting biotite gneiss

Green amazonite, white plagioclase, pink microcline, and colourless to smoky quartz are the principal constituents of the pegmatite. White peristerite, pink perthite, and pink and light green graphic granite are also present. The amazonite, peristerite, and graphic granite are suitable for lapidary purposes. Minerals occurring less commonly in the pegmatite are biotite, black tourmaline, actinolite, dark green massive chlorite, pyrite (coated with jarosite), and goethite.

The deposit has been exposed by a pit on the Albert Berger farm, about 7 km northwest of Eganville.

Road log from Highway 60 at **km 40.9** (*see* the Renfrew–Madawaska road log on p. 43):

km 0 Junction, highways 60 and 41 North; proceed onto Highway 41 North.

0.1 Junction; turn left onto Germanicus Road.

3.5 Junction, road to Berger farm on left; turn left.

3.8 Berger farmhouse; obtain permission to visit the occurrence. The Berger amazonite pit is in the pasture about 300 m west of the farmhouse.

Ref.: <u>166</u> p. 93.

Maps (T): 31 F/11 Golden Lake
(G): 53b Renfrew area, Ontario (OGS, 1:126 720)
P2356 Pembroke area, eastern part, southern Ontario (OGS, 1:63 360)
2459 Pembroke, Precambrian geology (OGS, 1:100 000)

Plate 15.

Berger amazonite occurrence, 1969. GSC 153182

Biederman (Germanicus) quarry

GRAPHITE, MICA, TREMOLITE, TOURMALINE, SERPENTINE, APATITE, CALCITE, QUARTZ

In crystalline limestone

The crystalline limestone is greyish white and contains disseminated grains of amber mica, graphite, light green and tan tremolite, orange tourmaline, green serpentine, and light blue apatite (uncommon). Crystals of amber mica 2 cm in diameter are common. Massive white calcite and colourless quartz are also present.

The quarry was worked in the 1930s for the production of lime for local use. A wood-burning kiln was operated at the quarry site. The quarry, now partly overgrown, is located near the top of the south slope of a ridge.

The quarry is about 9 km northeast of Golden Lake.

Road log from Highway 60 at **km 51.0** (*see* the Renfrew–Madawaska road log on p. 43):

km	0	Golden Lake, junction of Highway 60 and Renfrew County Road 30 (Reserve Road). Turn right (east) onto Renfrew County Road 30.
	2.8	*Roadcut* exposes crystalline limestone containing white hair-like aggregates of clinoamphibole, green clinopyroxene, titanite, quartz, pyrite, and magnetite. Black massive tourmaline and mica are associated with plagioclase-quartz masses. Rozenite occurs as white globular crusts on the rock.

4.4	*Roadcut* exposes biotite-plagioclase gneiss containing pink almandine garnet grains averaging 3 mm across, fibrous sillimanite, and titanite.
10.1	Junction; turn left (north). This junction is 6.2 km west of the junction of Highway 41 and Renfrew County Road 30.
11.2	Biederman (Germanicus) quarry on right, just south of the farm buildings.

Refs.: 64 p. 164–165; 118; 170 p. 109–110; 191 p. 52–54.

Maps   (T): 31 F/11 Golden Lake
(G): 53b Renfrew area, Ontario (OGS, 1:126 720)
P1980 Marbles of the Pembroke-Renfrew area, southern Ontario (OGS, 1:126 720)
P2356 Pembroke area, eastern part, southern Ontario (OGS, 1:63 360)
2459 Pembroke, Precambrian geology (OGS, 1:100 000)

Deady mine

QUARTZ CRYSTALS, GRAPHIC GRANITE

In granite pegmatite

Quartz crystals up to 2 cm in diameter occur in cavities in massive quartz and feldspar. The pegmatite is composed of microcline, quartz, plagioclase, chlorite, and mica. Medium-textured pink graphic granite is also present.

The Deady mine was operated in 1942 by Keystone Contractors, Limited. Small amounts of feldspar and quartz were recovered.

The mine is located at the west end of a small lake about 12 km northeast of Madawaska; it is visible from Highway 60. *See* Map 8 on p. 68. Access is by the single-lane road at **km 107.1** (*see* the Renfrew–Madawaska road log on p. 43).

Ref.:   170 p. 39.

Maps   (T): 31 F/12 Round Lake
(G): 53b Renfrew area, Ontario (OGS, 1:126 720)
P 2355 Pembroke area, western part, southern Ontario (OGS, 1:63 360)
2459 Pembroke, Precambrian geology (OGS, 1:100 000)

Bambrick mine

HEMATITE, MAGNETITE, MICROCLINE, PLAGIOCLASE

In granite pegmatite

Massive black hematite occurs with massive magnetite in pegmatite consisting of orange-red microcline, white plagioclase, colourless to smoky quartz, and biotite.

The deposit was originally worked by Mr. Bambrick of Ottawa in 1921, and by Canadian Non-Metallic Minerals Company of Montréal in 1922 and 1923. Production amounted to about 450 t of feldspar. The deposit was worked from an open cut in the side of a low ridge; the open cut measures about 180 m by 7.5 m and 7.5 m deep.

The mine is on the south side of Gun Lake Marsh, south of Aylen Lake, about 12 km northeast of Madawaska. *See* Map 8 on p. 68.

Road log from Highway 60 at **km 109.3** (*see* the Renfrew–Madawaska road log on p. 43):

km   0   Junction, Highway 60 and Aylen Lake Road; proceed north along Aylen Lake Road.

            5.1   Junction; turn right onto a single-lane road (former railway).

            9.7   Bambrick mine on right.

Refs.:   188 p. 52; 192 p. 153–154.

Maps   (T):   31 F/12 Round Lake
          (G):   53b Renfrew area, Ontario (OGS, 1:126 720)
                P2355 Pembroke area, western part, southern Ontario (OGS, 1:63 360)
                2459 Pembroke, Precambrian geology (OGS, 1:100 000)

Five Mile mine

ALLANITE, GARNET, CHLORITE, BIOTITE, PLAGIOCLASE, MICROCLINE, QUARTZ, GRAPHIC GRANITE, PYROXENE, TITANITE

In granite pegmatite

Allanite occurs as dull brown laths in white plagioclase. Associated with it are pink garnet and chlorite. The pegmatite is composed of plagioclase, microcline, quartz, and biotite. White graphic granite is also present. Excellent crystals of pyroxene (augite) and titanite occur in the pegmatite.

The mine was operated for feldspar by Keystone Contractors Limited in 1947, and by Opeongo Mining Company in 1948. Some 4535 t of feldspar were removed.

The mine is about 2 km west of Aylen Lake and 13 km northeast of Madawaska. *See* Map 8 on p. 68.

Road log from Highway 60 at **km 109.3** (*see* the Renfrew–Madawaska road log on p. 43):

km   0   Junction, Highway 60 and Aylen Lake Road; proceed north along Aylen Lake Road.

            5.9   Junction, single-lane road at gravel pits; turn left.

            6.1   Aylen River. Walk across the river and continue along the road for 1.2 km to a fork; follow the right fork for about 0.8 km to the Five Mile mine on the west side of the ridge.

Refs.:   60 p. 139; 75 p. 12; 85 p. 21; 192 p. 157–158; 213 p. 3.

Maps   (T):   31 F/12 Round Lake
          (G):   53b Renfrew area, Ontario (OGS, 1:126 720)
                P2355 Pembroke area, western part, southern Ontario (OGS, 1:63 360)
                2459 Pembroke, Precambrian geology (OGS, 1:100 000)

Spectacle Lake (Lake) mine

MICROCLINE, ALBITE, QUARTZ, GRAPHIC GRANITE, BIOTITE, CHLORITE, MAGNETITE, GARNET, MONAZITE, EUXENITE, SAMARSKITE, XENOTIME

In granite pegmatite

Part of 31 E/8, 31 E/9, 31 F/5 and 31 F/12

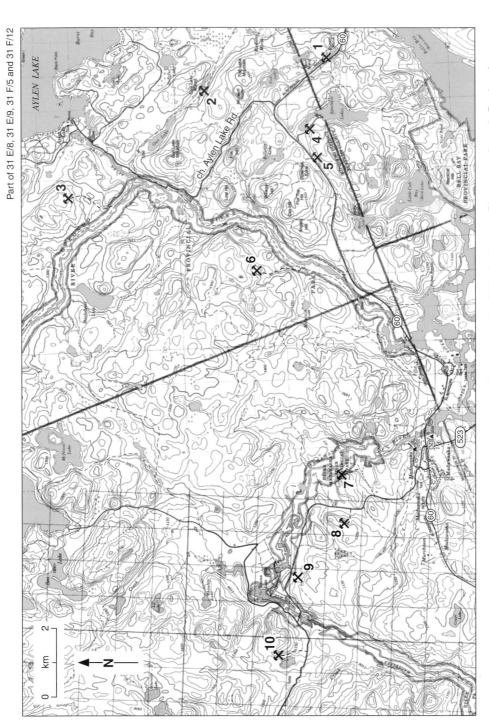

Map 8. Madawaska.

1. Deady mine 2. Bambrick mine 3. Five Mile mine 4. Spectacle Lake (Lake) mine 5. Plexman mine 6. Davis mine
7. Madawaska River mine 8. J.G. Gole (Comet) mine 9. Cameron and Aleck mine 10. Cameron mine

Pink microcline, greyish-white albite, colourless to white and smoky to black quartz, and pink and white fine- to medium-textured graphic granite are the chief constituents of the pegmatite. Accessory minerals include biotite, chlorite, magnetite, garnet, monazite, and euxenite. Samarskite and xenotime are also present (T.S. Ercit, pers. comm., 1995).

The deposit was worked in 1948–1949 by Opeongo Mining Company. About 379 t of feldspar were shipped. The mine consists of an open cut 25 m by 4.5 m and 9 m deep.

The Spectacle Lake (Lake) mine is on the east side of a ridge on the west side of Spectacle Lakes, about 10 km northeast of Madawaska. *See* Map 8 on p. 68.

Road log from Highway 60 at **km 110.5** (*see* the Renfrew–Madawaska road log on p. 43):

km   0   Junction, Highway 60 and Spectacle Lake Road; proceed southeast onto Spectacle Lake Road.

            0.6   Spectacle Lake (Lake) mine on right.

Refs.:   <u>60</u> p. 137 138; <u>75</u> p. 12; <u>85</u> p. 21, 65; <u>106</u> p. 142; <u>213</u> p. 3.

Maps   (T):   31 F/12 Round Lake
         (G):   53b Renfrew area, Ontario (OGS, 1:126 720)
                P2355 Pembroke area, western part, southern Ontario (OGS, 1:63 360)
                2459 Pembroke, Precambrian geology (OGS, 1:100 000)

Plexman mine

ALLANITE, MAGNETITE, MICROCLINE, PLAGIOCLASE, BIOTITE

In granite pegmatite

Allanite occurs as black, lustrous laths in pegmatite consisting of microcline, plagioclase, quartz, and biotite. Massive magnetite is also present. A black, glassy to dull mineral resembling euxenite has also been reported.

The pegmatite was explored by small pits and trenches as a feldspar prospect sometime before 1954. The openings are along the slope and crest of a ridge, and extend over a distance of about 60 m.

The Plexman mine is about 9 km northeast of Madawaska. It is just south of Highway 60 at **km 111.2** (*see* the Renfrew–Madawaska road log on p. 43); **km 111.2** is 0.75 km west of the junction of Spectacle Lake Road and Highway 60. To reach the mine, walk south from the highway for about 200 m, crossing a valley; the main opening begins about halfway up the ridge and extends to the crest. *See* Map 8 on p. 68.

Refs.:   <u>126</u> p. 44–45; <u>192</u> p. 159–161.

Maps   (T):   31 F/12 Round Lake
         (G):   53b Renfrew area, Ontario (OGS, 1:126 720)
                P2355 Pembroke area, western part, southern Ontario (OGS, 1:63 360)
                2459 Pembroke, Precambrian geology (OGS, 1:100 000)

Davis mine

ALLANITE, GARNET, MICROCLINE, OLIGOCLASE, PERISTERITE, MUSCOVITE, BIOTITE, MONAZITE, EUXENITE, SAMARSKITE, COLUMBITE

In granite pegmatite

Dark brown to black allanite and dark red garnet occur in pegmatite consisting of pink microcline, greenish-grey oligoclase, colourless to white quartz, muscovite, and biotite. Some oligoclase exhibits a blue iridescence (peristerite). Monazite, euxenite, samarskite, and columbite have been reported.

The deposit was originally explored sometime before 1936. In 1943, Canadian Flint and Spar Company Limited extracted about 313 kg of muscovite, 27 kg of K-feldspar, and 45 kg of plagioclase feldspar. The openings consist of an open cut 13.7 m by 4.5 m and 1.5 to 2.4 m deep, and another one 10.7 m long and up to 1.2 m deep.

The mine is on a ridge north of the Opeongo River about 7 km northeast of Madawaska. *See* Map 8 on p. 68.

Road log from Highway 60 at **km 116.5** (*see* the Renfrew–Madawaska road log on p. 43):

km	0	Junction, Highway 60 and a road leading north (on the west side of the bridge over Opeongo River); proceed north along this road.
	0.8	Junction; turn right onto a single-lane road (former railway).
	4.6	Cabin on left. A trail to the Davis mine leads north from the cabin along the east side of a ridge, then up a hill for a total distance of about 1200 m.

Refs.:   46 p. 424; 60 p. 135–136; 170 p. 122–123; 192 p. 155–156.

Maps   (T):   31 F/12 Round Lake
(G):   53b Renfrew area, Ontario (OGS, 1:126 720)
P2355 Pembroke area, western part, southern Ontario (OGS, 1:63 360)
2459 Pembroke, Precambrian geology (OGS, 1:100 000)

Madawaska River mine

MICROCLINE, PLAGIOCLASE, BIOTITE, MUSCOVITE, MAGNETITE, PYRITE, HEMATITE, GOETHITE

In granite pegmatite

Pyrite and hematite occur sparingly in pegmatite composed of microcline, plagioclase, quartz, muscovite, and biotite. Goethite occurs as an alteration product of the iron minerals.

The deposit was opened in 1924 by J.A. Cameron who extracted about 16 t of feldspar. The opening consists of an 18 m vertical open cut into the east side of a ridge.

The mine is 2.5 km north of Madawaska. *See* Map 8 on p. 68.

Road log from Highway 60 at **km 120.1** (*see* the Renfrew–Madawaska road log on p. 44):

km	0	Madawaska, at the junction of Highway 60 and Major Lake Road; proceed north along Major Lake Road.
	2.5	Junction; turn right onto a single-lane road.
	3.6	Junction; follow the road on left. At this point the road becomes an overgrown trail; continue walking north along the trail for about 500 m to the Madawaska River mine at the side of the ridge to the left of the trial.

Refs.:   60 p. 129–130; 85 p. 30; 192 p. 164–165.

Map   (T):   31 F/12 Round Lake
(G):   P2355 Pembroke area, western part, southern Ontario (OGS, 1:63 360)
2459 Pembroke, Precambrian geology (OGS, 1:100 000)

J.G. Gole (Comet) mine

PERISTERITE, SUNSTONE, MICROCLINE, PLAGIOCLASE, QUARTZ, BIOTITE, GRAPHIC GRANITE, CHLORITE, FERGUSONITE, ALLANITE, MAGNETITE, URANINITE

In granite pegmatite

Pink peristerite and greyish-pink sunstone (orthoclase) suitable for lapidary purposes occur in pegmatite. The sunstone has attractive reddish-gold flecks in it. The pegmatite consists of pink microcline, white to grey plagioclase, white to smoky quartz, biotite, and graphic granite. The plagioclase exhibits good twinning striations. Brownish-black fergusonite dipyramidal crystals up to 7.5 cm long and 2 cm wide occur in the pegmatite. Other accessory minerals include allanite, uraninite, chlorite, and magnetite. Allanite crystals and casts of crystals up to 60 cm long and 15 cm thick occur along the wall of the open cut. During mining operations large feldspar crystals were encountered, including one that yielded 272 t of feldspar.

This was the largest mine in the Madawaska district. It produced about 1383 t of feldspar and 7835 t of quartz. The mine consists of two open cuts on the southeast side of a hill. The main cut is 150 m long, 9 m wide, and 3 to 9 m deep; the smaller one is 21 m long, 5 m deep, with a 6 m face. Operators were J.G. Gole (1937–1941), D.L. Ross (1942–1944), and Comet Quartz Limited (1976–1977).

The mine is about 3 km northwest of Madawaska. *See* Map 8 on p. 68.

Road log from Highway 60 at **km 120.1** (*see* the Renfrew–Madawaska road log on p. 44):

km   0   Madawaska, at the junction of Highway 60 and Major Lake Road; proceed north along Major Lake Road.

Plate 16.

Muscovite crystal in pegmatite, J.G. Gole (Comet) mine. The crystal is 4 cm across. GSC 201420-G

Plate 17.

Fergusonite crystals in feldspar, J.G. Gole
(Comet) mine. The specimen is 7 cm from
top to bottom. GSC 201420-W

2.5 Junction, lane on right to Madawaska River mine; continue straight ahead.

3.2 Junction; turn left onto a single-lane road.

3.5 J.G. Gole (Comet) mine.

Refs.: 60 p. 127; 75 p. 12; 85 p. 21, 65; 91 p. 53–54; 106 p. 147; 170 p. 120; 192 p. 161–164; 201 p. 108.

Maps (T): 31 E/9 Opeongo Lake
(G): P2355 Pembroke area, western part, southern Ontario (OGS, 1:63 360)
2459 Pembroke, Precambrian geology (OGS, 1:100 000)

Cameron and Aleck mine

PERISTERITE, OLIGOCLASE, MICROCLINE, ALBITE, HORNBLENDE, BIOTITE, QUARTZ CRYSTALS, MUSCOVITE, TOURMALINE, ALLANITE, TITANITE, ANATASE, FERGUSONITE, ZIRCON, PYRITE, SERPENTINE, CHLORITE, URANINITE, APATITE, MAGNETITE, URANOPHANE, GRAPHIC GRANITE

In granite pegmatite

The pegmatite is composed principally of albite, oligoclase, microcline, and quartz. The plagioclase feldspars exhibit good twinning striations. Peristerite and sunstone (less common) are also present; crystal aggregates of lustrous black hornblende and large books of biotite are the most abundant accessory minerals. Cavities in massive quartz are lined with small crystals of quartz and of muscovite. Minerals occurring less abundantly in the pegmatite are tourmaline, as black massive patches; allanite, as dull black laths; titanite, as dark brown crystals; anatase, as cream-white compact masses in hornblende; fergusonite, as lustrous dark brown crystals; zircon, as brownish-pink turbid crystals less than 2 cm long; pyrite; serpentine, as dull greenish-black laths (alteration of pyroxene); chlorite, as greasy black flaky masses; uraninite, as small black masses in quartz and as microscopic grains and crystals in hornblende and in quartz; apatite, as amber patches in hornblende; and magnetite. The secondary uranium mineral, uranophane, occurs as a yellow waxy crust on hornblende associated with uraninite. Euxenite is reported to occur with biotite. Pink, fine-textured graphic granite also occurs in the deposit and is suitable for lapidary purposes.

The deposit was worked for feldspar in 1949–1950. About 1814 t of feldspar were produced. The open cut is on the north side of a wooded hill about 5.5 km northwest of Madawaska. *See* Map 8 on p. 68.

Road log from Highway 60 at **km 120.1** (*see* the Renfrew–Madawaska road log on p. 44):

km		
	0	Junction of Highway 60 and Major Lake Road in Madawaska; proceed north along Major Lake Road.
	3.2	Junction, lane to the J.G. Gole (Comet) mine on left, continue straight ahead.
	6.3	Junction, single-lane mine road on left; turn left. Small piles of feldspar, quartz, and accessory minerals from the quarry have been left in the lightly wooded area along the mine road.
	6.4	Cameron and Aleck mine.

Refs.:   60 p. 125–126; 75 p. 12; 85 p. 21, 65.

Maps   (T):   31 E/9 Opeongo Lake
    (G):   P2355 Pembroke area, western part, southern Ontario (OGS, 1:63 360)
       2459 Pembroke, Precambrian geology (OGS, 1:100 000)

Cameron mine

ALBITE, OLIGOCLASE, MICROCLINE, QUARTZ, HORNBLENDE, PYROXENE, TITANITE, EUXENITE, ALLANITE, EPIDOTE, PYRITE, HEMATITE, GRAPHIC GRANITE

In granite pegmatite

The main constituents of the pegmatite are albite, oligoclase, microcline, and colourless to smoky quartz. White platy albite (cleavelandite) is also present. Hornblende, pyroxene, and titanite are common accessories. Other minerals occurring in the deposit are euxenite, allanite, epidote, pyrite, and hematite. Medium-textured pink graphic granite occurs in the pegmatite.

The mine was originally operated in 1940 by W.B. Cameron. Subsequent operators were Keystone Contractors Limited, Canspar Mines Limited, Opeongo Mining Company, and Bowser Bros. Operations ended in 1950 after some 5440 t of feldspar had been mined. The opening on the southwest side of a hill is 91 m by 6 m and 9 m deep.

The mine is about 8 km northwest of Madawaska. See Map 8 on p. 68.

Road log from Highway 60 at **km 120.1** (*see* the Renfrew–Madawaska road log on p. 44):

km		
	0	Junction of Highway 60 and Major Lake Road in Madawaska; proceed north along Major Lake Road.
	3.2	Junction, lane on left to J.G. Gole (Comet) mine; continue straight ahead.
	6.3	Junction, lane on left to Cameron and Aleck mine; continue straight ahead.
	7.9	Bridge over Madawaska River.
	9.2	Junction, single-lane road on right; turn right.
	9.4	Fork; bear right. Proceed along the south end of a small lake, then along the west side of a hill to the mine.
	10.1	Cameron mine.

Refs.:   75 p. 12; 85 p. 21, 65; 170 p. 121; 213 p. 4.

Maps   (T):   31 E/9 Opeongo Lake
(G):   P2355 Pembroke area, western part, southern Ontario (OGS, 1:63 360)
2459 Pembroke, Precambrian geology (OGS, 1:100 000)

This is the end of the description of collecting localities between Ottawa and Renfrew. Collecting localities between Renfrew and North Bay are described in the text following the road log.

Renfrew to North Bay area – Highway 17 road log (resumed from p. 5)

km		
km	**62.1**	Junction, highways 17 and 60 (O'Brien Street), just east of Renfrew.
km	**64.3**	*Roadcuts* expose crystalline limestone containing orange-brown to brown tourmaline, colourless tremolite-actinolite, greyish-green clinopyroxene, serpentine, titanite, amber mica, graphite, and pyrite. Pink calcite veins cut the limestone.
km	**64.6**	Junction, Renfrew County Road 20 (on right) and Bruce Avenue (on left) to Renfrew County Road 4 roadcut (*see* p. 44).
km	**72.2**	*Roadcuts* expose crystalline limestone and fine-grained dioritic rock. The limestone contains finely disseminated graphite, pyrite, magnetite, pyrrhotite, green clinopyroxene, colourless tremolite, green serpentine, and amber mica. The dark dioritic rock is cut by veins of white calcite that fluoresce pink in short ultraviolet light. Biotite crystals and pyrite occur in the calcite.
km	**74.2**	*Roadcuts* expose crystalline limestone containing light green massive serpentine, pink and white calcite (white calcite fluoresces pink in short ultraviolet light), and prismatic aggregates of white diopside and white tremolite. Light blue apatite grains, amber mica, and pyrite occur sparingly.
km	**76.2**	Junction, Renfrew County Road 61 (on left), and Highway 653 (on right) to Wright mine (p. 77), Haley mine (p. 77), Smith mine (p. 79), and Rapides des Chenaux occurrence (p. 80).

km	80.8	*Roadcut* on left exposes pink calcite in crystalline limestone. The calcite contains pale green apatite crystals up to 2 cm in diameter, pyrite, titanite, black amphibole, dark green pyroxene, pink K-feldspar, and light yellow plagioclase. White massive calcite fluoresces pink in short ultraviolet light.
km	81.3	*Roadcut* on left exposes pink and grey coarsely crystalline calcite containing dark green massive pyroxene, dark brown massive titanite, biotite, light green and yellow apatite (massive and small crystals), black allanite crystals, magnetite, pyrite, and pyrrhotite.
km	83.6	*Historic site* on right. The site commemorates the area where Samuel de Champlain's astrolabe was lost during his first voyage up the Ottawa River in 1613, and found in 1867.
km	84.8	Junction, Ross Township No. 1 Sideroad.
		Roadcut on Ross Township No. 1 Sideroad, 0.4 km east of Highway 17, exposes microcline pegmatite containing black hornblende, colourless to violet fluorite, red and green apatite, dark green clinopyroxene, pink to white calcite, colourless quartz, titanite, and grains of magnetite, pyrite, and pyrrhotite.
km	86.8	Junction, Renfrew County Road 7 (to Beachburg and Foresters Falls) to Ross mine (p. 81), Elliott's mine (p. 82), Foresters Falls (Jamieson) quarry (p. 82), and Paquette Rapids occurrence (p. 83).
km	87.4	*Roadcut* exposes granitic rock containing granular masses of dark green pyroxene, dark brown titanite, yellow scapolite, and tiny grains of pink to tan zircon. Red apatite crystals, about 2 cm in diameter, occur in pink calcite veins cutting the granitic rock.
km	87.7	Cobden, junction of Renfrew County Road 8 to Eganville and to Cole mine (p. 85).
km	102.7	*Roadcuts* expose Ordovician limestone containing fossil shells and crinoids.
km	104.5	Junction, Renfrew County Road 40 (old Highway 17) to Morrison Island and Île aux Allumettes occurrences (p. 86) and Pembroke quarry (p. 86).
km	115.5	Junction, Highway 41. Occurrences in the Eganville–Quadeville–Combermere and Madawaska areas can be reached via Highway 41 (*see* p. 47).
		Roadcuts on Highway 41, 8.9 km south of Highway 17, expose Ordovician limestone containing brachiopods, gastropods, bryozoa, and crinoids.
		Roadcuts on Highway 41, 19.3 km south of Highway 17, expose granite pegmatite containing dull black bastnaesite, magnetite, titanite, and hornblende. The road log continues along Highway 17.
km	155.7	Junction, road to Atomic Energy of Canada Limited in Chalk River. For tours to the nuclear plant contact the Public Information Centre for arrangements.
km	184.0	Junction, Highway 635 in Rolphton.
km	186–190	*Roadcuts* expose biotite gneiss containing red garnet.
km	194.2	Junction, Mackey Creek Road in Mackey.

km	194.5	Junction, Jennings Road in Mackey to Carey (Mackey) mine (p. 87).
km	197.4	Junction, road to Driftwood Provincial Park.
km	201–213	*Roadcuts* expose feldspar-biotite gneiss containing red garnet crystals and grains up to 2 cm in diameter.
km	214.7	Junction, Bissett Creek Road to Bissett Creek mine (p. 89).
km	226.2	Gibson Lake Picnic Site.
km	227.3	*Roadcuts* expose dark red granitic rocks cut by a conspicuous zone of white massive quartz containing quartz crystals. Kaolinite and hematite occur as coatings on quartz.
km	234.7	Deux Rivières. The Deux Rivières outlier (p. 89) can be reached from the town by boat.
km	236.6	Junction, Brent Road to Muskwa Lake (Brent) mine (p. 90) and Brent Crater (p. 91).
km	261.6	Junction, road leading north to the McMeekin amazonite occurrence (p. 91).
km	268.5	Mattawa, junction of Highway 533 to Mattawa outlier (p. 92), Mattawan (O'Brien-Fowler) mine (p. 92), Purdy mine (p. 94), Croteau mine (p. 96), Mica Company of Canada mine (p. 97), Mattarig mine (p. 97), and Crocan Lake kyanite occurrence (p. 98).
km	281.0	Junction, road to Samuel de Champlain Provincial Park.
		Roadcuts along Highway 17 east and west of this junction expose biotite gneiss containing red garnet and some greyish-green tremolite.
km	287.0	Junction, Highway 630 to Eau Claire (MacLaren) beryl occurrence (p. 100).
km	289.0	*Roadcuts* expose feldspar-biotite gneiss containing red garnet, epidote, and magnetite.
km	290.7	*Roadcuts* expose crystalline limestone containing brucite, hydro-magnesite (white flaky aggregates), dolomite, serpentine, mica (light green), and graphite.
km	291.1	Bridge over Pimisi Bay.
km	291.7	*Roadcuts* expose light green quartzite containing aggregates of deep red garnet, amphibole, and titanite.
km	293.5	Junction, road on right to a gravel pit and Legendre mine (p. 100).
km	295–323	*Roadcuts* expose quartzite and biotite gneiss containing red garnet crystals and aggregates up to 2 cm across, some light green scapolite, and fracture fillings of white calcite that fluoresces bright pink in short ultraviolet light.
km	323.6	La Vase Portages Historic Site.
km	327.3	Junction, Highway 11 South. This is the starting point for occurrences in the North Bay–Huntsville area (p. 115).

| km | 328.1 | Junction, Highway 63 North in North Bay to Twenty Minute Lake occurrence, (p. 101), Niemetz and Ross quarries (p. 102), Nova Beaucage mine (p. 103), and to occurrences in the Témiscaming (Quebec) area (p. 109). |
| km | 330.5 | Junction, Highway 11 North in North Bay to River Valley garnet mine, (p. 105), Nipissing Black Granite quarry (p. 107), and Golden Rose (Afton) mine (p. 108). |

This is the end of the Highway 17 road log from Ottawa to North Bay.

Wright mine

TREMOLITE, DIOPSIDE, QUARTZ

In dolomitic crystalline limestone

Colourless, light blue, and green tremolite is abundant. It occurs as radiating bladed and acicular aggregates and as compact fibrous and columnar masses. White diopside (as flat prisms) is associated with tremolite. Colourless massive quartz is also present.

The deposit has been exposed by one large pit (6 m by 23 m and 2.4 m deep) and three small pits in a pasture on the farm of D. Wright. It was formerly worked for terrazzo.

The mine is about 2 km east of Haley Station. See Map 9 on p. 78.

Road log from Highway 17 at **km 76.2** (*see* Highway 17 road log on p. 74):

km	0	Junction of Highway 17, Highway 653, and Renfrew County Road 61; proceed southwest onto County Road 61.
	0.2	Junction; turn left (southeast) onto Ross Township Garden Road.
	1.2	Turn right to the D. Wright property and the Wright mine.

Ref.: 170 p. 107.

Maps (T): 31 F/10 Cobden
(G): 53b Renfrew area, Ontario (OGS, 1:126 720)
P1980 Marbles of the Pembroke-Renfrew area, southern Ontario (OGS, 1:126 720)
P2356 Pembroke area, eastern part, southern Ontario (OGS, 1:63 360)
2460 Cobden, Precambrian geology (OGS, 1:100 000)
GDIF 408 Ross Township, County of Renfrew (OGS, 1:31 680)

Haley mine

DOLOMITE, CALCITE, SERPENTINE, CHLORITE, TALC, TOURMALINE, TREMOLITE, RUTILE, PYRITE, HEMATITE, GRAPHITE, MARCASITE, CHONDRODITE

In dolomitic crystalline limestone

Dolomite is white to pink, granular massive. Other minerals occur sparingly, including white fibrous and white, pale blue, and pink crystalline calcite (the white calcite fluoresces pink when exposed to ultraviolet rays); light green and dark grey serpentine; dark green flaky chlorite; grey massive talc; light brown tourmaline (crystalline aggregates); white bladed tremolite; black metallic rutile (grains); pyrite; hematite, which in places produces a reddish colour in the host rock; graphite; and marcasite. Chondrodite has also been reported from the deposit.

Dominion Magnesium Limited (Timminco Limited) has operated the mine and processing plant for magnesium since 1941. The metal is used in the aeronautics industry. Two quarries have been opened in the deposit. Permission for entry must be obtained from the office.

The mine is about 4 km north of Haley Station. *See* Map 9 on p. 78.

Part of 31 F/10

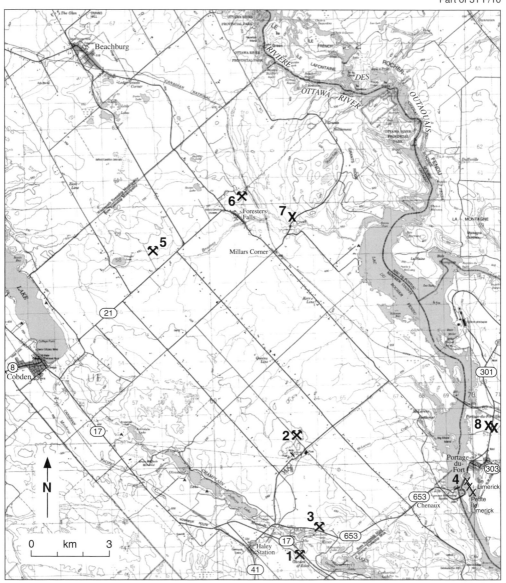

1. Wright mine   2. Haley mine   3. Smith mine   4. Rapides des Chenaux occurrence
5. Ross mine   6. Elliott's mine   7. Foresters Falls (Jamieson) quarry
8. Portage-du-Fort quarries

Map 9. Cobden–Portage-du-Fort.

Road log from Highway 17 at **km 76.2** (*see* Highway 17 road log on p. 74):

km	0	Junction of Highway 17, Highway 653, and Renfrew County Road 61; proceed northeast along Highway 653 toward Portage-du-Fort.
	0.6	Junction; turn left (north).
	3.3	Haley mine.

Refs.:   <u>81</u> p. 75; <u>110</u> p. 371; <u>111</u> p. 111–113; <u>170</u> p. 65–66.

Maps   (T): 31 F/10 Cobden
         (G): 53b Renfrew area, Ontario (OGS, 1:126 720)
         P1980 Marbles of the Pembroke-Renfrew area, southern Ontario (OGS, 1:126 720)
         P2356 Pembroke area, eastern part, southern Ontario (OGS, 1:63 360)
         2460 Cobden, Precambrian geology (OGS, 1:100 000)
         GDIF 408 Ross Township, County of Renfrew (OGS, 1:31 680)

Smith mine

TREMOLITE, MICA, TOURMALINE, APATITE, TALC, GRAPHITE, HEMATITE, GOETHITE, QUARTZ, SERPENTINE

In dolomitic crystalline limestone

The crystalline limestone (marble) is white with some grey and rose bands. It contains abundant colourless fibrous to columnar aggregates of tremolite, and greenish-yellow mica. Occurring less abundantly are yellow to yellowish-green granular tourmaline, light blue apatite, white talc, graphite, hematite, goethite, and quartz.

The mine was worked in the 1960s by Canadian Dolomite Company for the production of marble chips. It measures about 9 m by 6 m. Two nearby quarries are being worked by H & H Aggregates. One quarry, opened in 1985, is 50 m northwest of the original quarry. The other quarry, 50 m east of the original quarry, was opened in 1989; it produces serpentine marble.

The mine is about 3 km northeast of Haley Station. *See* Map 9 on p. 78

Road log from Highway 17 at **km 76.2** (*see* Highway 17 road log on p. 74):

km	0	Junction of Highway 17, Highway 653, and Renfrew County Road 61; proceed northeast onto Highway 653 toward Portage-du-Fort.
	1.6	*Roadcut* (on left) exposes crystalline limestone containing disseminations of graphite, mica, yellow chondrodite, orange tourmaline, brown titanite, light yellow clinoamphibole, magnetite, and pyrite.
	2.4	Turn left to the Smith mine.

Refs.:   <u>81</u> p. 79; <u>111</u> p. 115–117.

Maps   (T): 31 F/10 Cobden
         (G): 53b Renfrew area, Ontario (OGS, 1:126 720)
         P1980 Marbles of the Pembroke-Renfrew area, southern Ontario (OGS, 1:126 720)
         P2356 Pembroke area, eastern part, southern Ontario (OGS, 1:63 360)
         2460 Cobden, Precambrian geology (OGS, 1:100 000)
         GDIF 408 Ross Township, County of Renfrew (OGS, 1:31 680)

Rapides des Chenaux occurrence

DIOPSIDE, CHONDRODITE, SPINEL, CLINOAMPHIBOLE, TITANITE, PHLOGOPITE, SCAPOLITE, GARNET, WOLLASTONITE, VESUVIANITE, CLINOZOISITE, GRAPHITE, PYRITE, MAGNETITE, PYRRHOTITE, GOETHITE

In marble (crystalline limestone)

Marble is spectacularly exposed along the western side of Limerick Island in the channelway of the Ottawa River below the Chenaux dam. The marble mass contains both calcitic and magnesian marble, which are interbanded in places. Masses of dark brown gabbro composed of labradorite, hypersthene, and augite are also exposed. The marble is fine to medium grained, white grading to greyish white, and contains a variety of minerals as disseminated grains and as coarse aggregates of two or more minerals forming knobby and lense-like masses. These minerals include dark green diopside, orange chondrodite, pink spinel, smoky light brown clinoamphibole, titanite, phlogopite, scapolite, garnet, wollastonite, vesuvianite, clinozoisite, graphite, pyrite, magnetite, pyrrhotite, and goethite.

At one time, marble was produced from several small quarries on Limerick Island. The marble at Rapides des Chenaux is about 9 km east of Haley Station; it is visible from the road leading from Highway 17 to Portage-du-Fort, and is accessible from this road. Roadcuts along Highway 301 in Quebec expose the marble. *See* Map 9 on p. 78.

Road log from Highway 17 at **km 76.2** (*see* Highway 17 road log on p. 74):

km   0   Junction, Highway 17, Highway 653, and Renfrew County Road 61; proceed northeast onto Highway 653 toward Portage-du-Fort. Highway 653 connects onto Quebec Highway 301 at the Quebec border just west of Little Limerick Island.

Plate 18.

Spinel-bearing crystalline limestone, Ottawa River at Chenaux Dam, 1969. GSC 153191

8.7 Highway 301 crosses Little Limerick Island.

9.1 *Roadcut* exposes marble and hypersthene-augite gabbro. Pink calcite, green clinopyroxene, serpentine, pink spinel crystals, dolomite, and pyrite occur in marble. Pyrite and titanite occur in gabbro. Purple forsterite crystals to 1 cm across are reported to occur in calcite-dolomite marble exposed on this island (Ref.: 91).

9.4 Highway 301 enters Limerick Island. Marble exposures along the Ottawa River are visible from the bridge connecting Little Limerick and Limerick islands.

9.5 *Roadcut* exposes marble containing grains of graphite, mica, serpentine, grey olivine, and pyrite. Small brucite nodules, about 1 mm across, associated with pyroaurite and serpentine occur in the marble.

10.1 Portage-du-Fort, junction of highways 301 and 303. This junction is 13.6 km from the junction of highways 148 and 303, west of Shawville.

Refs.: 19 p. 3–5, 7–8; 63 p. 137; 91 p. 42–45; 99 p. 31–32.

Maps (T): 31 F/10 Cobden
(G): 660 Quebec and Ontario, parts of counties of Ottawa and Pontiac, Que. and Carleton and Renfrew, Ont. (Pembroke Sheet No. 122) (GSC, 1:253 440)
1804 Saint-Patrice Lake and Portage-du-Fort, electoral district of Pontiac-Témiscamingue (MRNQ, 1:126 720)

Ross mine

APATITE, TITANITE, PYROXENE, ZIRCON, CALCITE

In hornblende pegmatite

Light green and maroon-red apatite crystals occur with brown titanite, dark green pyroxene, and tiny pink zircon crystals in white to pink calcite. Small brown zircon crystals have been reported in the hornblende.

The deposit has been exposed by two small pits on the farm of Fred Ross, 0.8 km and 1.2 km west of the farmhouse. The openings and dumps are now overgrown.

The mine is about 6 km northeast of Cobden. *See* Map 9 on p. 78.

Road log from Highway 17 at **km 86.8** (*see* Highway 17 road log on p. 75):

km 0 Junction of Highway 17 and Renfrew County Road 7; proceed northeast onto County Road 7.

6.0 Junction, farm road on left leading north to the Ross farmhouse and the Ross mine.

Ref.: 170 p. 17.

Maps (T): 31 F/10 Cobden
(G): 53b Renfrew area, Ontario (OGS, 1:126 720)
P2356 Pembroke area, eastern part, southern Ontario (OGS, 1:63 360)
2460 Cobden, Precambrian geology (OGS, 1:100 000)
GDIF 408 Ross Township, County of Renfrew (OGS, 1:31 680)

Elliott's mine

APATITE, HORNBLENDE, PYROXENE, SCAPOLITE, TITANITE, FLUORITE, ORTHOCLASE, CALCITE, SPINEL, MOLYBDENITE

In crystalline limestone

Crystals of red apatite, black hornblende, dark green pyroxene, bluish-grey to grey scapolite, colourless to purple fluorite, and white orthoclase occur in white to pale pink calcite. The scapolite fluoresces pink when exposed to short ultraviolet rays. Spinel and molybdenite have been reported from the deposit.

The deposit has been exposed by a series of small pits, now moss covered and overgrown. In 1883, about 1 t of apatite crystals was mined.

The mine is about 1 km north of Foresters Falls. *See* Map 9 on p. 78.

Road log from Highway 17 at **km 86.8** (*see* Highway 17 road log on p. 75):

km		
	0	Junction of Highway 17 and Renfrew County Road 7; proceed northeast along County Road 7.
	6.0	Junction, farm road on left to the Ross mine; continue straight ahead toward Foresters Falls.
	9.6	Junction; turn left (northwest).
	10.1	Junction, at cemetery; turn right (northeast).
	10.9	Junction; turn right (southeast).
	11.2	The road bends sharply to the left. Park here and proceed to the woods on right. The Elliott's mine pits are along a ridge just beyond a swampy area, about 150 m from the road.

Refs.: 170 p. 17, 88; 214 p. 5, 8.

Maps (T): 31 F/10 Cobden
(G): 53b Renfrew area, Ontario (OGS, 1:126 720)
P2356 Pembroke area, eastern part, southern Ontario (OGS, 1:63 360)
2460 Cobden, Precambrian geology (OGS, 1:100 000)
GDIF 408 Ross Township, County of Renfrew (OGS, 1:31 680)

Foresters Falls (Jamieson) quarry

TREMOLITE, CLINOPYROXENE, PHLOGOPITE, GRAPHITE, PYRITE

In crystalline limestone

The crystalline limestone is white to grey. It contains some honey-yellow tremolite, dark green clinopyroxene, phlogopite, graphite, and pyrite.

The deposit was worked for lime many years ago by Jamieson Lime Company. The quarry consisted of three openings into a hillside; each opening was about 30 m in the longest dimension. There was a lime-burning kiln between the east and west openings, just below the third opening.

The quarry is about 2.5 km east of Foresters Falls. *See* Map 9 on p. 78.

Road log from Highway 17 at **km 86.8** (*see* Highway 17 road log on p. 75):

km	0	Junction of Highway 17 and Renfrew County Road 7; proceed northeast onto County Road 7.
	6.0	Junction, farm road on left leading to the Ross mine; continue straight ahead toward Foresters Falls.
	9.6	Junction; turn right (southeast) to Foresters Falls.
	12.2	Intersection; turn left (northeast).
	13.1	Junction; follow the road on left.
	13.8	Foresters Falls (Jamieson) quarry on the left (north) side of the road.

Refs.: 64 p. 167–168; 170 p. 108; 191 p. 66–67.

Maps (T): 31 F/10 Cobden
(G): 53b Renfrew area, Ontario (OGS, 1:126 720)
P1980 Marbles of the Pembroke-Renfrew area, southern Ontario (OGS, 1:126 720)
P2356 Pembroke area, eastern part, southern Ontario (OGS, 1:63 360)
2460 Cobden, Precambrian geology (OGS, 1:100 000)
GDIF 408 Ross Township, County of Renfrew (OGS, 1:31 680)

Paquette Rapids occurrence

FOSSILS

In limestone

Abundant fossils occur in Ordovician Black River limestone at Paquette Rapids. Fossils include corals, protozoa, hydrozoa, crinoid fragments, brachiopods, gastropods, pelecypods, cephalopods, ostracods, bryozoa, sponges, and trilobites. The fossils are silicified and stand out distinctly from the weathered, water-worn limestone.

The fossil-bearing rock is exposed as large ledges outcropping across the channel of the Ottawa River at Paquette Rapids, opposite the northeastern end of Île aux Allumettes. The best specimens are in the bed of the river, which may be accessible in times of low water in late summer. The locality is about 7 km north of Westmeath. *See* Map 10 on p. 84.

Road log from Highway 17 at **km 86.8** (*see* Highway 17 road log on p. 75):

km	0	Junction of Highway 17 and Renfrew County Road 7; proceed northeast onto County Road 7.
	7.3	Junction of Renfrew County Road 21 and County Road 7; turn left onto County Road 21 toward Beachburg.
	16.8	Junction at Beachburg; turn right (north) onto Renfrew County Road 49.
	20.2	Junction; turn left (northwest) onto Renfrew County Road 31.
	27.1	Junction of Renfrew County Road 12; turn right (north).
	28.1	Westmeath, at the junction of the road (on left) leading west 0.4 km to a boat launching site on the Ottawa River. Paquette Rapids is about 7.5 km north of this point by boat. The road log continues straight ahead. An alternate and shorter access by boat is given at the end of this road log.

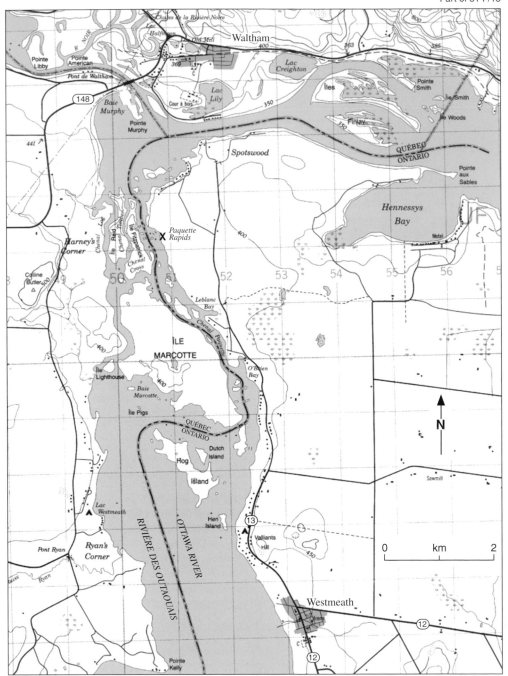

X Fossil occurrence

Map 10. Paquette Rapids.

28.4   Westmeath, at the junction of Renfrew County Road 50 to La Passe; continue north toward the Ottawa River.

36.75   Junction; follow the road on left.

37.2   Road ends at the Laurentian View Resort on the shore of the Ottawa River. Boat launching may be arranged at this resort. Proceed by boat 2 km southwest along the Ottawa River to the Paquette Rapids occurrence in Paquette Channel, which is between Fitzpatrick Island and the Westmeath peninsula.

Refs.:   4 p. 153–154; 42 p. 145; 44 p. 17, 36–39, 57–71; 114 p. 64; 116 p. 177; 216 p. 10; 217 p. 6; 218 p. 11; 220 p. 10; 221 p. 11.

Maps   (T):   31 F/15 Fort-Coulonge
         (G):   660 Quebec and Ontario, parts of counties of Ottawa and Pontiac, Que. and Carleton and Renfrew, Ont. (Pembroke Sheet No. 122) (GSC, 1:253 440)
               P2356 Pembroke area, eastern part, southern Ontario (OGS, 1:63 360)
               P2728 Fort Coulonge, southern Ontario, Paleozoic geology (OGS, 1:50 000)

Cole mine

MOLYBDENITE, PYRRHOTITE, PYRITE, CLINOPYROXENE, ACTINOLITE

In pyroxenite

Molybdenite occurs as coarse flakes up to 2.5 cm across in pyroxenite and in quartz-albite pegmatite stringers cutting the pyroxenite. Pyrrhotite and pyrite occur in small amounts. The pyroxenite is composed of green clinopyroxene with some actinolite, calcite, and plagioclase.

In 1916, J.E. Cole opened the deposit and shipped about 1.3 t of molybdenite to the Mines Branch in Ottawa for testing. In 1939 H. Edelstein did some surface work on the deposit and in 1939–1940 Puritan Mines Limited drove an adit 91.5 m eastward into the west side of a hill. A total of 19 pits were excavated on the hill in an area 76 m by 91 m, the largest measuring 4.6 m across and 3.7 m deep. Buckhorn Mines Limited excavated more pits in 1943.

The mine is about 8 km west of Cobden.

Road log from Highway 17 at **km 87.7** (*see* Highway 17 road log on p. 75):

km   0   Cobden, at the junction of Highway 17 and Renfrew County Road 8 to Eganville; proceed southwest along County Road 8.

4.2   Junction; turn right (northwest) onto the road to Osceola.

7.0   Junction; follow the road on left.

9.5   Junction, single-lane road on right; turn right.

10.4   Overgrown road on left leading west 750 m to the Cole mine.

Refs.:   21 p. 141–142; 37 p. 117; 145 p. 290; 170 p. 77–78.

Maps   (T):   31 F/10 Cobden
         (G):   53b Renfrew area, Ontario (OGS, 1:126 720)
               660 Quebec and Ontario, parts of counties of Ottawa and Pontiac, Que. and Carleton and Renfrew, Ont. (Pembroke Sheet No. 122) (GSC, 1:253 440)
               P2356 Pembroke area, eastern part, southern Ontario (OGS, 1:63 360)
               2460 Cobden, Precambrian geology (OGS, 1:100 000)

Morrison Island, Île aux Allumettes occurrences

FOSSILS, CALCITE CRYSTALS

In limestone

Fossils, including brachiopods and fucoids, occur in Ordovician sedimentary rocks exposed along the shores of Morrison Island and Île aux Allumettes in the vicinity of the Highway 148 bridge connecting the two islands. The sedimentary formations consist of grey fossiliferous limestone of the Ottawa Formation overlying light grey sandstone and greenish-grey shale of the Rockcliffe Formation. Small calcite crystals occur in the limestone. The fossiliferous limestone is also exposed at the rapids on the south side of Morrison Island and on the shore of Beckett Island. The sandstone from Morrison Island had been used for grindstones before 1845 when William E. Logan of the GSC examined the geology of the area. Logan observed fossils, including brachiopods and gastropods, in conglomerate below the sandstone formation.

The occurrences are about 7 km east of Pembroke.

Road log from Highway 17 at **km 104.5** (*see* Highway 17 road log on p. 75):

km		
	0	Junction of Highway 17 and Renfrew County Road 40; proceed onto County Road 40 toward Pembroke.
	9.5	Junction; turn right (east) onto Quebec Highway 148.
	11.7	Morrison Island, south end; Beckett Island is on the south side of Morrison Island and east of the highway.
	13.2	Île aux Allumettes.

Refs.: 44 p. 17–18, 50–51, 58; 99 p. 66–77, 102–106; 114 p. 65; 116 p. 125; 165; 221 p. 11.

Maps (T): 31 F/14 Pembroke
(G): 660 Quebec and Ontario, parts of counties of Ottawa and Pontiac, Que. and Carleton and Renfrew, Ont. (Pembroke Sheet No. 122) (GSC, 1:253 440)
1804 Saint-Patrice Lake and Portage-du-Fort, electoral district of Pontiac-Témiscamingue (MRNQ, 1:126 720)
P2356 Pembroke area, eastern part, southern Ontario (OGS, 1:63 360)
P2727 Pembroke area, southern Ontario, Paleozoic geology (OGS, 1:50 000)

Pembroke quarry

LIMESTONE

Brownish-grey, fine-grained, compact Ordovician limestone was formerly quarried in this and in adjacent quarries. It was originally used as a building stone for local buildings dating back to the 1850s. Several buildings in Pembroke, including the General Hospital, convent, and churches, were constructed of this stone. It was also used for rubble and crushed stone.

The quarry is water filled and partly overgrown. It is in Pembroke and belongs to the municipality of Pembroke.

Road log from Highway 17 at **km 104.5** (*see* Highway 17 road log on p. 75):

km		
	0	Junction of Highway 17 and Renfrew County Road 40; proceed onto County Road 40 toward Pembroke.
	9.5	Junction of Highway 148; continue along County Road 40.

11.0	Junction in Pembroke; turn left (west) onto Renfrew County Road 29 (Drive-In Road).
14.2	Junction; turn right.
14.4	Junction; continue straight ahead.
14.5	Gate to Pembroke quarry.

Refs.: 64 p. 162; 125 p. 161; 143 p. 195–197; 170 p. 106–107; 165; 194 p. 169.

Maps (T): 31 F/14 Pembroke
      (G): 660 Quebec and Ontario, parts of counties of Ottawa and Pontiac, Que. and Carleton and Renfrew, Ont. (Pembroke Sheet No. 122) (GSC, 1:253 440)
      P2356 Pembroke area, eastern part, southern Ontario (OGS, 1:63 360)
      P2727 Pembroke area, southern Ontario, Paleozoic geology (OGS, 1:50 000)

Carey (Mackey) mine

PERISTERITE, SUNSTONE, GRAPHIC GRANITE, MICROCLINE, QUARTZ, MUSCOVITE, BIOTITE, GARNET, MONAZITE, THORIANITE, SAMARSKITE, EUXENITE, BASTNAESITE, THORITE, ZIRCON, RUTILE, ANATASE, ARIZONITE, KAOLINITE, CHLORITE, MAGNETITE, HEMATITE, PYRITE

In granite pegmatite

Pink peristerite with a blue schiller is abundant in this deposit. It is suitable for lapidary purposes. Some sunstone is also present, but it is relatively uncommon. Pink graphic granite, also suitable for lapidary purposes, is common. The pegmatite is composed of pink microcline, colourless to smoky quartz, greenish-yellow muscovite, and biotite. Red almandine-spessartine garnet crystals to 2 cm in diameter are common in the feldspar. Samarskite and brown monazite crystals (5 cm in diameter) with thorianite crystals on their crystal faces are also present (T.S. Ercit, pers. comm., 1995). Also occurring in the deposit are patches of dark amber-brown euxenite, tabular yellow to brownish-red bastnaesite, brown thorite prisms, reddish-amber zircon prisms, brown rutile, tan anatase, brown arizonite, kaolinite, chlorite, magnetite, hematite, and pyrite.

The mine was opened on the James Carey farm in 1924 by Joseph Laberge of Eganville. It was worked until 1928 by Wanup Feldspar Mines Limited. About 2700 t of feldspar and some quartz were produced. The mine consists of a pit 30 m by 12 m and 12 m deep.

The mine is near the shore of the Ottawa River about 3 km northwest of Mackey. See Map 11 on p. 88.

Road log from Highway 17 at **km 194.5** (see Highway 17 road log on p. 76):

km	0	Junction, Highway 17 and Jennings Road; proceed north along Jennings Road.
	2.4	Junction, single-lane road on left; continue along the main road, which turns right at this point.
	3.0	Junction; turn right onto a single-lane road. (The main road continues straight ahead to Old Mackeys Park on the Ottawa River.)
	3.05	Cemetery on left; continue straight ahead.
	3.2	Carey (Mackey) mine.

Refs.: 52 p. 27; 60 p. 257–258; 85 p. 22; 188 p. 49; 194 p. 160; 195 p. 160.

Part of 31 K/SW and 31 L/SE

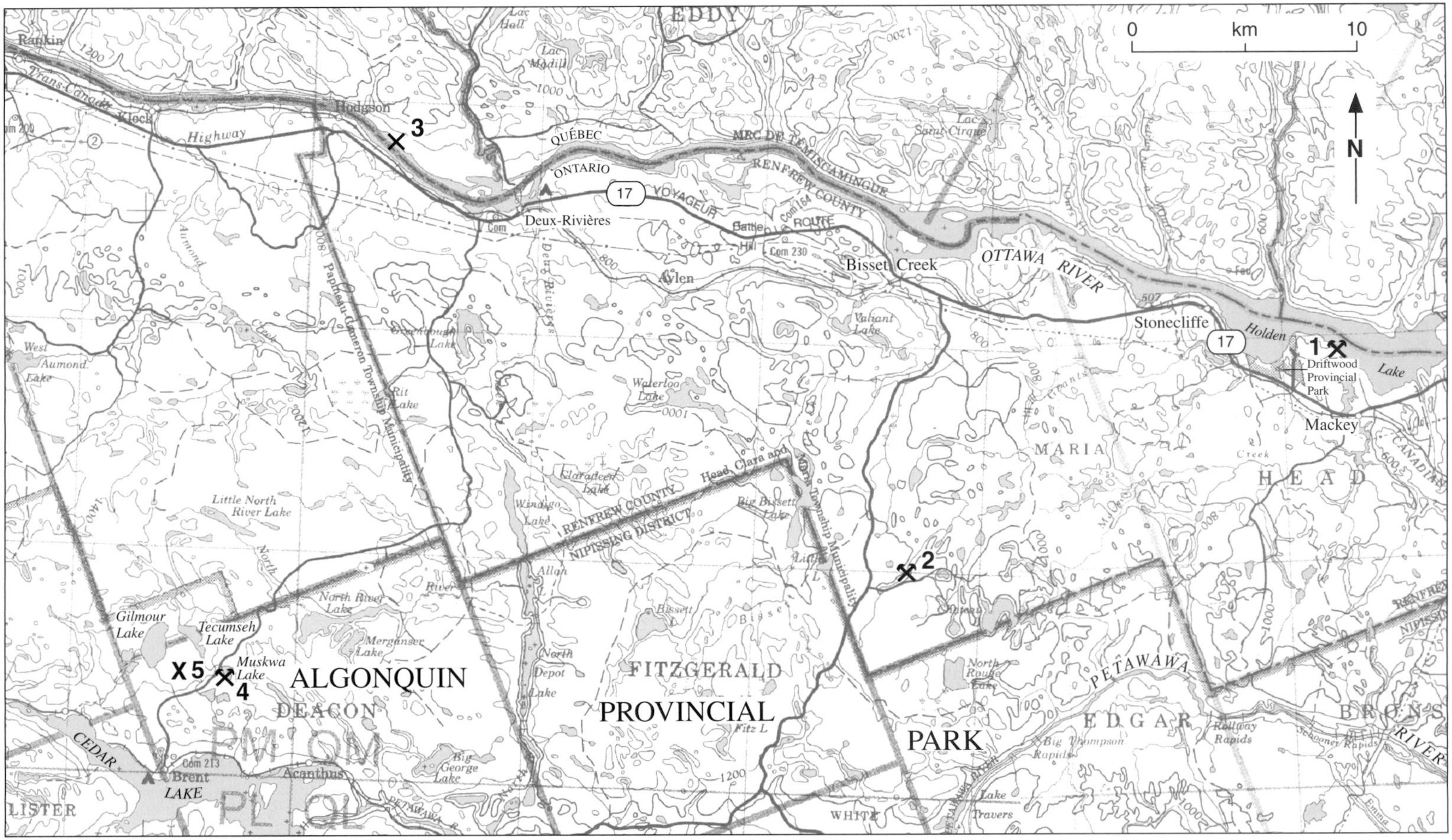

1. Carey (Mackey) mine 2. Bissett Creek mine 3. Deux Rivières outlier 4. Muskwa Lake (Brent) mine 5. Brent Crater

Map 11. Mackey–Deux Rivières.

Maps   (T):   31 K/4 Des Joachims
        (G):   P1197 Mattawa-Deep River area (eastern half), District of Nipissing and
               County of Renfrew (OGS, 1:63 360)

Bissett Creek mine

GRAPHITE, PYRITE, PYRRHOTITE, APATITE, TOURMALINE, CLINOAMPHIBOLE,
GOETHITE, GARNET, SILLIMANITE, TITANITE

In quartz-biotite-plagioclase gneiss

Graphite occurs as disseminated flakes and flaky aggregates in gneiss. Pyrite and pyrrhotite are
commonly associated with the graphite. Accessory minerals include microprisms of light blue
apatite, brown tourmaline (uvite), and light green clinoamphibole. Goethite occurs as a brownish-
yellow coating on weathered surfaces of the gneiss. Garnet, sillimanite, and titanite have been
reported from the deposit.

Investigation of the Bissett Creek graphite occurrence began in the early 1980s. In 1982,
Westcoast Charters did some trenching. In 1984–1987, Princeton Resources Corporation
explored the deposit by trenching and diamond drilling, and built a pilot plant for bulk sam-
pling. In 1988–1989, North Coast Industries Limited and Princeton Resources investigated the
deposit as a joint venture.

The mine is about 14 km south of Bissett Creek. *See* Map 11 on p. 88.

Road log from Highway 17 at **km 214.7** (*see* Highway 17 road log on p. 76):

km   0   Junction of Highway 17 and Bissett Creek Road; proceed south onto
                    Bissett Creek Road.

          0.4   Junction, road on left; continue straight ahead.

          1.2   Junction, road on left; continue straight ahead.

          2.3   Junction, road on left; continue straight ahead.

          5.2   Junction, road on right; continue straight ahead.

          9.4   Junction; continue along main road.

         11.5   Junction, road on left; continue straight ahead.

         13.6   Junction; turn left (east).

         15.3   Bissett Creek mine.

Refs.:   54 p. 112–120; 234 p. 342, 374; 235 p. 336; 236 p. 275.

Maps   (T):   31 L/1 Brent
        (G):   P1197 Mattawa-Deep River area (eastern half), District of Nipissing and
               County of Renfrew (OGS, 1:63 360)

Deux Rivières outlier

FOSSILS

In limestone

Ordovician fossils occur in grey-weathering, arenaceous limestone of the Deux-Rivières outlier. (An outlier is a body of sedimentary rock deposited by Paleozoic seas and surrounded by Precambrian rocks.) Species recorded include crinoids, bryozoa, protozoa, brachiopods, gastropods, trilobites, and coelenterates.

In the 1870s, a lime kiln was in operation at this locality and a quarry was worked for sandstone, which is associated with the fossiliferous limestone; the sandstone was used for making grindstones reputed to be of excellent quality.

The Deux Rivières outlier is exposed along the north shore of the Ottawa River, 6 to7 km west of Deux Rivières. *See* Map 11 on p. 88. Access is by boat from Deux Rivières on Highway 17 at **km 234.7** (*see* Highway 17 road log on p. 76).

Refs.: 5 p. 297–298; 11 p. 122; 42 p. 147–148; 114 p. 64; 203 p. 279.

Maps (T): 31 L/8 Maganasipi River
(G): P1196 Mattawa-Deep River area (western half), District of Nipissing (OGS, 1:63 360).

Muskwa Lake (Brent) mine

MICROCLINE, OLIGOCLASE, MUSCOVITE, BIOTITE, QUARTZ, ALLANITE, CHLORITE, MAGNETITE, SERPENTINE

In granite pegmatite

Microcline, oligoclase, muscovite, biotite, and quartz are the main constituents of the pegmatite. The oligoclase feldspar shows good twinning striations. Muscovite occurs as well formed, silvery-grey crystals. Accessory minerals include dull greenish-black allanite, chlorite, magnetite, and serpentine.

The mine was worked briefly for mica. North Bay Mica Company Limited produced about 1.3 t of muscovite between 1950 and 1953.

The mine is in a wooded area on the west side of Maskwa (formerly Muskwa) Lake, about 35 km southwest of Deux Rivières. *See* Map 11 on p. 88.

Road log from Highway 17 at **km 236.6** (*see* Highway 17 road log on p. 76):

km 0 Junction, Highway 17 and Brent Road; proceed south along Brent Road.

9.2 Junction; follow the road on right.

17.0 Junction; follow the road on right.

27.3 Algonquin Park boundary.

33.1 Junction, road on left leading to a gravel pit near the shore of Maskwa Lake. Park here, and walk south along the road about 50 m to a path on the left side of the road; follow this path for about 20 m to the Muskwa Lake (Brent) mine.

Refs.: 48 p. 113; 87 p. 86; 125 p. 214.

Maps (T): 31 L/1 Brent
(G): P1196 Mattawa-Deep River area (western half), District of Nipissing (OGS, 1:63 360)

Brent Crater

The Brent Crater, a rock-filled meteorite impact crater, is visible as a circular, smooth-surfaced topographical depression about 2900 m in diameter and 60 m deep. John A. Roberts of Spartan Air Services discovered it from aerial photographs in 1951. He brought it to the attention of C.S. Beals of the Dominion Observatory as a possible meteorite impact structure.

The Brent Crater is classified as a simple crater — a crater 90 m to 2 to 5 km in diameter with a bowl-shaped cavity rimmed by uplifted and overturned rocks, both meteorite and targeted rocks being subjected to shock. It is the world's largest known simple crater.

A theory regarding the origin of the Brent Crater proposes that the crater was excavated in the early part of the Ordovician Period by a chondrite stony meteorite estimated to be 220 m in diameter and impacting at 30 km per second. The crater is 880 m deep. The high-velocity impact on the existing Precambrian granodiorite gneiss and amphibolite brecciated these rocks, which then slumped into the newly formed cavity, filling the lower 630 m with a variety of breccia. Later, in mid-Ordovician time, sediments accumulated and covered the breccia with a 260 m layer of limestone and other sedimentary rocks. Subsequent erosion removed the rim of the crater, and Pleistocene sands and gravels mantled the crater and the surrounding area. Another theory suggests that the crater is the result of an explosive volcanic eruption that took place about 565 million years ago.

The Brent Crater is 4 km north of Brent. It encloses Gilmour and Tecumseh lakes. Its circular outline follows the western shore of Gilmour Lake, the northern and eastern shores of Tecumseh Lake, and streams south of these lakes. The densely wooded crater can be recognized only from the air; the location can be seen by looking to the right (west) from the Brent Road at a point about 300 m south of the Muskwa Lake (Brent) mine. An observation tower, built for the 1972 International Geological Congress field excursion to the site, provides a view across the crater from the southeastern rim. The tower is on the Brent Crater Trail, a 2 km loop that leads west from the Brent Road opposite Maskwa Lake.

Access to the Brent Crater is via the Brent Road, which leads south from Highway 17 at **km 236.6** (*see* Highway 17 road log on p. 76). The Brent Crater Trail leaves the Brent Road at a point 33.5 km south the junction of Highway 17 and Brent Road. *See* Map 11 on p. 88.

Refs.:   28 p. 481–496; 29 p. 84–85; 34 p. 11–18; 68; 131 p. 1–8; 137 p. 3, 9–10, 35–36, 106–110; 193.

Maps   (T):   31 L/1 Brent
        (G):   P1196 Mattawa-Deep River area, (western half), District of Nipissing (OGS, 1:63 360)
                1658A Terrestrial impact structures (GSC, 1:63 000 000)

McMeekin amazonite occurrence

AMAZONITE, PERTHITE, FLUORITE, MAGNETITE, NATIVE IRON, KAOLINITE, GOETHITE

In pegmatite

Bluish-green to emerald-green amazonite occurs with perthite in pegmatite dykes cutting biotite gneiss. Both minerals are suitable for cutting and polishing. The perthite is an intergrowth of brownish-pink orthoclase and white albite; internal light reflections from the albite produce a silky sheen, adding to the attractiveness of the stone. Bluish-green coarse cleavable fluorite is associated with the feldspars. Magnetite occurs with chlorite on fluorite. Pebbly granular magnetite occurs in kaolinite- and goethite-filled crevices in weathered perthite. Native iron occurs as dark grey metallic spherules about 0.5 mm in diameter forming the nuclei of magnetite granules.

The deposit was explored sometime before 1892 by four shallow pits in a search for apatite. When apatite was not found, work was abandoned. The deposit is on the McMeekin property on the north side of Highway 17 at **km 261.6** (*see* Highway 17 road log on p. 76).

Refs.:   11 p. 152–153, 159–190; 85 p. 21; 88 p. 23–24; 172 p. 236; 198 p. 203, 277.

Maps   (T):   31 L/7 Mattawa
           (G):   P1196 Mattawa-Deep River area (western half), District of Nipissing (OGS, 1:63 360)

Mattawa outlier

FOSSILS

In limestone

Ordovician fossils occur in grey-weathered arenaceous limestone of the Mattawa outlier. (An outlier is a body of sedimentary rock deposited by Paleozoic seas and surrounded by Precambrian rocks.) Species include crinoids, bryozoa, protozoa, brachiopods, gastropods, trilobites, and coelenterates.

The Mattawa outlier is exposed along the north shore of the Ottawa River, east of Mattawa, about 9.2 km downstream from the railway bridge in Mattawa and 1 km northwest of the Rankin railway station. Access is by boat.

Refs.:   5 p. 297–298; 11 p. 122–123; 114 p. 64; 153 p. 7.

Maps   (T):   31 L/7 Mattawa
           (G):   P1196 Mattawa-Deep River area (western half), District of Nipissing (OGS, 1:63 360)
                   1733 Beauchene and Bleu lakes, Temiskamingue County (MRNQ, 1:126 720)

Mattawan (O'Brien-Fowler) mine

MICROCLINE, PLAGIOCLASE, QUARTZ, BIOTITE, MUSCOVITE, EUXENITE

In granite pegmatite

The pegmatite comprises pink microcline, pink plagioclase, quartz, biotite, and muscovite. Crystals and aggregates of brilliant taffy-brown to black euxenite occur in microcline; black lustrous tabular masses up to 12 cm across have been found. The pegmatite dyke cuts biotite-hornblende gneiss.

The deposit was worked for feldspar in 1925 and 1926 by O'Brien and Fowler of Ottawa. It was the largest feldspar operation in the district. Production is estimated at 2798 t. Two pits, each about 40 m by 8 m, were dug on adjacent levels into the side of a ridge. Large dumps lie adjacent to the openings.

The mine is about 5 km west of Mattawa. *See* Map 12 on p. 93.

Road log from Highway 17 in Mattawa at **km 268.5** (*see* Highway 17 road log on p. 76):

km   0   Mattawa, at the junction of highways 17 and 533; proceed onto Highway 533.

              0.8   Junction; turn left onto Brydges Street.

              4.3   Junction; continue straight ahead.

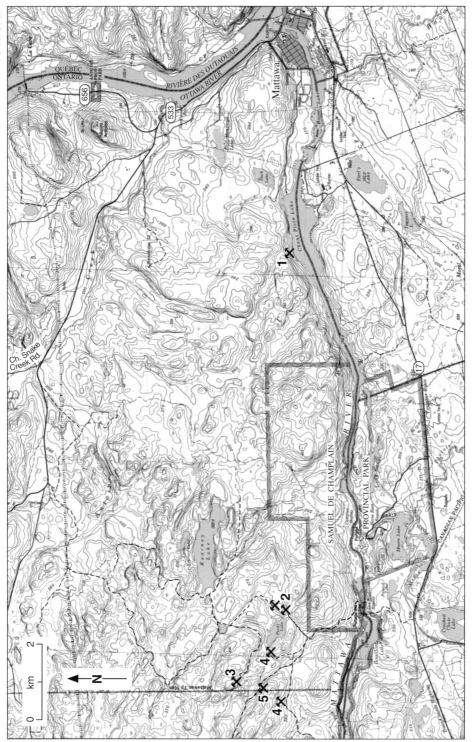

1. Mattawa (O'Brien-Fowler) mine   2. Purdy mine   3. Croteau mine   4. Mica Company of Canada mine   5. Mattarig mine

Map 12. Mattawan.

4.8   Junction, single-lane mine road on right. (This junction is just before a fork to the left.) Proceed on foot along the mine road, which leads west along the side of a ridge. Do not take any forks to the right off this road.

7.6   Mattawan (O'Brien-Fowler) mine.

Refs.:   45 p. 190–191; 60 p. 248–251; 71 p. 46–47; 85 p. 21, 65; 107 p. 147–148; 162 p. 28–29; 188 p. 52.

Maps   (T):   31 L/7 Mattawa
        (G):   53d Mattawan-Olrig area, District of Nipissing (OGS, 1:63 360)
                P1196 Mattawa-Deep River area (western half), District of Nippissing (OGS, 1:63 360)
                GDIF 138 Mattawan Township, District of Nipissing (OGS, 1:31 680)

Purdy mine

MUSCOVITE, BIOTITE, MICROCLINE, ALBITE, PERISTERITE, GARNET, ZIRCON, TOURMALINE, BERYL, EPIDOTE, HORNBLENDE, CHLORITE, MONAZITE, EUXENITE, FERGUSONITE, URANINITE, SAMARSKITE, ALLANITE, PYRITE, XENOTIME

In granite pegmatite

Plate 19.

Flake from large muscovite crystal 1.5 m long, Purdy mine, 1942. GSC 82692

Silvery-green muscovite occurs in microcline-albite-quartz pegmatite dykes cutting biotite-hornblende-feldspar gneiss. The deposit, formerly the largest muscovite producer in Canada, yielded exceptionally large muscovite crystals, including one measuring 2.9 m by 2.7 m and 0.9 m thick; this crystal was extracted by Justin Purdy, the discoverer of the deposit, from an outcrop that was later mined as No. 1 pit. The pegmatite contains considerable amounts of biotite and albite, including white translucent peristerite. Accessory minerals include red garnet, orange-red zircon, black tourmaline, light blue beryl, light green epidote, hornblende, chlorite, monazite, euxenite, fergusonite, uraninite, samarskite, allanite, and pyrite. Xenotime crystals up to 2 cm across occur in the pegmatite (T.S. Ercit, pers. comm., 1992).

Justin Purdy of Eau Claire originally discovered muscovite in a pegmatite dyke just east of Purdy Lake (then known as Grassy Lake) in the winter of 1941–1942. After the discovery, he teamed up with Huntley McDonald to continue prospecting. They staked three claims and discovered another mica-bearing dyke (No. 3) from which they extracted muscovite and shipped it to dressing plants in Ottawa and Hull. Further prospecting resulted in the discovery of 11 mica-bearing pegmatite dykes on the property. Justin Purdy was killed in a car accident in 1942 and his father, George Purdy, continued mining operations for a few months until Purdy Mica Mines Limited was formed to operate the deposit. This company continued production until 1945. The main production came from three dykes that were worked as pits No. 1, No. 2, and No. 3, with minor production from five other dykes. From 1942 to the end of 1944, the total production was sold to Colonial Mica Corporation for the United States strategic mica supply for the World War II effort. From 1949 to 1953, North Bay Mica Company conducted operations from the three main pits, and from the underground workings extending from them. The mica was processed in shops in Mattawa until 1944, and in North Bay from 1943 to 1945; the processing consisted of splitting (rifting), trimming or cutting, and sorting. Production from the mine to 1945 was 1 333 082 kg of mica valued at $1 578 128. In 1989–1990, J.M. Janveaux mined and hand cobbed about 80 t of feldspar and shipped it to Germany for possible use in the high-temperature ceramics industry.

The mine is about 14 km west of Mattawa. *See* Map 12 on p. 93.

Road log from Highway 17 at **km 268.5** in Mattawa (*see* Highway 17 road log on p. 76):

km	0	Mattawa, at the junction of highways 17 and 533; proceed onto Highway 533.
	12.3	Junction; turn left onto Kearney Lake Road. (This junction is 7.4 km from the junction of highways 533 and 656 and 0.5 km beyond the junction of Snake Creek Road.)
	14.1	Junction, road on right; continue straight ahead.
	14.5	Junction, road on right; continue straight ahead.
	15.6	Junction, road on right; continue straight ahead.
	17.5	Junction; continue straight ahead (west).
	18.3	Junction, road on right; continue straight ahead.
	18.5	Junction, road on right; continue straight ahead.
	19.0	Junction, road on right; continue straight ahead.
	19.4	Y-junction; follow the road on right leading west.
	20.5	Junction; continue straight ahead.
	23.2	Y-junction; follow the road on left.

24.0	Junction, road on right; continue straight ahead (south).
24.6	Junction, road on right; continue straight ahead. (The road on right leads to the Croteau mine.)
25.6	Clearing. The road turns right.
26.0	End of the road, just north of Purdy No. 3 pit and dumps. No. 3 pit is on the top of a hill and extends 107 m southward with a depth of 12 m. Two shafts were sunk at the south end of the pit, to 40 and 49 m. From there, an old mine road continues to pits No. 1 and No. 2 at the southern end of the Purdy mine workings. Proceed south along this road.
26.25	Junction, trail on right; this trail leads west 160 m to Purdy No. 2 pits.
	These pits consist of a series of benches cut into two parallel dykes, 61 m apart, on the southwestern slope of a hill. They extend over a length of 135 m with a depth of 11 m. The road log continues south.
26.65	Purdy No. 1 (Main) openings, the most southerly workings; they extend over 61 m with a depth of 12 m; a shaft at the south end of the main pit was sunk to about 18 m. An adit, driven 91 m from the base of the hill to No. 2 workings, was used to mine the dyke underground over a length of 107 m. The No. 2 pit is about 100 m north of the No. 1 pit. The East pit from which some muscovite was recovered is reached by a trail about 1150 m long leading east from the No. 1 workings.

Refs.:   13 p. 274; 60 p. 239–247; 71 p. 33–40, 42–43; 79 p. 181–185; 85 p. 31–35; 87 p. 72–78; 105 p. 305–312; 107 p. 147; 190 p. 1–17.

Maps   (T):   31 L/7 Mattawa
        (G):   53d Mattawa-Olrig area, District of Nipissing (OGS, 1:63 360)
               P1196 Mattawa-Deep River area (western half), District of Nipissing (OGS, 1:63 360)
               GDIF 138 Mattawan Township, District of Nipissing (OGS, 1:31 680)

Croteau mine

MUSCOVITE, MICROCLINE, PLAGIOCLASE, BIOTITE, GARNET, EPIDOTE, PYRITE

In granite pegmatite

Muscovite occurs in pegmatite dykes composed of pink microcline, plagioclase, and quartz with some biotite and garnet. Muscovite books 30 cm in diameter were recovered during mining operations. Epidote and pyrite occur in the walls of the dyke. The deposit consists of two pegmatite dykes, 60 m apart, in hornblende-biotite gneiss.

Paul and Wilfred Croteau discovered and staked the deposit in 1942. Inspiration Mining and Development Company Limited produced about 45 t of muscovite in the same year. Each dyke was opened by a pit: the East pit is 7.6 m deep and the West pit is 6.1 m deep.

The Croteau mine is on the south side of a hill, about 17 km northwest of Mattawa. It is northwest of the Purdy mine. See Map 12 on p. 93. Access is by a 2.5 km road at km 24.6 on the road log to the Purdy mine (p. 95).

Refs.:   71 p. 40–42; 87 p. 72–73; 105 p. 305–306.

Maps   (T):   31 L/7 Mattawa
      (G):   53d Mattawa-Olrig area, District of Nipissing (OGS, 1:63 360)
             P1196 Mattawa-Deep River area (western half), District of Nipissing (OGS,
             1:63 360)
             GDIF 138 Mattawan Township, District of Nipissing (OGS, 1:31 680)

Mica Company of Canada mine

MUSCOVITE, ORTHOCLASE, PLAGIOCLASE, BIOTITE, TOURMALINE

In granite pegmatite

Muscovite occurs in pegmatite composed of pink orthoclase, plagioclase, quartz, and some
biotite and tourmaline.

The property consists of a deposit (No. 1) near the west shore of Purdy Lake and another one
(No. 2) 1500 m farther west. In 1942, N. Vincent, George A. MacMillan, and Glen Wilton
staked muscovite-bearing pegmatite bodies in the Purdy Lake area. Mica Consolidated Mines
Limited (reorganized in 1943 under the name Mica Company of Canada Limited) worked the
deposits in 1942–1943 and processed 136 t of muscovite at its trimming plant in Bonfield. The
No. 1 workings consist of a shaft sunk from a pit to 20.7 m located 300 m west of Purdy Lake.
The No. 2 workings, on the southwest side of a hill, consist of a narrow pit 40 m long.

The mine is northwest of the Purdy mine. The pits are 16 km and 17 km west of Mattawa (*see*
Map 12 on p. 93). Access is by a road leading from the southern workings of the Purdy mine.

Road log from km 26.65 on the road log to the Purdy mine (p. 96):

km	0	Purdy mine, Main (No. 1) pit; proceed along the old mine road leading southwest toward the Mattawa River.
	1.0	Junction; turn right (northwest).
	1.2	Junction, mine road on right. Proceed along this road for 1.1 km to the Mica Company of Canada No. 1 workings. The road log continues to the No. 2 workings.
	1.9	Junction; follow the road on left leading west.
	3.3	Mica Company of Canada No. 2 workings, about 100 m north of this point.

Refs.:   71 p. 29–33; 85 p. 30.

Maps   (T):   31 L/7 Mattawa
      (G):   53d Mattawa-Olrig area, District of Nipissing (OGS, 1:63 360)
             P1196 Mattawa-Deep River area (western half), District of Nipissing (OGS,
             1:63 360)
             GDIF 137 Olrig Township, District of Nipissing (OGS, 1:31 680)
             GDIF 138 Mattawan Township, District of Nipissing (OGS, 1:31 680)

Mattarig mine

MUSCOVITE, FELDSPAR, BIOTITE, GARNET, TOURMALINE, PYRITE

In granite pegmatite

Muscovite crystals up to 10 cm in diameter were recovered from this deposit during mining operations. The muscovite occurred in pegmatite composed of K-feldspar, plagioclase, and quartz with some biotite, garnet, tourmaline, and pyrite.

The mine consists of a pit, 2.7 m deep, on the north side of a hill. Mattarig Mica Mining Syndicate Limited worked the deposit in 1942–1943. Some hand-cobbed muscovite was shipped to a trimming plant in Mattawa.

The mine is west of the Purdy mine and 17 km west of Mattawa. *See* Map 12 on p. 93.

Road log from km 26.65 on the road log to the Purdy mine (p. 96):

km	0	Purdy mine, Main (No. 1) pit; proceed along the old mine road leading southwest toward the Mattawa River.
	1.0	Junction; turn right (northwest).
	1.2	Junction, road on right to the Mica Company of Canada mine; continue straight ahead.
	1.9	Junction; follow the road on right leading northwest.
	2.7	Junction, trail on left. Follow this trail for 300 m to the Mattarig mine.

Refs.:   60 p. 247–248; 71 p. 28–29.

Maps   (T):   31 L/7 Mattawa
       (G):   53d Mattawa-Olrig area, District of Nipissing (OGS, 1:63 360)
              P1196 Mattawa-Deep River area (western half), District of Nipissing (OGS, 1:63 360)
              GDIF 138 Mattawan Township, District of Nipissing (OGS, 1:31 680)

Crocan Lake kyanite occurrence

KYANITE, GARNET, TOURMALINE, GRAPHITE

In muscovite-biotite gneiss

Kyanite occurs as colourless, light blue, and greenish-blue flat bladed crystals up to 7 to 8 cm long. Associated with it are abundant purplish-pink garnet crystals averaging 5 mm in diameter. Less common are tourmaline (as dark brown grains) and graphite. The kyanite content of the rock averages from 12 to 20 per cent.

Initial exploration of the deposit by trenching and drilling followed its discovery in 1951. The work was done by J. Kenmey and the Golwynne Chemical Corporation of New York. Additional trenching was done between 1967 and 1972 by Arrowhead Silica Corporation. In 1975, further investigation was undertaken by Kyanite Mining Corporation. The trenches are on a 55 m rise at the northeastern end of Crocan Lake. Outcrops of kyanite-bearing rock occur along the eastern shore of the lake, on a point on the west shore of the lake, and along a lumber road from Timber Creek to Crocan Lake. *See* Map 13 on p. 99.

The occurrence is about 31 km northwest of Mattawa.

Road log from Highway 17 at **km 268.5** in Mattawa (*see* Highway 17 road log on p. 76):

km	0	Junction of highways 17 and 533; proceed onto Highway 533.
	0.8	Junction, Brydges Street; continue along Highway 533.
	4.8	Junction; continue along Highway 533.

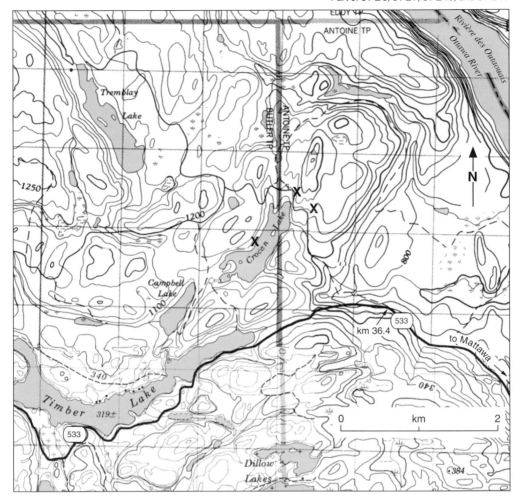

X Kyanite occurrences

Map 13. Crocan Lake.

36.4   Junction, single-lane road; turn right. (This junction is 16.9 km southeast of the junction of highways 533 and 63.)

36.7   Fork; bear right onto a rough, dry-weather road.

38.1   Crocan Lake kyanite occurrence on right, opposite the northeastern end of Crocan Lake.

Refs.:   76 p. 3–4; 95 p. 291–292; 96 p. 314–315; 123 p. 294; 209 p. 109–113.

Maps   (T):   31 L/10 Lac Beauchêne
               31 L/11 Témiscaming
       (G):   P679 Tomiko area (east half), District of Nipissing (OGS, 1:63 360)
               GDIF 129 Butler Township, District of Nipissing (OGS, 1:31 680)
               GDIF 130 Antoine Township, District of Nipissing (OGS, 1:31 680)

Eau Claire (MacLaren) beryl occurrence

BERYL, TOURMALINE, GARNET, PYROCHLORE, MICROCLINE, ALBITE, MUSCOVITE

In granite pegmatite

Beryl crystals occur in pegmatite composed of pink microcline, white albite (cleavelandite), quartz, and colourless to greenish-yellow muscovite. Accessory minerals include black tourmaline crystals to 20 cm long, red garnet, and brown pyrochlore. Yellow beryl crystals 2 to 7 cm in diameter were recovered from this deposit when it was first opened.

The deposit is exposed by three pits and some trenches over 60 m. These openings are in a wooded area and are partly overgrown. The occurrence is on the Fred Maxwell property, southeast of Eau Claire, and about 15 km southwest of Mattawa,

Road log from Highway 17 at **km 287.0** (*see* Highway 17 road log on p. 76):

km   0   Junction, highways 17 and 630; proceed south onto Highway 630.

          5.5   Crossroad; turn left (east).

          5.9   Fred Maxwell property on right. The Eau Claire (MacLaren) beryl occurrence is in an outcrop on the south side of the road about 700 m east of this point.

Refs.:   45 p. 188–189; 74 p. 314–316; 135 p. 85.

Maps   (T):   31 L/7 Mattawa
         (G):   P1196 Mattawa-Deep River area (western half), District of Nipissing (OGS, 1:63 360)

Legendre mine

PYROAURITE, BRUCITE, HYDROMAGNESITE, ARAGONITE, SERPENTINE, GRAPHITE, MAGNETITE, GOETHITE

In dolomitic crystalline limestone

Pyroaurite and brucite are common in this deposit. The pyroaurite occurs as transparent, greenish-blue, green, and tan (on weathered surfaces) fine flaky aggregates and as light green fibrous veinlets 5 mm wide. On exposed surfaces, the pyroaurite is lighter in colour and has a satin lustre. In some specimens it is closely associated with magnetite. The brucite occurs as white nodules up to 4 mm in diameter. It has a whorled structure and can be recognized readily by its chalk-white appearance, which contrasts with the translucent white of the enclosing limestone. Occurring much less abundantly are hydromagnesite, as colourless, very fine platy aggregates with silky lustre, and aragonite, as tiny white fibrous globules. Other minerals in the limestone are serpentine (as white, pale green, and olive green granular masses), graphite, magnetite, and goethite.

The mine was operated by L.P. Legendre in 1962–1963 for use in pulp and paper mills. The occurrence of brucite and pyroaurite in this area was discovered in 1937 by M.F. Goudge of the Canada Mines Branch. Several claims were staked in 1939 for brucite in the Pimisi Bay–Lake Talon area. A few pits and a shaft were sunk, but there was no further development of the deposit.

The Legendre mine is on the property of Russ James from whom permission to enter the mine must be obtained; the James farmhouse is on the north side of Highway 17 at **km 293.5** (*see* Highway 17 road log on p. 76). It is about 24 km west of Mattawa.

Road log from Highway 17 at **km 293.5** (*see* Highway 17 road log on p. 76):

km   0   Turn right onto the road leading to a gravel pit. This road proceeds along the right side of the pit, then to the mine.

                2.7   Legendre mine.

Refs.:   64 p. 130–132; 71 p. 25–26; 80 p. 12–13.

Maps   (T):   31 L/6 North Bay
          (G):   53d Mattawan-Olrig area, District of Nipissing (OGS, 1:63 360)
                 2361 Sudbury-Cobalt, Algoma, Manitoulin, Nipissing, Parry Sound, Sudbury and Timiskaming districts (OGS, 1:253 440)
                 GDIF 137 Olrig Township, District of Nipissing (OGS, 1:31 680)

North Bay area

Collecting localities in the North Bay area include Twenty Minute Lake occurrence (p. 101), Niemetz and Ross quarries (p. 102), Nova Beaucage mine (p. 103), River Valley garnet mine (p. 105), Nipissing Black Granite quarry (p. 107), and Golden Rose (Afton) mine (p. 108). The two starting points are along the Highway 17 road log in North Bay: at **km 328.1** at the junction of highways 17 and 63 North, and at **km 330.5** at the junction of highways 17 and 11 North.

Twenty Minute Lake occurrence

AMETHYST

In quartz

Amethyst crystals ranging from very pale to medium dark violet occur in massive quartz cutting diabase. The amethyst is used locally by lapidarists for jewellery.

The deposit has been exposed by a pit along the side of a ridge, about 1 km east of Twenty Minute Lake. Access to it is most practical in the autumn when the nearby swampy area is more accessible. *See* Map 14 on p. 102.

The occurrence is about 29 km northeast of North Bay.

Road log from Highway 17 at **km 328.1** (*see* Highway 17 road log on p. 77):

km   0   North Bay, junction of highways 17 and 63 North; proceed onto Highway 63 North.

                31.8   Junction, single-lane road to Twenty Minute Lake; turn right.

                32.0   Junction; bear right.

                32.2   Junction; continue straight ahead.

                32.5   Junction; continue straight ahead.

                33.8   Road widens at this point; park vehicle and follow the trail on left. The trail leads through the woods, through a swampy area, and around a small lake (Indian Lake) to a ridge.

                34.7   Twenty Minute Lake amethyst occurrence on the side of the ridge.

Maps   (T):   31 L/6 North Bay
        (G):   2216 North Bay area, Nipissing and Parry Sound districts (OGS, 1:126 720)
               2361 Sudbury-Cobalt, Algoma, Manitoulin, Nipissing, Parry Sound, Sudbury
               and Timiskaming districts (OGS, 1:253 440)

Niemetz and Ross quarries

GNEISS

Light green muscovite-quartz gneiss occurs in two quarries on Highway 63. The quarries produced building stone. The gneiss at the Ross quarry is associated with reddish quartzose rock.
This quarry, on the east side of Highway 63, consists of two levels: the upper quarry face
extends 43 m and the lower face extends 32 m. The gneiss at the Niemetz quarry contains

Part of 31 L/6

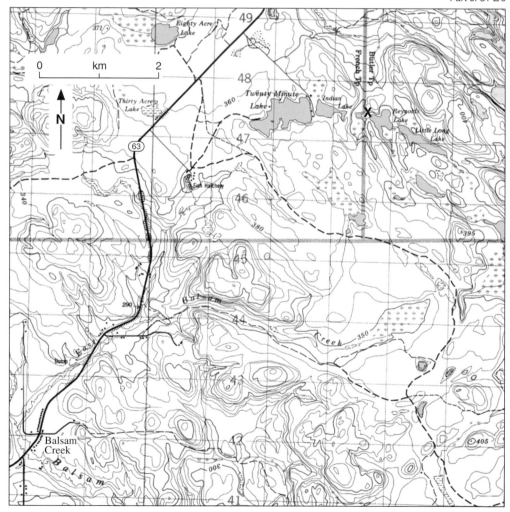

X Amethyst occurrence

Map 14. Twenty Minute Lake.

feldspar and garnet. This quarry is on the west side of Highway 63; its face extends 36 m. The quarries were operated by L. Ross and H. Niemetz, respectively. The muscovite-quartz gneiss is also exposed in a roadcut on the east side of the highway at the turnoff to the Ross quarry.

The quarries are on either side of Highway 63, 48 km from the junction of highways 17 and 63 in North Bay. They are just south of the highway bridge over Jocko River.

Road log from Highway 17 at **km 328.1** (*see* Highway 17 road log on p. 77):

km		
	0	North Bay, junction of highways 17 and 63; proceed onto Highway 63 North.
	31.8	Junction, road to Twenty Minute Lake; continue along the highway.
	35.0	*Roadcuts* expose muscovite gneiss containing garnet, magnetite, and pyrite.
	39.6	Junction, Highway 533; continue along Highway 63. (This junction is 17 km west of the turnoff from Highway 533 to the Crocan Lake kyanite occurrence described on p. 98.)
	48.0	Turnoffs to Niemetz quarry on left, and Ross quarry on right.

Ref.: 209 p. 44–47.

Maps (T): 31 L/11 Témiscaming
(G): P679 Tomiko area (east half), District of Nipissing (OGS, 1:63 360)
2361 Sudbury-Cobalt, Algoma, Manitoulin, Nipissing, Parry Sound, Sudbury and Timiskaming districts (OGS, 1:253 440)
GDIF 288 Jocko Township, District of Nipissing (OGS, 1:31 680)

Nova Beaucage mine

PYROCHLORE, ACMITE, FLUORITE, APATITE, CHLORITE, MONAZITE, HORNBLENDE, HEMATITE, MAGNETITE, PYRITE

In alkalic rock and carbonatite

Uranium-bearing pyrochlore was formerly mined from this deposit. It occurs as chocolate-brown crystals less than 3 mm in diameter, and as crystal aggregates. Associated with it are acmite, violet fluorite, light green apatite, chlorite, monazite, hornblende, hematite, magnetite, and pyrite. These minerals occur as aggregates of small crystals and grains. The pyrochlore contains approximately 10 per cent uranium oxide.

The deposit was discovered in 1952 by James Strohl of Tunkhannock, Pennsylvania, while prospecting outcrops on the Manitou Islands with a geiger counter. In 1953, Beaucage Mines Limited was formed to develop the deposit. The deposit extends from the east end of Newman Island eastward below the lake. Much of the diamond drilling was done from ice on the lake. A four-compartment shaft was sunk to a depth of 135 m. The underground workings extend eastward from the shaft on Newman Island and below the lake. A pilot plant was constructed on the site in 1955. Operations ended in 1956.

The Nova Beaucage mine is on the east end of Newman Island, one of the Manitou Islands, 10.5 km southwest of the wharf at North Bay. *See* Map 15 on p. 104. Boat rental arrangements may be made at the wharf in North Bay.

Refs.: 29 p. 80–81; 117 p. 81–83; 164 p. 45–62.

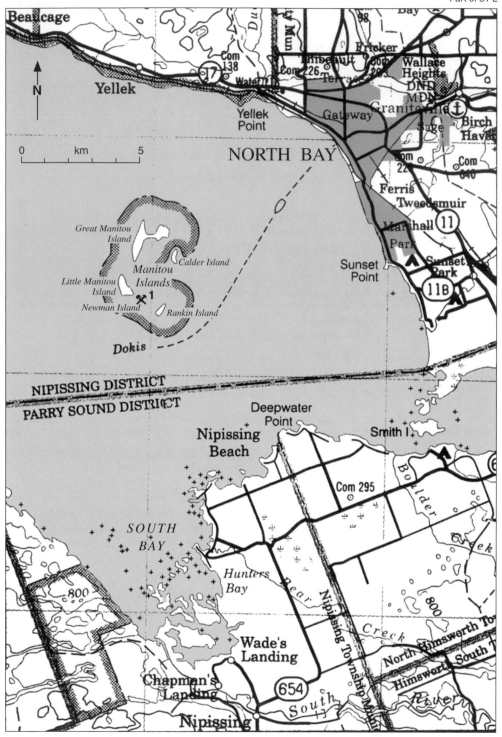

1. Nova Beaucage mine

Map 15. Newman Island.

Maps   (T):   31 L/5 Sturgeon Falls
         (G):   2216 North Bay area, Nipissing and Parry Sound districts (OGS, 1:126 720)
               2361 Sudbury-Cobalt, Algoma, Manitoulin, Nipissing, Parry Sound, Sudbury
               and Timiskaming districts (OGS, 1:253 440)

River Valley garnet mine

GARNET, CHLORITE

In biotite schist and biotite gneiss

Violet-red to red garnet crystals averaging 2 cm in diameter are enclosed in biotite. The garnet is of the almandine variety and crystals measuring up to 18 cm in diameter have been found. Some crystals are of gem quality. Some biotite has altered to green chlorite.

The deposit occurs on a ridge north of River Valley. It has been exposed by a few pits and strippings. The Niagara Garnet Company operated the deposit from 1943 to 1949. The company's mill was located in Sturgeon Falls. From 1960 to 1963, the deposit was operated by Industrial Garnet Company Limited.

The deposit is about about 9 km north of River Valley and about 38 km northwest of Sturgeon Falls. *See* Map 16 on p. 106.

Road log from Highway 17 at **km 330.5** (*see* Highway 17 road log on p. 77):

km		
	0	North Bay, junction of highways 17 and 11 North; proceed west along Highway 17.
	6.1– 7.2	*Roadcuts* expose hornblende-biotite gneiss containing magnetite and titanite.
	8.7	Junction, Nova Beaucage Road; continue on Highway 17. The Nova Beaucage Road leads to the Lake Nipissing shore. During mining operations at the Nova Beaucage mine, boat transportation to the mine was conducted from this point. The distance to the mine is about 12 km.
	13.0– 16.4	*Roadcuts* expose magnetite-bearing biotite-hornblende gneiss.
	17.7	Lake Nipissing Scenic Lookout on right.
	38.0	Sturgeon Falls, at the junction of Highway 64; turn right onto Highway 64.
	61.0	Field, at the junction of Highway 539; turn left onto Highway 539.
	75.9	Junction; turn right onto Highway 539A (Highway 539A becomes Highway 805 near Glen Afton).
	76.9	River Valley, at railway crossing.
	78.0	Bridge over Temagami River.
	78.4	Junction; continue straight ahead.
	79.5	Junction; turn right onto a gravel road.
	80.8	Fork; bear left.

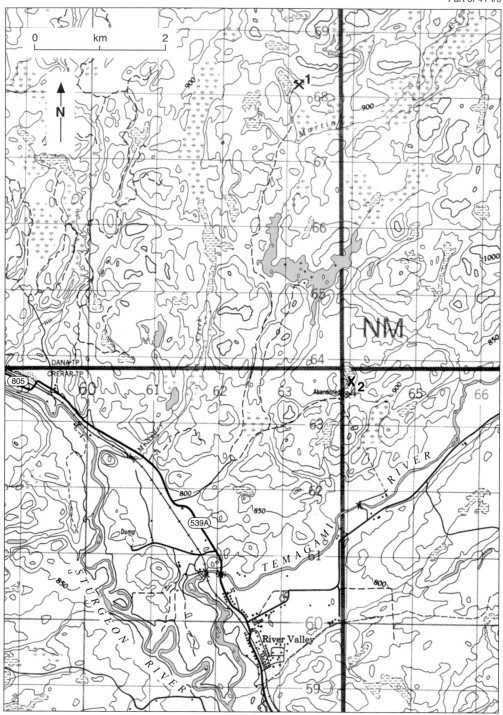

1. River Valley garnet mine   2. Nipissing Black Granite quarry

Map 16. River Valley.

81.7	Fork; bear right.
87.7	River Valley garnet mine.

Refs.:   163 p. 4–7; 209 p. 123–125.

Maps   (T):   4.1 I/9 Glen Afton
       (G):   P844 River Valley area, districts of Nipissing and Sudbury (OGS, 1:63 360)
              2361 Sudbury-Cobalt, Algoma, Manitoulin, Nipissing, Parry Sound, Sudbury
              and Timiskaming districts (OGS, 1:253 440)
              GDIF 246 Dana Township, District of Nipissing (OGS, 1:31 680)

Nipissing Black Granite quarry

ANORTHOSITE, NATROLITE, ANALCIME

Anorthosite, a medium-textured black igneous rock that takes an excellent polish, has been quarried at this locality for use as building and monument stone. It makes an attractive ornamental stone and is commercially known as 'Black Granite'. Joints in the rock are lined with thin layers of white radiating platy aggregates of natrolite. Patches of olive-green analcime occur on the natrolite.

The deposit has been quarried into the side of a hill. It was opened in 1948 by J. Theriault, who formed Nipissing Black Granite Company Limited to operate the deposit. This company produced blocks of 'granite' for use as a building stone until 1959. Subsequently the rock was produced for use as crushed stone aggregate. The producers were Industrial Garnet Company Limited (1959–1964) and Erana Mines Limited (1964–1980).

The deposit is 4 km northeast of River Valley, and about 33 km northwest of Sturgeon Falls. *See Map 16 on p. 106.*

Road log from Highway 17 at **km 330.5** (*see* Highway 17 load log on p. 77):

km	0	Junction of highways 17 and 11 North in North Bay; proceed west along Highway 17 and follow the road log for the River Valley garnet mine to km 79.5.
	79.5	Junction of Highway 539A and a gravel road; turn right onto the gravel road.
	80.8	Junction, road to River Valley garnet mine; bear right.
	81.6	Junction; continue straight ahead.
	83.2	Nipissing Black Granite quarry.

Refs.:   82 p. 30–32; 166 p. 49–50; 209 p. 15–20.

Maps   (T):   41 I/9 Glen Afton
       (G):   P844 River Valley area, districts of Nipissing and Sudbury (OGS, 1:63 360)
              2361 Sudbury-Cobalt, Algoma, Manitoulin, Nipissing, Parry Sound, Sudbury
              and Timiskaming districts (OGS, 1:253 440)
              GDIF 246 Dana Township, District of Nipissing (OGS, 1:31 680)

Plate 20.

Golden Rose mine, 1937. National Archives of Canada PA 15008

Golden Rose (Afton) mine

JASPILITE, NATIVE GOLD, PYRITE, DOLOMITE, GOETHITE, CHALCOPYRITE

In iron-formation

Jaspilite, a very attractive ornamental rock, occurs at this former gold mine. It consists of alternating bands of deep red siliceous hematite and bluish-black siliceous magnetite speckled with tiny grains and streaks of pyrite. It takes an excellent polish. Tiny fragments of native gold are associated with pyrite, which occurs as crystals up to 25 mm in diameter. The pyrite occurs in the iron-formation and in quartz and dolomite. Small amounts of goethite and chalcopyrite are associated with pyrite.

Gold was discovered in about 1897 in loose sand weathered from the iron-formation along the shore of Emerald Lake near the present mine site. The deposit was first worked in 1915–1916 by the Golden Rose Mining Company, which sank a 9 m shaft. In 1927, Afton Mines Limited deepened the shaft to 30 m, and in 1934 the property was acquired by the New Golden Rose Mines Limited, which was partly owned by the Consolidated Mining and Smelting Company. The latter company operated the mine from 1935 until it was closed in 1941. The workings consist of a three-compartment, 228 m shaft with drifts and crosscuts at several levels, and a 73 m adit near the water's edge. A mill, power house, and residential buildings had been erected near the mine. None of these buildings remain. A large dump is found near the shaft. Total production amounted to 1 412 512 g of gold and 258 124 g of silver from 130 822.9 t of ore.

The mine is on the northwestern shore of a peninsula on the east side of Emerald Lake, about 74 km northwest of Sturgeon Falls.

Road log from Highway 17 at **km 330.5** (*see* Highway 17 road log on p. 77):

km   0   North Bay, at the junction of highways 17 and 11 North; proceed west along Highway 17 and follow the road log for the River Valley garnet mine to km 79.5.

	79.5	Turnoff to River Valley garnet mine and Nipissing Black Granite quarry; continue straight ahead along Highway 539A.
	102.1	Fork; bear right.
	128.7	Junction; turn left onto a single-lane road to Camp Louise.
	129.4	Fork; bear right.
	130.2	Golden Rose (Afton) mine.

Refs.: 94 p. 93–94; 100 p. 131–133; 129 p. 46–50; 132 p. 38–39, 46–48.

Maps   (T): 41 I/16 Lake Temagami
       (G): 2361 Sudbury-Cobalt, Algoma, Manitoulin, Nipissing, Parry Sound, Sudbury and Timiskaming districts (OGS, 1:253 440)
           2385 Afton and Scholes townships, Sudbury and Nipissing districts (OGS, 1:31 680)
           GDIF 458 Afton Township (OGS, 1:31 680)

Témiscaming area

Collecting localities in the Témiscaming area of Quebec are described in the following text. They include the Narco mine (p. 109), Laniel garnet occurrence (p. 110), Kipawa occurrence (p. 111), and Sairs Lake occurrence (p. 114). The starting point is in Témiscaming, about 65 km from Highway 17 at **km 328.1** in North Bay (*see* Highway 17 road log on p. 77). Ontario Highway 63 North and Quebec Highway 101 connect Highway 17 to Témiscaming.

Narco mine

KYANITE, GARNET, GRAPHITE, APATITE, TOURMALINE

In biotite gneiss and schist

Kyanite occurs as colourless to ink-blue bladed aggregates associated with pink garnet crystals (less than 2 cm in diameter). Individual kyanite crystals measure up to 15 cm long. Graphite, as small flakes and aggregates, is common. Less abundant minerals are black tourmaline, amber to reddish-orange and yellow apatite, and pyrite; these minerals occur as small grains in gneiss. The kyanite from this locality is generally not sufficiently uniform in colour for use as a gemstone; its principal value is as specimen material. Particularly attractive are specimens consisting of blue kyanite crystals in the white quartz-rich layers of the gneiss.

The deposit was opened for kyanite by an open cut in 1967 by Narco Mines Limited; a test mill was installed to determine its potential use in the manufacture of refractories. There is no record of production and the mine is inactive.

The mine is about 16 km southeast of Témiscaming. *See* Map 18 on p. 113.

Road log from Témiscaming:

km	0	Témiscaming, junction of Highway 101 and Byrne Road; proceed east onto Byrne Road.
	0.2	Junction; turn right onto Murer Avenue.
	0.3	Junction; turn left onto the road to the golf club.

4.1 Junction; follow the road on left.

5.2 Junction; proceed along the road on right continuing south.

11.1 Junction; continue straight ahead and across a railway crossing.

12.1 Junction; follow the road on left.

12.4 Junction; follow the road on right leading south.

13.2 Junction; the road on left leads to Beauchêne Lake; continue straight ahead (south).

21.2 Narco mine.

Refs.: 152 p. 14–15; 153 p. 9.

Maps (T): 31 L/10 Lac Beauchêne
(G): 1733 Beauchene and Bleu lakes, Temiskamingue County (MRNQ, 1:63 360)
M-313 Feuille North Bay 31 L, Gîtes minéraux du Québec, région de l'Abitibi (MRNQ, 1:250 000)

Laniel garnet occurrence

GARNET, STAUROLITE, CLINOAMPHIBOLE, APATITE, KYANITE

In biotite schist

Almandine garnet crystals commonly 25 mm in diameter occur in biotite schist. The crystals are in the dodecahedral form and are dark red to brownish red; they vary from opaque to translucent. Staurolite occurs as dark brown prisms in garnet and in the host rock. Clinoamphibole occurs as black prisms and in massive form, and as dark grey prismatic aggregates. Some granular massive pinkish-grey apatite occurs in the schist.

The Laniel occurrence is exposed by a small open cut on a ridge in Laniel, about 39 km north of Témiscaming. A number of garnet and staurolite occurrences have been reported from the region between Laniel and the Ottawa River, including a garnet-staurolite-kyanite occurrence on the east shore of the Ottawa River where staurolite prisms are 5 to 6 cm long. The location of the occurrences are shown on Map 17 on p. 111.

Road log from Témiscaming:

km 0 Junction of Highway 101 and the road to Kipawa. (This junction is 4.3 km from the east end of the Highway 101 bridge over the Ottawa River.) Proceed north along Highway 101.

44.6 Laniel, at the bridge over the Kipawa River; continue along the highway.

45.6 Junction; turn left onto Dépotoir Road.

45.7 Path on left leads through the woods to the Laniel garnet occurrence. The distance is about 475 m.

Refs.: 8 p. 10; 152 p. 16–18; 155 p. 4–5.

Maps (T): 31 M/3 Fabre
(G): 1458 Fabre-Mazenod area, County of Temiscaming (MRNQ, 1:63 360)
1733 Beauchene and Bleu lakes, Temiskamingue County (MRNQ, 1:126 720)
M-311 Feuille Ville-Marie 31 M, Gîtes minéraux du Québec, région de l'Abitibi (MRNQ, 1:250 000)

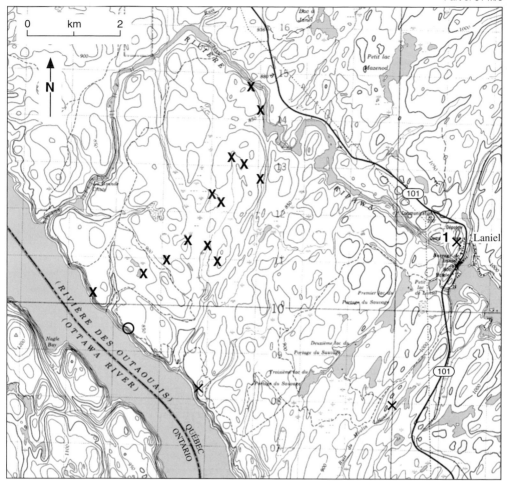

1. Laniel garnet occurrence **X** other garnet occurrences
O garnet-staurolite-kyanite occurrence

Map 17. Laniel.

Kipawa occurrence

EUDIALYTE, MOSANDRITE, BRITHOLITE, HIORTDAHLITE, VLASOVITE, GITTINSITE, AGRELLITE, MISERITE, ZIRCON, TITANITE, FLUORITE, APATITE, THORITE, OPAL, GAIDONNAYITE, MAGNETITE, GRAPHITE, GALENA, CHONDRODITE, NORBERGITE, CLINOHUMITE, DIOPSIDE, TREMOLITE, CLINOAMPHIBOLE, SCAPOLITE

In syenite gneiss and calc-silicate rocks

An unusual suite of yttrium and zirconium minerals occurs in a body of alkalic rocks known as the Kipawa complex. These minerals occur in a zone of syenite gneiss with pegmatitic lenses and minor calc-silicate rocks along a syenite-marble contact; coarse crystals of these minerals occur in albite-microcline pegmatitic lenses. The yttrium-bearing minerals are eudialyte,

111

mosandrite, britholite, hiortdahlite, miserite, titanite, fluorite, and apatite. The zirconium-bearing minerals are eudialyte, zircon, vlasovite, hiortdahlite, and gittinsite. This yttrium-zirconium mineralized zone is about 1300 m long and 10 to 30 m wide.

Eudialyte occurs as pink to red equant to flattened crystals (commonly 5 cm across) and as granular aggregates up to 30 cm across mainly in syenite gneiss. Associated with it are mosandrite, agrellite, vlasovite, thorite, miserite, fluorite, magnetite, and amphibole. Mosandrite occurs as brownish-yellow to tan tabular or prismatic crystals to 10 cm long. Agrellite occurs as white, greenish- or greyish-white crystals up to 10 cm long and as lenses of tabular crystals about 2 cm long. Zircon crystals are common and are radioactive due to the presence of thorium. Vlasovite occurs as clear brownish-yellow to light brown crystals to 15 cm long, as grains 1 to 2 cm across, and as white waxy grains (fluoresce yellow in ultraviolet light) in veins up to 5 cm thick in pegmatitic quartz syenite. Thorite occurs as reddish-brown to brick-red crystals to 10 mm long, and as granular masses. Miserite occurs as brownish-red disseminated grains and cleavage masses with scapolite in calc-silicate rock. Fluorite occurs as aggregates of crystals 2 to 3 cm long in calc-silicate rocks. Britholite occurs as light brown to brown microscopic grains and irregular granular aggregates forming streaks and veinlets to 4 cm wide and 10 to 20 cm long, and as crystals to 3 cm across in calc-silicate rock; it is commonly associated with apatite and thorite. Hiortdahlite occurs as light brown to brownish-orange microscopic crystals in streaks and veinlets up to 4 cm wide and 20 cm long in calc-silicate rock. Gittinsite, a new mineral species originally described from this locality, occurs as chalky-white to greyish-white fibrous to radiating aggregates intergrown with apophyllite in pods to 2 cm long, and as tiny prismatic crystals along cleavage planes in vlasovite; it occurs in pegmatitic lenses with eudialyte, fluorite, graphite, calcite, and opal. A potassian variety of gaidonnayite occurs as rare rims (0.1 mm wide) separating massive vlasovite from gittinsite-apophyllite intergrowths.

The syenite gneiss host rock is composed of dark green clinopyroxene, greenish-blue amphibole, albite, and microcline with some galena and magnetite. The calc-silicate rocks comprise calcite, feldspar, phlogopite, biotite, tremolite, diopside, apatite, chondrodite, norbergite, clinohumite, zircon, graphite, and diopside-phlogopite masses containing blue clinoamphibole and violet fluorite. A pegmatite dyke at the northwestern end of the deposit contains crystals of rare minerals including eudialyte, mosandrite, agrellite, vlasovite, gittinsite, britholite, and hiortdahlite.

The Kipawa thorium and rare-earth deposit was discovered in 1958 during a prospecting rush in the Kipawa area one year after the G. Jones discovery of uranium mineralization (uraninite, uranophane, soddyite, cuprosklodowskite in micaceous quartzite) just east of Hunter's Point. Hollinger Quebec Exploration Company discovered the rich thorium mineralization but withdrew from further exploration when uranium mineralization was not found. In 1969, Sturdy Mines Limited investigated the deposit and discovered zirconium and rare-earth mineralization and high thorium values in an alkalic complex. Unocal Canada Limited acquired the property in 1985 and investigated the deposit by diamond drilling and several trenches in 1987–1988.

The Kipawa occurrence is on a ridge on the east side of a widening of the Kipawa River (to form Sheffield Lake), about 50 km east of Témiscaming. A number of trenches extend in a northwest-southeast direction over a distance of about 3000 m along the ridge. *See* Map 18 on p. 113.

Road log from Témiscaming:

km	0	Junction of Highway 101 and the road to Kipawa (this junction is 4.3 km from the east end of the Highway 101 bridge over the Ottawa River); proceed along the road to Kipawa.
	8.2	Junction; turn right onto the road to Booth Lake and Grindstone Lake.
	44.8	Junction; turn left (north) onto the road to Chute-du-Pin-Rouge.

Part of 31 L

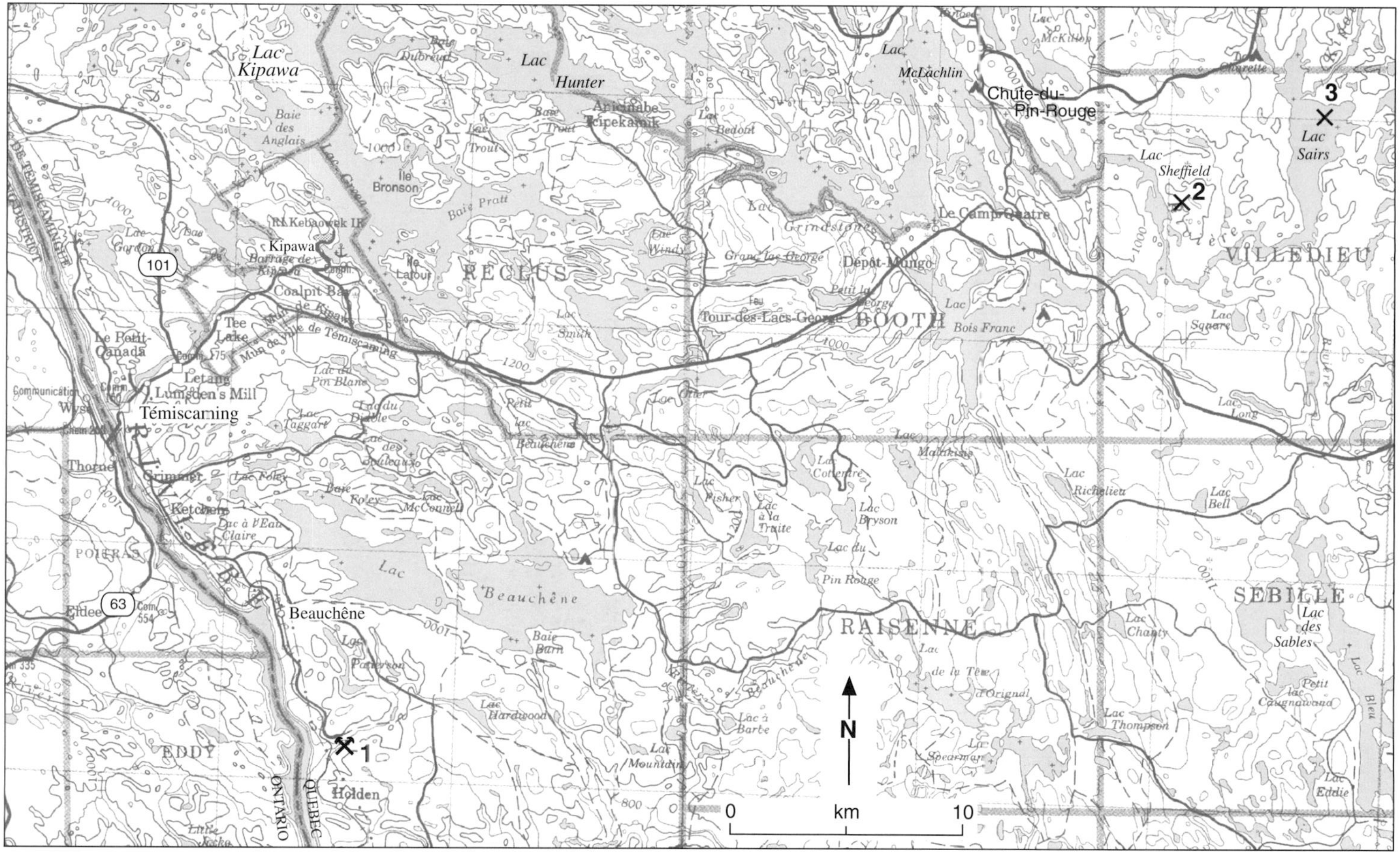

1. Narco mine 2. Kipawa occurrence 3. Sairs Lake occurrence

Map 18. Témiscaming–Kipawa.

52.8   Bridge over the Kipawa River at Chute-du-Pin-Rouge. From this point, proceed southeast by boat along the Kipawa River to the site of a mining camp on the east shore, a distance of about 13.5 km. From the camp, a trail about 1 km long leads east up the ridge to the Kipawa trenches.

Refs.:   1 p. 241–242; 3 p. 283–295; 7 p. 201–203; 15 p. 569; 29 p. 207; 30 p. 199–201; 40 p. 554–559; 57 p. 120–126; 58 p. 211–214; 120 p. 11–13; 152 p. 10–11; 154 p. 11; 156 p. 2–8; 157 p. 480–481; 182 p. 265–276; 199 p. 13–18.

Maps   (T):   31 L/15 Lac Grindstone
              31 L/16 Lac Sairs
        (G):   1278 McLachlan Booth area, electoral district of Témiscamingue (MRNQ, 1:63 360)
              1744 Ogascanane and Sairs lakes, Temiskaming County (MRNQ, 1:126 720)
              M-313 Feuille North Bay 31 L, Gîtes minéraux du Québec, région de l'Abitibi (MRNQ, 1:250 000)

Sairs Lake occurrence

AMAZONITE, CASSITERITE, FLUORITE, MANGANOCOLUMBITE, GALENA, NATIVE BISMUTH

In granite pegmatite

Bluish-green to green amazonite occurs as crystals up to 10 cm long in pegmatite. The amazonite is suitable for use as a gemstone. Brown cassiterite, violet fluorite, dark grey metallic manganocolumbite, galena, and native bismuth occur as grains and small granular aggregates in feldspar. Radioactivity has been detected in the pegmatite.

The deposit occurs near the top of a knoll on the south side of the largest of the three islands in the north-central part of Sairs Lake.

Sairs Lake is about 54 km northeast of Témiscaming and 5 km east of Sheffield Lake (a widening of the Kipawa River). Access is by boat by proceeding south from the Kipawa occurrence across Sheffield Lake, then along the Kipawa River to Sairs Lake; the distance is about 15 km. *See* Map 18 on p. 113.

Road log from Témiscaming:

km   0   Junction Highway 101 and the road to Kipawa. Proceed along the road to Kipawa and follow the road log to the Kipawa occurrence.

         52.8   Bridge over the Kipawa River at Chute-du-Pin-Rouge; continue north.

         55.5   Junction; continue straight ahead (east).

         55.7   Junction; continue straight ahead (east).

         69.0   Charette Lake campground. Proceed by boat via Charette Lake and connecting streams to Sairs Lake and to the largest island where the Sairs Lake occurrence is located. The distance from the campground to the Sairs Lake amazonite occurrence is about 5 km.

Refs.:   152 p. 11, 17; 154 p. 11; 198 p. 277.

Maps   (T):   31 L/16 Lac Sairs
        (G):   1744 Ogascanane and Sairs lakes, Temiskaming County (MRNQ, 1:126 720)
              M-313 Feuille North Bay 31 L, Gîtes minéraux du Québec, région de l'Abitibi (MRNQ, 1:250 000)

North Bay–Huntsville area – Highway 11 road log

Collecting localities between North Bay and Huntsville are described following the road log. A page reference is indicated in parentheses following the name of each mine or occurrence. The starting point is at the junction of highways 17 and 11 South, in North Bay. The collecting route is along Highway 11 South. Kilometre distances are shown in bold type.

North Bay–Huntsville road log along Highway 11 South

km	**0**	Junction of highways 11 and 17 in North Bay; proceed onto Highway 11 South.
km	**27.0**	Powassan, junction of Highway 534 to Nipissing, and to Nipissing amazonite occurrence (p. 115) and Nipissing mica mine (p. 116).
km	**38.6**	Trout Creek, junction of Highway 522 to Big Caribou Lake occurrences and mine (p. 116), and the road to Comet Quartz mine (p. 120).
km	**55.2**	South River, junction of the road to Mikesew Provincial Park, and to Magnetawan mine (p. 120), Bell-Tough mica occurrence (p. 121), Lount copper-garnet occurrence (p. 122), and South River quarry (p. 122).
km	**65.8**	Junction, Highway 124 to Blue Star mine (p. 123) and Lorimer Lake marble occurrence (p. 123).
km	**82.2**	Burk's Falls, junction of Highway 520 to Cecebe and to Jeffrey (Cecebe Lake) mine (p. 125), Bell (Cecebe) mine (p. 125), Hungry (Carmen) Lake mine (p. 127), Wheeling mine (p. 128), and Burcal mine (p. 129).
km	**95.3**	Elmsdale, junction of Highway 518 to Graphite Lake (Cal Graphite) mine (p. 129), and Sheehan beryl occurrence (p. 132).
km	**118.7**	Huntsville, junction of Highway 60 to International Quartz mine (p. 134).
km	**122.0**	Huntsville, junction of Vernon Lake Road (Muskoka Road 3) to McKay mine (p. 134).
End of road log.		

Nipissing amazonite occurrence

AMAZONITE, MUSCOVITE, GARNET, ZIRCON, HEMATITE, PYRITE, GRAPHIC GRANITE

In granite pegmatite dyke

Green amazonite occurs with muscovite in pegmatite composed of pink microcline and quartz. Crystals of garnet and zircon, and pink graphic granite, hematite, and pyrite also occur in the pegmatite. The pegmatite occurs in syenitic rocks.

The deposit was mined for muscovite and amazonite from a trench 27 m long, 3 m wide, and about 1.5 m deep. It is on a knoll about 11 km northwest of Nipissing and 3 km southwest of Muskie Bay, South Bay, Lake Nipissing.

Access to the Nipissing amazonite occurrence is by boat from Wade's Landing at South Bay to Muskie Bay, a distance of about 9 km. A trail leads 2.5 km southwest from Muskie Bay to a hunting camp; from the camp, walk southwest about 1200 m to the mine. There are beaver dams on the last part of the route so it is necessary to manoeuvre around them. *See* Map 19 on p. 117.

Wade's Landing is about 3 km north of Nipissing and about 17 km via Highway 534 from Powassan on Highway 11 South, at **km 27.0** (*see* North Bay–Huntsville road log on p. 115).

Ref.:   117 p. 89.

Maps   (T):   31 L/4 Nipissing
           (G):   2216 North Bay area, Nipissing and Parry Sound districts (OGS, 1:126 720)
                    2361 Sudbury-Cobalt, Algoma, Manitoulin, Nipissing, Parry Sound, Sudbury
                    and Timiskaming districts (OGS, 1:253 440)

Nipissing mica mine

MUSCOVITE

In granite pegmatite

Muscovite crystals up to 45 cm in diameter have been mined from a pegmatite composed of perthitic microcline and quartz. The pegmatite cuts gabbro.

The deposit was worked from an open cut 6 m by 3 m on the north side of a hill. The work was done in the 1940s; about 4000 t of muscovite were shipped to the North Bay Mica Company Limited.

The Nipissing mica mine is about 2 km southwest of Meadow Bay on the west side of South Bay, Lake Nipissing. Access is by boat from Wade's Landing at South Bay to Meadow Bay, a distance of about 13 km; from there a road leads southwest for about 2 km to a camp. A trail leads southeast about 600 m from the camp to the mine. *See* Map 19 on p. 117.

Wade's Landing is about 3 km north of Nipissing and about 17 km via Highway 534 from Powassan on Highway 11 South, at **km 27.0** (*see* North Bay–Huntsville road log on p. 115).

Ref.:   117 p. 89.

Maps   (T):   31 L/4 Nipissing
           (G):   2216 North Bay area, Nipissing and Parry Sound districts (OGS, 1:126 720)
                    2361 Sudbury-Cobalt, Algoma, Manitoulin, Nipissing, Parry Sound, Sudbury
                    and Timiskaming districts (OGS, 1:253 440)

Big Caribou Lake occurrences, mine

PERISTERITE, GARNET, ZIRCON, THORITE, XENOTIME, MUSCOVITE

In pegmatite

White peristerite, suitable for lapidary purposes, occurs in pegmatite composed of microcline, plagioclase, quartz, muscovite, and biotite. The peristerite is used locally for jewellery. Red garnet crystals up to 2 cm in diameter are common in mica and in feldspar. Other minerals found in the deposit include brownish-grey massive zircon, dull black thorite (laths), and black xenotime (grains). The peristerite occurrence is exposed along the side of a knoll on the south shore of the western narrows of Big Caribou Lake, about 5 km from the east end of the lake.

Part of 31 L/4

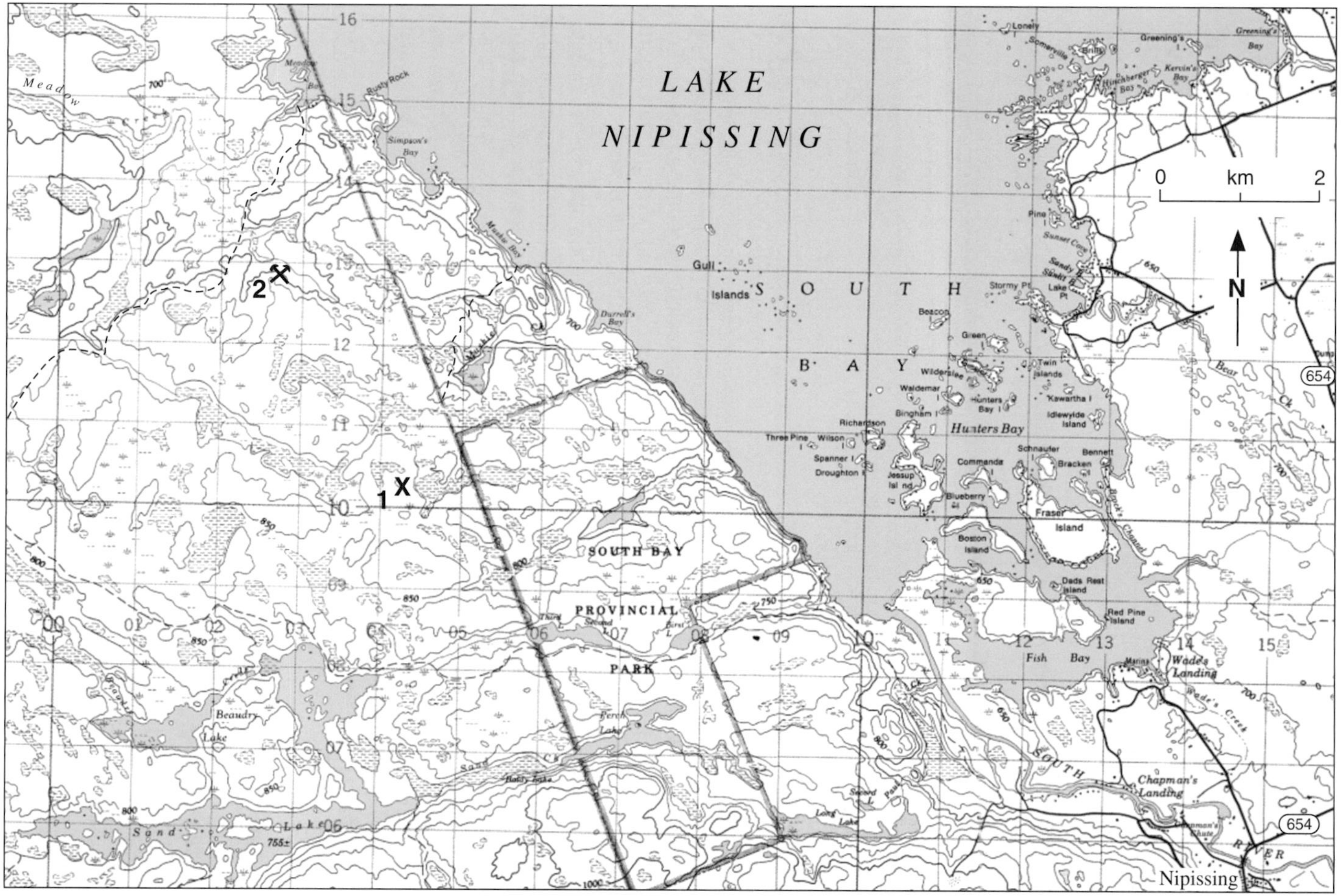

1. Nipissing amazonite occurrence 2. Nipissing mica mine

Map 19. Nipissing.

Plate 21.

Pegmatite knoll, Big Caribou Lake peristerite occurrence, 1969. GSC 153179

Two other pegmatite bodies were explored for feldspar by small pits on the south shore of Big Caribou Lake. One is on a point of land about 1200 m from the eastern end of the lake, and the other is on the west side of a knoll about 60 m south of the western arm of the lake. Another pit north of Big Caribou Lake exposes pegmatite composed of pink microcline and quartz. The pit is 4.5 m by 4.5 m and 1.2 m deep; it is at the top of a small ridge along the portage between Deep Bay (north side of Big Caribou Lake) and Burnt Lake. Fine specimens of peristerite are reported from a feldspar pit near a small pond east of the portage and just south of Burnt Lake.

Pegmatite dykes on the north side of the lake were worked for muscovite in 1952. These dykes are composed of microcline, albite, quartz, and muscovite with some biotite and garnet. During mining operations, muscovite books 10 to 45 cm in diameter were recovered. Inspiration Mining and Development Company Limited opened pits on three showings and produced about 9 t of muscovite. The main pit, from which most of the mica was recovered, is 8 m by 3 m and 2.5 m deep. The two other showings were explored by pits of about the same size, one north of the main pit and the other, northeast of it. The pits are northwest of the hunting camp at the north end of Deep Bay; they are just west of the feldspar pit on the portage between Deep Bay and Burnt Lake.

These occurrences are about 60 km west of Trout Creek. *See* Map 20 on p. 119.

Road log from Highway 11 at **km 38.6** in Trout Creek (*see* North Bay–Huntsville road log on p. 115):

km		
	0	Trout Creek, at the junction of highways 11 and 522; proceed west onto Highway 522.
	26.7	Junction of Highway 524; continue along Highway 522.
	52.0	*Rock exposures* along the highway, just southeast of Arnstein: garnet, kyanite, graphite, and pyrite occur in gneiss.
	59.6	Port Loring. Highway 522 turns north.
	65.8	Junction; turn right (north) onto Big Caribou Lake Road.

Part of 31 E/13 and 41 H/16

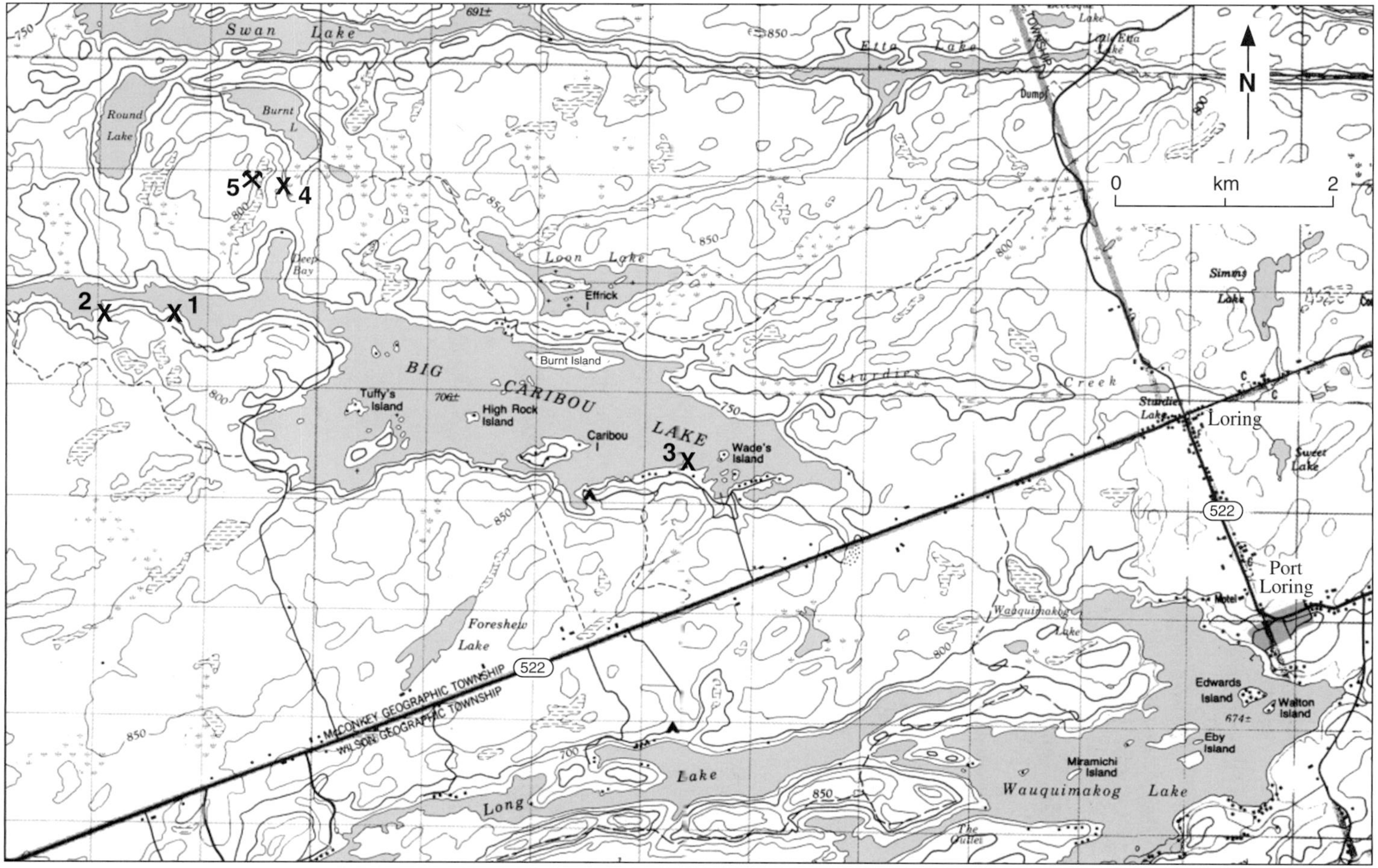

1. Peristerite occurrence   2, 3, 4. Feldspar occurrences   5. Muscovite mine

Map 20. Big Caribou Lake.

119

| | 66.8 | End of the road at the east end of Big Caribou Lake. Access to the pits is by boat from this point. |

Refs.:   32 p. 4; 85 p. 30, 35–36; 87 p. 78–81; 169 p. 58–59; 198 p. 9.

Maps   (T):   41 H/16 Noganosh Lake
(G):   51a Portions of the districts of Parry Sound and Muskoka, Province of Ontario (OGS, 1:126 720)

Comet Quartz mine

QUARTZ, ALBITE

In granite pegmatite

Massive white quartz occurs in quartz-albite pegmatite in biotite gneiss. Biotite, pyrite, and magnetite are minor accessories.

The deposit was investigated for quartz for use in the electronic industry. The exploration consisted of a pit about 12 m by 6 m; the work was done by the Comet Quartz Company in 1982–1983.

The mine is about 6 km southeast of Trout Creek.

Road log from Highway 11 at **km 38.6** in Trout Creek (*see* North Bay–Huntsville road log on p. 115):

km	0	Trout Creek, at the junction of highways 522 and 11 and Main Street; proceed east along Main Street.
	0.9	Turn right (south) onto a forest access road.
	8.5	Junction of a road on left just east of a swamp; turn left (north).
	8.8	Junction of a trail on left. Follow this trail for about 300 m to the Comet Quartz mine.

Refs.:   60 p. 162–164; 122 p. 372–374; 124 p. 104–105; 125 p. 257.

Maps   (T):   31 E/14 South River
(G):   51a Portions of the districts of Parry Sound and Muskoka, Province of Ontario (OGS, 1:126 720)

Magnetawan mine

MAGNETITE, HORNBLENDE, GARNET, PLAGIOCLASE, GOETHITE

In amphibolite

Massive magnetite was mined from this deposit. Associated with it are hornblende, granular garnet, and plagioclase. Goethite occurs as a rusty-yellow powder on ore specimens.

The deposit was worked by an open pit (15 m by 3 m and 4 to 7 m deep) and by a sidehill cut (4 m by 30 m). Operations were conducted from 1910 to 1912 by Cramp Steel Company Limited. Total production amounted to 5442 t. The openings and dumps are partly overgrown.

The mine is about 19 km southwest of South River.

Road log from Highway 11 at **km 55.2** in South River (*see* the North Bay–Huntsville road log on p. 115):

km	0	South River at the junction of Highway 11 and the road to Mikisew Provincial Park; proceed west toward Mikisew Provincial Park.
	13.8	The road turns south to Mikisew Provincial Park; continue straight ahead (west).
	21.1	Junction, road on right; continue straight ahead (west).
	23.5	Junction; turn left (south) onto the road to Magnetawan.
	28.0	Junction; turn right (south).
	30.1	Junction; turn right (west).
	32.3	Junction; continue along the road leading west.
	32.8	Magnetawan mine on right, opposite a farm lane, about 15 m from the road.

Refs.:   171 p. 32; 180 p. 283.

Maps   (T):   31 E/13 Golden Valley
(G):   1955-4 Township of Lount, District of Parry Sound (OGS, 1:31 680)

Bell-Tough mica occurrence

MUSCOVITE, K-FELDSPAR, OLIGOCLASE, ALLANITE

In pegmatite dyke

The occurrence consists of muscovite-bearing pegmatite dykes about 18 m apart in biotite gneiss. The eastern dyke contains muscovite books up to 7 cm in diameter in a quartz-K-feldspar pegmatite. The western dykes contain muscovite books up to 10 cm in diameter in pegmatite composed of quartz and white oligoclase with rod-shaped allanite crystals up to 7 cm long.

The deposit was worked first for muscovite by J. Bell, and for feldspar in 1941 by T.B. Tough. It was opened by a pit 6 m by 10.6 m and 1.2 m deep. Some muscovite was shipped from the deposit.

The occurrence is about 13 km southwest of South River.

Road log from Highway 11 at **km 55.2** in South River (*see* North Bay–Huntsville road log on p. 115):

km	0	South River at the junction of Highway 11 and the road to Mikisew Provincial Park; proceed west toward Mikisew Provincial Park, continuing along the road log toward the Magnetawan mine.
	13.8	The road turns south to Mikisew Provincial Park; continue straight ahead (west).
	16.6	Junction; turn right onto a road leading south.
	16.7	Trail on right leading west 300 m to the Bell-Tough mica occurrence.

Refs.:   85 p. 22, 30; 124 p. 106; 171 p. 41–42.

Maps   (T):   31 E/13 Golden Valley
(G):   1955-4 Township of Lount, District of Parry Sound (OGS, 1:31 680)

Lount copper-garnet occurrence

CHALCOPYRITE, PYRRHOTITE, GARNET, EPIDOTE, MAGNETITE, PYRITE

In amphibolite

Chalcopyrite and pyrrhotite occur in massive garnet rock associated with amphibolite containing garnet and epidote. These minerals occur in a copper prospect. Magnetite and pyrite occur in garnetiferous amphibolite in a nearby iron prospect.

Several copper and iron occurrences were found in Lount Township in 1908–1909. This copper prospect was opened by a shaft sunk to about 60 m. The shaft is now filled; some specimens and drill cores remain nearby. An adjacent iron prospect was investigated by a shallow pit 1.5 m in diameter.

The occurrence is about 22 km southwest of South River.

Road log from Highway 11 at **km 55.2** in South River (*see* North Bay–Huntsville road log on p. 115):

km   0   South River at the junction of Highway 11 and the road to Mikisew Provincial Park; proceed west toward Mikisew Provincial Park, continuing along the road log toward the Magnetawan mine.

          25.2   Junction; turn right onto a road leading southwest.

          25.8   Pits on the left (east) side of the road expose amphibolite containing small red garnets.

          27.0   Trail on left leads 100 m to pits exposing amphibolite containing garnet, and quartz-plagioclase pegmatite containing garnet and magnetite.

          28.6   Junction, road on left; continue straight ahead.

          30.5   Junction; turn right (northwest).

          31.6   Lount copper-garnet occurrence, about 60 m north of the road, just north of an outcrop clearing at the edge of a wooded area. The iron prospect pit is on the outcrop just south of the copper shaft.

Refs.:   122 p. 374; 171 p. 26–30.

Maps   (T):   31 E/13 Golden Valley
           (G):   1955-4 Township of Lount, District of Parry Sound (OGS, 1:31 680)

South River quarry

PYROCHLORE, GARNET

In granite

Small grains of brown pyrochlore and brownish-red garnet occur in pink granite. The granite was formerly quarried for building stone. The quarry is just north of the village of South River.

Road log from Highway 11 at **km 55.2** in South River (*see* North Bay–Huntsville road log on p. 115):

km   0   South River, at the junction of Highway 11 and the road heading west to Mikisew Provincial Park; proceed along the road leading east.

0.25   Intersection; turn left (north).

1.4   Entrance to the South River quarry on right.

Maps   (T):   31 E/14 South River
        (G):   51a Portions of the districts of Parry Sound and Muskoka, Province of Ontario
               (OGS, 1:126 720)

Blue Star mine

MICROCLINE (AMAZONITE), PLAGIOCLASE, QUARTZ, BIOTITE, HEMATITE, MAGNETITE, GARNET, CHLORITE, ILMENITE, PSEUDORUTILE, ANATASE, CASSITERITE, FLUORITE, SAMARSKITE, EUXENITE, PYROCHLORE, MANGANOCOLUMBITE

In granite pegmatite

Greenish blue amazonite, suitable for jewellery, occurs with plagioclase, colourless to smoky quartz, and biotite in a pegmatite dyke cutting biotite gneiss. Common accessory minerals include hematite, magnetite, garnet, and chlorite. Ilmenite, pseudorutile (pseudomorphs after ilmenite), anatase, cassiterite, fluorite, samarskite, euxenite, pyrochlore, and manganocolumbite have been reported.

The mine consists of an open cut on the east side of a ridge. It was operated by James Donald as a mineral-collecting site for tourists from 1984 to 1992.

The mine is about 10 km northeast of Magnetawan. *See* Map 21 on p. 124.

Road log from Highway 11 South at **km 65.8** (*see* North Bay–Huntsville road log on p. 115):

km   0   Junction of highways 11 and 124; proceed west along Highway 124 toward Magnetawan.

        17.8   Junction; turn right (north) onto Miller Road.

        20.1   Junction; continue along the main road on right.

        21.3   Junction; continue straight ahead.

        23.1   Blue Star mine.

Refs.:   46 p. 422–423; 60 p. 152–155; 204 p. 245; 205 p. 276; 206 p. 361.

Maps   (T):   31 E/12 Magnetawan
        (G):   51a Portions of the districts of Parry Sound and Muskoka, Province of Ontario
               (OGS, 1:126 720)

Lorimer Lake marble occurrence

GRAPHITE, CHONDRODITE, CLINOPYROXENE, SERPENTINE, SPINEL, MICA, APATITE, MAGNETITE, BRUCITE, PERICLASE

In crystalline limestone

Graphite, chondrodite, clinopyroxene, serpentine, spinel, mica, and apatite occur as disseminated grains in white crystalline limestone. Brucite and periclase have been reported.

123

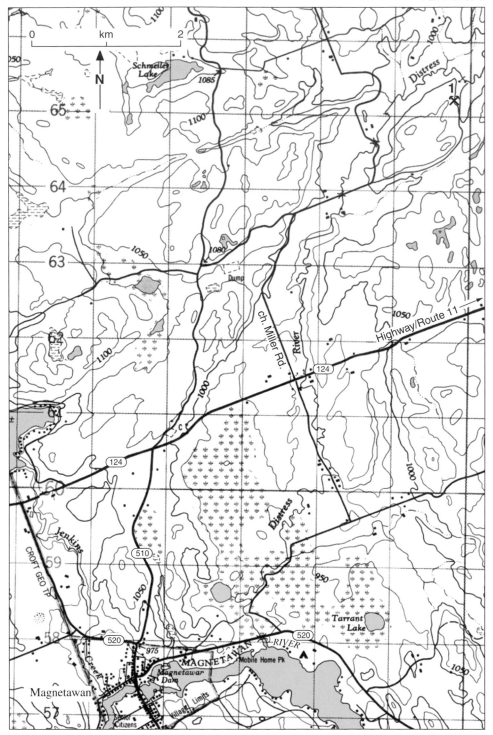

1. Blue Star mine

Map 21. Magnetawan.

The deposit is near the northeastern end of Lorimer Lake, about 40 km west of Burk's Falls. It was worked for marble by Cononaco Mines Limited in 1969. The openings consist of two pits, one on each side of Highway 124, 49.5 km from the junction of Highway 124 with Highway 11 at **km 65.8** (*see* North Bay–Huntsville road log on p. 115).

Refs.:   122 p. 405–411; 125 p. 183–184.

Maps   (T):   31 E/12 Magnetawan
        (G):   51a Portions of the districts of Parry Sound and Muskoka, Province of Ontario
               (OGS, 1:126 720)

Jeffrey (Cecebe Lake) mine

FELDSPAR, MUSCOVITE, BIOTITE, GARNET, ALLANITE, PYROCHLORE, ZIRCON

In granite pegmatite

Both plagioclase and microcline are present. Large books of light green muscovite up to 30 cm in diameter occur in the pegmatite. Less common in the deposit are biotite and deep red garnet crystals averaging 1 cm in diameter. Allanite, pyrochlore, and zircon also occur in the pegmatite (T.S. Ercit, pers. comm., 1987).

This mine was formerly worked for muscovite (1937–1938) and for feldspar (1941). It produced about 173 t of feldspar.

The mine is in a pegmatite outcrop at the top of a steep wooded ridge on the north shore of the eastern end of Cecebe Lake, about 9 km west of Burk's Falls. *See* Map 22 on p. 126.

Road log from Highway 11 at **km 82.2** (*see* North Bay–Huntsville road log on p. 115):

km   0   Burk's Falls, junction of highways 11 and 520; turn right (west) onto
                          Highway 520.

        12.1   Junction, single-lane road on left; turn left (south).

        12.7   Junction; turn right (west).

        13.7   Clearing on left. The old mine road begins in the clearing and leads south.
                  Proceed on foot along this road.

        14.5   Jeffery (Cecebe Lake) mine.

Refs.:   82 p. 12; 87 p. 98; 125 p. 212; 169 p. 60–61.

Maps   (T):   31 E/12 Magnetawan
        (G):   51a Portions of the districts of Parry Sound and Muskoka, Province of Ontario
               (OGS, 1:126 720)

Bell (Cecebe) mine

MICROCLINE, GRAPHIC GRANITE, CHLORITE, MAGNETITE, HEMATITE, GARNET, BASTNAESITE, EUXENITE, ZIRCON

In granite pegmatite

Part of 31 E/12

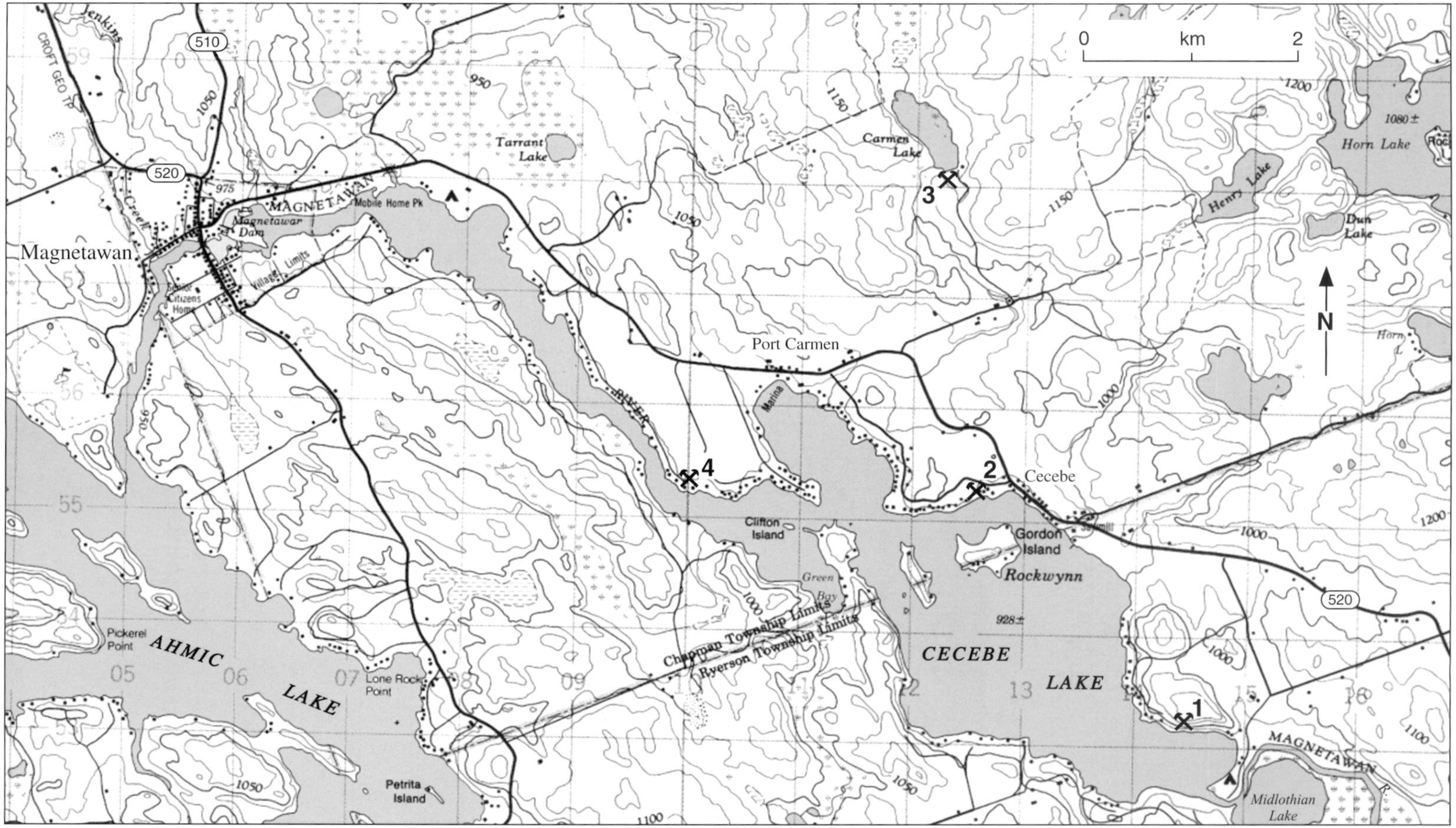

1. Jeffrey (Cecebe Lake) mine 2. Bell (Cecebe) mine 3. Hungry (Carmen) Lake mine 4. Wheeling mine

Map 22. Cecebe Lake.

Pink, fine- to medium-textured graphic granite suitable for lapidary purposes is abundant at this feldspar mine. It occurs in pegmatite composed of pink microcline, colourless to smoky quartz, muscovite, and biotite. Accessory minerals include chlorite, magnetite, hematite, garnet (tiny pink crystals), bastnaesite (dull black laths), euxenite (dark reddish-brown glassy grains), and zircon (tiny brown tetragonal prisms).

The deposit was worked for a brief time in 1948 by J. Bell of Burks Falls Feldspar Syndicate Limited. About 45 t of feldspar were removed from a pit 16 m by 3 m with a 7 m face.

The mine is in Cecebe village near the top of a steep ridge on the north side of Cecebe Lake, about 12 km northwest of Burk's Falls. *See* Map 22 on p. 126.

Road log from Highway 11 at **km 82.2** (*see* North Bay–Huntsville road log on p. 115):

km	0	Burk's Falls; junction of highways 11 and 520; turn right (west) onto Highway 520.
	12.1	Junction, road to Jeffrey (Cecebe Lake) mine; continue along the highway.
	14.2	Cecebe village, at the junction of Chapman Drive; turn left.
	14.6	Fork; bear left.
	14.8	Trail on left leads through a clearing then through a wooded area to the Bell (Cecebe) mine, a distance of about 100 m.

Refs.:   75 p. 12; 125 p. 59; 213 p. 1.

Maps   (T):   31 E/12 Magnetawan
        (G):   51a Portions of the districts of Parry Sound and Muskoka, Province of Ontario (OGS, 1:126 720)

Hungry (Carmen) Lake mine

MICROCLINE, QUARTZ, BIOTITE, GARNET, ZIRCON, EUXENITE, GRAPHIC GRANITE

In granite pegmatite

The pegmatite consists of pink to almost white microcline, colourless to smoky quartz, and biotite. Accessory minerals include red garnet (crystals averaging 5 mm in diameter), pink zircon (crystals about 2 mm long), and euxenite (T.S. Ercit, pers. comm., 1987). Some pale pink graphic granite occurs in the deposit.

The pegmatite dyke occurs in biotite gneiss.

The mine was operated for feldspar in 1941 by T.B. Tough. It consists of an open cut into the side of a hill at the south end of Hungry (Carmen) Lake. It is about 3 km north of Cecebe village and 13 km northwest of Burk's Falls. *See* Map 22 on p. 126.

Road log from Highway 11 at **km 82.2** (*see* North Bay–Huntsville road log on p. 115):

km	0	Burk's Falls, junction of highways 11 and 520; turn right (west) onto Highway 520.
	12.1	Junction, road to Jeffrey (Cecebe Lake) mine; continue along the highway.
	14.2	Junction, Chapman Drive; continue along the highway.

	15.9	Junction, gravel road; turn right.
	17.0	Junction, farm lane on left; turn left.
	17.4	Gate.
	18.5	Hungry (Carmen) Lake mine.

Refs.: 82 p. 12; 169 p. 56.

Maps (T): 31 E/12 Magnetawan
(G): 51a Portions of the districts of Parry Sound and Muskoka, Province of Ontario (OGS, 1:126 720)

Wheeling mine

K-FELDSPAR, BIOTITE, GRAPHIC GRANITE, CHLORITE, HEMATITE, MAGNETITE, ALLANITE

In granite pegmatite

The pegmatite comprises pink K-feldspar, white quartz, pink graphic granite, and biotite. Dark green chlorite flakes and grains of hematite and magnetite occur in feldspar. Allanite has been reported. The pegmatite occurs in granite gneiss.

The deposit was worked for feldspar between 1920 and 1923 by Wheeling Feldspar Company. About 787 t of stucco spar were produced from an open cut at the south side of a hill. The opening, which measures about 23 m wide and 6 m deep, is about 150 m from the shore of Cecebe Lake. During mining operations, a crushing plant operated at the shore of the lake. The crushed feldspar was shipped by scow to Burk's Falls for transport by rail.

The mine is on the north shore of Cecebe Lake at its western end, about 15 km northwest of Burk's Falls. *See* Map 22 on p. 126.

Road log from Highway 11 South at **km 82.2** in Burk's Falls (*see* North Bay–Huntsville road log on p. 115):

km	0	Burk's Falls, junction of highways 11 and 520; turn right (west) onto Highway 520.
	14.2	Cecebe village, at the junction of Chapman Drive; continue along Highway 520.
	18.2	Junction; turn left (south) onto Cecebe Lake road.
	18.8	Junction; turn right (west).
	19.0	Fork; follow the road on left.
	19.3	Wheeling mine.

Refs.: 75 p. 12; 169 p. 56; 188 p. 53.

Maps (T): 31 E/12 Magnetawan
(G): 51a Portions of the districts of Parry Sound and Muskoka, Province of Ontario (OGS, 1:126 720)

Burcal mine

CALCITE, CLINOAMPHIBOLE, CLINOPYROXENE, TITANITE, PHLOGOPITE, SCAPOLITE, APATITE, PLAGIOCLASE, CHLORITE, GRAPHITE, PYRITE

In crystalline limestone

White to pink coarse aggregates of calcite make up a band of almost pure calcite marble that was worked for industrial calcite. An impure marble associated with it contains disseminated grains and aggregates of the following minerals: black clinoamphibole, green clinopyroxene, brown titanite crystals up to 1 cm long, phlogopite, light yellowish-green scapolite crystals, light blue apatite crystals, colourless plagioclase, greyish-green chlorite, graphite, and pyrite.

Burcal Mines Limited worked the deposit between 1971 and 1975. The mine consists of a pit 61 m by 8 m and 10 m deep. The calcite was trucked to the company's crushing and processing plant in Burk's Falls.

The mine is south of Ahmic Lake and about 29 km west of Burk's Falls. *See* Map 23 on p. 130.

Road log from Highway 11 south at **km 82.2** in Burk's Falls (*see* North Bay–Huntsville road log on p. 115):

km		
	0	Burk's Falls, junction of highways 11 and 520; proceed onto Highway 520.
	4.0	Junction; turn left and leave Highway 520.
	6.6	*Ryerson Natural Stone quarry* on the right (north) side of the road. Biotite gneiss is exposed in the quarry.
	13.2	Crossroad; continue straight ahead.
	18.6	Junction; turn left (south).
	21.5	Junction; turn right (west).
	26.7	Junction; continue straight ahead (west).
	27.6	Junction, mine road; turn right (north).
	28.7	Burcal mine.

Ref.:   122 p. 416–420.

Maps   (T):   31 E/12 Magnetawan
       (G):   51a Portions of the districts of Parry Sound and Muskoka, Province of Ontario
              (OGS, 1:126 720)

Graphite Lake (Cal Graphite) mine

GRAPHITE, PYRITE, PYRRHOTITE, GARNET, TITANITE, APATITE, ALLANITE

In biotite schist and gneiss

Graphite occurs as disseminated flakes and flaky aggregates in biotite schist and, less abundantly, in biotite gneiss. K-feldspar, quartz, plagioclase, and dark green clinopyroxene are constituents of the host rocks. Several minerals occur as grains, including almandine garnet (averaging 2 mm in diameter), pyrite, pyrrhotite, titanite, and light blue apatite. Rusty-yellow goethite and white rozenite occur as coatings on the host rocks. Laths of reddish-brown allanite occur in biotite-quartz-feldspar pegmatite associated with the schist and gneiss. Sillimanite and scapolite have been reported from the deposit.

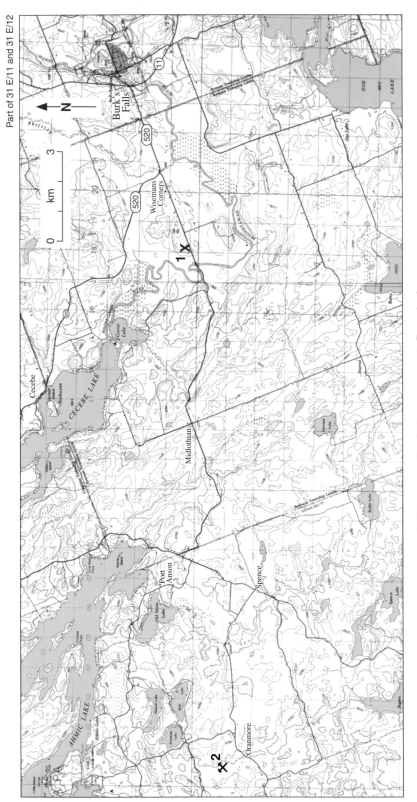

1. Ryerson natural stone quarry 2. Burcal mine

Map 23. Burk's Falls.

The deposit was originally staked in 1917. In 1942, it was staked by D.J. Sheehan of Kearney and investigated by stripping and small pits by Noranda Mines Limited. It was subsequently investigated by other companies. In 1985, Cal Graphite Corporation undertook development of the deposit. Production from an open pit began in 1990. In 1993, Applied Carbon Technology Inc. took over the deposit. Operations were suspended in June 1994. The ore, which grades 2.5 per cent graphite, was processed at a mill at the mine site.

The mine is on a hill overlooking the east end of Graphite Lake, about 28 km by road northeast of Kearney. *See* Map 24 on p. 133.

Road log from Highway 11 south at **km 95.3** in Elmsdale (*see* North Bay–Huntsville road log on p. 115):

km		
	0	Elmsdale, junction of highways 11 and 518; proceed east onto Highway 518.
	0.4	Junction of Highway 592; continue straight ahead along Highway 518.
	8.5	Junction, at Kearney; continue along Highway 518 toward Tim River and Algonquin Park.
	18.1	Junction of Kallio Road; continue along Highway 518.
	21.2	Junction of Perrys Road; continue along Highway 518.
	22.4	Junction; turn right (north) onto Forestry Tower Road to Tim River, Magnetawan Lake, and Algonquin Park.
	25.3	Junction; follow the road on right leading east toward Algonquin Park.
	26.8	Junction, single-lane road on right; continue straight ahead (east).
	27.5	Junction, road on right; continue straight ahead (north).
	28.2	Junction, road on left; continue straight ahead (north).
	30.5	Junction, single-lane road on right; continue straight ahead (north).
	31.1	Junction, single-lane road on left; follow the main road leading north.
	32.1	Junction, single-lane road on left; continue straight ahead (north).
	33.1	Junction, road on right leads to Tim River and Magnetawan Lake (to Sheehan and Rivers occurrences); continue straight ahead.
	33.2	Junction, single-lane road on right; follow the main road on left.
	36.1	Mill on left; the road continues straight ahead toward the mine.
	36.6	Turnoff (right) to the Graphite Lake (Cal Graphite) mine.

Refs.:   53 p. 332–334; 54 p. 82–95; 55 p. 14 23; 83 p. 40; 204 p. 242; 235 p. 92; 237 p. 72; 238 p. 40.

Maps   (T):   31 E/11 Burk's Falls
           (G):   P2563 Industrial minerals of the Algonquin region, Bracebridge area, Parry Sound, Muskoka, Nipissing districts and southern Ontario (OGS, 1:126 720)

Sheehan beryl occurrence

BERYL, K-FELDSPAR, MUSCOVITE, BIOTITE, MONAZITE, GARNET, MAGNETITE, EUXENITE, SAMARSKITE, ALLANITE, ZIRCON, APATITE

In granite pegmatite

Beryl crystals up to 5 cm in diameter occur in pegmatite. Faceted light blue beryl (aquamarine) stones from this locality are in the gem collections of the Royal Ontario Museum and the National Mineral Collection. The pegmatite is composed of K-feldspar and quartz with abundant muscovite. Other minerals occurring in the pegmatite include biotite, red-orange monazite, garnet, magnetite, euxenite, samarskite, allanite, zircon, and apatite (T.S. Ercit, pers. comm., 1995).

The deposit was worked for muscovite and beryl. The workings consist of two open cuts.

The occurrence is near the boundary of Algonquin Park, about 35 km by road northeast of Kearney. *See* Map 24 on p. 133.

Road log from Highway 11 south at **km 95.3** in Elmsdale (*see* North Bay–Huntsville road log on p. 115):

km		
	0	Elmsdale, junction of highways 11 and 518; proceed east onto Highway 518. Follow the road log to Graphite Lake (Cal Graphite) mine to km 33.1.
	33.1	Junction; turn right (east) onto the road leading to Tim River, Magnetawan Lake, and Algonquin Park. (The road straight ahead leads to the Graphite Lake (Cal Graphite) mine.)
	34.55	*Rivers occurrence.* Euxenite and zircon occur in granite pegmatite. The property was explored by stripping in 1953–1954. To reach it proceed south from km 34.55 to the Magnetawan River. The stripping is in a wooded area above the falls. *See* Map 24 on p. 133.
	35.3	Junction; turn left (north) onto the road to Tim River.
	37.7	Junction; continue straight ahead.
	37.9	Junction; follow the road on right. (The road on left leads 0.7 km to the Graphite Lake (Cal Graphite) mine.)
	39.2	Junction, road on right to Tim River; continue straight ahead (north).
	39.9	Junction; follow the road on right leading north.
	41.5	Junction at a gravel pit; continue straight ahead.
	43.0	T-junction; turn right (east).
	43.3	Shallow gravel pit on right. Continue along the road.
	43.5	Sheehan beryl occurrence to the north of the road. Walk north about 100 m to two shallow pits on the southeastern side (near the top) of a knob-like hill.

Refs.: 85 p. 38; 86 p. 47; 125 p. 15; 172 p. 61, 147; 210 p. 76.

Maps (T): 31 E/11 Burk's Falls
31 E/14 South River
(G): 1335A Southern Ontario, Ontario-Quebec-U.S.A. (GSC, 1:1 000 000)

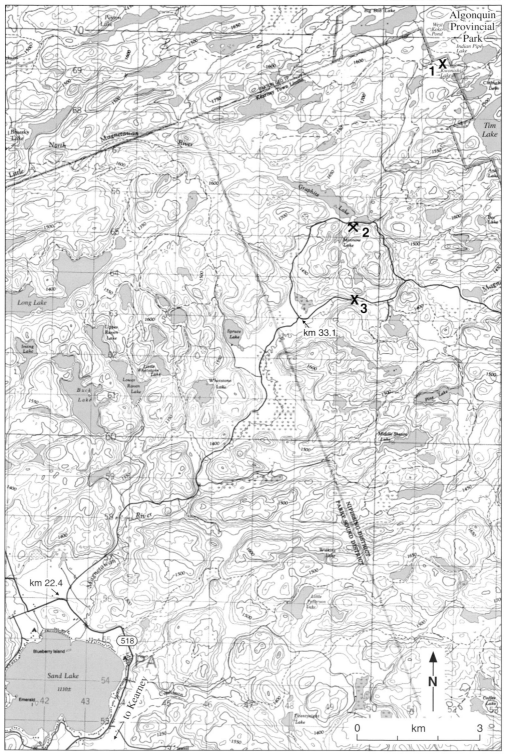

1. Sheehan beryl occurrence   2. Graphite Lake (Cal Graphite) mine   3. Rivers occurrence

Map 24. Kearney.

International Quartz mine

QUARTZ, K-FELDSPAR, MUSCOVITE, BIOTITE, EUXENITE, MAGNETITE, EPIDOTE, CHLORITE

In granite pegmatite

Massive white quartz and minor K-feldspar and plagioclase are the main constituents of the pegmatite. Muscovite, biotite, euxenite, magnetite, epidote, and chlorite have been reported. The pegmatite dyke cuts gabbro.

The deposit is exposed by two open cuts, the larger being 30 m by 7.6 m and 6 m high. International Quartz mined about 7200 t of quartz in the 1970s. Some of the quartz was used locally for decorative purposes.

The mine is on the south slope of a ridge overlooking the north shore of Fletcher Lake, 33 km east of Huntsville. *See* Map 25 on p. 135.

Road log from Highway 11 at **km 118.7** in Huntsville (*see* North Bay–Huntsville road log on p. 115):

km		
	0	Huntsville, junction of highways 60 and 11; proceed east along Highway 60.
	22.5	Junction, highways 60 and 35; proceed south along Highway 35.
	38.2	Junction; turn left onto the road leading northeast to Fletcher Lake.
	51.4	Junction; turn left (north) onto the road to Fletcher dam.
	51.6	Junction; follow the road on left.
	52.8	International Quartz mine.

Refs.:   60 p. 164–165; 125 p. 237–238.

Maps   (T):   31 E/7 Kawagama Lake
(G):   52a Haliburton area, Province of Ontario (OGS, 1:126 720)

McKay mine

MICROCLINE, PLAGIOCLASE, QUARTZ, BIOTITE, MAGNETITE, EUXENITE, SUNSTONE

In pegmatite

The pegmatite consists of microcline, plagioclase, and colourless to smoky quartz. Biotite occurs as crystals up to 4 cm in diameter. Magnetite occurs as grains and aggregates. Euxenite has been identified (T.S. Ercit, pers. comm., 1987). Some sunstone occurs in the feldspar.

The deposit was opened in 1941 by F.C. Hammond and Allan McKay. A test shipment of feldspar was mined from a pit measuring 7.5 m square and about 1.5 m deep.

The mine is on the north side of a wooded slope on the property of Alex McKay, about 8 km west of Huntsville. *See* Map 25 on p. 135.

Road log from Highway 11 at **km 122.0** in Huntsville (*see* North Bay–Huntsville road log on p. 115):

km		
	0	Huntsville, junction of Highway 11 and Vernon Lake Road; proceed onto Vernon Lake Road (Muskoka Road 3).
	7.7	Junction; turn left.

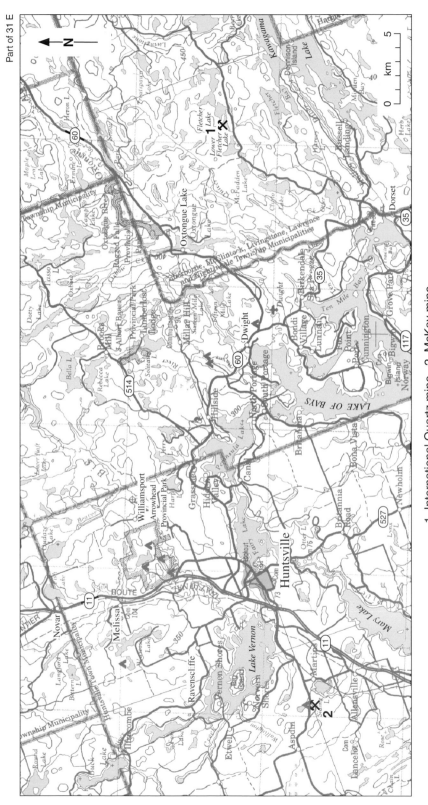

1. International Quartz mine   2. McKay mine

Map 25. Huntsville.

135

7.85 Turnoff (left) to the McKay property. The McKay mine is about 50 m from the farmhouse.

Refs.: 62 p. 22; 75 p. 11; 84 p. 45; 125 p. 85; 169 p. 61.

Maps (T): 31 E/6 Huntsville
(G): 2118 Parry Sound-Huntsville area, Ontario (OGS, 1:126 720)

GATINEAU (HULL) TO WALTHAM, QUEBEC

Collecting localities along Highway 148 between Gatineau (Hull) and Waltham, Quebec, are described following the road log. A page reference is indicated in parentheses following the name of each mine or occurrence. The main road log starts 3.5 km west of the main business section in Gatineau (Hull), proceeds west along Highway 148, and ends in Waltham, across the Ottawa River from Pembroke, Ontario. Along the route a side trip describes mineral occurrences in the Shawville–Otter Lake area.

Gatineau (Hull) to Waltham, Quebec area – Highway 148 road log

km	0	Gatineau (Hull), Highway 148 (Aylmer Road) at the junction of the road to Ottawa via the Champlain Bridge; proceed west along Highway 148.
km	3.5	Junction, Vanier Road to Lavigne quarries (p. 137). Dufferin Aggregates quarry (p. 138), and Deschênes quarry (p. 138).
km	6.5	Gatineau (Aylmer), at Principale Street (Highway 148) and a municipal park; the highway turns right.
km	43.2	Junction, Hammond Road to Godwin mine (p. 139).
km	47.0	Junction, Lac-des-Loups Road leading north to Moss mine (p. 140) and south to Quyon.
km	57.8	Junction, road to Bristol (Hilton) mine (p. 142).
km	69.8	Shawville, junction of Highway 303 (Centre Street). Several occurrences are described in the Shawville–Otter Lake area: Kirkham mine (p. 144), Welsh mine (p. 146), Father Ferary mine (p. 146), Kazabazua River (Milkie) asbestos occurrence (p. 147), Cawood mica occurrence (p. 148), Bretzlaff occurrence (p. 148), Zimmerling mine (p. 149), Richard cordierite occurrence (p. 149), Giroux mine (p. 150), Yates mine (p. 151), and Squaw Lake mine (p. 155).
km	71.2	Junction, Highway 303 South to Portage-du-Fort and Highway 301 South to the Rapides des Chenaux occurrence on Limerick and Little Limerick islands (p. 80), 14.5 km from this junction (see p. 80 for description and Map 9 on p. 78).
km	81.2	Junction, Highway 301 to Portage-du-Fort and the Portage-du-Fort quarries (p. 156).
km	82.1	Highway 148 (Bryson) roadcuts (p. 156).
km	82.8	Junction, road to Bryson and the Carswell quarry (p. 157) and Bryson marble blocks (p. 159).

km	84.7	Junction, road to Bryson and Île du Grand Calumet and to Bryson roadcuts 1 and 2 (p. 159, 160), New Calumet mine (p. 160), and Calumet uranium occurrence (p. 162).
km	91.4	Campbell's Bay, junction of Highway 301 to Otter Lake and the Lawless Lake occurrence (p. 163).
km	109.1	Fort-Coulonge, junction of Chemin de la Chute to the Gibson (Gib) Lake scapolite occurrence (p. 163).
km	118.5	Junction, road on left to Sèche Point occurrence (p. 164).
km	120.1	Junction, road on left to Devonshire Park occurrence (p. 164).
km	128.0	Waltham, junction of Highway 148 and the road to Chapeau and the Waltham mine (p. 165).
km	144.2	Highway 148 bridge over the Ottawa River connecting Île aux Allumettes and Morrison Island. The fossil occurrences on these islands are described on p. 86. Highway 148 continues across Morrison Island and Cotnam Island, and joins Renfrew County Road 40 (old Highway 17) at **km 104.5** of the Ottawa–North Bay road log (*see* p. 75).

End of the Highway 148 road log from Gatineau (Hull) to Waltham.

Lavigne quarries

CALCITE, FOSSILS

In limestone

Colourless to white calcite crystals occur along fractures in Ordovician limestone. Fossils including corals, crinoids, brachiopods, and gastropods are common; in places they are abundant and form a coquina limestone.

The quarries were formerly worked for road-building material. They are on the property of L.A. Lavigne, about 6 km north of Gatineau (Aylmer).

Road log from Highway 148 at **km 3.5** (*see* Highway 148 road log on p. 136):

km	0	Junction, Highway 148 (Aylmer Road) and Vanier Road; proceed north along Vanier Road.
	4.1	Inactive quarry on left; the limestone at this quarry is similar to the limestone at the Lavigne quarries. Continue along Vanier Road.
	6.4	Junction; turn left (west) onto Cook Road.
	8.0	Lavigne quarries on left.

Refs.: 63 p. 60; 90 p. 5; 222 p. 21–26.

Map (T): 31 G/5 Ottawa
(G): 7-1970 Gatineau Park – Parc de la Gatineau, Québec (GSC, 1:18 000)
414A Ottawa sheet (west half), Carleton and Hull counties, Ontario and Quebec (GSC, 1:63 360)
1508A Generalized bedrock geology, Ottawa-Hull, Ontario and Quebec (GSC, 1:125 000)

Dufferin Aggregates quarry

FOSSILS, CALCITE

In limestone

Ordovician fossils, including corals, crinoids, brachiopods, pelecypods, cephalopods, trilobites, and gastropods, occur in limestone. Crystals of colourless and white calcite occur in fractures in limestone.

The quarry and crushing plant are operated by Dufferin Aggregates. They are about 5 km northeast of Gatineau (Aylmer).

Road log from Highway 148 at **km 3.5** (*see* Highway 148 road log on p. 136):

km		
	0	Junction, Highway 148 (Aylmer Road) and Vanier Road; proceed north along Vanier Road.
	4.8	Junction; turn left (west) onto Pink Road.
	5.2	Junction, quarry road; turn left (south).
	5.4	Dufferin Aggregates quarry.

Refs.: 63 p. 59–60; 218 p. 11; 220 p. 10; 221 p. 11; 222 p. 21–26.

Maps (T): 31 G/5 Ottawa
(G): 414A Ottawa sheet (west half), Carleton and Hull counties, Ontario and Quebec (GSC, 1:63 360)
1508A Generalized bedrock geology, Ottawa-Hull, Ontario and Quebec (GSC, 1:125 000)

Deschênes quarry

FOSSILS, BARITE, CALCITE, PYRITE

In limestone

Ordovician fossils including corals, crinoids, brachiopods, trilobites, pelecypods, cephalopods, and gastropods are common in the limestone. The rock is medium grained, light grey, and is known as 'Black River limestone'. Calcite occurs as crystals and in massive form; the crystals are commonly coated with white platy barite. Pyrite occurs as nodules and in granular form.

The quarry and crushing plant are operated by Deschênes Construction Limited for road metal. They are about 4 km north of Gatineau (Aylmer).

Road log from Highway 148 at **km 3.5** (*see* Highway 148 road log on p. 136):

km		
	0	Junction, Highway 148 (Aylmer Road) and Vanier Road; proceed north along Vanier Road.
	4.8	Junction; turn left (west) onto Pink Road.
	7.5	Deschênes quarry, on left, at the junction of Klock Road.

Refs.: 63 p. 60; 218 p. 11; 220 p. 10; 221 p. 11; 222 p. 21–26.

Maps (T): 31 G/5 Ottawa
(G): 414A Ottawa sheet (west half), Carleton and Hull counties, Ontario and Quebec (GSC, 1:63 360)
1508A Generalized bedrock geology, Ottawa-Hull, Ontario and Quebec (GSC, 1:125 000)

Plate 22.
Deschênes quarry, 1969. GSC 153200

Godwin mine

MICA, PYROXENE, CALCITE, SCAPOLITE, HORNBLENDE, PYRITE

In pyroxenite

Mica was formerly mined from this deposit. Crystals up to 30 cm in diameter were obtained during mining operations. The crystals are amber with much darker edges. Massive pyroxene and pyroxene crystals occur with the mica in pink to orange calcite. Other minerals associated with the deposit are light greyish-green scapolite, hornblende, and pyrite. The mica-bearing pyroxenite dyke cuts syenite.

The deposit was first worked in 1900 by J.J. Godwin. It was operated again briefly in 1906. The pit measures 25 m by 3 m and 9 m deep. There is a small dump near the pit; both are now partly overgrown.

The mine, on the property of Paul J. Bourque, is about 7 km northeast of Quyon.

Road log from Highway 148 at **km 43.2** (*see* Highway 148 road log on p. 136):

km		
	0	Junction, Highway 148 and Hammond Road; turn right (north) onto Hammond Road.
	5.0	Junction. The road to the mine begins at the gate opposite this junction and leads north.
	6.4	Trail on left leading 30 m to the Godwin mine.

Refs.:   <u>173</u> p. 135–136; <u>224</u> p. 116–117.

Maps   (T):   31 F/9 Quyon
       (G):   660 Quebec and Ontario, parts of counties of Ottawa and Pontiac, Que. and
              Carleton and Renfrew, Ont. (Pembroke Sheet No. 122) (GSC, 1:253 440)
              1034 Onslow-Masham area, Pontiac and Gatineau counties (MRNQ, 1:63 360)
              1739 Portions of Bristol, Onslow, McNab, Fitzroy and Torbolton Townships,
              Quebec and Ontario (GSC, 1:63 360)

Moss mine

MOLYBDENITE, PYRITE, PYRRHOTITE, FLUORITE, MAGNETITE, CHLORITE, TITANITE, MICROCLINE, HEMATITE, PYROXENE, SIDERITE, BIOTITE, ALLANITE

In quartz syenite

Molybdenite occurs as flakes (averaging 2 cm in diameter) and as flaky aggregates in syenite. It is associated with aggregates of pyrite, pyrrhotite, violet fluorite, magnetite, chlorite, titanite, microcline, hematite, pyroxene, siderite, and biotite. Pyroxene crystals occur in the deposit but are uncommon. Allanite has been reported.

The molybdenite deposit, on the farm of Robert Steel, was discovered several years before it was first exploited in 1915. During World War I it was the world's leading producer of molybdenum and accounted for 80 per cent of the Canadian output. Operators included the Canadian Wood Molybdenite Company (1915–1916), Dominion Molybdenite Company (1917–1919), and Quyon Molybdenite Company (1938–1944). The workings consist of three pits and two shafts near the mill site, and a pit

Plate 23.
Moss mine, 1917. National Archives of Canada C 22964

Plate 24.

Dominion Molybdenite Company mill, Moss mine, 1917. GSC 40213

and shaft 450 m to the northwest. The largest pit measures 36 m by 15 m and is up to 9 m deep. All mine buildings have been dismantled, the pits are water filled, and only small dumps are found near the openings. Total production amounted to about 550 t of molybdenite.

The mine is about 6 km north of Quyon.

Road log from Highway 148 at **km 47.0** (*see* Highway 148 road log on p. 136):

km	0	Junction, Highway 148 and the road to Quyon and Lac-des-Loups Road; turn right (north) onto Lac-des-Loups Road.
	5.2	Junction; continue straight ahead. (The Godwin mine may be reached from this junction by proceeding east 4.5 km to the gate and turnoff to the mine.)
	5.6	Junction, mine road; turn right.
	5.75	Fork; bear left.
	5.9	Moss mine.

Refs.: 35 p. 408–409; 37 p. 150–155; 167 p. 6; 168 p. 38; 208 p. 186–194; 224 p. 64–77.

Maps (T): 31 F/9 Quyon
(G): 660 Quebec and Ontario, part of counties of Ottawa and Pontiac, Que. and Carleton and Renfrew, Ont. (Pembroke Sheet No. 122) (GSC, 1:253 440)
1034 Onslow-Masham area, Pontiac and Gatineau counties (MRNQ, 1:63 360)
1739 Portions of Bristol, Onslow, McNab, Fitzroy and Torbolton townships, Quebec and Ontario (GSC, 1:63 360)

Bristol (Hilton) mine

MAGNETITE, HEMATITE, HORNBLENDE, TALC, TREMOLITE, PYRITE, CHALCOPYRITE, CHLORITE, SERPENTINE, FELDSPAR, EPIDOTE, GARNET, SCAPOLITE, MARTITE

In amphibolite near its contact with crystalline limestone

Magnetite, the ore mineral, occurs as finely granular masses. Hematite is associated with it. Hornblende, grey massive talc, and light green fibrous tremolite occur commonly in the orebody. In places the fibrous tremolite is replaced by magnetite and/or pyrite retaining the fibrous structure. Grains and veinlets of pyrite and, less commonly, chalcopyrite are found in magnetite. Other minerals associated with the deposit include chlorite, serpentine, brick-red feldspar cut by epidote veinlets, orange-red garnet (grains associated with epidote), and greenish-grey scapolite. Martite, a hematite pseudomorph after magnetite, has been reported from the deposit.

The first report of iron ore in the area was made in 1847 by William E. Logan, director of the GSC, following a geological survey along the Ottawa River in 1845. John Moore discovered this deposit in about 1870. Taylor and Burns of Pittsburg began mining from open cuts in 1872–1873. This was followed by larger scale operations by Bristol Iron Company (1884–1889) and Ennis and Company of Philadelphia (1889–1894). Operations were conducted from shafts, 30 m and 61 m deep, and from several open cuts. Two roasting furnaces were used and about 14 510 t of ore were mined. The mine was inactive until 1958 when Hilton Mines Limited resumed operations from an open pit. The company installed concentrating and pelletizing plants at the mine site. Mining ended in 1977.

The Bristol (Hilton) mine is about 9 km southwest of Quyon. Access is by a 6.4 km long road leading south from Highway 148 at **km 57.8** (*see* Highway 148 road log on p. 136).

Plate 25.
Bristol (Hilton) mine, 1890. GSC 105346

Plate 26.
Bristol (Hilton) mine in 1969, just before operations ended. GSC 153194

Plate 27.

Tremolite partly replaced by magnetite, Bristol (Hilton) mine. The specimen is 14 cm from top to bottom. GSC 201420-N

Refs.: 25 p. 75–90; 41 p. 12–13; 44 p. 39–40; 69 p. 77–80; 114 p. 77–78; 161 p. 27–29; 224 p. 107–112.

Maps   (T):   31 F/9 Quyon
        (G):   660 Quebec and Ontario, parts of counties of Ottawa and Pontiac, Que. and Carleton and Renfrew, Ont. (Pembroke Sheet No. 122) (GSC, 1:253 440)
        1739 Portions of Bristol, Onslow, McNab, Fitzroy and Torbolton townships, Quebec and Ontario (GSC, 1:63 360)

Shawville–Otter Lake area

Collecting localities in the Shawville–Otter Lake area are described in the following text. The starting point is in Shawville at **km 69.8** (*see* Gatineau (Hull)–Waltham road log on p. 136). The following occurrences are described: Kirkham mine (p. 144), Welsh mine (p. 146), Father Ferary mine (p. 146), Kazabazua River (Milkie) asbestos occurrence (p. 147), Cawood mica occurrence (p. 148), Bretzlaff occurrence (p. 148), Zimmerling mine (p. 149), Richard cordierite occurrence (p. 149), Giroux mine (p. 150), Yates mine (p. 151), and Squaw Lake mine (p. 155).

Kirkham mine

MOLYBDENITE, PYRITE, PYRRHOTITE, CHALCOPYRITE, URANINITE, TITANITE, DIOPSIDE, TOURMALINE, SCAPOLITE, MAGNETITE, ZIRCON, ALLANITE, URANOTHORITE, ROZENITE, JAROSITE

In pyroxenite at the contact between crystalline limestone and gneiss

Molybdenite flakes up to 7 cm in diameter occur with pyrite, pyrrhotite, and chalcopyrite in light green pyroxenite. Grains of uraninite are associated with calcite, tremolite, titanite, diopside, black tourmaline, and scapolite. Titanite crystals occur in orange-pink calcite in trenches near No. 2 adit. In a pegmatite dyke associated with pyroxenite, the following minerals have been reported: pyroxene, magnetite, titanite, zircon, allanite, uranothorite, pyrite, and pyrrhotite. White rozenite and yellow jarosite occur as powdery coatings associated with pyrite and pyrrhotite.

The deposit was discovered by Bert Kirkham in 1951. Between 1952 and 1957, Quebec Metallurgical Industries Limited did some development work consisting of strippings, pits, trenches, and two adits. No. 1 adit was driven 244 m into a slope on the south side of a valley, and No. 2 adit was driven 91 m into the opposite side of the valley 152 m northeast of No. 1. Another molybdenite zone was exposed by stripping 300 m southeast of No. 1 adit.

The mine is about 11 km northeast of Shawville and about 3 km east of Charteris. *See* Map 26 on p. 145.

Road log from Highway 148 at **km 69.8** in Shawville (*see* Highway 148 road log on p. 136):

km   0   Shawville, junction of highways 148 and 303; proceed north along Highway 303.

          12.4   Junction; turn right (east) onto 15th Line Road.

          14.6   End of the road; a trail continues to the mine.

          15.0   Kirkham mine. No. 2 adit is to the left. Continue along the valley for about 150 m to No. 1 adit on the right side of the valley.

Refs.: 37 p. 143–144; 91 p. 39–40; 168 p. 39; 208 p. 173–179.

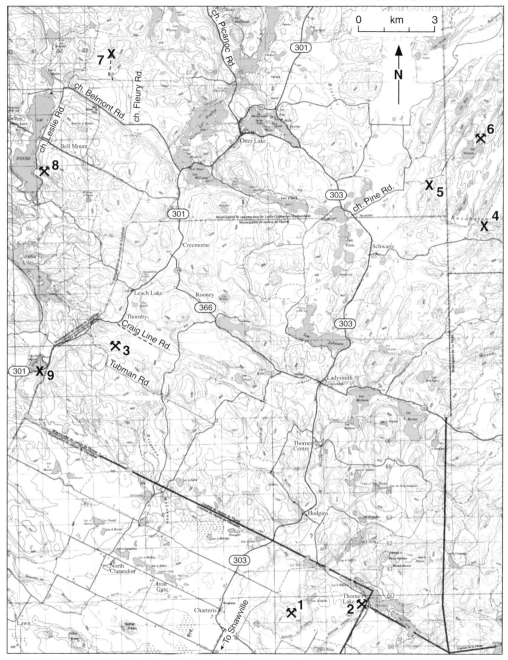

1. Kirkham mine   2. Welsh mine   3. Father Ferary mine   4. Kazabazua River (Milkie) asbestos occurrence   5. Bretzlaff occurrence   6. Zimmerling mine
7. Richard cordierite occurrence   8. Giroux mine   9. Lawless Lake occurrence

Map 26. Otter Lake.

Maps   (T):   31 F/9 Quyon
        (G):   660 Quebec and Ontario, parts of counties of Ottawa and Pontiac, Que. and
                Carleton and Renfrew, Ont. (Pembroke Sheet No. 122) (GSC, 1:253 440)
                1495 Bristol-Masham area, Pontiac and Gatineau counties (MRNQ, 1:63 360)

Welsh mine

MOLYBDENITE, PYRITE, CHALCOPYRITE, PYROXENE

In granite pegmatite and syenite gneiss

Molybdenite occurs as large, well formed flakes. Pyrite and some chalcopyrite are associated with it. Masses of green pyroxene occur in pegmatite.

The deposit was staked in about 1899 by Pat Welsh who mistook the molybdenite for silver. Sometime between 1916 and 1920, T.E. Richardson of Portage-du-Fort did a considerable amount of prospecting work on the occurrence. The work consisted of several pits and two shafts, each about 6 m deep. Adjacent to these openings is an adit driven 14 m into the north side of a low ridge; the adit cut into biotite gneiss but did not intersect the molybdenite zone.

The mine is just south of Thorne Lake on the property of J.E. Walsh, about 14 km northeast of Shawville. *See* Map 26 on p. 145.

Road log from Highway 148 at **km 69.8** in Shawville (*see* Highway 148 road log on p. 136):

km   0   Shawville, junction of highways 148 and 303; proceed north along
                    Highway 303.

          16.3   Junction; turn right (east).

          17.1   T-junction; turn right (south).

          21.2   Junction; turn right (south).

          21.25   Welsh mine on right.

Refs.:   37 p. 144–145; 168 p. 39; 208 p. 194.

Maps   (T):   31 F/9 Quyon
        (G):   660 Quebec and Ontario, parts of counties of Ottawa and Pontiac, Que. and
                Carleton and Renfrew, Ont. (Pembroke Sheet No. 122) (GSC, 1:253 440)
                1495 Bristol-Masham area, Pontiac and Gatineau counties (MRNQ, 1:63 360)

Father Ferary mine

PHLOGOPITE, SCAPOLITE, APATITE

In pyroxenite

Dark amber phlogopite occurs in a pink calcite vein in greyish-green pyroxenite. Greyish-white scapolite occurs as small crystals in cavities in the rock, and as abundant coarse crystals in the vein. Red apatite crystals occur in calcite.

The deposit was worked for mica by Father Ferary of Otter Lake in about 1900. The workings consist of an open cut into the side of a ridge and a small pit just below it. The open cut is 7.5 m deep and 9 m across. Several tonnes of mica are reported to have been removed from the deposit. The openings are overgrown.

The Father Ferary mine is on the property of Charles M. Atkinson of Ottawa; it is about 2.5 km northwest of Greer Mount and 19 km north of Shawville. *See* Map 26 on p. 145. Access is via the Craig Line Road or Tubman Road, which lead east from Highway 301 at points 10.5 km and 11.6 km respectively south of the junction of highways 301 and 303 in Otter Lake. For access to the mine, contact Cyrus Atkinson in Shawville.

Refs.:   44 p. 41–44; 173 p. 135.

Maps   (T):   31 F/16 Kazabazua
       (G):   660 Quebec and Ontario, parts of counties of Ottawa and Pontiac, Que. and Carleton and Renfrew, Ont. (Pembroke Sheet No. 122) (GSC, 1:253 440)
              1173 Thorne-Leslie-Clapham area, electoral district of Pontiac (MRNQ, 1:63 360)

Kazabazua River (Milkie) asbestos occurrence

CHRYSOTILE, SERPENTINE, PYROAURITE, CHLORITE, MICA, HEMATITE, PYRITE, MAGNETITE

In crystalline limestone

White chrysotile asbestos occurs as thin veinlets (less than 2 cm wide) in yellow, light green, and greenish-blue massive serpentine. Some serpentine is translucent and could be used for sculpting or cutting into small ornamental objects. Snow-white silky pyroaurite nodules (about 1 mm in diameter) are found sparingly in crystalline limestone. Flaky aggregates of light blue chlorite and colourless mica are relatively common. Other minerals found in the limestone rock are hematite, pyrite, and magnetite (as tiny crystals).

The deposit was opened by a small pit in 1955. It is located on the south side of a ridge overlooking the Kazabazua River, about 5 km east of Schwartz and 28 km northeast of Shawville. *See* Map 26 on p. 145.

Road log from Highway 148 at **km 69.8** in Shawville (*see* Highway 148 road log on p. 136):

km   0   Shawville, junction of highways 148 and 303; proceed north along Highway 303.

          27.2   Junction in Schwartz opposite a church; turn right (east) onto the road to Cawood.

          31.5   Junction; road to a red farmhouse on left. From this point a tractor road leads north to the mine. Proceed along this road.

          32.0   Fork; bear right (east) and proceed along the north bank of the Kazabazua River for a distance of 375 m to a fork at a fallen shack on left; follow the road on right for about 320 m to the Kazabazua River (Milkie) asbestos occurrence.

Refs.:   102 p. 5; 104 p. 288, 290.

Maps   (T):   31 F/16 Kazabazua
       (G):   660 Quebec and Ontario, parts of counties of Ottawa and Pontiac, Que. and Carleton and Renfrew, Ont. (Pembroke Sheet No. 122) (GSC, 1:253 440)
              1173 Thorne-Leslie-Clapham area, electoral district of Pontiac (MRNQ, 1:63 360)

Cawood mica occurrence

PHLOGOPITE, DIOPSIDE, TREMOLITE, APATITE, PYRITE, HEMATITE, STILPNOMELANE

In pyroxene skarn

Phlogopite occurs as sheets up to 18 cm across in white pyroxene skarn. Diopside occurs as white crystals up to 3 cm across, and as compact prismatic aggregates constituting the dominant mineral in the skarn. Some crystals are colourless, transparent, and of gem quality; faceted diopside gems from this occurrence are in the National Mineral Collection. Small diopside crystals also occur in sheets of phlogopite. White fibrous, columnar, and massive tremolite is associated with the diopside, and fibrous tremolite commonly cloaks diopside crystals. Apatite occurs as light blue crystals and granular aggregates. Massive and crystal aggregates of pyrite and grains of hematite are also present. Stilpnomelane occurs as black platy aggregates surrounding pyrite.

The deposit was explored for mica in about 1890. The occurrence consists of a small pit and a small dump in a wooded area on the David Early farm northwest of the former settlement of Cawood. The occurrence is about 34 km northeast of Shawville.

Road log from Highway 148 at **km 69.8** in Shawville (*see* Highway 148 road log on p. 136):

km		
	0	Shawville; junction of highways 148 and 303; proceed north along Highway 303.
	27.2	Junction in Schwartz, at a church. Turn right (east) onto the road to Cawood.
	34.8	Junction; turn left onto the Cawood–Ladysmith road.
	41.0	David Early farmhouse on left (north) side of the road. The Cawood mica pit is in a wooded area northwest of the farmhouse. Obtain permission to visit the occurrence from Mr. Early.

Refs.:   9 p. 15–16, 55; 97 p. 179; 104 p. 69–94; 159 p. 388; 212 p. 87.

Maps   (T):   31 F/16 Kazabazua
          (G):   660 Quebec and Ontario, parts of counties of Ottawa and Pontiac, Que. and Carleton and Renfrew, Ont. (Pembroke Sheet No. 122) (GSC, 1:253 440)

Bretzlaff occurrence

APATITE, SCAPOLITE, CLINOPYROXENE, MICA, GRAPHITE, PYRRHOTITE, PYRITE, MARCASITE, SPHALERITE, ARAGONITE, CALCITE

In crystalline limestone

Blue apatite occurs as small crystals and grains in crystalline limestone. Other minerals present are white to bluish-grey scapolite, colourless to grey and green clinopyroxene (crystals and massive), colourless mica, graphite, and grains of pyrrhotite, pyrite, marcasite, and sphalerite. White massive calcite fluoresces pink in short ultraviolet light. Aragonite occurs as botryoidal crusts on the rock.

The occurrence is exposed in a small pit on the property of Doug Bretzlaff, about 4 km northeast of Schwartz and 26 km northeast of Shawville. *See* Map 26 on p. 145.

Road log from Highway 148 at **km 69.8** in Shawville (*see* Highway 148 road log on p. 136):

km		
	0	Shawville, junction of highways 148 and 303; proceed north along Highway 303.

29.0   Junction; turn right (east) onto Pine Road.

31.6   Junction; turn right (east).

32.2   Bretzlaff occurrence on right.

Maps   (T): 31 F/16 Kazabazua
        (G): 660 Quebec and Ontario, parts of counties of Ottawa and Pontiac, Que. and
              Carleton and Renfrew, Ont. (Pembroke Sheet No. 122) (GSC, 1:253 440)
              1173 Thorne-Leslie-Clapham area, electoral district of Pontiac (MRNQ, 1:63 360)

Zimmerling mine

PHLOGOPITE, PYROXENE, CALCITE, APATITE, TITANITE, TOURMALINE, PYRITE

In pyroxenite

Books of deep amber phlogopite occur with greyish green pyroxene crystals in pale
salmon-pink calcite. The pyroxene crystals measure up to 2 cm in diameter. Pale blue apatite
grains, pyrite, and brown tourmaline are found in crystalline limestone. Mica, titanite, pyrite,
and greyish to light greenish-yellow tremolite are associated with quartz and feldspar in crystalline limestone. The pyroxenite dyke cuts crystalline limestone.

The deposit was worked from an open cut at the side of a hill by Adolph Zimmerling of Otter
Lake. It is just north of the northeastern end of Simpson Lake, about 6 km northeast of Schwartz
and 30 km northeast of Shawville. *See* Map 26 on p. 145.

Road log from Highway 148 at **km 69.8** in Shawville (*see* Highway 148 road log on p. 136):

km   0   Shawville; junction of highways 148 and 303; proceed north along
                 Highway 303.

            29.0   Junction; turn right (east) onto Pine Road.

            31.6   Junction; turn right.

            35.0   Fork; bear left.

            36.9   Zimmerling mine.

Refs.: 102 p. 5; 104 p. 289–291.

Maps   (T): 31 F/16 Kazabazua
        (G): 660 Quebec and Ontario, parts of counties of Ottawa and Pontiac, Que. and
              Carleton and Renfrew, Ont. (Pembroke Street No. 122) (GSC, 1:253 440)
              1173 Thorne-Leslie-Clapham area, electoral district of Pontiac (MRNQ, 1:63 360)

Richard cordierite occurrence

CORDIERITE, PYROXENE, SCAPOLITE, ALLANITE, TITANITE, GARNET, MICA, APATITE, PYRITE

In gneiss and pyroxenite

Blue cordierite occurs as pods up to 5 cm long in orthopyroxene-biotite gneiss. It is associated
with deep red granular garnet. Well formed pyroxene crystals occur in coarsely crystalline pink
calcite. Dark brown titanite crystals are found with white scapolite crystals in calcite and in feldspar. Crystals of allanite (platy), mica, apatite, and pyrite also occur in the deposit.

The deposit is exposed by an open cut on the southwest side of a hill. It was worked by Albert Richard for mineral specimens. Permission to visit the occurrence may be obtained from the owner of the property, John Telford of Quyon.

The occurrence is about 6 km northwest of Otter Lake and 31 km north of Shawville. *See* Map 26 on p. 145.

Road log from Otter Lake at the junction of highways 303 and 301, which is 36.5 km from Highway 148 at **km 69.8** in Shawville (*see* Highway 148 road log on p. 136):

km		
	0	Otter Lake, junction of highways 303 and 301; proceed south along Highway 301 toward Campbell's Bay.
	3.0	Junction; turn right (northwest) onto Belmont Road.
	6.0	Junction; turn right (north) onto Fleury Road.
	7.7	T-junction; turn left (west).
	8.5	Junction; turn right to the Telford property. The Richard cordierite occurrence is about 1 km from this turnoff.

Refs.:   102 p. 6; 104 p. 123; 166 p. 153.

Maps   (T):   31 F/16 Kazabazua
      (G):   660 Quebec and Ontario, parts of counties of Ottawa and Pontiac, Que. and Carleton and Renfrew, Ont. (Pembroke Sheet No. 122) (GSC, 1:253 440)
              1173 Thorne-Leslie-Clapham area, electoral district of Pontiac (MRNQ, 1:63 360)

Giroux mine

MOLYBDENITE, CLINOPYROXENE, SCAPOLITE, DATOLITE, TITANITE

In calcite skarn

Molybdenite was originally found here as large chunky flakes and aggregates, and as well formed crystals up to 8 cm across. Most crystals are 2 to 3 cm across. Crystals of green clinopyroxene, white scapolite, greenish datolite, and titanite occur in pink calcite.

The deposit was explored in the 1920s by Cadice Giroux who opened several small pits along the side of a ridge on his farm. Earlier, in about 1900, several pits had been excavated when the property was prospected for mica. Molybdenite was found in all the pits; some specimens recovered were up to 20 cm across.

The occurrence is near the east shore of Ours Lake (formerly Leslie Lake), near the southern end, about 8 km southwest of Otter Lake and 26 km northwest of Shawville. It is on the property of Pat Lawn. *See* Map 26 on p. 145.

Road log from Otter Lake at the junction of highways 303 and 301, which is 36.5 km from Highway 148 at **km 69.8** in Shawville (*see* Highway 148 road log on p. 136):

km		
	0	Otter Lake, junction of highways 303 and 301; proceed south along Highway 301 toward Campbell's Bay.
	3.0	Junction; turn right (northwest) onto Belmont Road.
	9.2	Junction; continue straight ahead (south) along Leslie Road. (Belmont Road leads west from this junction.)
	12.7	Junction; turn left to the Pat Lawn property and the Giroux mine.

Refs.:   37 p. 149; 104 p. 91, 93, 290–291; 208 p. 186; 215 p. 16.

Maps   (T):   31 F/15 Fort-Coulonge
       (G):   660 Quebec and Ontario, parts of counties of Ottawa and Pontiac, Que. and
             Carleton and Renfrew, Ont. (Pembroke Sheet No. 122) (GSC, 1:253 440)
             1165 Litchfield-Huddersfield area, electoral district of Pontiac (MRNQ,
             1:63 360)

Yates mine

URANOTHORITE, THORIANITE, THORITE, URANOPHANE, ALLANITE, APATITE,
PYROXENE, SCAPOLITE, MICROCLINE, FLUORITE, PHLOGOPITE, CALCITE,
STILBITE, HEULANDITE, TREMOLITE, TITANITE, CERITE

In calc-silicate rocks in skarn zones and in vein dykes

The Yates uranium deposit consists of uranium mineralization in six zones. The two main
radioactive zones on which most of the exploration work was done are known as the Camp and
Matte zones. They are about 1 km apart. Two other zones, the Bélanger and Bélisle zones, are
near the Camp zone, and another zone, the Lake zone, is near the Matte zone.

The Camp zone, the most important of the radioactive zones, is about 275 m long and is 15 to
30 m wide. It consists of calc-silicate skarn composed of salmon-pink calcite, white scapolite
(crystals to 5 cm long), dark green to greenish-black diopside (prisms to 5 cm long), green
fluorapatite (crystals), and phlogopite. The principal radioactive mineral is uranoan thorianite,
which occurs as tiny black cubes in granular diopside and in calcite-diopside-phlogopite rock.
Associated with it are thorite, red uranothorite, black platy and wedge-shaped allanite crystals
(to 5 cm wide), greenish-yellow scaly beta-uranophane aggregates, colourless lessingite grains,

Plate 28.
Apatite crystal in calcite, Yates mine. The crystal is 4 cm long.
GSC 201420-M

Plate 29.

Scapolite crystal, Yates mine. The crystal is 4.5 cm by 3 cm. GSC 201420-C

and yellow beta-uranophane. Uranothorite also occurs as lustrous black crystals to 5 mm in dark orange-red calcite. Other minerals occurring in this zone are green tremolite-actinolite crystals to 5 cm long, black titanite prisms to 1 cm long, massive violet fluorite, orange chondrodite, and molybdenite. Cavities in calcite are lined with sheaf-like aggregates of white stilbite and colourless to peach square crystals of heulandite. Dark pink microscopic grains of cerite occur in stilbite and in calcite at the edge of stilbite-heulandite-lined cavities. Clear calcite crystals (Iceland spar) and fluorescent calcite (bright pink in short ultraviolet rays) are also present.

Similar mineralization occurs in the nearby Bélanger and Bélisle zones. The Bélanger zone is exposed by a stripped area 36 m by 6 m. Uranoan thorianite occurs with smaller amounts of thorite, allanite, and beta-uranophane associated with fluorapatite, calcite, diopside, and tremolite. The Bélisle zone is notable for its large books of phlogopite to 15 cm across, and abundant large green fluorapatite crystals to 40 cm long and 15 cm across in pink calcite rock.

The Matte zone consists of salmon-pink calcite vein dykes in granite pegmatite. The zone is about 245 m long and up to 15 m wide. The veins contain massive violet fluorite, lustrous black diopside prisms to 3 cm long, green to reddish-brown fluorapatite prisms averaging 7 cm long, but as large as 25 cm long and 7 cm wide. Aggregates of small scapolite crystals, white microcline crystals to 5 cm long, peristerite, titanite, and chondrodite also occur in calcite. The radioactive minerals are uranothorite, as greyish-black prisms to 2.5 cm long and thin tetragonal crystals to 2 cm long in calcite and fluorite, thorite, as reddish-brown aggregates of crystals in fluorite, allanite, as black plates to 2.5 cm across and as platy aggregates in microcline and in calcite, and uranoan thorianite, as disseminations in calcite.

The Lake zone is a band of radioactive mineralization similar to the Matte zone, but smaller. It contains patches rich in greyish-black uranothorite. It is about 6 m wide and outcrops 975 m northwest of the Matte zone, of which it was thought to be an extension.

At some old mica pits immediately southwest and west of the Camp zone, phlogopite occurred as large crystals associated with brownish calcite veins in greyish-green pyroxenite. The veins contained well formed dark green pyroxene crystals, abundant violet fluorite, scapolite, and black allanite crystals.

The area was originally explored for phlogopite in the 1890s. Calumet Mica Company of Bryson first worked the deposit by several small pits, the largest being 6 m deep, in 1906 and 1907; the work was done by eight employees without machinery. The company did additional mining between 1914 and 1923. Since then, various operators, including A.G. Martin of Ottawa (pre-1939), Omer Bérard (1939), and Twin Valley Prospecting Syndicate (1944), worked the deposit for mica. In 1943–1944, Twin Valley Prospecting Syndicate mined 16.3 t of fluorite from the deposit. Bazel Reed and James Trudeau worked the dumps for mica in 1960. The main workings consisted of two open cuts, 45 m apart, driven southwest into the side of a ridge.

In 1953, when J.M. Yates discovered uranothorite in one of the old mica pits, attention turned to exploration for radioactive minerals. Yates Uranium Mines Incorporated was formed to develop the deposit. Development between 1953 and 1956 consisted of strippings and trenches in four zones. Development of the Camp zone consisted of a stripped area 160 m by 15 to 37 m with trenches in the southern part. Development of the Matte zone included a stripped area about 240 m by 37 m, trenches, and a 91 m adit driven from the south. A mining camp was built near the Camp zone.

The mine is about 4.5 km west of Sandy Creek, about 15 km north of Otter Lake, and 40 km northwest of Shawville. *See* Map 27 on p. 154.

Road log from Otter Lake at the junction of highways 303 and 301, which is 36.5 km from Highway 148 at **km 69.8** in Shawville (*see* Highway 148 road log on p. 136):

km		
	0	Otter Lake at the junction of highways 303 and 301; proceed north along Highway 301.
	0.5	Junction; turn left onto Picanoc Road.
	11.5	*Roadcuts*, on left, expose granite pegmatite containing dull black allanite and quartz veins containing epidote, titanite, clinopyroxene, and tremolite.
	14.6	Junction at Sandy Creek; turn left (west).
	15.1	Junction; follow the road on right.
	17.7	Junction; follow the road on right.
	19.0	Junction. The road on right leads to the Matte zone, the road on left to the Camp and other zones. To reach the Matte zone, proceed along the road leading northwest then north and northeast for a total of about 550 m to the Matte zone open cuts. This road continues northwest (just before the Matte zone is reached) for another 900 m to the Lake zone outcrop just south of Riendeau Lake.

To reach the other zones, proceed from the junction at km 19.0 along the road leading southwest toward the site of the former camp. The Camp zone is about 930 m from the junction. A trail from the Camp zone leads south then east for a total of 600 m to the Belisle zone, and another trail leads west then southwest for a total of 800 m to the Belanger zone. The old mica pits are just west of the second trail and about 150 m west of the Camp zone.

Refs.:   23 p. 71; 36 p. 34; 44 p. 41–42; 91 p. 40–41; 101 p. 5; 106 p. 212–213; 108 p. 359–363; 127 p. 330; 160 p. 727, 628; 166 p. 153–154; 173 p. 133–134; 176 p. 26–30; 177 p. 39–41; 178 p. 420–442; 232 p. 52–53.

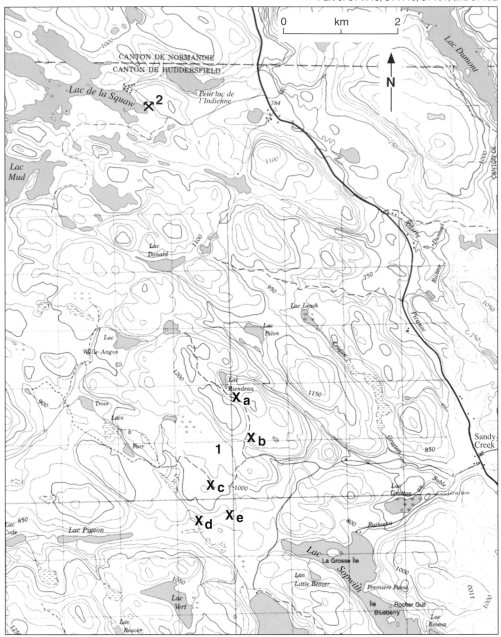

1. Yates mine: a. Lake zone b. Matte zone c. Camp zone d. Bélanger zone
e. Bélisle zone   2. Squaw Lake mine

Map 27. Sandy Creek.

Maps   (T):   31 F/15 Fort-Coulonge
        (G):   660 Quebec and Ontario, parts of counties of Ottawa and Pontiac, Que. and
               Carleton and Renfrew, Ont. (Pembroke Sheet No. 122) (GSC, 1:253 440)
               1165 Litchfield-Huddersfield area, electoral district of Pontiac (MRNQ,
               1:63 360)

Squaw Lake mine

MOLYBDENITE, PYRITE, PYRRHOTITE, DIOPSIDE, SCAPOLITE, PHLOGOPITE,
HORNBLENDE, APATITE, CALCITE, TITANITE, GRAPHITE, JAROSITE,
LEONHARDTITE

In pyroxenite and syenite gneiss

Flakes and flaky aggregates of molybdenite are associated with pyrite and pyrrhotite in
rusty-weathered rocks. Individual flakes about 2 cm in diameter have been found. Other minerals found in the deposit include green diopside (crystals averaging 2 cm in diameter), colourless
to grey scapolite, phlogopite, hornblende, green apatite (crystals), pink to white calcite, dark
brown titanite, fluorite, and graphite. Yellow jarosite and white leonhardtite occur as coatings
on the specimens.

The deposit is near the north shore of the east arm of Squaw Lake; it was exposed by five open
cuts and some trenches in 1971 by Wood Molybdenite Company of Ottawa. The largest pit
measures 25 m by 8 to 12 m and is up to 4 m deep. A concentrating mill was erected at the mine
site and 317 kg of concentrates were produced in 1918. The openings are largely overgrown;
the remnants of the old mill remain.

The mine is about 9 km northwest of Sandy Creek, 25 km northwest of Otter Lake, and 49 km
northwest of Shawville. *See* Map 27 on p. 154.

Road log from Otter Lake at the junction of highways 303 and 301, which is 36.5 km from
Highway 148 at **km 69.8** in Shawville (*see* Highway 149 road log on p. 136):

km   0   Otter Lake at the junction of highways 303 and 301; proceed north along
                    Highway 301.

            0.5   Junction; turn left onto Picanoc Road.

            14.6   Junction at Sandy Creek. This road leads to the Yates mine. Continue
                    straight ahead (north).

            22.6   Junction; turn left (west).

            24.7   Junction; follow the road on right.

            25.0   Junction of a trail on left. Proceed along this trail to the Squaw Lake mine
                    on a slope above the eastern end of Squaw Lake. The pits are about 75 m
                    southeast of the mill site.

Refs.:   10 p. 35–46; 37 p. 145–148; 103 p. 6; 208 p. 180–185; 224 p. 86–92.

Maps   (T):   31 K/2 Usborne Lake
        (G):   660 Quebec and Ontario, parts of counties of Ottawa and Pontiac, Que. and
               Carleton and Renfrew, Ont. (Pembroke Sheet No. 122) (GSC, 1:253 440)
               1211 Pontefract-Gillies area, electoral district of Pontiac (MRNQ, 1:126 440)
               M-314 Feuille Deep River 31 K, Gîtes minéraux du Québec, région de l'Abitibi
               (MRNQ, 1:150 000)

Portage-du-Fort quarries

MARBLE, TREMOLITE, SERPENTINE, MICA

In crystalline limestone

Dolomitic marble (crystalline limestone) is exposed in several quarries north of Portage-du-Fort. The marble is snow-white with some pink and light brown veinlets. It is generally pure containing very small amounts of colourless tremolite, pink calcite, colourless to light brown mica, and greenish-grey serpentine.

Quarrying of marble north of Portage-du-Fort began in about 1900 and was done by several operators. White Grit Company Limited produced crushed marble for stucco, terrazzo flooring, and poultry grit from 1924 to 1944 when operations were taken over by Canadian Dolomite Company. The current (1996) operator, Dufresnoy (SEM) inc., produces marble for decorative building stone and agricultural use.

Marble for building stone was formerly quarried just east of the village of Portage-du-Fort. This marble, a calcium marble, is bluish white to greenish white, or white with light blue bands, and contains small flakes of mica and graphite. The quarry was in operation from about the 1860s to 1923. Pontiac Marble and Lime Company Limited was the operator from 1913 to 1923. The quarry site is just east of the cemetery at Portage-du-Fort. Beautiful white marble of excellent quality was mined in the early 1860s from an opening about 135 m northeast of the main quarry for use in decorative pillars and columns in the Parliament Buildings in Ottawa.

There are three dolomitic marble quarries, including the currently active quarry, located along Highway 301 (Portage-du-Fort–Bryson Road), about 1.5 km north of Portage-du-Fort. *See* Map 9 on p. 78.

Road log from Highway 148 at **km 81.2** (*see* Highway 148 road log on p. 136):

km	0	Junction of highways 148 and 301; proceed onto Highway 301.
	7.2	Portage-du-Fort quarries on both sides of the road.

Refs.: 19 p. 19–21; 35 p. 529; 44 p. 15, 45; 59 p. 85; 63 p. 135–137; 99 p. 113–115; 116 p. 822; 144 p. 195–198; 230 p. 52.

Maps   (T):   31 F/10 Cobden
        (G):   660 Quebec and Ontario, parts of counties of Ottawa and Pontiac, Que. and Carleton and Renfrew, Ont. (Pembroke Sheet No. 122) (GSC, 1:253 440)
               1804 Saint-Patrice Lake and Portage-du-Fort, electoral district of Pontiac-Témiscamingue (MRNQ, 1:126 720)

Highway 148 (Bryson) roadcuts

MAGNETITE, PYROAURITE, SZAIBELYITE, SERPENTINE, MICA, ARAGONITE, PYRRHOTITE

In crystalline limestone

Dodecahedral crystals of magnetite up to 2 cm in diameter occur in the limestone. Of particular interest is the occurrence of the relatively rare minerals, pyroaurite and szaibelyite. The former occurs as light blue and white pearly nodules up to 2 mm in diameter, the latter as silky white fibrous, hair-like, or platy matted aggregates in cavities in the limestone and as patches on the limestone. Serpentine, as yellow, light green, and amber irregular masses, and mica, as deep greenish-blue flaky aggregates, are common. White aragonite occurs as coatings on pyroaurite and serpentine. Small grains of pyrrhotite are also present.

The occurrence is exposed by roadcuts on both sides of Highway 148 at **km 82.1**, 0.9 km north of the junction of highways 148 and 301. *See* Gatineau (Hull)–Waltham road log on p. 136 and Map 28 on p. 158.

Ref.:   <u>91</u> p. 41–42.

Maps   (T):   31 F/10 Cobden
         (G):   660 Quebec and Ontario, parts of counties of Ottawa and Pontiac, Que. and Carleton and Renfrew, Ont. (Pembroke Sheet No. 122) (GSC, 1:253 440)
              1804 Saint-Patrice Lake and Portage-du-Fort, electoral district of Pontiac-Témiscamingue (MRNQ, 1:126 720)

Carswell quarry

BRUCITE, SERPENTINE, DIOPSIDE, TREMOLITE, CHONDRODITE, MICA, PYRRHOTITE, GRAPHITE, OLIVINE, CORUNDUM

In crystalline limestone

Nodular, fibrous, foliated, and platy brucite occurs at this locality. Nodules up to 15 mm in diameter have been found, but the average size is about 2 to 3 mm. Minerals associated with brucite include white to light green or yellow serpentine (orange on weathered surfaces), green diopside, light green tremolite, pale yellow granular chondrodite, colourless mica, pyrrhotite, and graphite. Olivine crystals and large corundum crystals have been reported from the deposit. The crystalline limestone in which these minerals occur is white with blue and grey bands.

The cystalline limestone (marble) deposit was worked as far back as the 1860s to supply building stone for buildings in Bryson. The marble was used for decorative trim for the Bryson Court House built in 1891. Later, the deposit was worked for lime as well as for building stone. Two quarries were opened on the east side of a hill over which the road to Bryson passes. The quarries are about 10 m apart. The more westerly one is 23 m long and 12 m wide and was worked for lime. The smaller quarry to the northeast was worked for building stone. Operations were intermittent from the 1860s to the 1930s. R.B. Carswell operated the quarries from about 1914 to the late 1930s.

The quarry is just south of Bryson. *See* Map 28 on p. 158.

Road log from Highway 148 at **km 82.8** (*see* Highway 148 road log on p. 136):

km   0   Junction, Highway 148 and the road leading north to Bryson; proceed onto the road to Bryson.

              0.7   Gate to the Carswell quarry on right (east side of the road).

Refs.:   <u>35</u> p. 529–530; <u>63</u> p. 134–135; <u>65</u> p. 20–23; <u>66</u> p. 65; <u>73</u> p. 35–36; <u>99</u> p. 114; <u>166</u> p. 152–153.

Maps   (T):   31 F/10 Cobden
         (G):   549 Calumet Island area, Pontiac County (MRNQ, 1:31 360)
              660 Quebec and Ontario, parts of counties of Ottawa and Pontiac, Que. and Carleton and Renfrew, Ont. (Pembroke Sheet No. 122) (GSC, 1:253 440)
              1804 Saint-Patrice Lake and Portage-du-Fort, electoral district of Pontiac-Témiscamingue (MRNQ, 1:126 720)

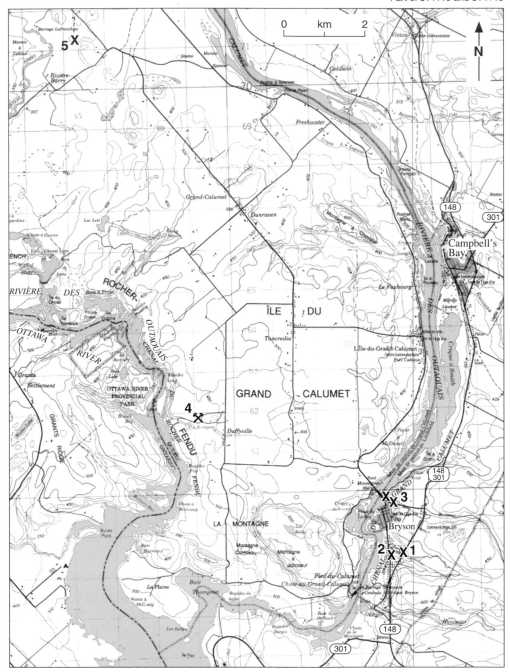

1. Highway 148 (Bryson) roadcuts   2. Carswell quarry   3. Bryson roadcuts
4. New Calumet mine   5. Calumet uranium occurrence

Map 28. Bryson–Grand Calumet.

Bryson marble blocks

GARNET, DIOPSIDE, BRUCITE, SPINEL, SERPENTINE, CHONDRODITE, APATITE, CALCITE, MICA, GRAPHITE, MAGNETITE, PYRITE, PYRRHOTITE, SPHALERITE

In crystalline limestone

An unusual occurrence at this locality is that of a light blue to white garnet; it is massive, transparent to translucent, and is intimately associated with light green diopside. Most of the garnet occurs as small irregular masses up to 3 mm across. Small white brucite nodules (about 2 mm in diameter) and microscopic mauve spinel crystals are found sparingly. Yellow, light green to olive-green, and dark brown serpentine occurs abundantly as irregular granules and in massive form. Other minerals found in the deposit include yellow granular chondrodite (uncommon), light blue apatite (uncommon), colourless calcite crystals (fluoresce bright pink under short ultraviolet rays), colourless to deep greenish-blue mica, graphite, magnetite, pyrite, pyrrhotite, and sphalerite.

The crystalline limestone (marble) containing these minerals is exposed as broken blocks along a short side road leading west from the road to Bryson, just beyond the Carswell quarry.

Road log from Highway 148 at **km 82.8** (*see* Highway 148 road log on p. 136):

km	0	Junction of the road to Bryson and Highway 148; proceed straight ahead toward Bryson village.
	0.7	Gate to Carswell quarry on right; continue straight ahead.
	0.8	Junction of a side road on left leading west. The Bryson marble is found along this road.

Maps (T): 31 F/10 Cobden
(G): 549 Calumet Island area, Pontiac County (MRNQ, 1:31 680)
660 Quebec and Ontario, parts of counties of Ottawa and Pontiac, Que. and Carleton and Renfrew, Ont. (Pembroke Sheet No. 122) (GSC, 1:253 440)
1804 Saint-Patrice Lake and Portage-du-Fort, electoral district of Pontiac-Témiscamingue (MRNQ, 1:126 720)

Bryson roadcut 1

MAGNETITE, SERPENTINE, CALCITE, CLINOPYROXENE, PYROAURITE, HYDROTALCITE, SPINEL, CHONDRODITE, DOLOMITE, HEMATITE, MICA, PYRITE, GRAPHITE

In crystalline limestone

Magnetite and serpentine are the most abundant minerals. Magnetite occurs in massive form and as well formed octahedral crystals; the best crystals are microscopic, occurring with calcite crystals in tiny cavities in the limestone. The serpentine occurs as grey, light green to olive-green, and dark brown nodules and irregular masses. Coarsely crystalline blue calcite is closely associated with some serpentine. Minerals occurring less commonly in the marble include light green clinopyroxene, light blue pyroaurite (tiny nodules), light brown hydrotalcite (grains), violet-pink and deep green spinel (microscopic crystals), pale yellow chondrodite (grains), dolomite (nodules), deep red hematite, pyrite, amber mica, and graphite.

The occurrence is exposed in a roadcut on the Bryson–Île du Grand Calumet road at a point 0.8 km west of the junction of this road with Highway 148 at **km 84.7** (*see* Highway 148 road log on p. 137). It is just east of the Bryson bridge. *See* Map 28 on p. 158.

Maps   (T):   31 F/10 Cobden
        (G):   549 Calumet Island area, Pontiac County (MRNQ, 1:31 680)
               660 Quebec and Ontario, parts of counties of Ottawa and Pontiac, Que. and
               Carleton and Renfrew, Ont. (Pembroke Sheet No. 122) (GSC, 1:253 440)
               1804 Saint-Patrice Lake and Portage-du-Fort, electoral district of Pontiac-
               Témiscamingue (MRNQ, 1:126 720)

Bryson roadcut 2

BRUCITE, PYROAURITE, SERPENTINE, SPINEL, CLINOHUMITE, OLIVINE,
DOLOMITE, MAGNETITE, GRAPHITE, PYRRHOTITE

In crystalline limestone

White brucite nodules 5 mm in diameter are abundant; on exposed surfaces the brucite is
cream-white to yellowish. Nodules of light blue pyroaurite up to 3 mm in diameter are fairly
common. Serpentine occurs as pale yellow, white, greenish-blue, and brown nodules and small
irregular masses. Less common in this deposit are spinel, as tiny mauve crystals and grains,
clinohumite, as yellow transparent grains, olivine, as colourless and pink transparent grains,
and white platy dolomite. Also present are crystals (octahedrons and dodecahedrons) and irregular masses of magnetite and disseminations of graphite and pyrrhotite.

The occurrence is exposed in a roadcut near the Bryson bridge. *See* Map 28 on p. 158.

Road log from Highway 148 at **km 84.7** (*see* Highway 148 road log on p. 137):

km   0   Junction of Highway 148 and the Bryson–Île du Grand Calumet road;
                     proceed west toward Bryson.

            0.8   Bryson roadcut 1 on right (*see* preceding description).

            1.0   Junction, just before the bridge; turn right (north).

            1.05   Bryson roadcut 2 on right.

Maps   (T):   31 F/10 Cobden
        (G):   549 Calumet Island area, Pontiac County (MRNQ, 1:31 360)
               660 Quebec and Ontario, parts of counties of Ottawa and Pontiac, Que. and
               Carleton and Renfrew, Ont. (Pembroke Sheet No. 122) (GSC, 1:253 440)
               1804 Saint-Patrice Lake and Portage-du-Fort, electoral district of Pontiac-
               Témiscamingue (MRNQ, 1:126 720)

New Calumet mine

GALENA, SPHALERITE, PYRITE, CHALCOPYRITE, PYRRHOTITE, MARCASITE,
ARSENOPYRITE, MAGNETITE, TETRAHEDRITE-TENNANTITE, NATIVE SILVER,
TITANITE, GARNET, TREMOLITE, DIOPSIDE, SCAPOLITE, ZIRCON, CHLORITE,
SILLIMANITE, APATITE, CLINOZOISITE

In amphibolite

The orebody consisted of lenses of argentiferous galena and dark brown sphalerite with minor
pyrrhotite and marcasite, and some pyrite, chalcopyrite, arsenopyrite, magnetite, and
tetrahedrite-tennantite. Silver values were obtained from tetrahedrite and from inclusions of
argentite or polybasite in galena. Crystals of galena, pyrite, and chalcopyrite occurred in the
orebody. The sulphide mineralization occurred in carbonate amphibolite associated with biotite

gneiss and crystalline limestone. Carbonate lenses in the amphibolite contained tremolite, diopside, scapolite, clinozoisite, apatite, calcite, phlogopite, green hornblende, titanite, andesine, chlorite, and serpentine; these calc-silicate minerals were noted in the dumps at the St. Anne, Lawn, Bowie, and Longstreet workings. Granite pegmatite consisting of microcline, quartz, and phlogopite contained apatite, zircon, muscovite, chlorite, serpentine, and sillimanite (needles); the pegmatite was found in the dumps at the Lawn and St. Anne workings. Zircon was also found in amphibolite wall rock. Titanite, garnet, and tremolite occurred in biotite gneiss.

The main mineralized zone extended north-south for 800 m. The workings along it, from south to north, include the Bowie shaft and pits, on the south side of a creek and about 150 m south of the Main new (No. 1) shaft; the McDonald shaft (new No. 2 shaft), 300 m north of the Main shaft; the Lawn shaft and pit, about 35 m west of the McDonald; the Russell pit, 240 m north of the McDonald; the St. Anne shaft and Galena pits, 200 m north of the Russell pit. There was a smaller mineralized zone 300 m east of the main zone and parallel to it. The Longstreet shaft, 290 m northeast of the Main shaft, is at the south end of this zone; it cut into a high-grade galena lens. The Belgian pits, about 350 m north of the Longstreet shaft, are at the north end of this zone.

The mine produced lead and zinc and some silver and gold. It operated at various times between 1893 and 1968. John Lawn discovered the lead-zinc mineralization in 1893, staked the property, and turned it over to James and Calvin Russell who developed it and shipped 12 t of ore to England in the same year. Grand Calumet Mining Company of Ottawa worked the mine in 1897–1898 and shipped 998 t of ore to Belgium. Calumet Metals Company operated the mine between 1910 and 1912, and installed the first concentrating mill; the mill was destroyed by fire in 1916. The next operations were by Calumet Zinc and Lead Company (1913–1914) and British Metals Corporation (Canada) Limited (1926). Development to then consisted of seven shafts, ranging from 5.5 to 44 m deep, and several open cuts. In 1937, Calumet Mines Limited sank a new shaft, the Main or No. 1 shaft. New Calumet Mines Limited acquired the property in 1942, installed a mill, and mined the deposit until 1968. Operations were from three shafts extending to 227 m (No. 1), 469 m (No. 2), and 822 m (No. 4) from the surface. Total production from the mine was 200 451 091 kg zinc, 56 399 872 kg lead, 1 471 414 kg copper, 1 687 959.8 g gold, and 321 812 756 g silver. In 1986, Lacana Mining Corporation explored the deposit by trenching and drilling; results indicated concentrations of gold throughout the ore zone from the St. Anne to the Bowie workings, and in the Longstreet zone.

The mine is on the southwest side of Île du Grand Calumet, about 6 km northwest of Bryson. *See* Map 28 on p. 158.

Road log from Highway 148 at **km 84.7** (*see* Highway 148 road log on p. 137):

km		
	0	Junction of Highway 148 and the road to Bryson; turn left (west) onto the road to Bryson and Île du Grand Calumet.
	1.4	Junction; continue straight ahead. The road on left leads 2.6 km to the Bryson dam where crystalline limestone containing disseminations of pink spinel, yellow clinohumite, mica, and serpentine is exposed.
	1.5	*Roadcuts* expose crystalline limestone containing serpentine, phlogopite, chlorite, magnetite, pyrite, and tremolite. Green apatite crystals (5 mm in diameter), dark green pyroxene, and brown titanite grains occur in pink calcite masses enclosed by the limestone.
	2.2	Junction; turn left.
	3.8	Junction; turn left.
	5.6	Junction; turn right.

6.6　　　Junction, mine road; turn left.

7.3　　　New Calumet mine (Main Shaft).

Refs.:　2 p. 121–126; 44 p. 41; 61 p. 116–122; 133 p. 617–626; 138 p. 12–25; 202 p. 6–7; 207 p. 35–39; 229 p. 169–170; 233 p. 245.

Maps　　(T):　31 F/10 Cobden
　　　　(G):　191A Calumet Island, Pontiac District, Quebec (GSC, 1:47 520)
　　　　　　　549A Calumet Island area, Pontiac County (MRNQ, 1:126 720)
　　　　　　　660 Quebec and Ontario, parts of counties of Ottawa and Pontiac, Que. and Carleton and Renfrew, Ont. (Pembroke Sheet No. 122) (GSC, 1:253 440)

Calumet uranium occurrence

URANOTHORITE, FLUORITE, PYROXENE, SCAPOLITE, HORNBLENDE, CALCITE, PHLOGOPITE, APATITE, ALLANITE, CHONDRODITE, THORIANITE

In skarn zone in pegmatite

Dark brown prisms of uranothorite occur in massive violet fluorite. Other minerals occurring in this radioactive skarn zone include dark green pyroxene crystals 15 mm in diameter, light green scapolite crystals, black hornblende crystals, allanite crystals, pink calcite, dark amber phlogopite, and light green apatite. Chondrodite and black thorianite cubes occur in pink calcite in crystalline limestone.

The deposit has been exposed by strippings and trenches. The exploration was conducted by Calumet Uranium Mines Limited between 1953 and 1955. The openings are moss covered and partly overgrown.

The occurrence is about 5 km northwest of Dunraven on Île du Grand Calumet, and 15 km northwest of Bryson. *See* Map 28 on p. 158.

Road log from Highway 148 at **km 84.7** (*see* Highway 148 road log on p. 137):

km　　　　0　　　Junction of Highway 148 and the road to Bryson; turn left (west) onto the road to Bryson and Île du Grand Calumet, and proceed toward the New Calumet mine.

　　　　　3.8　　Junction; turn right. (The road on the left goes to the New Calumet mine.)

　　　　　16.0　Junction; turn right.

　　　　　17.1　Gate on left across the road from a farmhouse. A trail leads southwest about 500 m from the gate to the Calumet uranium trenches in an outcrop area at the edge of the woods. A few more openings are found farther into the wooded area.

Refs.:　175 p. 20–21; 177 p. 30–32; 178 p. 423.

Maps　　(T):　31 F/15 Fort Coulonge
　　　　(G):　191A Calumet Island, Pontiac District, Quebec (GSC, 1:47 520)
　　　　　　　660 Quebec and Ontario, parts of counties of Ottawa and Pontiac, Que. and Carleton and Renfrew, Ont. (Pembroke Sheet No. 122) (GSC, 1:253 440)
　　　　　　　1165 Litchfield-Huddersfield area, electoral district of Pontiac (MRNQ, 1:63 360)

Lawless Lake occurrence

PYROXENE, ALLANITE, PHLOGOPITE, TREMOLITE, QUARTZ CRYSTALS, SCAPOLITE, HORNBLENDE, TITANITE, TOURMALINE, PYRITE, EPIDOTE, FLUORITE, CHLORITE, K-FELDSPAR

In skarn zone between gneiss and granite

Green pyroxene is the most abundant mineral in the skarn; it occurs as crystals up to several centimetres long. Allanite and phlogopite occur as pockets of crystals. Crystal aggregates of green tremolite and colourless quartz are common. Scapolite occurs as large white crystals that fluoresce reddish pink in short ultraviolet rays. Other minerals found in the skarn include hornblende, titanite, tourmaline, pyrite, epidote, fluorite, pink calcite, chlorite, and K-feldspar. The skarn zone is about 12 m thick and lies between gneiss and granite. Allanite crystals occur in grey granite pegmatite dykes cutting gneiss that underlies the skarn.

The Lawless Lake occurrence consists of a roadcut on Highway 301 opposite Lawless Lake. It is 7 km from the junction of highways 148 and 301 at **km 91.4** in Campbell's Bay (*see* Highway 148 road log on p. 137), and 14 km from Otter Lake. *See* Map 26 on p. 145.

Ref.:   <u>104</u> p. 79–80.

Maps   (T):   31 F/15 Fort-Coulonge
        (G):   660 Quebec and Ontario, parts of counties of Ottawa and Pontiac, Que. and Carleton and Renfrew, Ont. (Pembroke Sheet No. 122) (GSC, 1:253 440)
        1165 Litchfield-Huddersfield area, electoral district of Pontiac (MRNQ, 1:63 360)

Gibson (Gib) Lake scapolite occurrence

SCAPOLITE, PARGASITE

In skarn

Massive scapolite occurs in skarn enclosed in banded phlogopite marble near the southeast end of Gibson (Gib) Lake. The scapolite is violet-blue with stringers and minute patches of white albite, calcite, and dolomite; these white inclusions produce a mottled effect on the polished surface.

The scapolite forms the central core of a zoned skarn nodule. Surrounding the scapolite core is a zone of greyish-green pargasite and some albite and phlogopite; in places the pargasite occurs as coarse bladed crystals. Orange-brown grains of serpentinized forsterite occur in marble near its contact with the skarn.

The scapolite skarn nodule is exposed in a low marble cliff, 9 m above the water's edge, on the east side of the southern end of Gibson (Gib) Lake. When the occurrence was first reported, the skarn nodule was 1.5 m high and 1 m wide; much of the scapolite has since been removed.

The occurrence is about 15 km due north of Fort Coulonge. *See* Map 29 on p. 165.

Road log from Highway 148 at **km 109.1** in Fort Coulonge (*see* Highway 148 road log on p. 137):

km   0   Fort Coulonge, junction of Highway 148 and Chemin de la Chute; proceed north onto Chemin de la Chute.

          5.6   T-junction; the main road turns left (west).

          13.7   Junction, road on right to Hickey Lake; continue straight ahead.

          16.7   Junction, road to Gibson (Gib) Lake on left (just after the road crosses a creek); turn left (west) to Gibson (Gib) Lake.

19.5   The road bends sharply to the right.

20.0   Bridge over a creek.

21.3   Junction of a trail on right; proceed east along this trail.

22.1   Trail crosses a creek at the south end of Gibson (Gib) Lake. Cross the creek, then turn left and walk to the Gibson (Gib) Lake scapolite-bearing marble exposure at the south end of the lake.

Refs.:   104 p. 91; 179 p. 577–585.

Maps   (T):   31 F/15 Fort-Coulonge
        (G):   660 Quebec and Ontario, parts of counties of Ottawa and Pontiac, Que. and Carleton and Renfrew, Ont. (Pembroke Sheet No. 122) (GSC, 1:253 440)
              1165 Litchfield-Huddersfield area, electoral district of Pontiac (MRNQ, 1:63 360)

Sèche Point, Devonshire Park occurrences

FOSSILS

In limestone

Fossils are abundant along shoreline exposures at Sèche Point and at Devonshire Park on the north shore of the Ottawa River. They occur in dark grey Black River limestone of Ordovician age. The fossils include corals, cephalopods, pelecypods, trilobites, brachiopods, gastropods, ostracods, bryozoa, and crinoid fragments.

At one time, the limestone was quarried at both locations. The Sèche Point limestone was used locally as a building stone and for road metal, and the Devonshire Park limestone was processed into lime in kilns on the site. At Devonshire Park, the limestone band, 122 m long and 46 m wide, is in contact with Precambrian quartz-feldspar gneiss, which forms Mount Devonshire. Cottages have been built along the limestone band.

The fossil-bearing limestone is exposed as flat-lying ledges at Sèche Point and along the shore of Devonshire Park, about 2 km farther upstream. The localities are on the north shore of the Coulonge Lake expansion of the Ottawa River, 6 to 8 km upstream from Fort Coulonge. *See* Map 29 on p. 165.

Road log from Highway 148 at **km 118.5** (*see* Highway 148 road log on p. 137):

km   0   Junction of Highway 148 and a road leading south; turn left (south).

         1.8   Junction; turn right onto a road leading south.

         2.1   Junction; follow the road on right leading west.

         2.9   End of the road at Sèche Point.

To reach the Devonshire Park shore, follow the road leading south from Highway 148 at **km 120.1** for about 600 m.

Refs.:   44 p. 16–17, 34, 44–45, 50, 64–65; 99 p. 73–77, 115; 114 p. 64–65; 151 p. 99–100, 107; 216 p. 10; 217 p. 6; 221 p. 11.

Maps   (T):   31 F/15 Fort-Coulonge
        (G):   249 Coulonge and Black rivers area, County of Pontiac (MRNQ, 1:190 080)
              660 Quebec and Ontario, parts of counties of Ottawa and Pontiac, Que. and Carleton and Renfrew, Ont. (Pembroke Sheet No. 122) (GSC, 1:253 440)

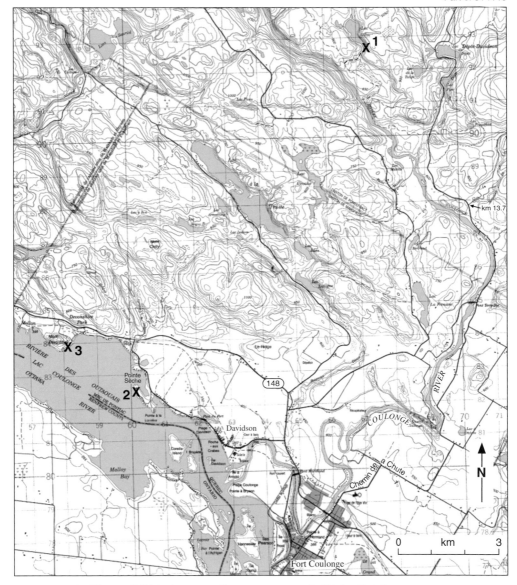

1. Gibson (Gib) Lake scapolite occurrence   2. Sèche Point occurrence
3. Devonshire Park occurrence

Map 29. Fort-Coulonge.

Waltham mine

FELDSPAR, PERISTERITE, HORNBLENDE, PYROXENE, TITANITE, MAGNETITE, EPIDOTE, SERPENTINE, MICA, ALLANITE, PYRITE, CALCITE, MOLYBDENITE

In granite pegmatite dyke cutting granite gneiss

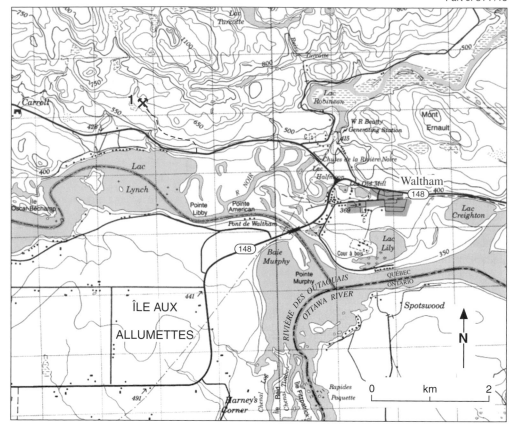

1. Waltham mine

Map 30. Waltham.

Pink to grey peristerite with blue iridescence occurs in this inactive feldspar mine. The chief constituents of the pegmatite are pink to grey feldspar, and quartz. Pink perthite is the main feldspar. Black massive hornblende and crystal aggregates of pyroxene and titanite are common. Less abundant accessories include magnetite, epidote, serpentine, mica, allanite, pyrite, and calcite. Molybdenite has been reported.

The deposit was worked in 1915 by Rock Products Company of New Jersey. Two small open cuts have been made into a wooded cliff on the east side of a creek; the cuts extend 30 m up the cliff. The property belongs to William Lamarche of Waltham.

The mine is about 4 km west of Waltham. *See* Map 30 on p. 166.

Road log from Waltham at **km 128.0** on Highway 148 (*see* Highway 148 road log on p. 137):

km		
	0	Waltham, junction of Highway 148 and the road to Chapeau; proceed west along the road to Chapeau.
	2.8	Junction, single-lane road on right. Proceed along this road for about 800 m to a creek; turn right and proceed along the east side of the creek for approximately 350 m to the Waltham mine on the right. At this point, some feldspar blocks occur in the creek bed.

Refs.:　　151 p. 104–105; 174 p. 44.

Maps　　(T):　31 F/15 Fort Coulonge
　　　　(G):　249 Coulonge and Black rivers area, County of Pontiac (MRNQ, 1:190 080)
　　　　　　　660 Quebec and Ontario, parts of counties of Ottawa and Pontiac, Que. and
　　　　　　　Carleton and Renfrew, Ont. (Pembroke Sheet No. 122) (GSC, 1:253 440)
　　　　　　　1804 Saint-Patrice Lake and Portage-du-Fort, electoral district of Pontiac-
　　　　　　　Témiscamingue (MRNQ, 1:126 720)

ADDRESSES FOR MAPS AND REPORTS

Geological maps and reports published by the Government of Canada

GSC Ottawa
601 Booth Street, Room 107
Ottawa, Ontario
K1A 0E8
Tel.: (613) 995-4342 or
1-888-252-4301 (toll free)
Fax: (613) 943-0646

GSC Pacific
101-605 Robson Street
Vancouver, British Columbia
V6B 5J3
Tel.: (604) 666-0529
Fax: (604) 666-1337

GSC Calgary
3303-33rd Street N.W.
Calgary, Alberta
T2L 2A7
Tel.: (403) 292-7030
Fax: (403) 299-3542

or

Authorized agents (*see* Book Dealers, yellow pages of the telephone directory)

For topographic maps published by the Government of Canada, *see* list of authorized agents under Maps, yellow pages of the telephone directory.

Geological maps and reports published by the governments of Ontario and Quebec

Mines and Minerals Information Centre
Ministry of Northern Development and Mines
Macdonald Block, 2nd Floor, Room M217
900 Bay Street
Toronto, Ontario M7A 1C3
Tel.: (416) 314-3790
Fax: (416) 314-3797

Ministry of Northern Development and Mines
Publication Sales
933 Ramsey Lake Road, Level B2
Sudbury, Ontario P3E 6B5
Tel.: (705) 670-5691 or 1-888-415-9845
Fax: (705) 670-5770

Ministère des Ressources naturelles
Gouvernement du Québec
Centre de diffusion
5700, 4e Avenue Ouest
Charlesbourg, Quebec G1H 6R1
Tel.: (418) 643-4601
Fax: (418) 644-3814

Road maps and travel information

Ontario Travel
Queen's Park
Toronto, Ontario M7A 2E5
Tel.: (416) 314-6557 or
1-800-668-2746
Fax: (416) 314-7372
http://www.ontariotravel.net

Tourisme Québec
C.P. 979
Montréal, Quebec G1K 7X2
Tel.: (514) 837-2015 or
1-877-266-5687
http://www.bonjourquebec.com

MINERAL AND ROCK DISPLAYS

Écomusée de Hull
170, rue Montcalm
Gatineau, Quebec J8X 2M3
Tel.: (819) 595-7790
Fax: (819) 595-0332

Haileybury Campus (School of Mines)
Ontario College of Applied Arts and
Technology
Haileybury, Ontario P0J 1K0
Tel.: (705) 672-3376
Fax: (705) 672-2014
http://www.northernc.on.ca/about/haileyb
ury.html

Lake Timiskaming Fossil Centre
5, rue Principale, P.O. Box 296
Notre-Dame-du-Nord, Quebec J0Z 3B0
Tel.: (819) 723-2500
Fax: (819) 773-2369
http://www.fossiles.qc.ca/index2.html

Geological Survey of Canada
Logan Hall
601 Booth Street
Ottawa, Ontario K1A 0E8
Tel.: (613) 995-4261
Fax: (613) 996-8059
http://www.gsc.nrcan.gc.ca/hist/logan/log
anhall_e.php

Carleton University
Department of Earth Sciences,
Tory Building
Ottawa, Ontario K1S 8B6
Tel.: (613) 788-4400
http://www.earthsci.carleton.ca

Canadian Museum of Nature
249 McLeod Street
Ottawa, Ontario K1A 0M8
Tel.: (613) 566-4700 or
1 (800) 263-4433 (toll free)
Fax: (613) 995-3040
http://www nature.ca/nature_e.cfm

Ontario Geological Survey
Willet Green Miller Centre
933 Ramsey Lake Road,
3rd Floor
Sudbury, Ontario P3E 6B5
Tel.: (705) 670-5741
Fax: (705) 670-5818
http://www.mndm.gov.on.ca/MNDM/MIN
ES/ogs/default_e.asp

Science North
100 Ramsey Lake Road
Sudbury, Ontario P3E 5S9
Tel.: (705) 522-3701 or
1 (800) 461-4898 (toll free)
Fax: (705) 522-4954
http://www.sciencenorth.on.ca/

REFERENCES

1. **Aarden, H.M. and Gittins, J.**
   1974: Hiortdahlite from Kipawa River, Villedieu Township, Temiscaming Country, Québec, Canada; The Canadian Mineralogist, v. 12, p. 241–247.

2. **Alcock, F.J.**
   1930: Zinc and lead deposits of Canada; Geological Survey of Canada; Economic Geology Series 8, 406 p.

3. **Allan J.F.**
   1992: Geology and mineralization of the Kipawa yttrium-zirconium prospect, Quebec; Exploration and Mining Geology, v. 1, p. 183–295.

4. **Ami, H.M.**
   1896: Notes on some fossil organic remains comprised in the geological formations and outliers of the Ottawa Paleozoic basin; Royal Society of Canada, Proceedings and Transactions, Second Series, v. 2, 1896, p. 151–158.

5. 1899: On some Cambro-Silurian fossils from Lake Temiscaming, Lake Nipissing and Mattawa outliers; *in* Report on the Geology and Natural Resources of the Area Included by the Nipissing and Temiscaming Map-sheets Comprising Portions of the District of Nipissing, Ontario, and the County of Pontiac, Quebec, by A.E. Barlow; Geological Survey of Canada, Annual Report 1897, New Series, v. 10, pt. I, p. 289–302.

6. 1904: Appendix; *in* Report on the Geology of a Portion of Eastern Ontario, by R.W. Ellis; Geological Survey of Canada, Annual Report 1901, v. 14, pt. J, p. 80–89.

7. **Ansell, H.G., Roberts, A.C., Plant, A.G., and Sturman, B.D.**
   1980: Gittinsite, a new calcium zirconium silicate from the Kipawa agpaitic syenite complex, Quebec; The Canadian Mineralogist, v. 18, p. 201–203.

8. **Avramtchev, L. and LeBel-Drolet, S.**
   1989: Catalogue des gîtes minéraux du Québec — Région de l'Abitibi; ministère de l'Énergie et des Ressources, Québec, DPV-744, 98 p.

9. **Baker, D.B.**
   1977: Aylwin–Cawood area, Pontiac and Gatineau counties; ministère des Richesses naturelles, DP-510, 80 p.

10. **Bancroft, J.A.**
    1918: The molybdenite deposits in the vicinity of Big Squaw Lake, Huddersfield Township, Pontiac County, P.Q.; *in* Report on Mining Operations in the Province of Quebec During the Year 1917, by Théo. C. Denis; Quebec Department of Colonization, Mines and Fisheries, p. 35–46.

11. **Barlow, A.E.**
    1899: Report on the geology and natural resources of the area included by the Nipissing and Temiscaming map-sheets comprising portions of the District of Nipissing, Ontario, and the County of Pontiac, Quebec; Geological Survey of Canada, Annual Report 1897, New Series, v. 10, pt. I, 302 p.

12. 1915: Corundum, its occurrence, distribution exploitation and uses; Geological Survey of Canada, Memoir 57, 377 p.

13. **Basa, E.**
    1991: Cobalt resident geologist's district — 1990; *in* Report of Activities 1990, Resident Geologists, (ed.) K.G. Fenwick, J.W. Newsome, and A.E. Pitts; Ontario Geological Survey, Miscellaneous Paper 152, p. 261–279.

14. **Bates, R.L. and Jackson, J.A.**
1980: Glossary of Geology, 2nd edition; American Geological Institute, Falls Church, Virginia, 749 p.

15. **Berry, L.S., Lin, H., and Davis, G.C.**
1972: A new occurrence of miserite from the Kipawa Lake area, Temiscamingue County, Quebec; The Canadian Mineralogist, v. 11, p. 569.

16. **Berry, L.G. and Mason, B.**
1983: Mineralogy, Concepts, Descriptions, Determinations, 2nd edition revised by R.B. Dietrich; W.H. Freeman and Company, San Francisco, California, 561 p.

17. **Blue, A.**
1896: Section 1. General introduction; Ontario Bureau of Mines, Annual Report 1895, v. 5, p. 7–46.

18. 1897: Section 1. General introduction; Ontario Bureau of Mines, Annual Report 1896, v. 6, p. 7–70.

19. **Brun, J.**
1984: Géologie de la région de Portage-du-Fort; ministère de l'Énergie et des Ressources, Québec, ET-83-03, 87 p.

20. **Carlson, H.D.**
1954: Craigmont corundum deposits; *in* Geology of the Brudenell–Raglan Area, by D.F. Hewitt; Ontario Department of Mines, Annual Report, v. 62, pt. 5, 1953, Appendix A, p. 102–116.

21. **Carter, T.R., Colvine, A.C., and Meyn, H.D.**
1980: Geology of base metal, precious metal, iron and molybdenum deposits in the Pembroke–Renfrew area; Ontario Geological Survey, Mineral Deposits Circular 20, 196 p.

22. **Charlton, J., Bell, R., Coe, W., Merritt, W.H., and Blue, A.**
1890: Report of the Royal Commission on the mineral resources of Ontario and measures for their development; printed by order of the Legislative Assembly, Toronto, 566 p.

23. **Cirkel, F.**
1905: Mica, its occurrence, exploitation and uses; Canada Department of Mines, Mines Branch, Publication 10, 148 p.

24. 1907: Graphite, its properties, occurrence, refining and uses; Canada Department of Mines, Mines Branch, Publication 18, 307 p.

25. 1909: Report on the iron ore deposits along the Ottawa (Quebec side) and Gatineau rivers; Canada Department of Mines, Mines Branch, Publication 23, 147 p.

26. **Clark, A.M.**
1993: Hey's Mineral Index, Mineral Species, Varieties and Synonyms, 3rd edition; Chapman & Hall, London, England, 848 p.

27. **Cole, L.H.**
1930: The gypsum industry of Canada; Canada Department of Mines, Mines Branch, Publication 714, 164 p.

28. **Currie, K.L.**
1971: A study of potash fenitization around the Brent Crater, Ontario — A Paleozoic alkaline complex; Canadian Journal of Earth Sciences, v. 8, p. 481–497.

29. 1976: The alkaline rocks of Canada; Geological Survey of Canada, Bulletin 239, 228 p.

30. **Currie, K.L. and Gittins, J.**
1993: Preliminary report on peralkaline silica-undersaturated rocks in the Kipawa syenite gneiss complex, western Quebec; *in* Current Research, Part E; Geological Survey of Canada, Paper 93-1E, p. 197–205.

31. **Dana, E.S.**
1904: The System of Mineralogy of James Dwight Dana, 6th edition; John Wiley & Sons, New York, New York, 1134 p.

32.   **Davidson, A.**
        1982:   Graphite occurrences in the Algonquin region, Grenville province, Ontario; Geological
                Survey of Canada, Open File 870, 7 p.

33.   **Dawson, K.R.**
        1985:   Geology of barium, strontium, and fluorine deposits in Canada; Geological Survey of
                Canada, Economic Geology Report 34, 136 p.

34.   **Dence, M.R. and Guy-Bray, J.V.**
        1972:   Some astroblemes, craters and cryptovolcanic structures in Ontario and Quebec; 24th
                International Geological Congress, Field Excursion A65 Guidebook, Montréal,
                Quebec, 1972, 61 p.

35.   **Dresser, J.A. and Denis, T.C.**
        1949:   Geology of Quebec, Volume III, Economic Geology; Quebec Department of Mines,
                Geological Report 20, 562 p.

36.   **Drolet, P.**
        1955:   Mining operations in 1953, Metals; *in* The Mining Industry of the Province of Quebec
                in 1953; Quebec Department of Mines, p. 12–36.

37.   **Eardley-Wilmot, V.L.**
        1925:   Molybdenum, metallurgy and uses, and the occurrence, mining and concentration of its
                ores; Canada Department of Mines, Mines Branch, Publication 592, 292 p.

38.   1927:   Abrasives, Part II, corundum and diamond; Canada Department of Mines, Mines
                Branch, Publication 675, 51 p.

39.   1927:   Abrasives, Part III, garnet; Canada Department of Mines, Mines Branch, Publication
                677, 69 p.

40.   **Edgar, A.D. and Blackburn, C.E.**
        1972:   Eudialyte from the Kipawa area, Temiscamingue Co., Quebec; The Canadian
                Mineralogist, v. 11, p. 554–559.

41.   **Ells, R.W.**
        1890:   Report on the mineral resources of the province of Quebec; Geological Survey of
                Canada, Annual Report 1888-89, New Series, v. 4, pt. K, 159 p.

42.   1896:   Paleozoic outliers in the Ottawa River basin; Royal Society of Canada, Proceedings
                and Transactions, Second Series, v. 2, p. 137–149.

43.   1904:   Report on the geology of a portion of eastern Ontario; Geological Survey of Canada,
                Annual Report 1901, New Series, v. 14, pt. J, 89 p.

44.   1907:   Report on the geology and natural resources of the area included in the northwest
                quarter sheet, Number 122 of the Ontario and Quebec series comprising portions of the
                counties of Pontiac, Carleton and Renfrew; Geological Survey of Canada, Separate
                Report no. 977, 71 p.

45.   **Ellsworth, H.V.E.**
        1932:   Rare-element minerals in Canada; Geological Survey of Canada, Economic Geology
                Series 11, 272 p.

46.   **Ercit, T.S.**
        1994:   The geochemistry and crystal chemistry of columbite-group minerals from granitic
                pegmatites, southwestern Grenville Province, Canadian Shield; The Canadian
                Mineralogist, v. 32, p. 421–438.

47.   **Evans, A.M.**
        1964:   Ashby and Denbigh township; Ontario Department of Mines, Geological Report 26,
                39 p.

48.   **Field, D.J.**
        1955:   Mining operations in 1953; Ontario Department of Mines, Annual Report v. 63, pt. 2,
                1954, 155 p.

49. **Fleischer, M. and Mandarino, J.A.**
    1995:   Glossary of Mineral Species 1995, 7th edition; the Mineralogical Record Inc., Tucson, Arizona, 280 p.

50. **Ford, D.C.**
    1961:   The Bonnèchere caves, Renfrew County, Ontario; The Canadian Geographer, v. 5, no. 3, p. 22–25.

51. **Fréchette, H.**
    1910:   On a number of iron ore properties in northeastern Ontario; Summary Report for 1909; Canada Department of Mines, Mines Branch, Publication 63, p. 81–88.

52. **Freeman, B.C.**
    1936:   Mineral deposits in Renfrew County and vicinity; Geological Survey of Canada, Memoir 195, 34 p.

53. **Garland, M.I.**
    1987:   A detailed petrological study of the Cal Graphite Limited Graphite deposit in Butt Township, Central Ontario; *in* Summary of Field Work and Other Activities, 1987, (ed.) R.B. Barlow, M.E. Cherry, A.C. Colvine, B.O. Dressler, and O.L. White; Ontario Geological Survey, Miscellaneous Paper 137, p. 332–334.

54.   1987:   Graphite in the central gneiss belt of the Grenville Province of Ontario; Ontario Geological Survey, Open File Report 5649, 198 p.

55.   1991:   Geology of the Cal Graphite flake graphite deposit; Ontario Geological Survey, Open File Report 5816, 61 p.

56. **Gerow, M.C., Sherlock, E.J., and Bellinger, J.A.**
    1991:   Soapstone in Ontario; Ontario Geological Survey, Open File Report 5764, 208 p.

57. **Gittins, J., Bown, M.G., and Sturman, D.**
    1976:   Agrellite, a new rock-forming mineral in regionally metamorphosed agpaitic alkalic rocks; The Canadian Mineralogist, v. 14, p. 120–126.

58. **Gittins, J., Gasparrini, E.L., and Fleet, S.G.**
    1973:   The occurrence of vlasovite in Canada; The Canadian Mineralogist, v. 12, p. 211–214.

59. **Globensky, Y.**
    1994:   District minier de Montréal-Laurentides; *in* Rapport des géologues résidents sur l'activité minière régionale, (ed.) G. Cockburn, F. Dompierre et M. Germain; ministère des Ressources naturelles, Québec, D.V. 94-01, p. 81–102.

60. **Goad, B.E.**
    1990:   Granitic pegmatites of the Bancroft area, southeastern Ontario; Ontario Geological Survey, Open File Report 5717, 459 p.

61. **Goranson, R.W.**
    1927:   Calumet Island, Pontiac County, Quebec; Geological Survey of Canada, Summary Report 1925, pt. C, p. 105–124.

62. **Gordon, J.B., Lovell, H.L., de Grijs, J., and Davie, R.F.**
    1979:   Gold deposits of Ontario Part 2, part of District of Cochrane, districts of Muskoka, Nipissing, Parry Sound, Sudbury, Timiskaming, and counties of southern Ontario; Ontario Geological Survey, Mineral Deposits Circular 18, 253 p.

63. **Goudge, M.F.**
    1935:   Limestones of Canada, their occurrence and characteristics, Part III, Quebec; Canada Department of Mines, Mines Branch, Publication 755, 274 p.

64.   1938:   Limestones of Canada, their occurrence and characteristics, Part IV, Ontario; Canada Department of Mines, Mines Branch, Publication 781, 362 p.

65.   1939:   A preliminary report on brucite deposits in Ontario and Quebec, and their commercial possibilities; Canada Department of Mines, Mines Branch, Memorandum Series 75, 57 p.

66.   1957:   Brucite; *in* The Geology of Canadian Industrial Mineral Deposits; 6th Commonwealth Mining Metallurgical Congress, 1956, Toronto, Ontario, Canada, p. 61–69.

67.   **Grice, J.D. and Gault, R.A.**
    1982:   The Lake Clear–Kuehl Lake area, Renfrew County, Ontario; The Mineralogical Record, v. 13, p. 209–214.

68.   **Grieve, R.A.F. and Robertson, P.D.**
    1987:   Terrestrial impact structures; Geological Survey of Canada, Map 1658A, scale 1:63 000 000.

69.   **Gross, G.A.**
    1967:   Geology of iron deposits in Canada, Volume 11, Iron deposits in the Appalachian and Grenville regions of Canada; Geological Survey of Canada, Economic Geology Report 22, 111 p.

70.   **Guillet, G.R.**
    1963:   Barite in Ontario; Ontario Department of Mines, Industrial Mineral Report 10, 42 p.

71.   **Harding, W.D.**
    1946:   Geology of the Mattawa–Olrig area; Ontario Department of Mines, Annual Report, v. 53, pt. 6, 1944, 47 p.

72.   **Hardman, J.E.**
    1917:   The Kingdon Lead mine; Transactions of the Canadian Mining Institute, v. 20, p. 180–187.

73.   **Hébert, Y. and Paré, C.**
    1990:   Les ressources en minéraux de magnésium et leur utilisation au Québec; ministère de l'Énergie et des Ressources, Québec, MB 90-31, 55 p.

74.   **Heinrich, E.W.**
    1962:   Some mineral occurrences near Eau Claire, Ontario; The Canadian Mineralogist, v. 7, p. 314–318.

75.   **Hewitt, D.F.**
    1952:   Feldspar in Ontario; Ontario Department of Mines, Industrial Mineral Circular 3, 13 p.

76.   1952:   Kyanite and sillimanite in Ontario; Ontario Department of Mines, Industrial Mineral Circular 4, 9 p.

77.   1954:   Geology of Brudenell–Raglan area; Ontario Department of Mines, Annual Report, v. 62, pt. 5, 1953, 123 p.

78.   1955:   Geology of Monteagle and Carlow townships; Ontario Department of Mines, Annual Report, v. 63, pt. 6, 1954, 78 p.

79.   1957:   The Purdy mica mine; *in* The Geology of Canadian Industrial Mineral Deposits; 6th Commonwealth Mining and Metallurgical Congress, 1956, Toronto, Ontario, Canada, p. 181–185.

80.   1964:   The limestone industry of Ontario 1958–1963; Ontario Department of Mines, Industrial Mineral Report 13, 77 p.

81.   1964:   Building stones of Ontario; Part III, marble; Ontario Department of Mines, Industrial Mineral Report 16, 89 p.

82.   1964:   Building stones of Ontario, Part V, granite and gneiss; Ontario Department of Mines, Industrial Mineral Report 19, 51 p.

83.   1965:   Graphite in Ontario; Ontario Department of Mines, Industrial Mineral Report 20, 66 p.

84.   1967:   Geology and mineral deposits of the Parry Sound–Huntsville area; Ontario Department of Mines, Geological Report 52, 65 p.

85.   1967:   Pegmatite mineral resources of Ontario; Ontario Department of Mines, Industrial Mineral Report 21, 83 p.

86.   1967:   Uranium and thorium deposits of southern Ontario; Ontario Department of Mines, Mineral Resources Circular 4, 76 p.

87. **Hoadley, J.W.**
     1960: Mica deposits of Canada; Geological Survey of Canada, Economic Geology Series 19, 141 p.

88. **Hoffmann, G.C.**
     1895: Chemical contributions to the geology of Canada from the laboratory of the Survey; Geological Survey of Canada, Annual Report 1892-93, v. 6, pt. R, 93 p.

89. 1898: Report of the section of chemistry and mineralogy; Geological Survey of Canada, Annual Report 1896, New Series v. 9, pt. R, 53 p.

90. **Hogarth, D.D.**
     1970: Geology of the southern part of Gatineau Park, National Capital region; Geological Survey of Canada, Paper 70-20, 8 p.

91. **Hogarth, D.D., Moyd, L., Rose, E.R., and Steacy, H.R.**
     1972: Classic mineral collecting localities in Ontario and Quebec; Field excursion A47-C47, XXIVth International Geological Congress, Montréal, Quebec, 1972, 79 p. (reprinted as Geological Survey of Canada, Miscellaneous Report 37).

92. **Ingall, E.D.**
     1898: Section of mineral statistics and mines, Annual report for 1897; Geological Survey of Canada, Annual Report 1897, New Series, v. 10, pt. S, 232 p.

93. 1901: Report on the iron ore deposits along the Kingston and Pembroke railway in eastern Ontario; Geological Survey of Canada, Annual Report, New Series, v. XII, 1899, pt. I, 91 p.

94. **Inspectors, Ontario Department of Mines**
     1946: Mines of Ontario in 1941; Ontario Department of Mines, Annual Report, v. 51, pt. 1, 1942, 282 p.

95. **Ireland, J.C., Basa, E.M., Zalnieriunas, R.V., Beecham, A.W., and Lovell, H.**
     1992: Cobalt resident geologist's district — 1991; in Report of Activities 1991, Resident Geologists, (ed.) K.G. Fenwick, J.W. Newsome, and A.E. Pitts, Ontario Geological Survey, Miscellaneous Paper 158, p. 285–309.

96. **Ireland, J.C., Zalnieriunas, R.V., and Basa, E.M.**
     1993: Cobalt resident geologist's district — 1992; in Report of Activities 1992, Resident Geologists, (ed.) K.G. Fenwick, J.W. Newsome, and A.E. Pitts; Ontario Geological Survey, Miscellaneous Paper 161, p. 307–333.

97. **Johnston, R.A.A.**
     1915: A list of Canadian mineral occurrences; Geological Survey of Canada, Memoir 74, 275 p.

98. **Johnstone, F.J.**
     1968: Molybdenum deposits in Ontario; Ontario Department of Mines, Mineral Resources Circular 7, 98 p.

99. **Katz, M.B.**
     1976: Région/area Portage-du-Fort & Lac Saint-Patrice; ministère des Richesses naturelles, Québec, Rapport géologique 170, 122 p.

100. **Kindle, E.D.**
     1936: Gold occurrences of Ontario east of Lake Superior; Geological Survey of Canada, Memoir 192, 167 p.

101. **Kretz, R.**
     1957: Preliminary report on Litchfield–Huddersfield area, Pontiac electoral district; Quebec Department of Mines, Preliminary Report no. 338, 7 p.

102. 1957: Preliminary report on Thorne–Leslie–Clapham area, Pontiac electoral district; Quebec Department of Mines, Preliminary Report no. 346, 6 p.

103. 1957: Preliminary report on Pontefract–Gillies area, Pontiac electoral district; Quebec Department of Mines, Preliminary Report no. 357, 7 p.

104.   1977:   Fort-Coulonge–Otter Lake–Kazabazua area, Pontiac–Témiscamingue and Gatineau electoral districts; ministère des Richesses naturelles, Québec, DPV-514, 309 p.

105.   **Lang, A.H.**
     1943:   Geology of Eau Claire mica deposits; Transactions of the Canadian Institute of Mining and Metallurgy, v. 46, p. 305–312.

106.   1952:   Canadian deposits of uranium and thorium (interim account); Geological Survey of Canada, Economic Geology Series 16, 173 p.

107.   **Lang, A.H., Griffith, J.W., and Steacy, H.R.**
     1962:   Canadian deposits of uranium and thorium, 2nd edition; Geological Survey of Canada, Economic Geology Series 16, 324 p.

108.   **Leavitt, D.L.**
     1981:   Minerals of the Yates uranium mine, Pontiac County. Quebec; The Mineralogical Record, v. 12, p. 359–363.

109.   **LeBaron, P.S. and van Haaften, S.**
     1989:   Talc in southeastern Ontario; Ontario Geological Survey, Open File Report 5714, 240 p.

110.   **LeBaron, P.S., Kingston, P.W., Papertzian, V.C., van Haaften, S., Meyn, H.D., and Caley, W.F.**
     1993:   Southeastern resident geologist's district — 1992; *in* Report of Activities, 1992, Resident Geologists, (ed.) K.G. Kenwick, J.W. Newsome, and A.E. Pitts; Ontario Geological Survey, Miscellaneous Paper 161, p. 371–392.

111.   **LeBaron, P.S. and MacKinnon, A.**
     1990:   Precambrian dolomite resources in southeastern Ontario; Ontario Geological Survey, Open File Report 5712, 134 p.

112.   **Lentz, D.R.**
     1991:   U-, Mo- and REE-bearing pegmatites, skarns and veins in the central metasedimentary belt, Grenville Province, Ontario; Geological Association of Canada/Mineralogical Association of Canada, Toronto 1991, Field Trip A9, Guidebook, 61 p.

113.   **Lindeman, E. and Bolton, L.L.**
     1917:   Iron ore occurrences in Canada, volume II, descriptions of iron ore occurrences; Canada Department of Mines, Mines Branch, Publication 217, 222 p.

114.   **Logan, W.E.**
     1847:   On the topography and geology of the Ottawa River and some of its tributaries with notes on economic minerals; Geological Survey of Canada, Report of Progress for the year 1845-46, p. 1–98.

115.   1850:   Catalogue of some of the economic minerals and deposits of Canada with their localities; Geological Survey of Canada, Report of Progress for the year 1849-50, p. 107–115.

116.   1863:   Geology of Canada; Report of Progress from Commencement to 1863; Geological Survey of Canada, 983 p.

117.   **Lumbers, S.B.**
     1971:   Geology of the North Bay area, districts of Nipissing and Parry Sound; Ontario Department of Mines and Northern Affairs, Geological Report 94, 104 p.

118.   1980:   Geology of Renfrew County; Ontario Geological Survey, Open File Report 5282, 94 p.

119.   1982:   Summary of metallogeny, Renfrew County area; Ontario Geological Survey, Report 212, 58 p.

120.   **Lyall, H.B.**
     1959:   Preliminary report on McLachlin–Booth area, Temiscamingue electoral district; Quebec Department of Mines, Preliminary Report no. 391, 13 p.

121.   **Marmont, C.R.**
     1988:   Limestone (crystalline marble) in the Parry Sound–Huntsville area; Ontario Geological Survey, Open File Report 5687, 71 p.

122.   1991:   Building stone, feldspar and limestone resources in central Ontario; Ontario Geological Survey, Open File Report 5760, 499 p.

123.   1993:   Project 5.6. Industrial minerals and building stone in the districts of Nipissing, Parry Sound and Sudbury; *in* Summary of Field Work and Other Activities 1993, (ed.) C.L. Baker, B.O. Dressler, H.A.F. de Souza, K.G. Fenwick, J.W. Newsome, and L. Owsiacki; Ontario Geological Survey, Miscellaneous Paper 162, p. 292–295.

124.   **Marmount, C.R. and Johnston, M.**
        1987:   Mineral deposits studies in the Huntsville–Parry Sound–Powassan area — a progress report; Ontario Geological Survey, Open File Report 5647, 221 p.

125.   **Martin W.**
        1983:   Industrial minerals of the Algonquin region; Ontario Geological Survey, Open File Report 5425, 316 p.

126.   **Masson, S.L. and Gordon, J.B.**
        1981:   Radioactive mineral deposits of the Renfrew–Pembroke area; Ontario Geological Survey, Mineral Deposits Circular 23, 155 p.

127.   **Maurice, O.D.**
        1973:   Annotated list of occurrences of industrial minerals and building materials in Quebec; ministère des Richesses naturelles, Québec, DP-184, 580 p.

128.   **Meen, V.B. and Gorman, D.H.**
        1953:   Mineral occurrences of Wilberforce, Bancroft and Craigmont–Lake Clear areas, southeastern Ontario; Geological Society of America and Geological Association of Canada, Field Trip No. 2 Guidebook, November 12–14, 1953, Toronto, Ontario, 23 p.

129.   **Meyn, H.D.**
        1977:   Geology of Afton, Scholes, Macbeth, and Clement townships, districts of Sudbury and Nipissing; Ontario Geological Survey, Report 170, 77 p.

130.   **Miller, J.E.**
        1898:   Economic geology of eastern Ontario; Ontario Bureau of Mines, 7th Report, 1897, pt. 3, p. 207–250.

131.   **Millman, P.M.**
        1960:   The Brent crater, Part 1, General considerations; *in* The Brent Crater, by P.M. Millman, B.A. Liberty, J.F. Clark, P.L. Willmore and M.J.S. Innes; Publication of Dominion Observatory, Ottawa, v. 24, no. 1, p. 1–8.

132.   **Moore, E.S.**
        1937:   Geology of the Afton–Scholes area; Ontario Department of Mines, Annual Report, v. 45, pt. 6, 1936, p. 38–48.

133.   **Moorhouse, W.W.**
        1941:   Geology of the zinc-lead deposit on Calumet Island, Quebec; Geological Society of America, Bulletin, v. 52, p. 601–632.

134.   **Mulligan, R.**
        1960:   Beryllium occurrences in Canada; Geological Survey of Canada, Paper 60-21, 40 p.

135.   1968:   Geology of Canadian beryllium deposits; Geological Survey of Canada, Economic Geology Report 23, 109 p.

136.   **Nickel, E.H. and Nichols, M.C.**
        1991:   Mineral Reference Manual; Van Nostrand Reinhold, New York, New York, 250 p.

137.   **Ogilvie, B.Y., Robertson, P.B., and Grieve, R.A.F.**
        1985:   Meteorite impact features in Canada, an inventory and an evaluation; National Parks Branch, Canada Department of Environment, 180 p.

138.   **Osborne, F.F.**
        1944:   Calumet Island area, Pontiac County; Quebec Department of Mines, Geological Report 18, 30 p.

139. **Palache, C., Berman, H., and Frondel, C.**
   1944:   Dana's System of Mineralogy, 7th Edition, v. I; John Wiley & Sons Inc., New York, New York, 834 p.

140.   1951:   Dana's System of Mineralogy, 7th Edition, v. II; John Wiley & Sons Inc., New York, New York, 1124 p.

141.   1962:   Dana's System of Mineralogy, 7th Edition, v. III; John Wiley & Sons Inc., New York, New York, 334 p.

142. **Papertzian, V.C., Kingston, P.W., LeBaron, P.S., van Haaften, S., Meyn, H.D., Caley, W.F., and Kipouros, G.J.**
   1992:   Southeastern resident geologist's district — 1991; *in* Report of Activities, 1991, Resident Geologists, (ed.) K.G. Fenwick, J.W. Newsome, and A.E. Pitts; Ontario Geological Survey, Miscellaneous Paper 158, p. 351–368.

143. **Parks, W.A.**
   1912:   Report on the building and ornamental stones of Canada, Vol. I; Canada Department of Mines, Mines Branch, Publication 100, 376 p.

144.   1914:   Report on the building and ornamental stones of Canada, Vol. III; Canada Department of Mines, Mines Branch, Publication 279, 304 p.

145. **Parsons, A.L.**
   1917:   Molybdenite deposits of Ontario; Ontario Bureau of Mines, Annual Report, v. 26, no. 4, p. 275–313.

146.   1931:   The mode of occurrence of the giant zircons from Brudenell Township, Ontario; *in* Contributions to Canadian Mineralogy; University of Toronto Studies, Geological Series, no. 30, p. 21–24.

147. **Pauk, L.**
   1984:   Geology of the Lavant area, Frontenac and Lanark counties; Ontario Geological Survey, Open File Report 5519, 129 p.

148.   1989:   Geology of the Lavant area, Frontenac and Lanark counties; Ontario Geological Survey, Report 253, 61 p.

149. **Peach, P.A.**
   1958:   The geology of Darling Township and part of Lavant Township; Ontario Department of Mines, Annual Report 1956, v. 65, pt. 7, p. 47–60.

150. **Quinn, H.A.**
   1952:   Renfrew map-area, Renfrew and Lanark coounties; Geological Survey of Canada, Paper 51-27, 79 p.

151. **Retty, J.A.**
   1933:   Reconnaissance along the Coulonge and Black rivers, Pontiac County; Quebec Bureau of Mines, Report of the Minister of Mines of the Province of Quebec 1932–1933, pt. D, p. 85–107.

152. **Rive, M.**
   1972:   Mineralization in the south part of Temiskamingue County and the west part of Pontiac County; Québec Department of Natural Resources, Open File Manuscript, DP-106, 20 p.

153.   1973:   Geology of the Beauchene and Bleu lakes area; Quebec Department of Natural Resources, Preliminary Report no. 580, 17 p.

154.   1973:   Geology of the Ogascannane and Sairs lakes area, Temiskaming County; ministère des Richesses naturelles, Québec, Preliminary Report no. 606, 16 p.

155. **Robert, J.-L.**
   1962:   Preliminary report on Fabre–Mazenod area, Témiscamingue County; Quebec Department of Natural Resources, Preliminary Report no. 485, 9 p.

156.   1963:   Geology of Kipawa area, Témiscamingue County; Quebec Department of Natural Resources, Preliminary Report no. 502, 8 p.

157.   **Roberts, A.C. and Bonardi, M.**
        1983:   Potassian gaidonnayite from the Kipawa agpaitic syenite complex, Quebec; *in* Current
                Research, Part A; Geological Survey of Canada, Paper 83-1A, p. 480–482.

158.   **Roberts, W.L., Campbell, Thomas, J., and Rapp, G.R., Jr.**
        1990:   Encyclopedia of Minerals, 2nd edition; Van Nostrand Reinhold, New York, New York,
                979 p.

159.   **Robinson, G.W. and King,V.T.**
        1993:   What's new in minerals? Annual world summary of mineral discoveries, covering
                April 1992 through April 1993; The Mineralogical Record, v. 24, p. 381–394.

160.   **Robinson, S.C. and Sabina, A.P.**
        1955:   Uraninite and thorianite from Ontario and Quebec; The American Mineralogist, v. 40,
                p. 624–633.

161.   **Rose, E.R.**
        1958:   Iron deposits of eastern Ontario and adjoining Quebec; Geological Survey of Canada,
                Bulletin 45, 120 p.

162.   1960:   Rare-earths of the Grenville sub-province, Ontario and Quebec; Geological Survey of
                Canada, Paper 59-10, 41 p.

163.   **Ross, J.S.**
        1959:   An investigation of garnet from the Sudbury area, Ontario; Canada Department of
                Mines, Mines Branch, Investigation Report 59-65, 26 p.

164.   **Rowe, R.B.**
        1958:   Niobium (columbium) deposits of Canada; Geological Survey of Canada, Economic
                Geology Series 18, 108 p.

165.   **Russell, D.J. and Willims, D.A.**
        1985:   Paleozoic geology of the Pembroke area, southern Ontario; Ontario Geological Survey,
                Preliminary Map p. 2727, scale 1:50 000.

166.   **Sabina, A.P.**
        1964:   Rock and mineral collecting in Canada, Vol. II, Ontario and Quebec; Geological
                Survey of Canada, Miscellaneous Series 8, 252 p.

167.   **Sabourin, R.-J.-E.**
        1954:   Preliminary report on Onslow–Masham area, Pontiac and Gatineau counties; Quebec
                Department of Mines, Preliminary Report no. 293, 6 p.

168.   1965:   Bristol–Masham area, Pontiac and Gatineau counties; Quebec Department of Natural
                Resources, Geological Report 110, 44 p.

169.   **Satterly, J.**
        1943:   Mineral occurrences in the Parry Sound district; Ontario Department of Mines, Annual
                Report, v. 51, pt. 2, 1942, 86 p.

170.   1945:   Mineral occurrences in the Renfrew area; Ontario Department of Mines, Annual
                Report, v. 53, pt. 3, 1944, 139 p.

171.   1956:   Geology of Lount Township; Ontario Department of Mines, Annual Report, v. 64, pt. 6,
                1955, 46 p.

172.   1977:   A catalogue of the Ontario localities represented by the mineral collection of the Royal
                Ontario Museum; Ontario Geological Survey, Miscellaneous Paper 70, 463 p.

173.   **de Schmid, H.S.**
        1912:   Mica, its occurrence, exploitation and uses, second edition; Canada Department of
                Mines, Mines Branch, Publication 118, 411 p.

174.   1916:   Feldspar in Canada; Canada Department of Mines, Mines Branch, Publication 401,
                125 p.

175.   **Shaw, D.M.**
        1955:   Geology of the north part of Calumet Island, Pontiac County; Quebec Department of
                Mines, DP-09, 25 p.

176. 1956: Uranium; *in* Mining Operations in 1954, Metals; The Mining Industry of the Province of Quebec in 1954; Quebec Department of Mines, p. 6–30.

177. 1958: Radioactive mineral occurrences of the province of Quebec; Quebec Department of Mines, Geological Report 80, 52 p.

178. **Shaw, D.M., Moxham, R.L., Filby, R.H., and Laprowsky, W.W.**
      1963: The petrology and geochemistry of some Grenville skarns, Part I: geology and petrography; The Canadian Mineralogist, v. 7, p. 420–442.

179. **Shaw, D.M., Schwarcz, H.P., and Sheppard, S.M.F.**
      1965: The petrology of two zoned scapolite skarns; Canadian Journal of Earth Sciences, v. 2, p. 577–595.

180. **Shklanka, R.**
      1968: Iron deposits of Ontario; Ontario Department of Mines, Mineral Resources Circular 11, 489 p.

181. 1969: Copper, nickel, lead and zinc deposits of Ontario; Ontario Department of Mines, Mineral Resources Circular 12, 394 p.

182. **Sinclair, W.D., Jambor, J.L., and Birkett, T.C.**
      1992: Rare earths and the potential for rare-earth deposits in Canada; Exploration and Mining Geology, v. 1, p. 265–281

183. **Soever, A. and Meusy, G.**
      1987: The Cadieux (Renprior) zinc deposit; *in* Livret-guide excursion gîtes métallifères dans le sud du Grenville québecois, 25-26-27 mai, 1987, (éd.) André Vallières; ministère de l'Énergie et des Ressources, Québec, MB 88-10, p. 45–47.

184. **Spence, H.S.**
      1920: Phosphate in Canada; Canada Department of Mines, Mines Branch, Publication 396, 156 p.

185. 1920: Graphite; Canada Department of Mines, Mines Branch, Publication 511, 202 p.

186. 1922: Barium and strontium in Canada; Canada Department of Mines, Mines Branch, Publication 570, 100 p.

187. 1929: Mica; Canada Department of Mines, Mines Branch, Publication 701, 142 p.

188. 1932: Feldspar; Canada Department of Mines, Mines Branch, Publication 731, 145 p.

189. 1940: Talc, steatite, and soapstone; pyrophyllite; Canada Department of Mines, Mines Branch, Publication 803, 146 p.

190. 1947: The 'Bonanza' mica operation of Purdy Mica Mines, Limited, Mattawan Township, Ontario; American Institute of Mining Engineers, Technical Publication no. 2154, p. 1–17.

191. **Storey, C.C. and Vos, M.A.**
      1981: Industrial minerals of the Pembroke–Renfrew area, Part 1: marble; Ontario Geological Survey, Mineral Deposits Circular 21, 132 p.

192. 1981: Industrial minerals of the Pembroke–Renfrew area, Part 2; Ontario Geological Survey, Mineral Deposits Circular 22, 214 p.

193. **Strickland, D.**
      1987: Brent Crater Trail, History of the Crater; The Friends of Algonquin Park, Whitney, Ontario, 14 p.

194. **Sutherland, T.F., Collins, E.A., McMillan, J.G., and Bartlett, J.**
      1915: Mines of Ontario; Ontario Bureau of Mines, Annual Report, v. 24, pt. 1, 1915, p. 94–170.

195. **Sutherland, T.F., McMillan, J.G., Bartlett, J., Cole, G.E., and Webster, A.R.**
      1926: Mines of Ontario in 1924; Ontario Department of Mines, Annual Report, v. 34, pt. 1, 1925, p. 66–169.

196. **Themistocleous, S.G.**
1981: Geology of the Clontarf area, Renfrew County; Ontario Geological Survey, Report 209, 64 p.

197. 1981: Geology of the Khartum area, Renfrew County; Ontario Geological Survey, Report 211, 55 p.

198. **Traill, R.J.**
1983: Raw materials of Canada's mineral industry; Geological Survey of Canada, Paper 80-18, 432 p.

199. **Tremblay-Clark, P. and Kish, L.**
1978: Le district radioactif de Kipawa; ministère des Richesses naturelles, Québec, DPV-597, 28 p.

200. **Tremblay, M.**
1948: Statistical review of the mineral industry of Ontario for 1945; Ontario Department of Mines, Annual Report 1946, v. 55, pt. 1, p. 1–61.

201. **Trusler, J.R. and Villard, D.J.**
1978: 1977 Report of the Algonquin regional geologist; *in* Annual Report of the Regional and Resident Geologists 1977, (ed.) C.R. Kustra; Ontario Geological Survey, Miscellaneous Paper 78, p. 100–108.

202. **Uglow, W.L.**
1916: Lead and zinc deposits in Ontario and in eastern Canada; Ontario Bureau of Mines, Annual Report, v. 25, pt. 2, 1916, 56 p.

203. **Vennor, H.G.**
1878: Progress report of explorations and surveys made during the years 1875 and 1876, in the counties of Renfrew, Pontiac and Ottawa, together with additional notes on the iron ores, apatite, and plumbago deposits of Ottawa County; Geological Survey of Canada, Report of Progress for 1876-77, pt. 10, p. 244–320.

204. **Villard, D.J. and Garland, M.**
1985: Huntsville resident geologist area, Algonquin region; *in* Report of Activities, 1984, Regional and Resident Geologists, (ed.) C.R. Kustra; Ontario Geological Survey, Miscellaneous Paper 122, p. 242–246.

205. 1986: Huntsville resident geologist area, Algonquin region; *in* Report of Activities, 1985, Regional and Resident Geologists, (ed.) C.R. Kustra; Ontario Geological Survey, Miscellaneous Paper 128, p. 273–277.

206. **Villard, D.J., Keevil, R., and Marmont, C.**
1993: Algonquin resident geologist's district — 1992; *in* Report of Activities, 1992, Resident Geologists, (ed.) K.G. Fenwick, J.W. Newsome, and A.E. Pitts; Ontario Geological Survey, Miscellaneous Paper 161, p. 361–370.

207. **Villeneuve, D.**
1987: The Calumet project; *in* Livret-guide excursion gîtes métallifères dans le sud du Grenville québecois, 25-26-27 mai, 1987, (éd.) André Vallières; ministère de l'Énergie et des Ressources, Québec, MB 88-10, p. 35–39.

208. **Vokes, F.M.**
1983: Molybdenum deposits of Canada; Geological Survey of Canada, Economic Geology Series 20, 332 p.

209. **Vos, M.A., Smith, B.A., and Stevanato, R.J.**
1981: Industrial minerals of the Sudbury area; Ontario Geological Survey, Open File Report 5329, 148 p.

210. **Waite, G.G.**
1945: Notes on Canadian gems and ornamental stones; *in* University of Toronto Studies, Geological Series no. 49, Contributions to Canadian Mineralogy, 1944, p. 75–78.

211.   **Walker, T.L.**
       1911:   Report on the molybdenite ores of Canada; Canada Department of Mines, Mines Branch, Publication 93, 64 p.

212.   **Wight, W.**
       1995:   Canadian gemstones: old & new; The Canadian Gemmologist, v. 16, no. 3, p. 82–87.

213.   **Williams, I.**
       1950:   Mines of Ontario in 1948; Ontario Department of Mines, Annual Report, v. 58, pt. 2, 1949, 111 p.

214.   **Willimott, C.W.**
       1994:   Report on observations in 1883 on some mines and minerals in Ontario, Quebec and Nova Scotia; Geological Survey of Canada, Report of Progress 1882-83-84, pt. L, 28 p.

215.   1904:   Notes on molybdenite; *in* Bulletin on Molybdenum and Tungsten, by R.A.A. Johnston; Geological Survey of Canada, Publication no. 872, p. 15–16.

216.   **Wilson, A.E.**
       1946:   Brachiopoda of the Ottawa Formation of the Ottawa–St. Laurence Lowland; Geological Survey of Canada, Bulletin 8, 149 p.

217.   1948:   Miscellaneous classes of fossils, Ottawa Formation of the Ottawa–St. Lawrence valley; Geological Survey of Canada, Bulletin 11, 116 p.

218.   1951:   Gastropoda and conularida of the Ottawa Formation of the Ottawa–St. Lawrence Lowland; Geological Survey of Canada, Bulletin 17, 149 p.

219.   1956:   A guide to the geology of the Ottawa district; Canadian Field Naturalist, v. 70, no. 1, 68 p.

220.   1956:   Pelecypoda of the Ottawa Formation of the Ottawa–St. Lawrence Lowland; Geological Survey of Canada, Bulletin 28, 102 p.

221.   1961:   Cephalopoda of the Ottawa Formation of the Ottawa–St. Lawrence Lowland; Geological Survey of Canada, Bulletin 67, 106 p.

222.   1964:   Geology of the Ottawa–St. Lawrence Lowland, Ontario and Quebec; Geological Survey of Canada, Memoir 241, 66 p.

223.   **Wilson, M.E.**
       1921:   Mineral deposits in the Ottawa Valley; Geological Survey of Canada, Summary Report 1919, pt. E, p. 19–44.

224.   1924:   Arnprior–Quyon and Maniwaki areas, Ontario and Quebec, Geological Survey of Canada, Memoir 136, 152 p.

Anonymous publications

225.   1885:   Fitzroy lead mine; *in* The Canadian Mining Review, v. 3, no. 4, p. 6.

226.   1885:   Galetta lead mine; *in* The Canadian Mining Review, v. 3, no. 6, p. 5.

227.   1893:   Our mineral exhibits at the World's Fair; *in* The Canadian Mining and Mechanical Review, v. 12, no. 10, p. 170–172.

228.   1900:   Descriptive Catalogue of a Collection of the Economic Minerals of Canada, Paris International Exhibition 1900; Canadian Commission for the Exhibition, Ottawa, Ontario, 217 p.

229.   1945:   Canadian Mines Handbook 1945; Northern Miner Press Limited, Toronto, Ontario, 322 p.

230.   1945:   Mining operations in 1944: the mining industry of the province of Quebec in 1944; Quebec Department of Mines, p. 13–53.

231.   1949:   Canadian Mines Handbook 1949; Northern Miner Press Limited, Toronto, Ontario, 360 p.

232.   1956:   Description of mining properties visited in 1952 and 1953, an outline of geology and exploratory work; Quebec Department of Mines, Preliminary Report no. 330, 104 p.

233.   1970:   Canadian Mines Handbook 1969-70; Northern Miner Press, Toronto, Ontario, 456 p.

234.   1988:   Canadian Mines Handbook 1988-89; Northern Miner Press, Toronto, Ontario, 604 p.

235.   1990:   Canadian Mines Handbook 1990-91; Northern Miner Press, Toronto, Ontario, 588 p.

236.   1991:   Canadian Mines Handbook 1991-92; Southern Business Communications, Inc., Don Mills, Ontario, 536 p.

237.   1993:   Canadian Mines Handbook 1993-94; Southam Magazine Group, Don Mills, Ontario, 555 p.

238.   1994:   Canadian Mines Handbook 1994-95; Southam Magazine Group, Don Mills, Ontario, 567 p.

GLOSSARY

Acanthite. Ag_2S. H = 2–2.5. Iron-black, metallic, prismatic aggregates. Sectile. Low-temperature form of silver sulphide, argentite being the high-temperature form. Ore of silver associated with other silver minerals.

Acmite. Not a valid mineral name; renamed 'aegirine'.

Actinolite. $Ca_2(Mg,Fe)_5Si_8O_{22}(OH)_2$. H = 5–6. Bright green to greyish-green, columnar, fibrous, or radiating prismatic aggregates. Occurs in metamorphic rocks. Commonly associated with epidote. Monoclinic variety of amphibole.

Adularia. Transparent to translucent, generally colourless variety of K-feldspar; may exhibit an opalescent effect, or schiller, as in moonstone. Occurs as pseudorhombohedra in low-temperature hydrothermal veins in schist and gneiss.

Aegirine. $NaFeSi_2O_6$. H = 6. Dark green to almost black or greenish-brown; prismatic, commonly elongated and striated crystals. Monoclinic variety of pyroxene.

Agate. Patterned and variously coloured variety of microcrystalline quartz (chalcedony). Translucent to opaque; colours are due to metallic oxide mineral impurities. Used as an ornamental stone.

Agglomerate. Rock formed by the consolidation of angular fragments ejected by volcanoes.

Agrellite. $NaCa_2Si_4O_{10}F$. H = 5.5. White, greyish, or greenish flat prismatic crystals with excellent cleavage; pearly lustre. Occurs in alkalic rocks. Originally described from the Kipawa area, Quebec.

Akermanite. $Ca_2MgSi_2O_7$. H = 5. Colourless, greyish-green, brown to black; generally massive. Vitreous to resinous lustre. Subconchoidal fracture. Not readily distinguished in the hand specimen from other members of group. Melilite group.

Aktashite. $Cu_6Hg_3As_4S_{12}$. Grey, metallic. Occurs as grains with other mercury sulphide minerals.

Alaskite. Granitic rock composed of microcline, orthoclase, and quartz with few or no dark minerals such as amphibole, biotite, or pyroxene.

Albertite. Hydrocarbon. H = 1–2. Black with brilliant lustre. Occurs in shale in Albert County, New Brunswick. Also known as 'albert coal'. Name is derived from the locality.

Albite. $NaAlSi_3O_8$. H = 6. White, tabular, striated crystals, or cleavable masses. Vitreous lustre. Variety of plagioclase feldspar. Used in the manufacture of ceramics.

Allanite. $(Ce,Ca,Y)_2(Al,Fe)_3(SiO_4)_3(OH)$. H = 6.5. Black or dark brown tabular aggregates, or massive with conchoidal fracture. Vitreous or pitchy lustre. Generally occurs in granitic rocks, in pegmatite, and is commonly surrounded by an orange halo. Distinguished by its weak radioactivity.

Allargentum. $Ag_{1-x}Sb_x$. Grey, metallic grains occurring in native silver or as veinlets in calcite containing high-grade silver ore.

Allemontite. A mixture of stibarsen and arsenic or antimony. Not a valid mineral species.

Alloclasite. (Co,Fe)AsS. Light grey, metallic; compact radiating crystal aggregates. Occurs in cobalt deposits.

Allophane. Amorphous hydrous aluminosilicate. $H = 3$. Light blue, green, brown, yellow, or colourless encrustations or powdery masses, also stalactitic or mammillary. Vitreous to waxy. Decomposition product of aluminous silicates such as feldspar. Not a valid mineral species.

Alluaudite. (Na,Ca)Fe(Mn,Fe,Mg)$_2$(PO$_4$)$_3$. $H = 5$–5.5. Yellow to brownish-yellow, massive granular or compact radiating fibrous aggregates. Generally opaque. Occurs as an alteration of varulite-hühnerkobelite in pegmatite.

Almandine. Fe$_3$Al$_2$(SiO$_4$)$_3$. $H = 7$–7.5. Dark red transparent to opaque dodecahedral or trapezohedral crystals; also massive. Generally occurs in mica schist or gneiss; also in granite and pegmatite. Used as an abrasive (sand paper); transparent variety used as a gemstone. Garnet group.

Altaite. PbTe. $H = 3$. Light grey, metallic, with bronze tarnish. Generally massive, but may occur as cubic or cubo-octahedral crystals. Sectile with perfect cleavage. Occurs with native gold and with other tellurides and sulphides in vein deposits.

Alunogen. Al$_2$(SO$_4$)$_3$•17H$_2$O. $H = 1.5$–2. White fibrous crusts; powdery. Vitreous to silky lustre. Acid, sharp taste. Secondary mineral associated with pyrite or marcasite.

Amazonite. KAlSi$_3$O$_8$. $H = 6$. Green variety of microcline feldspar. Colour is due to natural irradiation of microcline containing Pb and H$_2$O. Occurs in pegmatite. Used as a gemstone and for ornamental purposes.

Amethyst. Violet variety of quartz. Colour is due to natural irradiation of quartz containing Fe. Generally occurs in igneous and volcanic rocks. Transparent variety is used as a gemstone.

Amphibole. A mineral group consisting of complex silicates including tremolite, actinolite, and hornblende. Common rock-forming mineral.

Amphibolite. A metamorphic rock composed essentially of amphibole and plagioclase.

Amygdaloidal lava. Fine-grained lava (basalt) with cavities (amygdales) that may be filled with quartz, calcite, chlorite, zeolites, etc.

Analcime (Analcite). NaAlSi$_2$O$_6$•H$_2$O. $H = 5$–5.5. Colourless, white, yellowish, or greenish vitreous, transparent, trapezohedral crystals, or massive granular. Distinguished from garnet by its inferior hardness. Often associated with other zeolites.

Anatase. TiO$_2$. $H = 5.5$–6. Yellowish or reddish-brown pyramidal or tabular crystals with adamantine lustre; also grey or blue. Massive. Also known as 'octahedrite'.

Ancylite. SrCe(CO$_3$)$_2$(OH)•H$_2$O. $H = 4$–4.5. Light yellow, yellowish-brown, or grey translucent prismatic crystals or rounded crystal aggregates. Splintery fracture. Soluble in acids. Rare mineral.

Andalusite. Al_2SiO_5. H = 7.5. White, grey, rose red, or brown prismatic crystals with almost square cross-section. Vitreous to dull lustre. Transparent to opaque. Chiastolite variety has carbonaceous inclusions arranged in crossed lines that are evident in cross-section. Occurs in metamorphosed shale. Used in the manufacture of mullite refractories, spark plugs; transparent variety used as a gemstone.

Andesite. A dark-coloured volcanic rock composed mainly of plagioclase feldspar with amphibole or pyroxene.

Andorite. $PbAgSb_3S_6$. H = 3–3.5. Dark grey, metallic, striated prismatic or tabular crystals; massive. Conchoidal fracture. Black streak. Soluble in HCl. Associated with sulphides and other sulphosalts.

Andradite. $Ca_3Fe_2(SiO_4)_3$. H = 7. Yellow, green, brown or black dodecahedral or trapezohedral crystals; massive. Occurs in chlorite schist, serpentinite, crystalline limestone. Gem varieties are demantoid (green), topazolite (yellow), and melanite (black). Garnet group.

Anglesite. $PbSO_4$. H = 2.5–3. Colourless to white, greyish, yellowish, or bluish tabular or prismatic crystals, or granular. Adamantine to resinous lustre. Characterized by high specific gravity (6.37) and adamantine lustre. Effervesces in HNO_3. Secondary mineral, generally formed from galena. Ore of lead.

Anhydrite. $CaSO_4$. H = 3–3.5. White, bluish, or greyish with vitreous lustre. Generally granular massive. Alters to gypsum by absorption of water. Distinguished from gypsum by its superior hardness. Used as a soil conditioner and in portland cement.

Ankerite. $Ca(Fe,Mg,Mn)(CO_3)_2$. Variety of dolomite from which it cannot be distinguished in the hand specimen.

Annabergite. $Ni_3(AsO_4)_2 \bullet 8H_2O$. H = 1.5–2.5. Light green, finely crystalline or earthy encrustations. Soluble in acids. Secondary mineral formed by oxidation of cobalt and nickel arsenides. Colour and association with nickel minerals are distinguishing characteristics. Referred to as 'nickel bloom'.

Anorthite. $CaAl_2Si_2O_8$. H = 6. White or greyish cleavable masses; prismatic, striated crystals. Plagioclase feldspar.

Anorthoclase. $(Na,K)AlSi_3O_8$. H = 6–6.5. Colourless, white with reddish, greenish, or yellowish tint. May exhibit polysynthetic twinning. Occurs in volcanic and other igneous rocks. Feldspar group.

Anorthosite. An igneous rock composed almost entirely of plagioclase.

Anthophyllite. $(Mg,Fe)_7Si_8O_{22}(OH)_2$. H = 6. White, light grey to brown fibrous or prismatic aggregates with vitreous or silky lustre. Distinguished from tremolite by its fibrous habit and silky lustre. Fibrous variety resembles asbestos, but is more brittle. Used in asbestos cement, for boiler coverings, and fireproof paints because of its resistance to heat. Orthorhombic variety of amphibole.

Anthraxolite. Hydrocarbon. H = 3–4. Black, massive. Submetallic to pitchy lustre. Uneven to conchoidal fracture. Friable, combustible. Exposed surface partly altered to orange powder.

Antigorite. $Mg_3Si_2O_5(OH)_4$. H = 2.5. Green translucent variety of serpentine with lamellar structure.

Antimony. Sb. H = 3–3.5. Light grey, metallic, cleavable, massive, also radiating or botryoidal. Perfect cleavage. Occurs in hydrothermal veins with silver, antimony, and arsenic ores. Minor source of antimony for use in alloys of lead and tin, and for flame-proofing textiles, paints, and ceramics.

Antiperthite. Lamellar intergrowth of potassium and sodium feldspars in which sodium feldspar is dominant.

Antlerite. $Cu_3SO_4(OH)_4$. H = 3.5. Emerald-green to dark green, tabular, prismatic, or acicular microscopic crystals. Vitreous lustre. Secondary mineral occurring in copper deposits. Ore of copper.

Apatite. $Ca_5(PO_4)_3(F,Cl,OH)$. H = 5. Green to blue, colourless, brown, or red hexagonal crystals or granular to sugary massive. Vitreous lustre. May be fluorescent. Distinguished from beryl and quartz by its inferior hardness; massive variety is distinguished from calcite and dolomite by lack of effervescence in HCl, and from diopside and olivine by its inferior hardness. Used in the manufacture of fertilizers and in the production of detergents. Apatite is a mineral group that includes the species fluorapatite, chlorapatite, hydroxylapatite, carbonate-fluorapatite.

Aplite. A light-coloured igneous (dyke) rock with fine-grained granitic texture and composition similar to granite.

Aplowite. $(Co,Mn,Ni)SO_4 \bullet 4H_2O$. H = 3. Pink, powdery, with vitreous lustre and white streak. Occurs as coatings on barite-siderite-sulphide specimens. Soluble in water. Originally described from the Magnet Cove barite mine, Walton, Nova Scotia, and named in honour of A.P. Low, director of the Geological Survey of Canada (1906–1907).

Apophyllite. $KCa_4(Si_4O_{10})_2(F,OH) \bullet 8H_2O$. H = 5. Colourless, grey, white, green, yellow, or less commonly, pink square, prismatic, or pyramidal crystals with pearly or vitreous lustre. Perfect basal cleavage and pearly lustre on cleavage face are diagnostic. Commonly associated with zeolites in basalt.

Aragonite. $CaCO_3$. H = 3.5–4. Colourless to white or grey and, less commonly, yellow, blue, green, violet, or rose-red prismatic or acicular crystals; also columnar, globular, or stalactitic aggregates. Vitreous lustre. Transparent to translucent. Distinguished from calcite by its cleavage, superior hardness, and higher specific gravity (2.93). Effervesces in dilute HCl. Pearly inner surfaces of sea shells and pearls are composed of aragonite.

Arfvedsonite. $Na_3(Fe,Mg)_4FeSi_8O_{22}(OH)_2$. H = 5–6. Greenish-black to black tabular or long prismatic crystals. Vitreous lustre. Occurs in alkalic igneous rocks. Monoclinic variety of amphibole.

Argentite. Ag_2S. H = 2–2.5. Dark grey, metallic, cubic or octahedral crystals; arborescent, massive. Very sectile. Occurs in sulphide deposits with other silver minerals. Inverts to acanthite at temperatures below 180°C.

Argentopentlandite. $Ag(Fe,Ni)_8S_8$. Bronze-brown metallic octahedral crystals; massive. Associated with pyrite, cubanite, and chalcopyrite in veins and in sulphide deposits.

Argillite. A clayey sedimentary rock without slaty cleavage or shaly fracture.

187

Arizonite. $Fe_2Ti_3O_9$. H = 3.5. Brown to black, platy or granular. Opaque; submetallic lustre. Reddish-brown streak. Alteration product of ilmenite.

Arkose. A sandstone in which feldspar grains predominate over quartz.

Armenite. $BaCa_2Al_6Si_9O_{30} \bullet 2H_2O$. H = 7.5. Colourless, white, or greyish-green prismatic crystals. Vitreous lustre. Associated with axinite, zoisite.

Arsenic. As. H = 3.5. Light grey to black, submetallic. Massive, reniform, or stalactitic. Volatile without fusion, giving off garlic odour. Occurs in veins with silver, cobalt, and nickel ores.

Arsenolite. As_2O_3. H = 1.5. White, botryoidal, stalactitic, earthy encrustations. Vitreous to silky lustre. Sweetish astringent taste. Secondary mineral formed by oxidation of arsenopyrite, smaltite, and other arsenic minerals.

Arsenopyrite. FeAsS. H = 5.5–6. Light to dark grey, metallic, striated prisms with characteristic wedge-shaped cross-section; also massive. Tarnishes to bronze colour. Ore of arsenic; may contain gold or silver.

Artinite. $Mg_2(CO_3)(OH)_2 \bullet 3H_2O$. H = 2.5. White acicular crystals; fibrous aggregates forming botryoidal, spherical masses and crossfibre veinlets. Transparent with vitreous, silky, or satin lustre. Occurs in serpentine. Distinguished from calcite by its form and lustre.

Asbestos. Fibrous variety of certain silicate minerals such as serpentine (chrysotile) and amphibole (anthophyllite, tremolite, actinolite, crocidolite) characterized by flexible, heat- and electrical-resistant fibres. Chrysotile is the only variety produced in Canada; it occurs as veins with fibres parallel (slip fibre) or perpendicular (crossfibre) to the vein walls. Used in the manufacture of asbestos cement sheeting, shingles, roofing, and floor tiles, millboard, thermal insulating paper, pipe covering, clutch and brake components, reinforcing in plastics, etc.

Asbolite. A mixture of manganese oxides (wad) containing cobalt oxide with or without oxides of nickel and copper. Occurs as dull-black earthy or compact masses.

Ashcroftine. $K_9Na_9(Y,Ca)_{12}Si_{28}O_{70}(OH)_2(CO_3)_8 \bullet 3H_2O$. Pink fibrous, prismatic, or powdery aggregates. Occurs in alkalic igneous rocks.

Asterism. Intersecting lines or bands of light forming a star, as seen in transmitted light in mica, or in reflected light in cabochon-cut sapphire, garnet, etc. Caused by light reflected from microscopic inclusions arranged along crystallographic directions.

Astrophyllite. $(K,Na)_3(Fe,Mn)_7Ti_2Si_8O_{24}(O,OH)_7$. H = 3. Golden-yellow to bronze-brown elongated crystals or blades, often radiating; also micaceous with pearly or splendent lustre. More brittle than mica. Generally occurs in nepheline syenite.

Atacamite. $Cu_2Cl(OH)_3$. H = 3–3.5. Green, prismatic, tabular aggregates; granular massive, fibrous. Adamantine to vitreous lustre. Soluble in acids. Associated with other secondary copper minerals.

Augite. $(Ca,Na)(Mg,Fe,Al,Ti)(Si,Al)_2O_6$. Dark green to black. Important constituent of basic and ultrabasic rocks. Monoclinic variety of pyroxene.

Augite syenite. A relatively coarse-textured igneous rock composed mainly of feldspar and pyroxene (augite) with little or no quartz. Used as a building stone.

Aurichalcite. $(Zn,Cu)_5(CO_3)_2(OH)_6$. H = 1–2. Light green or blue silky to pearly acicular or lath-like crystals forming tufted, feathery, plumose, laminated, or granular encrustations. Transparent. Soluble in acids and in ammonia. Secondary mineral occurring in oxidized zones of copper and zinc deposits, associated with other secondary copper and zinc minerals.

Aurostibite. $AuSb_2$. H = 3. Dark grey, metallic. Occurs as grains with gold and sulphide minerals. Resembles galena. Not readily identified in hand specimen.

Axinite. $(Ca,Mn,Fe,Mg)_3Al_2BSi_4O_{15}(OH)$. H = 7. Violet, pink, yellow to brown wedge-shaped crystals or massive, lamellar. Vitreous lustre. Fuses readily with intumescence. Occurs commonly in contact-altered calcareous rocks. Transparent varieties are used as gemstones.

Azurite. $Cu_3(CO_3)_2(OH)_2$. H = 3.5–4. Azure-blue to inky blue tabular or prismatic crystals; also massive, earthy, stalactitic with radial or columnar structure. Vitreous lustre; transparent. Secondary copper mineral. Effervesces in acids. Ore of copper.

Baddeleyite. ZrO_2. H = 6.5. Cream-white, yellowish, or amber scaly, finely granular, powdery aggregates. Greasy to dull lustre. Associated with fluorite, dawsonite at the Francon Quarry, Montréal.

Barite. $BaSO_4$. H = 3–3.5. White, pink, yellowish, or blue tabular or prismatic crystals; granular massive. Vitreous lustre. Characterized by high specific gravity (4.5) and perfect cleavage. Used in glass, paint, rubber, and chemical industries, and in oil-drilling technology.

Barylite. $BaBe_2Si_2O_7$. H = 7. Colourless, white, or bluish tabular, prismatic crystals, or massive. Transparent, vitreous. Perfect cleavage.

Basalt. Dark, fine-grained volcanic rock or lava composed predominantly of an amphibole or a pyroxene with plagioclase. Amygdaloidal basalt contains cavities that may be hollow or occupied by one or more minerals.

Basaluminite. $Al_4(SO_4)(OH)_{10} \bullet 5H_2O$. White, powdery to compact, massive. Dull lustre. Conchoidal fracture. Secondary mineral, associated with gypsum, aragonite.

Bassanite. $2CaSO_4 \bullet H_2O$. White microscopic prisms, fibres, plates. Silky to dull lustre. Associated with gypsum on which it may form chalky coatings. Dehydration product of gypsum; also occurs in volcanic rocks.

Bastnaesite. $(La,Ce)(CO_3)F$. H = 4–4.5. Yellowish to reddish-brown and grey platy, lath-shaped, or granular masses with dull, greasy, or pearly lustre; also greenish brown, earthy. Occurs with other rare-element minerals. Soluble in HCl. Difficult to identify in hand specimen.

Batholith. A very large body of coarse-textured igneous rocks such as granite or diorite.

Baumhauerite. $Pb_3As_4S_9$. H = 3. Grey, metallic, striated prismatic or tabular crystals. Brown streak. Occurs with other lead sulphosalt minerals.

Bavenite. $Ca_4Be_2Al_2Si_9O_{26}(OH)_2$. H = 5.5. White; greenish-, pinkish-, or brownish-white prismatic crystals; also fibrous or radiating lamellar aggregates. Vitreous lustre. Associated with beryl in granite pegmatite.

Behoite. $Be(OH)_2$. H = 4. Colourless, white pseudo-octahedral crystals. Vitreous lustre. Occurs in granitic pegmatite and in syenite.

Berthierite. $FeSb_2S_4$. H = 2–3. Dark steel-grey, metallic, striated prismatic crystals; fibrous or granular masses. Tarnished surface is iridescent or brown. Generally associated with stibnite and not readily distinguished from it in hand specimen.

Bertrandite. $Be_4Si_2O_7(OH)_2$. H = 6–7. Colourless or light yellow tabular or prismatic crystals. Vitreous or pearly lustre. Associated with beryl in granite pegmatite.

Beryl. $Be_3Al_2Si_6O_{18}$. H = 8. White, yellow, green, or blue hexagonal prisms, or massive with conchoidal or uneven fracture. Vitreous lustre; transparent to translucent. Distinguished from apatite by superior hardness, from topaz by its lack of perfect cleavage; massive variety distinguished from quartz by its higher density. Ore of beryllium with numerous uses in nuclear energy, space, aircraft, electronic, and scientific equipment industries; used as alloying agent with copper, nickel, iron, aluminum, and magnesium. Gem varieties include emerald and aquamarine.

Betafite. $(Ca,Na,U)_2(Ti,Nb,Ta)_2O_6(OH)$. H = 4–5.5. Brown to black, waxy to submetallic octahedral or modified octahedral crystals. Metamict. Occurs with euxenite, fergusonite, cyrtolite in granite pegmatite and in calcite veins.

Beta-uranophane. $(H_3O)_2Ca(UO_2)_2(SiO_4)_2 \bullet 3H_2O$. H = 2.5–3. Yellow to yellowish-green aggregates of acicular crystals or short prismatic crystals. Silky to waxy lustre. May fluoresce green in ultraviolet light. Secondary mineral occurring in granitic rocks and calcite veins containing uranium minerals.

Beudantite. $PbFe_3(AsO_4)(SO_4)(OH)_6$. H = 3.5–4.5. Dark green, brown, or black rhombohedral crystals; also yellow earthy or botryoidal masses. Vitreous, resinous to dull lustre. Secondary mineral occurring in iron and lead deposits. Difficult to distinguish in hand specimens from other yellowish secondary minerals.

Beyerite. $(Ca,Pb)Bi_2(CO_3)_2O_2$. H = 2–3. White, yellow, greenish-yellow to green or grey platy, tabular crystals, or earthy. Vitreous to dull lustre. Occurs as encrustations, or fillings in cavities and fractures. Secondary mineral formed from bismuth minerals.

Bindheimite. $Pb_2Sb_2O_6(O,OH)$. H = 4–4.5. Yellow to brown, white to grey or greenish powdery to earthy encrustations; also nodular. Secondary mineral found in antimony-lead deposits. Difficult to identify except by X-ray methods.

Biomicrite. Limestone composed of skeletal fossil debris and carbonate mud (micrite). Described by major fossil type present, e.g. crinoid biomicrite.

Biotite. $K(Mg,Fe)_3(Al,Fe)Si_3O_{10}(OH,F)_2$. H = 2.5–3. Dark brown or greenish-black, transparent, hexagonal, platy crystals; platy or scaly aggregates. Splendent lustre. Occurs in pegmatite, calcite veins, pyroxenite. Constituent of igneous rocks (granite, syenite, diorite, etc.) and metamorphic rocks (gneiss, schist). Elasticity of individual plates or sheets distinguishes it from chlorite. Sheet mica is used as electrical insulators and for furnace and stove doors (isinglass); ground mica is used in the manufacture of roofing materials, wallpaper, lubricants, and fireproofing material. Mica group.

Birnessite. $Na_4Mn_{14}O_{27} \bullet 9H_2O$. H = 1.5. Black opaque grains, granular aggregates, earthy. Dull lustre. Secondary mineral associated with other manganese minerals. Difficult to identify except by X-ray methods.

Bismoclite. BiOCl. H = 2–2.5. Cream-white to grey, brownish; greasy to silky, or dull lustre. Massive, earthy, columnar, fibrous, or scaly. Soluble in acids. Secondary mineral formed by alteration of bismuthinite or native bismuth.

Bismuth. Bi. H = 2–2.5. Light grey, metallic, reticulated crystal aggregates; also foliated or granular. Iridescent tarnish. Used as a component of low melting-point alloys and in medicinal and cosmetic preparations.

Bismuthinite. Bi_2S_3. H = 2. Dark grey, striated, prismatic, acicular crystals; also massive. Iridescent on tarnished surface. Ore of bismuth.

Bismutite. $Bi_2(CO_3)O_2$. H = 2.5–3.5. Yellowish-white to brownish-yellow, light green, or grey earthy or pulverulent masses; also fibrous crusts, spheroidal aggregates, scaly, or lamellar. Dull, vitreous, or pearly lustre. Effervesces in HCl. Uncommon secondary mineral formed by alteration of bismuth minerals.

Bitumen. Natural mixture of hydrocarbons that may be liquid (petroleum) or solid (asphalt or mineral pitch).

Bityite. $CaLiAl_2(AlBeSi_2)O_{10}(OH)_2$. H = 5.5. White, yellow, or brownish-white transparent tabular, pseudohexagonal crystals, or micaceous. Associated with lithium minerals in granite pegmatite.

"Black diamond". A siliceous hematite that, when polished, takes a high, mirror-like lustre. Used as a gemstone.

Boehmite. AlO(OH). H = 3. White with pearly to silky lustre. Flaky, fibrous, granular, or powdery aggregates; also pisolitic. Associated with other aluminum minerals.

Bog iron ore. Loose porous iron ore formed by precipitation of water in bogs or swampy areas. Ore consists of limonite, goethite, and/or hematite.

Bohdanowiczite. $AgBiSe_2$. H = 3. Dark grey, metallic, microscopic grains associated with other selenides and with sulphides.

Boltwoodite. $(H_3O)K(UO_2)(SiO_4)$. H = 3.5–4. Light yellow acicular, fibrous aggregates. Silky, vitreous, to dull lustre. Fluoresces dull green in ultraviolet light. Secondary mineral formed from uranium minerals.

Boracite. $Mg_3B_7O_{13}Cl$. H = 7–7.5. Colourless, white, yellow, green, or grey cubic or dodecahedral crystals; fibrous or granular aggregates. Transparent with vitreous lustre. Occurs in gypsum, halite, and potash deposits. Soluble in HCl.

Bornite. Cu_5FeS_4. H = 3. Reddish-brown, metallic. Usually massive. Tarnishes to iridescent blue, purple, etc. Ore of copper. Also known as 'peacock ore', 'variegated copper', 'vitreous copper', and 'purple copper ore'.

Botallackite. $Cu_2Cl(OH)_3$. Light green to bluish-green columnar crystals forming crusts. Secondary mineral associated with other copper minerals.

Boulangerite. $Pb_5Sb_4S_{11}$. H = 2.5–3. Dark bluish-grey, metallic; striated, elongated, prismatic to acicular crystals; also fibrous, plumose aggregates. Fibrous cleavage is distinguishing characteristic. Ore of antimony.

Bournonite. $PbCuSbS_3$. $H = 2.5–3$. Grey to blackish-grey, metallic. Short prismatic or tabular crystals with striations; massive. Occurs in veins with sulphides and sulphosalts. Not readily identified in the hand specimen.

Brannerite. $(U,Ca,Y,Ce)(Ti,Fe)_2O_6$. $H = 4.5$. Black opaque grains, prismatic crystals, granular masses. Resinous to dull lustre. Brownish-yellow on weathered surfaces. Conchoidal fracture. Radioactive. Ore of uranium.

Bravoite. $(Ni,Fe)S_2$. Yellow to grey, metallic, with violet tinge. Pyrite group. Resembles pyrite except for colour.

Breccia. A rock composed of angular fragments; may be attractively patterned and coloured and used as an ornamental rock.

Breithauptite. $NiSb$. $H = 5.5$. Light copper-red with violet tint. Metallic lustre. Occurs as disseminated grains, massive, arborescent, and rarely as tabular or prismatic crystals. Reddish-brown streak. Associated with silver and nickel minerals in vein deposits.

Breunnerite. A variety of magnesite containing iron. White, yellowish- to brownish-white.

Britholite. $(Y,Ce,Ca)_5(SiO_4,PO_4)_3(OH,F)$. Tan to brown prisms, platy aggregates, and massive. Resinous lustre. Difficult to distinguish in the hand specimen.

Brochantite. $Cu_4(SO_4)(OH)_6$. $H = 3.5–4$. Green acicular crystal aggregates; massive, granular. Vitreous lustre. Secondary mineral formed by oxidation of copper minerals. Distinguished from malachite by lack of effervescence in HCl.

Brookite. TiO_2. $H = 5.5–6$. Dark brown to black tabular or pyramidal crystals with metallic, adamantine lustre. Not readily identifiable in the hand specimen.

Brucite. $Mg(OH)_2$. $H = 2.5$. White, grey, light blue, or green tabular, platy, foliated, or fibrous aggregates; also massive. Pearly or waxy lustre. Soluble in HCl. Distinguished from gypsum and talc by its superior hardness and lack of greasy feel. Resembles asbestos, but lacks silky lustre. More brittle than muscovite. Used for refractories and as a minor source of magnesium metal.

Brugnatellite. $Mg_6Fe(CO_3)(OH)_{13}•4H_2O$. $H = 2$. White silky, pearly, or waxy; flaky, aggregates, or foliated lamellar nodules; may be tinted reddish, yellowish, brownish. Associated with brucite and serpentine.

Burbankite. $(Na,Ca)_3(Sr,Ba,Ce)_3(CO_3)_5$. $H = 3.5$. Tiny yellow or greyish-yellow hexagonal crystals, massive; also colourless to reddish-pink fine hair-like aggregates in cavities with calcite. Associated with other rare-element minerals. Effervesces in HCl. Not readily identifiable in the hand specimen.

Cabochon. A polished gemstone having a convex surface; translucent or opaque minerals such as opal, agate, jasper, and jade are generally cut in this style.

Cadmoselite. $CdSe$. $H = 4$. Black microscopic grains with resinous to adamantine lustre. Rare mineral associated with other selenium and cadmium minerals.

Cafarsite. $Ca_8(Ti,Fe,Mn)_{6-7}(AsO_3)_{12}•4H_2O$. Dark brown cubic, octahedral, or dodecahedral crystals. Opaque. Conchoidal fracture. Yellowish-brown streak.

Calaverite. $AuTe_2$. H = 2.5–3. Brass-yellow to silver-white, metallic, bladed, lath-like, or striated short prismatic crystals. Fuses readily; on charcoal, gives bluish-green flame and gold globules. Ore of gold. Occurs in veins with pyrite, native gold.

Calcite. $CaCO_3$. H = 3. Colourless or white rhombohedral, scalenohedral crystals; cleavable, granular massive. May be variously coloured due to impurities. Transparent to opaque. Vitreous, pearly, or dull lustre. May fluoresce in ultraviolet light. Effervesces in dilute HCl. Distinguished from dolomite by its inferior hardness and superior solubility in HCl. Major constituent of chalk and limestone.

Cancrinite. $Na_6Ca_2Al_6O_{24}(CO_3)_2$. H = 6. Yellow, pink, or grey massive or prismatic crystals; vitreous to greasy lustre. Effervesces in warm HCl. Associated with nepheline and sodalite in nepheline syenite.

Carbonate-cyanotrichite. $Cu_4Al_2(CO_3,SO_4)(OH)_{12}•2H_2O$. H = 2. Light blue to medium blue, finely granular encrustations with vitreous lustre; also silky fibrous. Secondary mineral formed from copper minerals and associated with other secondary copper minerals. Dissolves in HCl.

Carbonatite. Carbonate rock formed by the reaction of basic magma with limestone and dolomite.

Carletonite. $KNa_4Ca_4Si_8O_{18}(CO_3)_4(F,OH)•H_2O$. H = 4–4.5. Colourless, pink, or light blue flakes. Transparent to translucent; vitreous to pearly. New species originally described from Mount Saint-Hilaire, Quebec, where it is associated with pectolite, albite, arfvedsonite, calcite, fluorite, and apophyllite. Named in honour of Carleton University where this and several other new species have been identified.

Carnallite. $KMgCl_3.•6H_2O$. H = 2.5. Colourless to white tabular crystals, or granular massive. Greasy or dull lustre. Deliquescent and soluble in water. Bitter taste. Occurs with halite and sylvite.

Carnelian. Red to reddish-brown or reddish-yellow translucent variety of chalcedony. Used as a gemstone.

Carrollite. $Cu(Co,Ni)_2S_4$. H = 4.5–5.5. Grey, metallic; tarnishes to copper-red or violet-grey. Granular massive; octahedral crystals. Occurs with other sulphide minerals in vein deposits.

Cassiterite. SnO_2. H = 6–7. Yellow to brown prismatic crystals; twinning common. Also radiating fibrous, botryoidal, or concretionary masses; granular. Adamantine to splendent lustre. White to brownish or greyish streak. Distinguished from other light-coloured nonmetallic minerals by its high specific gravity (6.99), from wolframite by its superior hardness. Ore of tin. Concentrically banded variety is used as a gemstone. Occurs with gold in placers in Yukon Territory.

Catapleiite. $Na_2ZrSi_3O_9•2H_2O$. H = 6. Light yellow, tan, yellowish-brown, or colourless hexagonal plates with vitreous to greasy lustre. Occurs in nepheline syenite where it can be distinguished by its platy habit.

Cattierite. CoS_2. H = 4. Pinkish metallic granular intergrowths with other sulphide minerals; cubic crystals to 1 cm across.

Caysichite. $Ca,GdY_4Si_8O_{20}(CO_3)_6(OH) \bullet 2H_2O$. Colourless, white, yellow, or green coatings or encrustations with divergent columnar structure. Associated with other yttrium minerals. Originally described from the Evans-Lou mine near Wakefield, Quebec. Named for the elements Ca, Y, Si, C, H.

Celadonite. $K(Mg,Fe)(Fe,Al)Si_4O_{10}(OH)_2$. $H = 2$. Bluish-green to greyish-green scaly, fibrous, or earthy compact masses. Occurs in basalt with zeolites and quartz. Mica group.

Celestine. $SrSO_4$. $H = 3–3.5$. Transparent, colourless, white, or light blue tabular crystals; also fibrous, massive. Vitreous lustre. Perfect cleavage. Flame test produces crimson colour. Resembles barite but not as heavy. Ore of strontium.

Cement rock. *See* waterlime.

Cenosite. *See* kainosite.

Cernyite. Cu_2CdSnS_4. $H = 4$. Steel-grey, metallic. Occurs as rare grains in pegmatite at the type locality, the Bernic Lake (Tanco) mine, in Manitoba. Named in honour of Professor Petr Cerny, University of Manitoba.

Cerussite. $PbCO_3$. $H = 3–3.5$. Transparent white, grey, or brownish tabular crystals with adamantine lustre; also massive. High specific gravity (6.5) and lustre are distinguishing features. Secondary mineral formed by oxidation of lead minerals. Fluoresces yellow in ultraviolet light. Soluble in dilute HNO_3. Ore of lead.

Cervantite. Sb_2O_4. $H = 4–5$. Yellow to yellowish-white powdery or fibrous crust. Greasy, pearly, or earthy lustre. Secondary mineral formed by oxidation of antimony minerals.

Chabazite. $CaAl_2Si_4O_{12} \bullet 6H_2O$. $H = 4$. Square colourless, white, yellowish, or pinkish crystals. Vitreous lustre. Occurs in cavities in basalt. Distinguished from other zeolites by its almost cubic crystal form, from calcite by its superior hardness and its lack of effervescence in HCl.

Chalcanthite. $CuSO_4 \bullet 5H_2O$. $H = 2.5$. Light to dark blue tabular or short prismatic crystals; massive, granular. Vitreous lustre. Metallic taste. Secondary mineral formed in copper sulphide deposits. Distinguished from azurite by lack of effervescence in HCl.

Chalcedony. SiO_2. $H = 7$. Translucent microcrystalline variety of quartz. Colourless, grey, bluish, yellowish, reddish, brown. Formed from aqueous solutions. Attractively coloured chalcedony is used for ornamental objects and jewellery. Varieties include agate, carnelian, jasper, etc.

Chalcoalumite. $CuAl_4(SO_4)(OH)_{12} \bullet 3H_2O$. $H = 2.5$. Light blue, bluish-green, or bluish-grey, transparent to translucent, platy, fibrous aggregates. Vitreous to dull lustre. Secondary mineral associated with copper minerals.

Chalcocite. Cu_2S. $H = 3.5–4$. Dark grey to black, metallic; massive. Tarnishes to iridescent blue, purple, etc. Also referred to as 'vitreous copper', 'sulphurette of copper', and 'copper glance'. Soluble in HNO_3. Black colour and slight sectility distinguish it from other copper sulphides. Ore of copper.

Chalcopyrite. $CuFeS_2$. $H = 3.5–4$. Brass-yellow, massive, or as tetrahedral crystals. Iridescent tarnish. Brass colour distinguishes it from pyrrhotite. Distinguished from pyrite by its inferior hardness, from gold by its superior hardness and lower density. Also called 'copper pyrite' and 'yellow copper'. Ore of copper.

Chalcostibite. $CuSbS_2$. H = 3–4. Dark grey metallic blade-like crystals, or massive. Associated with copper and antimony minerals.

Chamosite. $(Fe,Mg)_5Al(Si_3Al)O_{10}(O,OH)_8$. H = 3. Yellowish to dull green or grey earthy or clay-like masses. Occurs in some sedimentary iron deposits. Chlorite group.

Chapmanite. $SbFe_2(SiO_4)_2(OH)$. H = 2. Yellowish-green lath-shaped crystals; powdery. Alteration product of silver-antimony minerals. Associated with native silver. Originally described from the Keeley mine, Cobalt district, Ontario. Named in honour of Edward J. Chapman, professor of mineralogy (1853–1895), University of Toronto.

Chert. SiO_2. H = 7. Massive opaque variety of chalcedony; generally drab colours: various tints of grey or brown.

Chloanthite. $(Ni,Co)As_3$. Member of the skutterudite series, high in nickel. Not distinguishable in hand specimen from other members of the series — smaltite and skutterudite in which the cobalt nickel content is variable. Variety of nickel-skutterudite; not a valid mineral name.

Chlorite. $(Mg,Fe,Al)_6(Al,Si)_4O_{10}(OH)_8$. H = 2–2.5. Transparent green flaky aggregates. Distinguished from mica by its colour and by its flexible, but nonelastic, flakes. Occurs in metamorphic, igneous, and volcanic rocks. Alteration product of amphibole, pyroxene, biotite.

Chloritoid. $(Fe,Mg,Mn)_2Al_4Si_2O_{10}(OH)_4$. H = 6.5. Dark grey to black tabular crystals; also platy, scaly, foliated aggregates and massive. Translucent. Pearly lustre. Occurs in schist, lava.

Chlorophane. A variety of fluorite that phosphoresces bright green when heated. Not a valid mineral name.

Chondrodite. $(Mg,Fe)_5(SiO_4)_2(F,OH)_2$. H = 6–6.5. Orange-yellow grains and granular masses. Vitreous to slightly resinous lustre. Subconchoidal to uneven fracture. Occurs in crystalline limestone and in skarn deposits. Orange colour is distinguishing feature. Distinguished from tourmaline by its inferior hardness, from apatite by its superior hardness. Humite group.

Chrome-mica. Green chromium-bearing mica. Also known as "fuchsite".

Chromite. $FeCr_2O_4$. H = 5.5. Black metallic octahedral crystals (rare); generally massive. Distinguished from magnetite by its brown streak and weak magnetism. Commonly associated with serpentine. Ore of chromium.

Chrysoberyl. $BeAl_2O_4$. H = 8.5. Yellow, green, or brown tabular or short prismatic crystals commonly striated and twinned forming six broad radiating spokes. Vitreous; transparent to opaque. Transparent variety is used as a gemstone. Other gem varieties include alexandrite, which is green in natural light and red in artifical light, and cat's-eye, which exhibits a movable streak of light when cut in the cabochon style. Occurs in pegmatite and in mica schist.

Chrysocolla. $(Cu,Al)_2H_2(Si_2O_5)(OH)_4 \bullet nH_2O$. H = 2–4. Blue to blue-green, earthy, botryoidal, or fine grained massive. Conchoidal fracture. Secondary mineral found in oxidized zones of copper-bearing veins. Often intimately mixed with quartz or chalcedony, producing attractive patterns; being mixed with these minerals gives chrysocolla a superior hardness that renders it suitable for use in jewellery and ornamental objects. Minor ore of copper.

Chrysotile. Fibrous variety of serpentine (asbestos).

Cinnabar. HgS. H = 2–2.5. Orange-red to brownish-red, dark grey, rhombohedral, tabular, or prismatic crystals; also granular to earthy massive. Adamantine, metallic, or dull lustre. Opaque. Perfect cleavage. Occurs in veins formed at low temperatures. Commonly associated with pyrite, marcasite, and stibnite in silica-carbonate gangue. Ore of mercury.

Clausthalite. PbSe. H = 2.5–3. Dark grey metallic with bluish tint. Granular massive, foliated. Associated with other selenides in ore deposits.

Cleavelandite. Platy, tabular, or lamellar variety of albite; white with pearly lustre.

Clinopyroxene. Monoclinic. Pyroxene group. Includes aegirine, augite, clinoenstatite, diopside.

Clinosafflorite. $(Co,Fe,Ni)As_2$. Monoclinic variety of safflorite. Associated with skutterudite in cobalt deposits.

Clinozoisite. $Ca_2Al_3(SiO_4)_3(OH)$. H = 7. Light green to greenish-grey prismatic crystals; also granular or fibrous masses. Vitreous lustre. Perfect cleavage. Epidote group. Occurs in metamorphic rocks.

Cobalt bloom. Term used by miners for erythrite.

Cobaltite. CoAsS. H = 5.5. Light grey metallic crystals (cubes, pyritohedrons), or massive. Perfect cleavage. Pinkish tinge distinguishes it from other grey metallic minerals. Crystals resemble pyrite, but differ in colour. Associated with cobalt and nickel sulphides or arsenides. Ore of cobalt.

Cobalt pentlandite. Co_9S_8. A rare mineral intimately associated with sulphides and arsenides in ore deposits at Cobalt, Ontario.

Coffinite. $U(SiO_4)_{1-x}(OH)_{4x}$. H = 5–6. Black with adamantine lustre; dull brown. Finely granular massive. Associated with uraninite from which it is indistinguishable in the hand specimen.

Colemanite. $Ca_2B_6O_{11} \bullet 5H_2O$. H = 4.5. Colourless to white prismatic crystals; cleavable or granular massive. Transparent to translucent with vitreous lustre. Flame test produces green colour. Occurs in borate and gypsum deposits.

Colerainite. $(Mg,Fe)_5Al(Si_3Al)O_{10}(OH)_8$. Thin, colourless to white, hexagonal plates forming rosettes and botryoidal aggregates. Pearly lustre. Associated with serpentine. Named for Coleraine Township, Quebec, where it was first found. Variety of clinochlore. Not a valid mineral name.

Coloradoite. HgTe. H = 2.5. Dark grey to black, metallic, granular masses. Soluble in HNO_3. Occurs with gold and silver tellurides.

Columbite. $(Fe,Mn)(Nb,Ta)_2O_6$. H = 6–7. Brownish-black to black prismatic or tabular crystals forming divergent or parallel groups; also massive. Submetallic lustre. Black to reddish-brown streak. Occurs in pegmatite. Ore of niobium used in high-temperature steel alloys.

Colusite. $Cu_{26}V_2(As,Sn,Sb)_6S_{32}$. H = 3–4. Bronze-yellow to bronze-brown granular massive or tetrahedral crystals. Associated with other copper minerals in ore deposits.

Concretion. Rounded mass formed in sedimentary rocks by accretion of some constituent (iron oxides, silica, etc.) around a nucleus (mineral impurity, fossil fragment, etc.).

Conglomerate. A sedimentary rock composed of rounded pebbles or gravel.

Connellite. $Cu_{19}Cl_4(SO_4)(OH)_{32} \bullet 3H_2O$. H = 3. Light azure-blue, translucent, acicular crystals. Vitreous lustre. Distinguished from azurite by lack of effervescence in HCl and by lighter colour.

Cookeite. $LiAl_4(Si_3Al)O_{10}(OH)_8$. H = 2.5–3.5. White, pink, greenish, yellowish, or brown pseudohexagonal plates; also scaly. Transparent to translucent with pearly or silky lustre. Occurs with lithium minerals in granite pegmatite. Chlorite group.

Copiapite. $Fe_5(SO_4)_6(OH)_2 \bullet 20H_2O$. H = 2.5–3. Light yellow to orange-yellow and greenish-yellow granular to scaly aggregates; also tabular crystals. Transparent to translucent. Vitreous to pearly lustre. Secondary mineral formed by oxidation of sulphides, especially pyrite. Yellow colour is characteristic.

Copper. Cu. H = 2.5–3. Massive, filiform, or arborescent; crystals (cubic or dodecahedral) rare. Hackly fracture. Ductile and malleable. Occurs in lava.

Coquimbite. $Fe_2(SO_4)_3 \bullet 9H_2O$. H = 2.5. White, yellowish, greenish, or violet, massive; also prismatic crystals. Vitreous lustre. Astringent taste. Secondary mineral formed from pyrite ore.

Cordierite. $Mg_2Al_4Si_5O_{18}$. H = 7. Blue to purplish-blue, bluish-grey, or colourless massive or irregular grains. Vitreous lustre. Subconchoidal fracture. Alters readily to muscovite or chlorite. Distinguished by its colour and by its alteration products. Occurs in metamorphic rocks (schist, gneiss). Gem variety is known as iolite.

Cordylite. $(Ce,La)_2Ba(CO_3)_3F_2$. H = 4.5. Short colourless or yellowish hexagonal prisms. Transparent; greasy to adamantine, pearly lustre. Occurs in nepheline syenite rocks.

Corundum. Al_2O_3. H = 9. Blue, red, yellow, violet, or brown hexagonal prisms or barrel-shaped, pyramidal, or flat tabular crystals. Uneven to conchoidal fracture. Adamantine to vitreous lustre. Distinguished by its hardness and characteristic barrel-shaped form. Used as an abrasive. Transparent red (ruby), blue (sapphire), yellow, and violet varieties are used as gemstones. Translucent varieties may produce star ruby and star sapphire gemstones.

Cosalite. $Pb_2Bi_2S_5$. H = 2.5–3. Dark grey, metallic, prismatic, needle-like, fibrous, or feathery aggregates; massive. Soluble in HNO_3. Associated with smaltite and cobaltite.

Covellite. CuS. H = 1.5–2. Inky blue, metallic; iridescent in shades of brass yellow, purple, coppery red. Massive; platy crystals (hexagonal) rare. Distinguished from chalcocite and bornite by its perfect cleavage and colour.

Crandallite. $CaAl_3(PO_4)_2(OH)_5 \bullet H_2O$. H = 5. Minute yellow to white or grey prisms; also fibrous, nodular, or finely granular massive. Transparent to translucent with vitreous or dull lustre. Occurs with other secondary phosphate minerals.

Criddleite. $TlAg_2Au_3Sb_{10}S_{10}$. Fine grey metallic grains (up to 50 µm) associated with aurostibite; recognized only by microscopic examination of polished sections. Occurs in the Hemlo gold deposit, the type locality. Named in honour of ore mineralogist Alan J. Criddle, British Museum, London.

Cristobalite. SiO_2. H = 6.5. White, grey, bluish octahedral (less than 1 mm) crystals; fibrous, massive, stalactitic, botryoidal. Translucent to opaque; vitreous to dull lustre. Occurs in volcanic rocks.

Crocidolite. Blue or bluish-grey asbestiform variety of riebeckite (amphibole). Known as 'blue asbestos'. Used as an insulator. Not a valid mineral name.

Crocoite. $PbCrO_4$. H = 2.5–3. Red-orange to yellow prismatic crystals; massive. Transparent to translucent; adamantine to vitreous lustre. Secondary mineral formed by oxidation of minerals containing lead and chromium.

Cryolite. Na_3AlF_6. H = 2.5. Colourless, yellow, reddish, or brownish, massive granular; crystals with cubo-octahedral aspect. Transparent; vitreous to greasy. Appears to disappear when immersed in water. Soluble in H_2SO_4.

Cryptomelane. KMn_8O_{16}. H = 6–6.5. Grey, greyish-black to black compact to loosely granular massive; also radiating fibres, botryoidal. Metallic to dull lustre. Brownish-black streak. Secondary mineral associated with manganese minerals.

Crystalline limestone. A limestone that has been metamorphosed or recrystallized. Also known as 'marble'. Used as building, monument, and ornamental stone. Dolomitic crystalline limestone contains a high proportion of dolomite.

Cubanite. $CuFe_2S_3$. H = 3.5. Brass-yellow to bronze-yellow tabular crystals, or massive. Distinguished from chalcopyrite by its strong magnetism. Associated with other copper-iron sulphides. Rare mineral.

Cuprite. Cu_2O. H = 3.5–4. Red to almost black octahedral, dodecahedral, or cubic crystals, massive, earthy. Adamantine, submetallic, or earthy lustre. Brownish-red streak. Distinguished from hematite by its inferior hardness, from cinnabar and proustite by its superior hardness. On charcoal, it is reduced to a metallic globule of copper. Soluble in concentrated HCl. Associated with native copper and other copper minerals. Ore of copper.

Curite. $Pb_2U_5O_{17}•4H_2O$. H = 4–5. Orange, yellow-brown, greenish yellow to greenish-brown, finely granular. Waxy to dull lustre. Strongly radioactive. Associated with uraninite.

Cyanotrichite. $Cu_4Al_2(SO_4)(OH)_{12}•2H_2O$. Minute sky-blue to azure-blue acicular crystals commonly radiating; also extremely fine, plush or wool-like aggregates. Silky lustre. Secondary mineral found sparingly in copper deposits.

Cyrtolite. A radioactive zircon containing uranium and rare elements. Not a valid mineral name.

Dachiardite. $(Ca,Na_2,K_2)_5Al_{10}Si_{38}O_{96}•25H_2O$. H = 4–4.5. Colourless to white prismatic crystals, or fibres forming parallel, divergent groups. Transparent; vitreous to silky lustre. Zeolite group.

Dacite. An igneous rock composed mainly of plagioclase with some quartz and pyroxene or hornblende.

Danaite. $(Fe,Co)AsS$. Variety of arsenopyrite containing up to 9% cobalt. Not a valid mineral name.

Danburite. $CaB_2(SiO_4)_2$. H = 7. Transparent colourless, light yellow prismatic crystals; white nodules. Clear, colourless danburite is used as a gemstone.

Datolite. $CaBSiO_4(OH)$. H = 6.5. Short, transparent, colourless, light yellow, green, or white prismatic crystals; also botryoidal porcelain-like masses, or granular. Vitreous lustre. Easily fusible. Distinguished by its colour, glassy appearance, crystal form, and ease of fusibility.

Dawsonite. $NaAl(CO_3)(OH)_2$. H = 3. Transparent, striated, square prismatic crystals; rosettes or encrustations of bladed or acicular crystals; tufts of colourless needles; also very fine micaceous aggregates. Lustre is vitreous or pearly in crystals, and silky in micaceous variety. Effervesces in HCl. Distinguished by its striated crystal form. Generally difficult to identify in the hand specimen because crystals are very small. Originally found in Montréal, Quebec, near the McGill University campus. Named for John William Dawson (1820–1899), geologist and principal of McGill University.

Devilline. $CaCu_4(SO_4)_2(OH)_6 \bullet 3H_2O$. H = 2.5. Bright green to bluish-green, transparent, platy crystals forming rosettes or tiny masses. Associated with azurite, malachite on copper-bearing rocks; not readily distinguishable from other secondary copper minerals in the hand specimen.

Diabase. Dark-coloured igneous rock composed mostly of lath-shaped crystals of plagioclase and pyroxene. Used as a building, ornamental, and monument stone.

Diaspore. $AlO(OH)$. H = 6.5–7. White, grey, yellow, brown, light violet, pink, or colourless foliated, scaly, granular, or massive aggregates. Platy or acicular crystals. Pearly, vitreous, or brilliant lustre. Associated with aluminous minerals in igneous and metamorphic rocks.

Diatomite. Pulverulent material composed of the siliceous remains of tiny organisms (diatoms), which accumulated on the bottoms of lakes and swamps in Recent geological time. Lightweight and resembles chalk. Used for insulation, filtration, abrasives, absorbents, etc.

Digenite. Cu_9S_5. H = 2.5–3. Bluish-black to black with submetallic lustre. Occurs as pseudocubic crystals or as intergrowths with other copper sulphides.

Diopside. $CaMgSi_2O_6$. H = 6. Colourless, white, grey, green, blue. Transparent to opaque with vitreous lustre. Occurs as short prisms or granular masses in calcium-rich metamorphic rocks. Monoclinic variety of pyroxene.

Diorite. A dark-coloured igneous rock composed mainly of plagioclase and amphibole or pyroxene.

Djurleite. $Cu_{1.96}S$. Properties similar to those of chalcocite from which it is indistinguishable in the hand specimen. Occurs in some Cobalt, Ontario, ore deposits.

Dolomite. $CaMg(CO_3)_2$. H = 3.5–4. Colourless, white, pink, yellow, or grey rhombohedral or saddle-shaped crystals; also massive. Vitreous to pearly lustre. Slightly soluble in cold HCl. Common vein-filling mineral in ore deposits and essential constituent of dolomitic limestone and dolomitic marble. Ore of magnesium used in the manufacture of lightweight alloys.

Dolomitic limestone. Limestone containing 10% to 50% dolomite.

Domeykite. Cu_3As. H = 3–3.5. Light grey, metallic; massive, reniform, or botryoidal. Becomes yellowish to brown or iridescent when tarnished. Occurs with other copper minerals. Soluble in HNO_3 but not in HCl.

Donnayite. $NaCaSr_3Y(CO_3)_6•3H_2O$. H = 3. Yellow, colourless, white, grey, brown, or red-dish-brown platy, tabular, columnar, or granular aggregates. Vitreous lustre. Associated with microcline, analcime, calcite, natrolite, chlorite, aegirine, and arfvedsonite in nepheline syenite at the type locality, Mount Saint-Hilaire, Quebec. It was named in honour of Professors J.D.H. Donnay and Gabrielle Donnay, McGill University.

Doverite. *See* synchysite-Y.

Doyleite. $Al(OH)_3$. H = 2.5–3. White platy crystals forming rosettes; pulverulent to compact globules, crusts. Dull lustre. Originally described from Mount Saint-Hilaire, Quebec, where it occurs in albitite, and from Francon quarry, Montréal, where it occurs on weloganite, calcite, and quartz. Named in honour of its discoverer, mineral collector E.J. Doyle of Ottawa.

Dresserite. $Ba_2Al_4(CO_3)_4(OH)_8•3H_2O$. H = 2.5–3. White to colourless spheres commonly 3 to 4 mm in diameter; blade-like crystals with oblique terminations forming tufts, spheres. Transparent to translucent, opaque; silky to vitreous lustre. Effervesces in HCl. Distinguished from dawsonite by its oblique termination. Associated with weloganite in quartz-albite-lined cavities in igneous sill rock at the Francon quarry, Montréal, Quebec, the type locality. Named in honour of geologist John A. Dresser (1866–1954) in recognition of his geological work in the Monteregian Hills, Quebec.

Dufrenoysite. $Pb_2As_2S_5$. H = 3. Long, grey, metallic, striated tabular crystals. Reddish-brown streak. Perfect cleavage. Associated with sphalerite and arsenic minerals.

Dumortierite. $Al_7(BO_3)(SiO_4)_3O_3$. H = 7. Blue, violet, or greenish-blue columnar or fibrous masses; also massive. Vitreous or dull lustre. Transparent to translucent. Difficult to distinguish from cordierite except by X-ray methods. Used in the manufacture of porcelain spark plugs and as a gemstone.

Dundasite. $PbAl_2(CO_3)_2(OH)_4•H_2O$. H = 2. White silky to vitreous radiating crystals, spherical aggregates, matted encrustations. Effervesces in acids. Secondary mineral associated with lead minerals.

Dunite. Fine-grained, dull grey-black ultramafic igneous rock composed mainly of olivine.

Dyke. A long narrow body of igneous rock cutting across the structure of other rocks that it intrudes.

Dyscrasite. Ag_3Sb. H = 3.5–4. Light grey, metallic, tarnishing to dark grey. Granular massive, foliated; also pyramidal crystals. Sectile. Occurs in veins with silver minerals and sulphide minerals. Decomposed by HNO_3.

Ekanite. $ThCa_2Si_8O_{20}$. H = 5. Dark reddish-brown, yellow, or green tetragonal prisms, or massive. Vitreous lustre. Transparent variety is used as a gemstone. Originally found in gem gravel of Sri Lanka.

Electrum. (Au,Ag). H = 2.5–3. Yellow, metallic. Natural alloy of gold and silver with 20% gold content.

Ellsworthite. Amber yellow to dark brown, massive; adamantine lustre. Originally found in 1922 at the McDonald mine near Bancroft, Ontario, and named in honour of H.V. Ellsworth, mineralogist, Geological Survey of Canada. Subsequently found to be a uranpyrochlore. Not a valid mineral name.

Elpidite. $Na_2ZrSi_6O_{15}\bullet3H_2O$. H = 7. White, light green, or grey fibrous, prismatic crystals or massive. Vitreous or silky lustre. Found in nepheline syenite. Not readily identifiable in the hand specimen.

Enargite. Cu_3AsS_4. H = 3. Greyish-black to iron-black, metallic (dull when tarnished), prismatic or tabular crystals; also massive or granular. When twinned, it forms star-shaped cyclic trillings. Perfect cleavage. Associated with pyrite, galena, sphalerite, and copper sulphides. Good cleavage is characteristic. Ore of copper.

Enstatite. $MgSiO_3$. H = 6. White, green, or brown with vitreous lustre. Occurs as coarse cleavable masses in pyroxenite, peridotite. Orthorhombic variety of pyroxene.

Epididymite. $NaBeSi_3O_7(OH)$. H = 5.5. White prismatic crystals, massive. Silky lustre. Occurs sparingly in nepheline syenite. Not readily identifiable in the hand specimen.

Epidote. $Ca_2(Al, Fe)_3(SiO_4)_3(OH)$. H = 6–7. Yellowish-green massive or fibrous aggregates. Vitreous lustre. Often associated with quartz and pink feldspar, producing attractive mottled or veined patterns (unakite). Forms during metamorphism of igneous rocks and limestone, and in veins. Takes a good polish and can be used for jewellery and other ornamental objects.

Epistilbite. $CaAl_2Si_6O_{16}\bullet5H_2O$. H = 4. Colourless to reddish twinned prismatic crystals, spherical aggregates, or granular massive. Vitreous lustre. Occurs with stilbite and other zeolite minerals in cavities in basalt. Zeolite group.

Erythrite. $Co_3(AsO_4)_2\bullet8H_2O$. H = 1.5–2.5. Rose-red to crimson globular, radial, or reniform aggregates; also earthy or pulverulent; prismatic to acicular crystals (rare). Dull to adamantine lustre. Soluble in HCl. Secondary mineral formed by the oxidation of cobalt arsenides. Referred to as 'cobalt bloom'.

Esker. A long stream-deposited ridge or mound formed by the accumulation of sand, gravel, and boulders left by retreating glaciers.

Eucairite. CuAgSe. H = 2.5. Light grey, metallic; tarnishes to a bronze colour. Granular massive. Associated with other selenides in copper deposits.

Eucryptite. $LiAlSiO_4$. H = 6.5. Short colourless or white hexagonal prisms; more commonly massive granular. Transparent with vitreous lustre. Fluoresces pink in ultraviolet light. Occurs with lithium minerals in granite pegmatite.

Eudialyte. $Na_4(Ca,Ce)_2(Fe,Mn,Y)ZrSi_8O_{22}(OH,Cl)_2$. H = 5–5.5. Pink, red, yellow, brown, massive; as grains, or tabular or rhombohedral crystals. Transparent with vitreous lustre. Occurs in nepheline syenite. Difficult to identify in the hand specimen.

Eulytite. $Bi_4(SiO_4)_3$. H = 4.5. Yellow, grey, light green, brown, or white tetrahedral crystal aggregates, also spherical forms. Associated with bismuth minerals.

Euxenite. $(Y,Ca,Ce,U,Th)(Nb,Ta,Ti)_2O_6$. H = 5.5–6.5. Black massive or prismatic crystals forming parallel or radial groups. Brilliant, submetallic, or greasy lustre. Conchoidal fracture. Radioactive. Distinguished from other radioactive minerals by X-ray methods.

Evaporite. Sedimentary rock formed by evaporation of minerals such as gypsum or halite from saline waters.

Ewaldite. $Ba(Ca,Y,Na,K)(CO_3)_2$. Bluish-green aggregates of microcrystals; tiny white tabular crystals. Associated with mckelveyite.

Facet cut. Polished gemstone featuring numerous flat surfaces, as in diamond.

Facies. A distinctive rock type corresponding to a certain environment or mode of origin.

Fairfieldite. $Ca_2(Mn,Fe)(PO_4)_2•2H_2O$. H = 3.5. White, greenish-white, or yellow transparent prismatic crystals; also foliated, fibrous, lamellar, or radiating aggregates. Brilliant or pearly lustre. Soluble in acids. Occurs in granite pegmatite.

Faujasite. $(Na_2,Ca)Al_2Si_4O_{12}•8H_2O$. H = 5. Colourless or white octahedral crystals. Vitreous lustre. Distinguished from fluorite by its superior hardness.

Fault. Structural feature produced by the movement of one rock mass relative to another; the terms 'shear zone', 'brecciated zone', and 'fault zone' refer to the region affected by the movement.

Feldspar. A mineral group consisting of aluminosilicates of potassium and barium (monoclinic or triclinic), and of sodium and calcium (triclinic). Orthoclase and microcline belong to the first group, plagioclase to the second. Used in the manufacture of glass, ceramics, porcelain enamel, porcelain, pottery, scouring powders, and artificial teeth.

Felsic. A term describing an igneous rock composed mostly of light-coloured minerals such as feldspar, feldspathoids, quartz, and muscovite.

Felsite. A dense, fine-grained, light-coloured (pink or grey) igneous rock composed mainly of feldspar with little or no quartz.

Ferberite. $FeWO_4$. H = 4–4.5. Black striated wedge-shaped prisms; also bladed or massive. Metallic lustre. Brownish-black to black streak. Weakly magnetic. Ore of tungsten.

Fergusonite. $(Y,Ce,La,Nd)(Nb,Ti)O_4$. H = 5.5–6.5. Black prismatic or pyramidal crystals; also massive. Brilliant to submetallic lustre on fresh surfaces; grey, yellowish, or brownish on exposed surfaces. Subconchoidal fracture. Radioactive. Occurs in granite pegmatite. Distinguished from other radioactive minerals by X-ray methods.

Fersmite. $(Ca,Ce,Na)(Nb,Ta,Ti)_2(O,OH,F)_6$. H = 4–4.5. Dark brown to black striated prisms; also tabular. Subvitreous to resinous lustre. Greyish-brown streak. Occurs with niobium minerals in marble and in pegmatite.

Fibroferrite. $Fe(SO_4)(OH)•5H_2O$. H = 2.5. White, yellow, or greenish fibrous masses; also radiating fibres. Silky or pearly lustre. Formed by oxidation of pyrite and associated with other secondary iron minerals from which it is distinguished by X-ray methods.

Fischesserite. Ag_3AuSe_2. H = 2. Metallic grains associated with clausthalite, native gold, chalcopyrite, pyrite, and other selenides.

Flint. Yellowish-grey or brown, dark grey to black opaque variety of chalcedony. Used by primitive peoples for tools.

Fluoborite. $Mg_3(BO_3)(F,OH)_3$. H = 3.5. Colourless, white, or pink transparent to translucent hexagonal prisms, prismatic or granular aggregates; vitreous, silky, or pearly lustre. May fluoresce white in ultraviolet light. Resembles apatite, but has an inferior hardness. Occurs in crystalline limestone.

Fluorescence. Property of certain substances to glow when exposed to ultraviolet light, X-rays, or cathode rays. It is caused by impurities in the substance or by defects in its crystal structure. Two wavelengths are commonly used to produce ultraviolet fluorescence: long wave (320 to 400 nm), short wave (253.7 nm).

Fluorite. CaF_2. H = 4. Transparent, colourless, blue, green, violet, or yellow cubic or, less commonly, octahedral crystals; also granular massive. Vitreous lustre. Good cleavage. Often fluorescent; this property derives its name from the mineral. Used in optics, steel-making, ceramics.

Fluor-richterite. $Na(Ca,Na) Mg_3Si_8O_{22}F_2$. H = 5–6. Dark grey to dark greenish-grey long prismatic crystals or aggregates of crystals. Fluorine-rich variety of richlerite; amphibole group. Not a valid mineral name.

Forsterite. Mg_2SiO_4. H = 6.5. White or light green square prismatic or tabular crystals; also massive. Vitreous lustre. Conchoidal fracture. Member of the olivine group; distinguished from other members of the group by X-ray methods. Used in the manufacture of refractory bricks.

Franconite. $Na_2Nb_4O_{11}•9H_2O$. White microscopic globules and globular aggregates (about 0.5 mm across) with vitreous to silky lustre. Dissolves in HCl. Occurs on weloganite, calcite, and quartz crystals at the Francon quarry, Montréal, the type locality. Named for the locality.

Freibergite. $(Ag,Cu,Fe)_{12}(Sb,As)_4S_{13}$. A silver-rich member of the tetrahedrite-tennantite series.

Freieslebenite. $AgPbSbS_3$. H = 2–2.5. Grey, metallic, striated prismatic crystals. Grey streak. Associated with silver and lead ores.

Frohbergite. $FeTe_2$. H=4. Pinkish white, metallic. Occurs as intergrowths with other telluride minerals, chalcopyrite, and native gold. Distinguishable from other metallic minerals only by microscopic examination of polished surfaces. Originally found in the Robb-Montbray mine, near Arntfield, Quebec. Named in honour of mining geologist Dr. M.H. Frohberg of Toronto, Ontario.

Froodite. $PdBi_2$. H = 2. Grey, metallic grains associated with arsenic-lead-copper ores. Originally described from the Frood mine, Sudbury district, Ontario, for which it is named.

Fuchsite. An emerald-green chromian muscovite. Not a valid mineral name. Also called chrome-mica.

Gabbro. A dark, coarse-grained igneous rock composed mainly of calcic plagioclase and pyroxene. Used as a building stone and monument stone.

Gadolinite. $(Ce,La,Nd,Y)_2FeBe_2Si_2O_{10}$. H = 6.5–7. Black prismatic crystals, or massive. Vitreous lustre. Occurs in pegmatite.

Gahnite. $ZnAl_2O_4$. H = 7.5–8. Dark blue-green, yellow, or brown octahedra, rounded grains, massive. Vitreous lustre. Occurs in granite pegmatite and in marble. Spinel group.

Gaidonnayite. $Na_2ZrSi_3O_9•2H_2O$. Colourless, white to light yellowish-brown striated bladed crystals. Transparent; vitreous. Occurs in nepheline syenite at Mount Saint-Hilaire, Quebec, as crystals on analcime, in cavities in natrolite; also occurs in pegmatite dykes with catapleiite, elpidite, hilairite, albite, microcline, chlorite, aegirine, epididymite, and goethite. Named in honour of Gabrielle Donnay, professor of crystallography, McGill University.

Galena. PbS. H = 2.5. Dark grey, metallic, cubic crystals or crystal aggregates; also massive. Perfect cleavage. Distinguished by its high specific gravity (7.58) and perfect cleavage. Ore of lead; may contain silver.

Galkhaite. $(Cs,Tl)(Hg,Cu,Zn)_6(As,Sb)_4S_{12}$. H = 3. Orange-red cubic crystals; granular aggregates. Vitreous to adamantine lustre. Occurs in arsenic-antimony-mercury deposits.

Garnet. Silicate of Al, Mg, Fe, Mn, Ca. H = 6.5–7.5. Transparent red dodecahedral crystals, or massive; also colourless, yellow, brown, orange, green, black. Used as an abrasive; transparent garnet is used as a gemstone. Distinguished by its crystal form. Mineral group consisting of several species including almandine, grossular, pyrope, spessartine.

Genthelvite. $Zn_4Be_3(SiO_4)_3S$. H = 6–6.5. Light yellow to brown, yellowish-green, or reddish-brown tetrahedral crystals, and massive. Vitreous lustre. Uneven to conchoidal fracture. Helvite group.

Genthite. Hydrous nickel silicate, also known by the general term 'garnierite'. Not a valid mineral species.

Gersdorffite. NiAsS. H = 5.5. Light to dark grey, metallic; octahedral, pyritohedral crystals or granular massive. Associated with other nickel minerals in vein deposits.

Getchellite. $AsSbS_3$. H = 1.5–2. Dark red, resinous, microscopic crystals; also granular or micaceous. May show violet or green iridescence. Associated with stibnite, realgar, orpiment.

Gibbsite. $Al(OH)_3$. H = 2.5–3.5. White, six-sided, tabular crystals; massive. Translucent, vitreous to pearly, or dull; earthy. Secondary mineral formed by alteration of aluminum minerals.

Gittinsite. $CaZrSi_2O_7$. H = 3.5–4. White fibrous radiating masses. Occurs as intergrowths with apophyllite in pegmatite. Originally described from the Kipawa area, Quebec, and named in honour of Professor John Gittens, University of Toronto.

Gladite. $PbCuBi_5S_9$. Dark grey, metallic, prismatic crystals. Associated with other lead-bismuth sulphide minerals.

Glaucodot. (Co,Fe)AsS. H = 5. Light grey to reddish-grey, metallic, striated prismatic crystals, or massive. May form cruciform twins. Decomposed by HNO_3 forming a pink solution. Associated with cobaltite from which it is distinguished by crystal form and colour.

Glauconite. $(K,Na)(Fe,Al,Mg)_2(Si,Al)_4O_{10}(OH)_2$. H = 2. Greyish, bluish, or yellowish-green fine platy aggregates. Commonly occurs in sedimentary rocks. Mica group.

Gmelinite. $(Na_2,Ca)Al_2Si_4O_{12} \bullet 6H_2O$. H = 4.5. Colourless, white, light yellow, green, or pink striated tabular, pyramidal, or rhombohedral crystals. Transparent, vitreous. Occurs in basalt and other igneous rocks. Zeolite group.

Gneiss. A coarse-grained, foliated, metamorphic rock composed mainly of feldspar, quartz, and mica. Used as a building stone and as monument stone.

Godlevskite. $(Ni,Fe)_7S_6$. Light yellow, metallic. Occurs as microscopic grains and aggregates associated with nickel and copper ores.

Goethite. FeO(OH). H = 5–5.5. Dark brown, reddish- or yellowish-brown earthy, botryoidal, fibrous, bladed, or loosely granular masses; also prismatic, acicular, or tabular crystals, or scaly. Characteristic yellowish-brown streak. Weathering product of iron-rich minerals. Ore of iron.

Gold. Au. H = 2.5–3. Yellow, metallic, irregular masses, plates, scales, nuggets. Rarely as crystals. Distinguished from other yellow metallic minerals by its hardness, malleability, high specific gravity (19.3). Precious metal.

Gossan. Rusty oxidation product consisting of hydrated iron oxides derived from the weathering of pyrite and pyrrhotite. Commonly occurs as an outcrop of the upper zone of pyrite-bearing veins.

Götzenite. $Na_2Ca_5Ti(Si_2O_7)_2F_4$. Light yellowish-brown to colourless radiating acicular aggregates. Vitreous lustre. Rare mineral, difficult to identify in the hand specimen. Occurs with pectolite, natrolite, apophyllite at Mount Saint-Hilaire, Quebec.

Granite. Relatively coarse-grained grey to reddish igneous rock composed mainly of feldspar and quartz. Used as a building stone and as monument stone.

Granite gneiss. Gneiss having the mineral composition of granite.

Granite pegmatite. Pegmatite having the mineral composition of granite.

Granodiorite. A coarse-grained igneous rock with composition intermediate between granite and diorite.

Graphic granite. A granitic rock composed of a regular intergrowth of quartz and K-feldspar producing a geometric pattern resembling hieroglyphic writing. An attractive ornamental stone.

Graphite. C. H = 1–2. Dark grey to black, metallic, flaky or foliated masses. Flakes are flexible. Greasy to touch. Black streak and colour distinguish it from molybdenite. Usually occurs in metamorphic rocks. Used as a lubricant in the manufacture of 'lead' pencils and refractories.

Greenockite. CdS. H = 3–3.5. Yellow earthy coating; rarely as pyramidal crystals. Resinous to adamantine lustre. Associated with sphalerite. Dissolves in HCl giving strong H_2S odour.

Greenstone. A metamorphosed volcanic rock composed mainly of chlorite.

Greywacke. Sedimentary rock containing large amounts of amphibole or pyroxene and feldspar.

Grossular. $Ca_3Al_2(SiO_4)_3$. H = 6.5–7. Colourless, white, yellow, pink, orange, brown, red, black, or green, transparent to opaque, dodecahedral or trapezohedral crystals; massive granular. Vitreous lustre. Occurs in metamorphosed limestone and skarn zones with other calcium silicates. Transparent varieties are used as a gemstone. Garnet group.

Groutite. MnO(OH). H = 5.5. Black, lustrous, acicular, prismatic, wedge-shaped crystals. Associated with other manganese minerals.

Gudmundite. FeSbS. H = 6. Light to dark grey, metallic, elongated, striated prismatic crystals; also massive, lamellar. Light bronze when tarnished. Not readily distinguishable from other grey metallic sulphides in the hand specimen.

Gunningite. $ZnSO_4 \cdot H_2O$. H = 2.5. White powder occurring as an efflorescence on sphalerite from which it has oxidized. First described from the Keno Hill, Yukon Territory, deposits, and named for Dr. H.C. Gunning, a former geologist with the Geological Survey of Canada and later head of the Geology Department, University of British Columbia.

Gustavite. $PbAgBi_3S_6$. Dark grey, metallic, tabular grains. Rare mineral associated with bismuth-lead-silver sulphosalt minerals.

Gypsum. $CaSO_4 \cdot 2H_2O$. H = 2. White, grey, light brown, granular massive; also fibrous (satin spar), or colourless transparent (selenite). Distinguished from anhydrite by its inferior hardness. Occurs in sedimentary rocks. Used in the construction industry (plaster, wallboard, cement, tiles, paint) and as a soil conditioner and fertilizer. Satin spar, selenite, and alabaster (fine-grained translucent variety) are used for carving into ornamental objects.

Gyrolite. $NaCa_{16}(Si_{23}Al)O_{60}(OH)_5 \cdot 15H_2O$. H = 3–4. Colourless to white concretions with a radiating internal structure. Vitreous lustre. Associated with zeolite minerals in cavities in basalt. Zeolite group.

Hackmanite. $Na_8Al_6Si_6O_{24}Cl_2S$. H = 6. Light violet to bluish-violet, massive. Fades on exposure to sunlight. Vitreous to greasy lustre. Fluoresces yellow when exposed to ultraviolet rays. Variety of sodalite.

Halite. NaCl. H = 2.5. Colourless, white, grey, yellow, or blue, transparent to translucent vitreous crystals (cubes), or granular masses. May be fluorescent. Water soluble. Occurs in sedimentary rocks, in springs, seas, and salt lakes, and in dried inland lake basins. Used for the production of sodium, chlorine, hydrochloric acid, and in natural state as table salt.

Halotrichite. $FeAl_2(SO_4)_4 \cdot 22H_2O$. H = 1.5. White hair-like crystals; spherical aggregates. Vitreous lustre. Astringent taste. Secondary mineral formed by weathering of pyrite.

Harmotome. $(Ba,K)_{1-2}(Si,Al)_8O_{16} \cdot 6H_2O$. H = 4.5. Colourless, white, grey, yellow, pink, or brown cruciform penetration twins or radiating aggregates. Transparent to translucent, vitreous. Occurs in basalt and other igneous rocks. Zeolite group.

Hatchettolite. H = 4. Amber to black irregular masses. Occurs with radioactive zircon (cyrtolite) in pegmatite. Not a valid mineral name. Accepted name is 'uranpyrochlore'.

Hauchecornite. $Ni_9Bi(Sb,Bi)S_8$. H = 5. Light yellow, metallic, tarnishing to dark bronze; tabular, bipyramidal, prismatic crystals. Conchoidal fracture. Black streak. Occurs in nickel-bismuth ores.

Hausmannite. Mn_3O_4. H = 5.5. Brownish-black, greasy to submetallic, fine grained massive. Associated with other manganese minerals and difficult to distinguish from them in the hand specimen. Ore of manganese.

Hawleyite. CdS. Bright yellow powdery coating; earthy. Associated with sphalerite and siderite. First described from the lead-silver-zinc deposit at the Hector-Calumet mine, Elsa, Yukon Territory. Named for Professor J.E. Hawley, Queen's University, Kingston.

Heazlewoodite. Ni_3S_2. H = 4. Yellow, metallic; massive, granular, or platy aggregates. Distinguished from pyrite by its inferior hardness.

Hedenbergite. $CaFeSi_2O_6$. H = 6. Green to black short prismatic crystals or massive. Translucent to opaque; vitreous to dull. Monoclinic variety of pyroxene.

Hellandite. $(Ca,Y)_6(Al,Fe)Si_4B_4O_{20}(OH)_4$. H = 5.5. Red to brown tabular, prismatic crystals. Occurs with tourmaline and rare-earth minerals in granite pegmatite.

Hematite. Fe_2O_3. H = 5.5–6.5. Reddish-brown to black, massive, botryoidal, or earthy; also foliated or micaceous with high metallic lustre (specularite). Characteristic red streak. Greasy to dull lustre. Ore of iron.

Hemimorphite (Calamine). $Zn_4Si_2O_7(OH)_2•H_2O$. H = 5. White, brownish, light blue, or green thin tabular crystals; also massive, stalactitic, or mammillary. Vitreous lustre. Associated with smithsonite in zinc deposits; distinguished from it by lack of effervescence in HCl and superior hardness. Minor ore of zinc.

Hemloite. $(As,Sb)_4(Ti,Fe,V,Al)_{24}(O,OH)_{48}$. Black, metallic to submetallic, with black streak. Occurs as grains associated with rutile, molybdenite, titanite, pyrite, sphalerite, arsenopyrite, vanadian muscovite, microcline, and quartz in the Hemlo gold deposit, the type locality. Named for the locality.

Hessite. Ag_2Te. H = 2–3. Grey, metallic, finely granular, massive. Sectile. Occurs with native gold and with other tellurides in vein deposits.

Heterogenite. $CoO(OH)$. H = 3–4. Black to dark brown, reddish globular or reniform masses with conchoidal fracture. Alteration product of smaltite.

Heulandite. $(Na,Ca)_{2-3}Al_3(Al,Si)_2Si_{13}O_{36}•12H_2O$. H = 3–4. Colourless, white, pink, or orange tabular crystals. Vitreous or pearly lustre. Distinguished from other zeolites by its crystal form.

Hexahydrite $MgSO_4•6H_2O$. Colourless, white, finely fibrous, columnar; also globular encrustations. Pearly to vitreous lustre. Bitter, saline taste. Occurs sparingly as an alteration product of epsomite. Originally found at a Bonaparte River locality in British Columbia. Associated with other sulphates from which it is not readily distinguished.

Hibschite. $Ca_3Al_2(SiO_4)_{3-x}(OH)_{4x}$. H = 6. Colourless, light yellow, or greenish-white octahedral crystals (minute), or massive. Vitreous to greasy lustre. Uncommon mineral, not readily identifiable in hand specimen. Garnet group.

Hilairite. $Na_2ZrSi_3O_9•3H_2O$. H = +4. Very small, trigonal, light brown, transparent crystals, and pink, porcelain-like, opaque crystals. Associated with analcime, natrolite, microcline, catapleiite, elpidite, aegirine, and chlorite in nepheline syenite at Mount Saint-Hilaire, Quebec, the type locality for which the mineral was named.

Hilgardite. $Ca_2B_5O_9Cl•H_2O$. H = 5. Colourless, transparent, tabular crystals. Vitreous lustre. Occurs in salt deposits and in gypsum or anhydrite deposits.

Hiortdahlite. $(Ca,Na)_3(Zr,Ti)Si_2O_7(O,F)_2$. H = 5.5. Yellow to brown tabular crystals. Translucent to transparent; vitreous. Occurs in alkalic igneous rocks.

Hisingerite. $Fe_2Si_2O_5(OH)_4•2H_2O$. H = 3. Black to brownish-black, compact, massive with conchoidal fracture. Greasy to dull lustre. Alteration product of iron-bearing minerals.

Hochelagaite. $(Ca,Na,Sr)Nb_4O_{11} \cdot 8H_2O$. H ~ 4. White microscopic globules composed of radiating blades. Vitreous lustre. Occurs on crystals of weloganite, calcite, and quartz at the Francon quarry, Montréal, the type locality. Indistinguishable from franconite in the hand specimen. Named for Hochelaga, the original name for Montréal.

Hollingworthite. $(Rh,Pt,Pd)AsS$. H = 6. Grey, metallic grains intergrown with platinum minerals such as sperrylite.

Holmquistite. $Li_2(Mg,Fe)_3Al_2Si_8O_{22}(OH)_2$. H = 5–6. Violet to light blue prismatic, acicular to fibrous aggregates; also massive. Transparent to translucent with vitreous lustre. Associated with lithium-rich pegmatite occurring in wall rock. Orthorhombic member of amphibole.

Hornblende. $Ca_2(Fe,Mg)_4Al(Si_7Al)O_{22}(OH,F)_2$. H = 6. Dark green, brown, or black prismatic crystals, or massive. Vitreous lustre. Common rock-forming mineral. Monoclinic variety of amphibole.

Howlite. $Ca_2B_5SiO_9(OH)_5$. H = 3.5. Colourless to white, vitreous, granular masses; transparent elongated tabular crystals; compact nodular masses. Crystals distinguished from selenite by superior hardness. Occurs in sedimentary rocks. Named after Henry How, Nova Scotia mineralogist who first described it in 1868.

Humite. $(Mg,Fe)_7(SiO_4)_3(F,OH)_2$. H = 6–6.5. Yellow to orange, granular or massive. Vitreous to resinous lustre. Difficult to distinguish from other members of the humite group (chondrodite, norbergite, clinohumite). Occurs in crystalline limestone.

Hydroboracite. $CaMgB_6O_8(OH)_6 \cdot 3H_2O$. H = 2–3. Colourless, transparent, vitreous, prismatic crystals; white fibrous masses with silky lustre. Occurs in salt and borate deposits. Soluble in acids.

Hydrocarbon. Naturally occurring compounds of carbon and hydrogen such as paraffin, and compounds of carbon, hydrogen, and oxygen such as amber, petroleum, coal. Compounds are of organic origin and are not classified as minerals.

Hydrocerussite. $Pb_3(CO_3)_2(OH)_2$. H = 3.5. Tiny colourless to white or grey hexagonal scales and plates. Transparent to translucent with adamantine or pearly lustre. Associated with cerussite from which it is not readily distinguished. Alteration product of lead, galena.

Hydrodresserite. $BaAl_2(CO_3)_2(OH)_4 \cdot 3H_2O$. H = 3–4. White spheres and hemispheres (2 to 4 mm across) composed of radiating blades. Translucent to opaque. Dehydrates to dresserite from which it cannot be distinguished in hand specimen. Effervesces in HCl. Occurs with quartz, dawsonite, and weloganite at the Francon quarry, Montréal, the type locality. Named for its chemical relationship to dresserite.

Hydromagnesite. $Mg_5(CO_3)_4(OH)_2 \cdot 4H_2O$. H = 3.5. Colourless or white, transparent, flaky, acicular, or bladed crystals, aggregates forming tufs, rosettes, or encrustations; also massive. Vitreous, silky, or pearly lustre. Associated with serpentine, brucite, magnesite. Effervesces in acids. Distinguished from calcite by its habit.

Hydronepheline. Pink to orange-red nodular or irregular patches in nepheline syenite. Not a valid species. In the Bancroft, Ontario, area, what was referred to as 'hydronepheline' is natrolite.

Hydrotalcite. $Mg_6Al_2(CO_3)(OH)_{16} \cdot 4H_2O$. H = 2. White, transparent, foliated, lamellar aggregates; also platy. Pearly to waxy lustre. Greasy feel. Distinguished from talc by its effervescence in dilute HCl and by its superior hardness. Associated with talc, serpentine deposits.

Hydroxylbastnaesite. $(Ce,La)(CO_3)(OH,F)$. $H = 4$. Yellow to brown, pinkish-brown, or dark green, opaque, irregular to reniform masses. Waxy, greasy, or resinous lustre. Associated with other rare-earth minerals.

Hydrozincite. $Zn_5(CO_3)_2(OH)_6$. $H = 2$–2.5. White to grey, yellowish, brownish, or pinkish, fine- grained, compact to earthy or gel-like masses; also stalactitic, reniform, pisolitic, concentrically banded, or radially fibrous aggregates; flat, blade-like crystals. Dull, silky, or pearly lustre. Fluoresces light blue or light violet in ultraviolet light. Secondary mineral found in oxidized zones in zinc deposits.

Hypersthene. $(Mg,Fe)_2Si_2O_6$. $H = 6$. Brown to blackish-brown prismatic crystals or granular to cleavable masses. May have a bronze lustre (bronzite). Occurs in anorthosite, peridotite, and pyroxenite. Intermediate member of the orthorhombic enstatite-ferrosilite series, pyroxene group. Bronze variety used as a gemstone.

Igneous. Rocks that have crystallized from magma or from the melting of other rocks; usually composed of feldspar, quartz, and hornblende, pyroxene, or biotite.

Ilesite. $(Mn,Zn,Fe)SO_4•4H_2O$. Green to white, loose prismatic crystal aggregates. A secondary mineral formed by oxidation in sulphide veins.

Illite. $(K,H_3O)(Al,Mg,Fe)_2(Si,Al)_4O_{10}(OH)_2•H_2O$. $H = 1$-2. White, finely micaceous to clay-like. Dull lustre. Perfect cleavage. Mica-clay mineral.

Ilmenite. $FeTiO_3$. $H = 5$–6. Black, metallic to submetallic. Compact or granular massive; thick tabular crystals. Black streak distinguishes it from hematite. Ore of titanium.

Ilmenomagnetite. Titanium-bearing magnetite containing ilmenite in exsolution. Not a valid mineral name.

Ilmenorutile. $(Ti,Nb,Fe)_3O_6$. $H = 6$. Black to greenish-black plates, rosettes. Opaque; velvety to submetallic lustre. Occurs in dawsonite, calcite at the Francon Quarry, Montréal.

Insizwaite. $Pt(Bi,Sb)_2$. Metallic grains and massive. Associated with pentlandite, chalcopyrite, and nickel and platinum minerals.

Inyoite. $Ca_2B_6O_6(OH)_{10}•8H_2O$. $H = 2$. Colourless, transparent, prismatic to tabular crystals; granular massive. Vitreous lustre. Occurs in gypsum and borate deposits. Soluble in dilute acids and in hot water.

Irarsite. $(Ir,Ru,Rh,Pt)AsS$. Black, metallic, massive. Associated with platinum minerals.

Iridosmine. (Os,Ir). $H = 6$–7. Light grey, metallic, tabular, or rarely, short prismatic crystals; flakes, flattened grains. Perfect cleavage. Associated with gold and platinum in placer deposits.

Iron. Fe. $H = 4$. Dark grey to greyish-black metallic blebs, or massive. Malleable and magnetic. Soluble in dilute HCl and in acetic acid. Occurs in meteorites. Terrestrial native iron (uncommon) occurs in volcanic rocks.

Iron-formation. Metamorphosed sediment containing iron minerals and silica.

Ixiolite. $(Ta,Nb,Sn,Fe,Mn)_4O_8$. $H = 6$–6.5. Grey, metallic, prismatic crystals. Occurs in granite pegmatite.

Jade. Term used for two gemstones, nephrite and jadeite.

Jamesonite. $Pb_4FeSb_6S_{14}$. H = 2.5. Dark grey, metallic, acicular, fibrous, columnar, or plumose aggregates commonly striated. Iridescent tarnish. Decomposes in HNO_3. Occurs in veins with other lead sulphosalts and sulphides.

Jarosite. $KFe_3(SO_4)_2(OH)_6$. H = 2.5–3.5. Yellow to brownish pulverulent coating associated with iron-bearing rocks and with coal. Distinguished from iron oxides by giving off SO_2 when heated.

Jasper. An opaque, dark red to brown, yellow, green, or light violet variety of chalcedony. Used as an ornamental stone and as a gemstone.

Jaspilite. A rock consisting of alternating bands of red jasper and iron oxides. An attractive ornamental rock.

Joaquinite. $Ba_2NaCe_2Fe(Ti,Nb)_2Si_8O_{26}(OH,F)_2$. H = 5.5. Yellow to brown tabular or stubby pyramidal crystals. Transparent to translucent; vitreous. Occurs with aegirine and microcline in cavities in breccia at Mount Saint-Hilaire, Quebec. Rare mineral.

Junoite. $Pb_3Cu_2Bi_8(S,Se)_{16}$. Metallic grains (up to 0.5 mm across) associated with chalcopyrite, sphalerite, colbaltite, kesterite, and mawsonite in the Kidd Creek mine, Timmins, Ontario.

Kaersutite. $NaCa_2(Mg,Fe)_4Ti(Si_6Al_2)O_{22}(OH)_2$. H = 5–6. Dark brown to black short prismatic crystals, or massive. Translucent to opaque; vitreous to resinous. Occurs in volcanic rocks. Amphibole group.

Kainosite (cenosite). $Ca_2(Y,Ce)_2Si_4O_{12}(CO_3)•H_2O$. H = 5–6. Yellow to brown, colourless, or pink prismatic crystals. Transparent, vitreous. Occurs in igneous rocks.

Kaolinite. $Al_2Si_2O_5(OH)_4$. H = 2. White, greyish, yellowish, or brownish earthy masses. Dull lustre. Clay mineral formed chiefly by decomposition of feldspars. Becomes plastic when wet. Used as a filler (in paper) and in the manufacture of ceramics.

Karpinskyite. Mixture of leifite $[Na_2(Si,Al,Be)_7(O,OH,F)_{14}]$ and zinc-bearing montmorillonite. Not a valid mineral name.

Kasolite. $Pb(UO_2)SiO_4•H_2O$. H = 4–5. Yellow, greenish-yellow, or brown, finely granular; also minute prismatic crystals. Dull to resinous lustre. Radioactive. Soluble in acids. Associated with uraninite and secondary radioactive minerals from which it is not easily distinguished in the hand specimen.

Kermesite. Sb_2S_2O. H = 1–1.5. Red hair-like or tufted radiating aggregates of lath-shaped crystals. Translucent with adamantine to semimetallic lustre. Sectile. Alteration product of stibnite. Colour and habit are characteristic. Minor ore of antimony.

Kesterite. $Cu_2(Zn,Fe)SnS_4$. H = 4.5. Greenish black, opaque, massive. Associated with sulphide minerals. Related structurally to stannite.

K-feldspar. $KAlSi_3O_8$. H = 6. Potassium feldspar includes sanidine (colourless), orthoclase (white, pink), and microcline (white, pink, green).

Kiddcreekite. Cu_6SnWS_8. Microscopic metallic irregular grains. Originally found intimately associated with scheelite, clausthalite, tennantite, and tungstenite in a bornite zone in the Kidd Creek mine, Timmins, Ontario. Named for the locality. Identified by microscopic examination of polished surfaces.

Kieserite. $MgSO_4 \cdot H_2O$. H = 3.5. White, granular, massive. Occurs in salt deposits. Dissolves slowly in water.

Kimberlite. Porphyritic igneous rock composed mainly of serpentinized olivine and chloritized phlogopite forming phenocrysts and the fine-grained matrix enclosing them. Common host rock for diamond.

Klockmannite. CuSe. H = 2–3. Grey, metallic, tarnishing to bluish black. Granular aggregates; tabular. Associated with other selenides in ore deposits.

Kornerupine. $Mg_4(Al,Fe)_6(Si,B)_4O_{21}(OH)$. H = 6.5. Yellow, brown, red, blue, and green elongated prisms; also fibrous and columnar. Vitreous lustre. Transparent. Occurs in metamorphic rocks. Transparent variety used as a gemstone.

Kotulskite. Pd(Te,Bi). Metallic minute grains intergrown with chalcopyrite and platinum-group minerals. Identified by microscopic examination of polished surfaces.

Krennerite. $AuTe_2$. H = 2–3. Light grey to yellow, metallic, prismatic, striated crystals. Occurs with other gold tellurides and with native gold in vein deposits.

Kyanite. Al_2SiO_5. H = 4–5, 6–7. Blue, green, greyish-blue, long, bladed crystals and bladed masses. Vitreous to pearly lustre. Hardness is 4 to 5 along the length of the crystal and 6 to 7 across it. Occurs in schist and gneiss. Colour and varied hardness are distinguishing characteristics. Used in the manufacture of mullite refractories.

Labradorite. $(Ca,Na)(Al,Si)AlSi_2O_8$. H = 6. Grey, vitreous, transparent to translucent. Commonly exhibits blue, green, yellow, or bronze iridescence and is used as a gemstone. Chief constituent of anorthosite and gabbro. Named for Labrador. Variety of plagioclase feldspar.

Labuntsovite. $(K,Ba,Na)(Ti,Nb)(Si,Al)_2(O,OH)_7 \cdot H_2O$. H = 6. Pink, orange, red, or brownish-yellow prismatic, acicular crystals. Perfect cleavage. Occurs in nepheline syenite at Mount Saint-Hilaire, Quebec.

Laitakarite. $Bi_4(Se,S)_3$. H = soft. Grey, metallic, foliated plates and sheets to 2 mm across. Associated with junoite in the bornite zone at the Kidd Creek mine, Timmins, Ontario.

Lamprophyre. A dark porphyritic igneous rock with hornblende, pyroxene, and biotite forming phenocrysts in a fine-grained matrix composed of the same mafic minerals.

Langisite. (Co,Ni)As. Pinkish, light brown, metallic. Occurs as grains, lamellae in safflorite. Named for the Langis mine, Cobalt, Ontario, where it was orignally found.

Langite. $Cu_4(SO_4)(OH)_6 \cdot 2H_2O$. H = 2.5–3. Transparent tiny blue crystals forming aggregates on copper-bearing rocks. Vitreous to silky lustre. Formed by oxidation of copper sulphides. Difficult to distinguish from other copper sulphates in the hand specimen.

Lapieite. $CuNiSbS_3$. H = 4–5. Grey, metallic, microscopic grains associated with pyrite, polydymite, gersdorffite, and millerite in a matrix consisting of quartz with altered spinel, magnesite, and bright green mica. Named for the Lapie River, Yukon Territory, which was named for an Indian guide to explorer Robert Campbell.

Larosite. $(Cu,Ag)_{21}(Pb,Bi)_2S_{13}$. Whitish, light brown, acicular crystals associated with chalcocite, stromeyerite in silver-copper ores. Originally found in the Foster mine, Cobalt, Ontario. Named for Mr. Fred LaRose, one of the discoverers of silver-cobalt ore in Cobalt.

Latite. A porphyritic igneous rock consisting of approximately equal amounts of plagioclase and K-feldspar phenocrysts, with little or no quartz, in a fine-grained to glassy matrix.

Laumontite. $CaAl_2Si_4O_{12} \bullet 4H_2O$. H = 4. White to pink or reddish-white, vitreous to pearly, prismatic crystal aggregates; also friable, chalky due to dehydration. Characteristic alteration distinguishes it from other zeolites.

Lava. Rock resulting from a volcanic eruption; also referred to as volcanic rock.

Lavenite. $(Na,Ca)_2(Mn,Fe)(Zr,Ti)Si_2O_7(O,OH, F)_2$. H = 6. Yellow to dark brown or brownish-red, prismatic, fibrous, acicular aggregates, or massive. Translucent; vitreous to greasy or dull lustre. Occurs in alkalic igneous rocks.

Lazulite. $MgAl_2(PO_4)_2(OH)_2$. H = 5.5–6. Blue pyramidal or tabular crystals; massive. Vitreous lustre. Soluble in hot acids. Transparent variety used as a gemstone.

Lead. Pb. H = 1.5. Grey, metallic, platy, dendritic, rounded masses; less commonly octahedral, dodecahedral, or cubic crystals. Malleable and ductile. Rare mineral occurring in various rock environments and in placer deposits. Decomposes readily in HNO_3.

Leadhillite. $Pb_4(SO_4)(CO_3)_2(OH)_2$. H = 2.5–3. Colourless, white, light blue to green tabular or prismatic crystals, or granular massive. Secondary lead mineral associated with galena and other lead minerals. Soluble in HNO_3. Exfoliates in hot water.

Lemoynite. $(Na,Ca)_3Zr_2Si_8O_{22} \bullet 8H_2O$. H = 4. White or yellowish-white, minute, prismatic crystals, spheres. Occurs in nepheline syenite associated with microcline at Mount Saint-Hilaire, Quebec, the type locality. Named for Charles Lemoyne and his sons, seventeenth century explorers of New France.

Leonhardtite. Not a valid mineral name. Renamed starkeyite.

Lepidocrocite. FeO(OH). H = 5. Reddish-brown, submetallic, scaly or fibrous masses. Characteristic orange streak. Associated with goethite as an oxidation product of iron minerals.

Lessingite. $(Ce,Ca)_5(SiO_4)_3F$. H = 4.5. Colourless, greenish, or reddish yellow. Vitreous lustre. Occurs with allanite, bastnaesite, cerite.

Leucophanite. $(Ca,Na)_2BeSi_2(O,F,OH)_7$. H = 4. Green to greenish-yellow tabular crystals with vitreous lustre. Occurs sparingly in nepheline syenite. Not readily distinguished in the hand specimen.

Leucosphenite. $BaNa_4Ti_2B_2Si_{10}O_{30}$. H = 6.5. Light blue, white prismatic crystals; also tabular. Vitreous lustre. Occurs sparingly in nepheline syenite. Not readily distinguished in the hand specimen.

Leucoxene. A general term for alteration products of ilmenite. Not a valid mineral species.

Levyne. $(Ca,Na_2,K_2)Al_2Si_4O_{12} \bullet 6H_2O$. H = 4–4.5. Colourless, transparent, tabular crystals or sheaf-like aggregates; also reddish or yellowish. Vitreous lustre. Occurs in cavities in basalt. Zeolite group.

Liebigite. $Ca_2(UO_2)(CO_3)_3 \bullet 11H_2O$. H = 2.5–3. Light green, or yellowish-green short prismatic crystals; also scaly, granular, botryoidal aggregates. Transparent to translucent with vitreous to pearly lustre. Fluoresces green in ultraviolet light. Secondary mineral formed in uranium deposits.

Limestone. Soft, white, grey, or greyish-brown sedimentary rock formed by deposition of calcium carbonate. Dolomitic limestone contains varied proportions of dolomite and is distinguished from normal limestone by its weaker (or lack of) effervescence in HCl. Used as a building stone and as road metal. Shell limestone (coquina) is a porous rock composed mainly of shell fragments. Crystalline limestone (marble) is a metamorphosed limestone and is used as a building and ornamental stone, as a filler for paper and paints, for the production of magnesium metal, and as crushed stone.

Limonite. Field term referring to natural hydrous iron oxides. Yellow-brown to dark brown, earthy, porous, ochreous masses; also stalactitic or botryoidal. Secondary product of iron minerals. Not a valid mineral species.

Linnaeite. Co_3S_4. H = 4.5–5.5. Light to dark grey, metallic, tarnishing to copper-red. Octahedral crystals, massive. Decomposed by HNO_3. Uncommon mineral associated with cobalt ores.

Lithiophilite. $LiMnPO_4$. H = 4–5. Yellow, yellowish-brown, brown, pink, cleavable to compact massive; crystals (prismatic) are rare. Transparent to translucent with vitreous to subresinous lustre. Becomes brown, dark grey to black on weathered surfaces. Soluble in acids. Occurs with other lithium and phosphate minerals in granite pegmatite. Forms a series with triphylite.

Lithiophosphate. Li_3PO_4. H = 4. Colourless, white, or pink prismatic crystals, or massive. Vitreous lustre. Perfect cleavage. Occurs with other lithium minerals in granite pegmatite.

Loellingite. $FeAs_2$. H = 5–5.5. Light to dark grey, metallic, prismatic crystals; also pyramidal crystals or massive. Occurs with nickel and cobalt minerals in the Cobalt, Ontario, deposits.

Lokkaite. $CaY_4(CO_3)_7 \bullet 9H_2O$. White radiating fibrous aggregates; massive. Alteration product of yttrium minerals.

Ludwigite. Mg_2FeBO_5. H = 5. Greenish-black, opaque, longitudinally striated prisms; dull to submetallic lustre. Also fibrous, acicular, or granular masses. Occurs with brucite, serpentine in contact metamorphic zones.

Lyndochite. Th-Ca-Euxenite. H = 6.5. Black, lustrous, flat, prismatic crystals. Conchoidal fracture. Vitreous lustre. Occurs in pegmatite. Named for Lyndoch Township, Ontario. Not a valid mineral species.

Mackinawite. $(Fe,Ni)_9S_8$. H = 2.5. Yellow, metallic; light grey metallic on freshly broken surfaces. Tetragonal, platy, or pyramidal crystals; also massive, finely lamellar aggregates. Associated with sulphide ore minerals.

Mafic. A term describing an igneous rock composed mostly of dark (ferromagnesian) minerals such as amphibole, pyroxene, biotite.

Magnesite. $MgCO_3$. H = 4. Colourless, white, greyish, yellowish to brown, lamellar, fibrous, granular, or earthy masses; crystals rare. Vitreous, transparent to translucent. Distinguished from calcite by lack of effervescence in cold HCl and by superior hardness. Used in the manufacture of refractory bricks, cements, flooring, and magnesium metal.

Magnetite. Fe_3O_4. H = 5.5–6.5. Black metallic octahedral, dodecahedral, or cubic crystals; massive granular. Occurs in vein deposits, in igneous and metamorphic rocks, and in pegmatite. Strongly magnetic. Ore of iron.

Malachite. $Cu_2CO_3(OH)_2$. H = 3.5–4. Green granular, botryoidal, earthy masses; usually forms coatings with other secondary copper minerals on copper-bearing rocks. Distinguished from other green copper minerals by effervescence in HCl. Ore of copper.

Manganite. $MnO(OH)$. H = 4. Steel-grey to iron-black, metallic, prismatic striated crystal aggregates; also columnar, fibrous, stalactitic, finely granular. Not readily distinguishable from other black manganese minerals in the hand specimen. Ore of manganese.

Manganocolumbite. $(Mn,Fe)(Nb,Ta)_2O_6$. H = 6. Black, brownish-black tabular crystals. Occurs in granite pegmatite. Forms series with manganotantalite and ferrocolumbite.

Manganotantalite. $MnTa_2O_6$. H = 6–6.5. Brownish-black, tabular, short prismatic crystals, or massive. Dark red streak. Vitreous to resinous lustre. Iridescent on tarnished surfaces. Occurs in granite pegmatite. Columbite group.

Manganous manganite. $Na_4Mn_{14}O_{27} \cdot 9H_2O$. H = 1.5. Occurs as black to bluish-black, submetallic to dull, fine-grained powdery coating associated with other manganese minerals and hematite. Synonym for birnessite.

Marble. *See* limestone.

Marcasite. FeS_2. H = 6–6.5. Light bronze to grey, metallic, radiating, stalactitic, globular, or fibrous; twinning produces cockscomb and spear shapes. Yellowish to dark brown tarnish. Massive variety is difficult to distinguish from pyrite in the hand specimen.

Mariposite. Bright green. Chrome variety of muscovite. Not a valid mineral name.

Martite. Fe_2O_3. H = 5.5–6.5. Black octahedral crystals. Dull to splendent lustre. Hematite pseudomorphous after magnetite.

Matildite. $AgBiS_2$. H = 2.5. Black to grey, metallic, granular massive; striated indistinct prismatic crystals (rare). Uneven fracture. Occurs intergrown with galena from which it alters. Associated with sulphide minerals in deposits formed at moderate to high temperatures.

Mattagamite. $CoTe_2$. Grey, metallic, with violet to pink tinge. Occurs as microscopic grains and bladed aggregates with altaite, pyrrhotite, and chalcopyrite. Named for Mattagami Lake, Quebec, which is near the mine where it was originally found.

Maucherite. $Ni_{11}As_8$. H = 5. Grey, metallic, with reddish tinge tarnishing to copper-red. Tabular or pyramidal crystals; also massive, granular, or radiating fibrous. Decomposed by acids. Associated with cobalt-nickel ores.

Mawsonite. $Cu_6Fe_2SnS_8$. H = 3.5–4. Metallic microscopic irregular to rounded grains associated with bornite and other copper sulphide minerals.

Mckelveyite. $Ba_3Na(Ca,U)Y(CO_3)_6 \cdot 3H_2O$. Green, yellowish-green, or yellow crystal aggregates or platy crystals. Occurs with donnayite, natrolite, microcline in carbonate cavities at Mount Saint-Hilaire, Quebec.

Mckinstryite. $(Ag,Cu)_2S$. Steel grey, metallic, becoming black on exposure to air. Associated with silver ore minerals. Originally found in the Foster mine, Cobalt, Ontario.

Melaconite. CuO. Dull powdery coatings or masses; lustrous, resembling coal; reniform or colloform masses. Soluble in HCl or HNO_3. Known as 'copper pitch ore'. Name changed to tenorite.

Melanterite. $FeSO_4 \cdot 7H_2O$. H = 2. Greenish-white to green or blue, massive, pulverulent; also stalactitic, concretionary, fibrous, or capillary; short prismatic crystals (less common). Vitreous to dull lustre. Metallic, astringent taste. Soluble in water. Secondary mineral associated with pyrite and marcasite.

Melilite. $(Ca,Na)_2(Mg,Fe,Al)(Al,Si)O_7$. H = 5. White, light yellow, greenish; square or octagonal prisms. Vitreous to resinous lustre. Conchoidal to uneven fracture. Difficult to identify in the hand specimen.

Melonite. $NiTe_2$. H = 1–1.5. Reddish-white, metallic, tarnishing to brown. Tiny hexagonal plates or lamellae. Dark grey streak. Perfect cleavage. Occurs with sulphides and other tellurides in nickel-copper deposits.

Meneghinite. $Pb_{13}Sb_7S_{24}$. H = 2.5. Blackish-grey, metallic. Slender, striated prismatic crystals, fibrous, massive. Oxidized by HNO_3. Associated with sulphides and sulphosalts.

Merenskyite. $(Pd,Pt)(Te,Bi)_2$. Minute metallic grains intergrown with platinum minerals. Distinguished from associated minerals by microscopic examination of polished surfaces.

Mertieite. $Pd_{11}(Sb,As)_4$. Yellow metallic grains, massive. Sparingly associated with platinum minerals.

Mesolite. $Na_2Ca_2Al_6Si_9O_{30} \cdot 8H_2O$. H = 5. Colourless or white acicular crystals and radiating aggregates; as tufts. Vitreous lustre. Generally associated with other zeolites in amygdaloidal basalt and distinguished from them by X-ray methods.

Metagabbro. A metamorphosed gabbro.

Metamict mineral. Mineral rendered amorphous by the destruction of its crystal structure by radiation from radioactive elements it contains. Zircon and allanite may be metamict.

Metasedimentary rock. Metamorphosed sedimentary rock.

Metavolcanic rock. Metamorphosed volcanic rock.

Miargyrite. $AgSbS_2$. H = 2.5. Black to dark grey, metallic, striated tabular crystals; massive. Red streak. Occurs with other silver sulphosalts and with sulphide minerals in low-temperature hydrothermal veins.

Mica. A mineral group of hydrous aluminum silicates characterized by sheet-like platy structure producing perfect basal cleavage. Muscovite, biotite, and phlogopite are common members of this group.

Michenerite. $(Pd,Pt)BiTe$. H = 2.5. Greyish-white, metallic, minute grains; massive. Black streak. Associated with gold, platinum, and bismuth minerals. Originally described from the Frood mine, Sudbury, Ontario, and named in honour of geologist C.E. Michener who discovered the mineral.

Microcline. $KAlSi_3O_8$. H = 6. White, pink to red, or green (amazonite) crystals or cleavable masses. Distinguished from other feldspars by X-ray diffraction and chemical analysis. Triclinic member of K-feldspar.

Microlite. $(Ca,Na)_2Ta_2O_6(O,OH,F)$. H = 5–5.5. Yellow to brown, reddish octahedral crystals, grains, or massive. Translucent to opaque with vitreous lustre. Occurs with lithium minerals in granite pegmatite.

Micropegmatite. A granitic rock composed of an irregular microscopic intergrowth of quartz and K-feldspar. Synonym of granophyre.

Millerite. NiS. H = 3–3.5. Light brass-yellow, slender, elongated, striated crystals; acicular radiating or hair-like aggregates. Grey iridescent tarnish. Distinguished from pyrite by its crystal form and its inferior hardness. Ore of nickel.

Minium. Pb_3O_4. H = 2.5. Bright red to brownish-red, earthy, pulverulent masses with greasy to dull lustre. Orange-yellow streak. Affected by HCl and HNO_3. Secondary mineral formed by alteration of galena, cerussite.

Miserite. $K(Ca,Ce)_6Si_8O_{22}(OH,F)_2$. H = 5.5–6. Pink to light violet fibrous, scaly, or cleavable masses. Vitreous or pearly lustre. Associated with wollastonite, eudialyte, scapolite.

Mixite. $BiCu_6(AsO_4)_3(OH)_6 \bullet 3H_2O$. H = 3–4. Green acicular crystals with brilliant lustre; hair-like tufts; compact spherical masses. Occurs in copper and bismuth deposits.

Molybdenite. MoS_2. H = 1–1.5. Dark bluish-grey, metallic, tabular, foliated, scaly aggregates or hexagonal crystals; also massive. Sectile with greasy feel. Distinguished from graphite by its bluish-lead-grey colour and by its streak (greenish on porcelain, bluish grey on paper). Ore of molybdenum.

Molybdite. MoO_3. Very soft, yellow, fibrous or earthy crusts or coatings. Secondary mineral formed by alteration of molybdenite.

Molybdomenite. $PbSeO_3$. H = 3.5. Colourless to white, yellowish-white scaly aggregates. Pearly to greasy lustre. Occurs with clausthalite from which it forms.

Monadnock. A residual hill or mountain rising conspicuously above a peneplain having resisted the long erosion that produced the plain.

Monazite. $(Ce,La,Nd,Th)PO_4$. H = 5–5.5. Yellow, reddish-brown, or brown equant or flattened crystals and grains. Resinous to vitreous lustre. Radioactive. Resembles zircon, but it is not as hard. Distinguished from titanite by its superior hardness and radioactivity. Occurs in granitic rocks. Ore of thorium.

Montbrayite. $(Au,Sb)_2Te_3$. H = 2.5. Greyish-white to yellowish-white, metallic. Occurs as intergrowths with other telluride minerals, chalcopyrite, and native gold. Distinguishable from other metallic minerals only by microscopic examination of polished surfaces. Originally found in the Robb-Montbray mine, Montbray Township, near Arntfield, Quebec. Named for the type locality.

Monteregianite. $(Na,K)_6(Y,Ca)_2Si_{16}O_{38} \bullet 10H_2O$. H = 3.5. Colourless, white, grey, rarely light violet or light green. Transparent; vitreous to silky lustre. Acicular radiating or tabular crystals. Occurs in cavities in nepheline syenite at Mount Saint-Hilaire, Quebec, the type locality, where it is associated with calcite, pectolite, microcline, albite, aegirine, arfvedsonite. Named for the Monteregian Hills, Quebec, igneous monadnocks protruding from Ordovician limestone; Mount Saint-Hilaire is one of the Monteregian Hills.

Monticellite. $CaMgSiO_4$. H = 5. Colourless, grey, small prismatic crystals or grains. Vitreous lustre. Occurs in calcite and crystalline limestone. Related to the olivine group. Not readily identifiable in the hand specimen.

Montmorillonite. $(Na,Ca)_{0.3}(Al,Mg)_2Si_4O_{10}(OH)_2 \cdot nH_2O$. H = 1–2. White, grey, greenish, yellowish, flaky or finely granular massive. Waxy to dull lustre; opaque. Expands with absorption of water, becoming viscose, gelatinous.

Montroyalite. $Sr_4Al_8(CO_3)_3[(OH),F]_{26} \cdot 10–11H_2O$. H = 3.5. White, translucent, distorted spheres (1 mm across) with bumpy to botryoidal surface. Dull lustre. Soluble in HCl. Fluoresces white in ultraviolet light. Occurs on platy albite and quartz lining of cavities in silicocarbonatite sill at the Francon quarry, Montréal, the type locality. Named after Mont Royal, the name given by Jacques Cartier to Mount Royal from which the name Montréal is derived.

Moorhouseite. $(Co,Ni,Mn)SO_4 \cdot 6H_2O$. H = 2.5. Pink, powdery, with vitreous lustre and white streak. Occurs as coatings on barite-siderite-sulphide specimens. Soluble in water. Originally described from the Magnet Cove barite mine, Walton, Nova Scotia, and named in honour of W. Wilson Moorhouse, professor of geology, University of Toronto.

Mordenite. $(Ca,Na_2,K_2)Al_2Si_{10}O_{24} \cdot 7H_2O$. H = 3–4. White, pink, or reddish tabular crystals; also as spheres or nodules with compact fibrous structure. Crystal form is not easily distinguished from other zeolites; compact fibrous structure is characteristic. Named for Morden, Nova Scotia, where it was first found.

Morenosite. $NiSO_4 \cdot 7H_2O$. H = 2–2.5. Light green to greenish-white fibrous encrustations; stalactitic. Generally translucent to opaque. Vitreous to dull lustre. Astringent metallic taste. Soluble in water. Secondary mineral formed by oxidation of nickel sulphide minerals.

Mosandrite. Alteration product of rinkite. Not a valid mineral name.

Mudstone. Hardened mud-like sediment composed chiefly of clay minerals.

Muscovite. $KAl_2(Si_3Al)O_{10}(OH,F)_2$. H = 2–2.5. Colourless or light green, grey, brown; transparent with splendent or pearly lustre. Tabular hexagonal crystals, sheet-like, platy, or flaky aggregates. Occurs in pegmatite. Constituent of granitic and metamorphic rocks. Sericite is a white, silky, fine, scaly aggregate of muscovite that occurs as an alteration of minerals such as topaz, kyanite, feldspar, spodumene, and andalusite. Used as electrical and heat insulator; in cosmetics, paints, and wallpaper to produce a pearly lustre; in the manufacture of simulated pearls; as a filler for plastics.

Mylonite. Chert-like rock with streaky, banded, or flow structure.

Nacrite. $Al_2Si_2O_5(OH)_4$. H = 2–2.5. White thin tabular crystals; scaly or granular massive. Silky to earthy lustre. Kaolinite group.

Nahcolite. $NaHCO_3$. H = 2.5. Colourless, white prismatic crystals; fibrous, concretionary; fibrous, porous masses. Transparent to translucent; vitreous to resinous. Associated with sodium chloride, carbonate, borate, and sulphate minerals.

Narsarsukite. $Na_2(Ti,Fe)Si_4(O,F)_{11}$. H = 7. Yellow tabular or short prismatic crystals. Vitreous lustre. Weathers to brownish grey or brownish yellow. Rare mineral occurring in nepheline syenite and pegmatite.

Natrojarosite. $NaFe_3(SO_4)_2(OH)_6$. H = 3. Yellow to brownish-yellow, earthy, minute tabular crystals. Dull lustre. Secondary mineral formed from alteration of iron minerals such as pyrite, marcasite.

Natrolite. $Na_2Al_2Si_3O_{10}•2H_2O$. H = 5. Colourless, white, reddish needle-like crystals often forming radiating or nest-like aggregates; also nodular or slender prisms. Vitreous to pearly lustre. May be distinguished from other zeolites by its acicular habit. Occurs with other zeolite minerals in amygdaloidal basalt and in some igneous rocks.

Naumannite. Ag_2Se. H = 2.5. Dark grey to black, metallic, tarnishing to iridescent brown. Granular massive, platy; cubic crystals. Associated with copper minerals and gold in vein deposits.

Nemalite. A fibrous variety of brucite.

Nenadkevichite. $(Na,Ca)(Nb,Ti)Si_2O_7•2H_2O$. H = 5. Dark brown to pink foliated masses. Opaque; dull lustre. Occurs in alkalic igneous rocks.

Nepheline. $(Na,K)AlSiO_4$. H = 6. White to grey irregular masses, less commonly as hexagonal prisms. Greasy to vitreous lustre. Distinguished from feldspar and scapolite by its greasy lustre and by its gelatinizing in HCl. Used in the manufacture of glass and ceramics.

Nephrite. $Ca_2(Fe,Mg)_5Si_8O_{22}(OH)_2$. H = 6. Dense, compact, fibrous variety of tremolite-actinolite group. Green to black, grey, white. Occurs in metamorphic rocks, peridotite, or serpentinite. Very tough. Nephrite is one variety of jade used as a gemstone and as an ornamental stone; another variety is jadeite.

Neptunite. $KNa_2Li(Fe,Mn)_2Ti_2Si_8O_{24}$. H = 5–6. Black, dark red, prismatic crystals. Vitreous lustre. Occurs in nepheline syenite. Rare mineral.

New mineral. A mineral approved by the Commission on New Minerals and New Mineral Names of the International Mineralogical Association upon determining that the mineral's physical, structural, optical, and chemical properties are distinct from those of any known mineral. The proposed name of the new mineral must also be approved.

Niccolite. *See* nickeline.

Nickel bloom. Term used by miners for annabergite.

Nickeline. NiAs. H = 5–5.5. Copper-coloured to pinkish coppery, metallic, massive, reniform with columnar structure; crystals (tabular, pyramidal) rare. Exposed surfaces alter readily to annabergite. Occurs in veins with cobalt arsenides and native silver. Colour is distinctive. Formerly known as 'niccolite'.

Niggliite. PtSn. H = 3. Silver-white, metallic, minute grains. Associated with platinum and palladium minerals.

Niocalite. $Ca_{14}Nb_2(Si_2O_7)_4O_6F_2$. H = 6. Yellow prismatic crystals with vitreous lustre; also massive granular. Occurs commonly as twinned crystals. Associated with other niobium minerals. Granular variety resembles apatite, but is harder. Originally found in the niobium deposit at Oka, Quebec; named for the elements niobium and calcium.

Norbergite. $Mg_3(SiO_4)(F,OH)_2$. H = 6–6.5. Yellow to orange, transparent to translucent squat crystals, grains. Vitreous to resinous lustre. Occurs in crystalline limestone. Humite group; distinguished from other members of the group by X-ray diffraction and chemical analysis.

Nordmarkite. A quartz-bearing syenite. Used as a building stone and an ornamental stone.

Nordstrandite. $Al(OH)_3$. H = 3. Colourless to white, yellowish, or greyish-white transparent, tabular, blade-like crystals or fine crystal aggregates. Vitreous, pearly to greasy lustre. Occurs in limestone and altered igneous rocks.

Norite. A gabbro with orthopyroxene (hypersthene) as the dominant ferromagnesian component.

Ochre. Impure iron oxides composed of limonite or goethite (yellow ochre), or of hematite (red ochre). Pulverulent, yellow, brownish red, massive. Used as a pigment.

Okenite. $Ca_{10}Si_{18}O_{46}•18H_2O$. H = 4.5–5. White, vitreous to pearly, blade-like crystals; compact fibrous massive. Occurs in amygdaloidal basalt.

Oligoclase. $(Na,Ca)(Al,Si)Si_2O_8$. H = 6–6.5. Colourless, white, pink, grey, greenish, yellowish, or brown transparent to translucent cleavable masses; tabular crystals (less common). Vitreous to pearly lustre. Occurs in pegmatite, granitic rocks. Plagioclase feldspar group.

Olivine. $(Mg,Fe)_2SiO_4$. H = 6.5. Yellowish- to brownish-green, vitreous, granular masses or rounded grains; also colourless, yellowish to brownish, black. Distinguished from quartz by its cleavage, from other silicates by its yellowish-green colour. Used in the manufacture of refractory bricks; transparent variety (peridot) used as a gemstone. Mineral group that includes the fayalite-forsterite series.

Opal. $SiO_2•nH_2O$. H = 5.5–6.5. Colourless, green, grey to black with waxy lustre, and iridescence (play of colour) in gem varieties. Common or nongem variety lacks iridescence, is translucent to opaque, colourless to white, red, brown, grey, green, yellow, etc. Massive, botryoidal, mammillary, or pisolitic forms. Distinguished from chalcedony by its inferior hardness, lower specific gravity. Formed at low temperatures by silica-bearing waters seeping into fissures and cavities in sedimentary and volcanic rocks; silica is in the form of cristobalite.

Orpiment. As_2S_3. H = 1.5–2. Yellow foliated, columnar, fibrous, reniform, botryoidal, granular to powdery aggregates; short prismatic crystals (rare). Transparent to translucent with pearly or resinous lustre. Alteration product of arsenic minerals, notably realgar. Associated with arsenic and antimony minerals.

Orthoclase. $KAlSi_3O_8$. H = 6. Colourless, white, pink, green, grey, yellow transparent to translucent squat prismatic or tabular crystals; cleavable massive. Vitreous to pearly lustre. Perfect cleavage. Occurs as a constitutent of pegmatite and granitic rocks. Distinguished from plagioclase feldspar by the absence of twinning striations. Monoclinic variety of K-feldspar.

Orthogneiss. A gneiss derived from the metamorphism of an igneous rock.

Orthopyroxene. Orthorhombic variety of pyroxene, including enstatite and hypersthene.

Ottrelite. $(Mn,Fe,Mg)_2Al_4Si_2O_{10}(OH)_4$. H = 6.5. Green, grey to black tabular crystals; also scaly, platy, or foliated. Lamellar varieties resemble mica or chlorite, but are distinguished by their brittleness and hardness. Occurs in metamorphosed sedimentary rocks.

Overite. $CaMgAl(PO_4)_2(OH)•4H_2O$. H = 3.5–4. Light green to colourless platy crystals and aggregates; massive. Vitreous lustre. Soluble in hot HNO_3. Associated with other phosphate minerals.

Paragneiss. A gneiss derived from a sedimentary rock.

Parapierrotite. $Tl(Sb,As)_5S_8$. Black, semimetallic, small prismatic crystals. Occurs in cavities in realgar.

Pararammelsbergite. $NiAs_2$. H = 5. Light grey, metallic, rectangular tablets, or massive. Exposed surfaces alter readily to erythrite. Associated with nickel and cobalt minerals in the Cobalt district, Ontario.

Pararealgar. AsS. H = 1–1.5. Yellow, orange-yellow to orange-brown powdery to granular aggregates. Vitreous to resinous lustre. Associated with realgar, stibnite.

Paratacamite. $Cu_2(OH)_3Cl$. H = 3. Green, dark green to greenish-black vitreous, translucent, to semi-opaque rhombohedral crystals; also granular massive, powdery encrustations, or fibrous or spherulitic aggregates. Easily soluble in acids. Secondary mineral formed by alteration of copper minerals.

Pargasite. $NaCa_2(Mg,Fe)_4Al(Si_6Al_2))_{22}(OH)_2$. H = 5–6. Bluish-green, light brown to brown, grey prismatic crystals, or massive. Occurs in igneous and metamorphic rocks. Monoclinic member of the amphibole group.

Parisite. $Ca(Ce,La)_2(CO_3)_3F_2$. H = 4.5. Yellow, brownish, or greyish-yellow hexagonal pyramids or rhombohedral crystals. Striated. Transparent to translucent; vitreous, resinous, or pearly lustre. Soluble in hot acids.

Parkerite. $Ni_3(Bi,Pb)_2S_2$. H = 2. Bronze, metallic. Exhibits lamellar twinning. Occurs as microscopic grains intimately associated with bismuthinite, native bismuth, cobalt pentlandite, siegenite, and bravoite at the Langis mine, Cobalt, Ontario. Effervesces in dilute HNO_3.

Pavonite. $AgBi_3S_5$. Grey, metallic, lath-like or elongated grains. Occurs in bismuthinite-matildite-native bismuth intergrowths in the Keeley mine, Cobalt, Ontario.

Pearceite. $Ag_{16}As_2S_{11}$. H = 3. Black, metallic, hexagonal tabular prisms with bevelled edges and triangular striations on the basal face. Decomposed by HNO_3. Associated with silver minerals such as argentite, native silver.

Pectolite. $NaCa_2Si_3O_8(OH)$. H = 5. White needle-like crystals forming radiating and globular masses. Silky to vitreous lustre. Decomposed by warm dilute HCl. Associated with zeolites in basalt. Blue gem variety known as 'larimar stone'.

Pegmatite. A very coarse-grained igneous rock occurring as dykes, lenses, and veins at the margins of batholiths.

Pekoite. $PbCuBi_{11}(S,Se)_{18}$. Grey, metallic, thin-bladed crystals associated with lead-bismuth minerals.

Pentlandite. $(Fe,Ni)_9S_8$. H = 3.5–4. Light bronze-yellow, massive, granular aggregates. Octahedral parting distinguishes it from pyrrhotite with which it is commonly associated. Non-magnetic. Ore of nickel.

Periclase. MgO. H = 5.5. Colourless to grey and, less commonly, yellow, green, or black octahedrons or grains. Transparent with vitreous lustre. Soluble in dilute HCl. Distinguished from spinel by its inferior hardness; spinel is not soluble in HCl.

Peridotite. An igneous rock consisting almost entirely of olivine and pyroxene with little or no plagioclase feldspar.

Peristerite. White or reddish albite having a blue schiller (iridescence). Intergrowth of K-feldspar and albite. Also called moonstone. Used as a gemstone.

Perovskite. $CaTiO_3$. H = 5.5. Reddish-brown to black cubic or octahedral crystals; also granular massive. Adamantine to metallic lustre. Uneven fracture. White to grey streak. Distinguished from titanite by its crystal form, from pyrochlore by its lustre and streak.

Perrierite. $(Ca,Ce,Th)_4(Mg,Fe)_2(Ti,Fe)_3Si_4O_{22}$. H = 5.5. Dark reddish-brown to black, opaque, striated tabular plates, or flat prismatic crystals; resinous to greasy lustre. Occurs in crystalline limestone, in weathered tuff. Resembles titanite; striations, platy habit, and lustre distinguish it from titanite.

Perthite. A subparallel intergrowth of pink microcline or orthoclase and colourless albite. Exhibits silky sheen with golden aventurescence. Named for Perth, Ontario, where it was originally found. Used as a gemstone. Not a valid mineral species.

Petalite. $LiAlSi_4O_{10}$. H = 6–6.5. Colourless, white, grey, or yellow, cleavable, massive. Vitreous to pearly lustre. Transparent to translucent. Associated with lepidolite in granite pegmatite.

Petarasite. $Na_5Zr_2Si_6O_{18}(Cl,OH) \bullet 2H_2O$. H = 5–5.5. Amber yellow, greenish yellow, massive. Transparent to translucent; vitreous. Associated with biotite, microcline, catapleiite, apatite, zircon, aegirine in nepheline syenite at Mount Saint-Hilaire, Quebec, the type locality. Named in honour of Dr. Peter Tarassoff, collector and amateur mineralogist from Dollard-des-Ormeaux, Quebec.

Petzite. Ag_3AuTe_2. H = 2.5–3. Light to dark grey, metallic; massive granular. Associated with other tellurides in vein deposits. Decomposed by HNO_3.

Phenocryst. Distinct crystal in a fine-grained igneous rock referred to as porphyry.

Phillipsite. $(K,Na,Ca)_{1-2}(Si,Al)_8O_{16} \bullet 6H_2O$. H = 4–4.5. White radiating aggregates of prismatic crystals with pyramidal terminations. Translucent to opaque, vitreous. Associated with other zeolites in basalt.

Phlogopite. $KMg_3Si_3AlO_{10}(F,OH)_2$. H = 2.5. Amber to light brown variety of mica. Used in the electrical industry.

Phosphorescence. Property of certain substances to continue to glow after heating or exposure to ultraviolet rays.

Phyllite. A lustrous metamorphic rock with a texture between that of schist and slate.

Picrolite. A nonflexible fibrous variety of antigorite (serpentine).

Piemontite. $Ca_2(Al,Mn,Fe)_3(SiO_4)_3(OH)$. Violet-red, reddish-brown to reddish-black prismatic or acicular crystals; also fibrous, massive. Occurs in igneous rocks and in schists. Epidote group. Also known as piedmontite.

Pitchblende. Massive uraninite containing trace amounts of thorium and rare earths. Not a valid mineral name.

Placer. Sand or gravel deposit containing gold and/or other heavy minerals; generally refers to deposits in paying quantities.

Plagioclase. $(Na,Ca)Al(Al,Si)Si_2O_8$. H = 6. White or grey tabular crystals and cleavable masses having twinning striations on cleavage surfaces. Vitreous to pearly lustre. Distinguished from other feldspars by its twinning striations. Feldspar group.

Platinum. Pt. H = 4–4.5. Grey, metallic grains, scales, nuggets, cubic crystals (rare). Hackly fracture. Malleable and ductile. Occurs in mafic and ultramafic igneous rocks and in placers.

Plumbojarosite. $PbFe_6(SO_4)_4(OH)_{12}$. Yellowish-brown to dark brown, dull to silky, powdery, earthy, or compact encrustations; microscopic hexagonal plates. Soft, and feels like talc. Dissolves slowly in acids. Oxidation product of lead ores. Not readily identified in the hand specimen.

Pollucite. $(Cs,Na)_2Al_2Si_4O_{12}•H_2O$. H = 6.5–7. Colourless, white, grey, massive; crystals (cubic) are rare. Transparent to translucent with vitreous to pearly lustre. Conchoidal to uneven fracture. Associated with spodumene, amblygonite in granite pegmatite. Resembles quartz, but has a slightly greasy lustre. Zeolite group. Ore of cesium.

Polybasite. $(Ag,Cu)_{16}Sb_2S_{11}$. H = 2–3. Black, metallic, tabular crystals, or massive. Thin splinters are dark red. Decomposed by HNO_3. Occurs with silver-bearing minerals in veins.

Polycrase. $(Y,Ca,Ce,U,Th)(Ti,Nb,Ta)_2O_6$. H = 5.5–6.5. Black prismatic crystals; parallel to radial aggregates of crystals, or massive. Submetallic to greasy lustre. Yellowish, greyish, or reddish-brown streak. Radioactive. Conchoidal fracture. Occurs in granite pegmatite.

Polydymite. Ni_3S_4. H = 4.5–5.5. Grey, metallic, octahedral crystals, massive. Associated with other sulphide minerals in hydrothermal vein deposits.

Polylithionite. $KLi_2AlSi_4O_{10}(F,OH)_2$. H = 2.5–4. White, pink, micaceous; tabular crystals. Pearly lustre. Variety of lepidolite.

Polymorph. Mineral having the same chemical composition as another mineral, but a different crystal structure.

Porphyroblast. A large crystal formed in a metamorphic rock by recrystallization, e.g. garnet in schist. Also referred to as metacryst.

Porphyry. A dyke rock consisting of distinct crystals (phenocrysts) in a fine-grained matrix. The matrix may be diorite, diabase, rhyolite, etc.; these terms are then used to describe the rock.

Posnjakite. $Cu_4(SO_4)(OH)_6•H_2O$. H = 2–3. Minute, blue, flaky, radiating, sheaf-like aggregates on copper-bearing rocks. Associated with other secondary copper minerals; not readily distinguished from them in the hand specimen.

Prehnite. $Ca_2Al_2Si_3O_{10}(OH)_2$. H = 6.5. Light green, globular, stalactitic masses with fibrous or columnar structure; tabular crystals. Vitreous lustre. Colour and habit are distinguishing features. Associated with zeolite minerals in basalt, and as an alteration of plagioclase.

Priceite. $Ca_4B_{10}O_{19}•7H_2O$. H = 3–3.5. White, earthy, nodular or irregular masses. Occurs in gypsum and borate deposits. Soluble in acids.

Pringleite. $Ca_9B_{26}O_{34}(OH)_{24}Cl_4•13H_2O$. H = 3–4. Colourless or orange prismatic crystals and platy aggregates. Transparent to translucent with vitreous lustre. Occurs with hilgardite, halite, and sylvite. Originally described from the Penobsquis potash mine, Sussex, New Brunswick, and named in honour of Gordon J. Pringle, Geological Survey of Canada.

Probertite. $NaCaB_5O_7(OH)_4 \bullet 3H_2O$. $H = 3.5$. Colourless, transparent acicular crystals; radiating crystal aggregates; massive. Occurs with other borate minerals. Soluble in dilute acids.

Proustite. Ag_3AsS_3. $H = 2–2.5$. Red with adamantine lustre. Prismatic crystals or massive. Associated with other silver minerals. Known as ruby silver. Ore of silver.

Pseudoixiolite. A disordered columbite-tantalite. Not a valid mineral name.

Pseudorutile. Renamed 'arizonite'.

Psilomelane. $(Ba,H_2O)Mn_5O_{10}$. $H = 5–6$. Black, massive, botryoidal, stalactitic, or earthy. Dull to submetallic lustre. Black streak. Associated with other manganese minerals, from which it is distinguished by superior hardness, black streak, and amorphous appearance. Ore of manganese. Not a valid mineral name. Renamed romanechite.

Pumpellyite. $Ca_2(Mg,Fe)Al_2(SiO_4)(Si_2O_7)(OH)_2 \bullet H_2O$. $H = 5.5$. Bluish-green to green or white tiny fibrous aggregates; also platy, massive. Silky to vitreous lustre. Occurs in amygdaloidal basalt and in metamorphic rocks.

Pyrargyrite. Ag_3SbS_3. $H = 2.5$. Dark red prismatic crystals, or massive. Adamantine lustre. Dark red streak. Occurs in veins carrying other silver minerals. Known as ruby silver. Ore of silver. Colour is identifying characteristic.

Pyrite. FeS_2. $H = 6–6.5$. Light brass-yellow (iridescent when tarnished) metallic crystals (cube, pyritohedron, octahedron), or massive granular. Distinguished from other sulphides by colour, crystal form, and superior hardness. Source of sulphur.

Pyroaurite. $Mg_6Fe_2(CO_3)(OH)_{16} \bullet 4H_2O$. $H = 2.5$. Colourless, yellowish, blue, green, or white, flaky, nodular or fibrous. Pearly or waxy lustre. Crushes to talc-like powder. Effervesces in HCl. Becomes golden yellow and magnetic when heated. Occurs with brucite in serpentine and in crystalline limestone.

Pyrochlore. $(Na,Ca)_2Nb_2O_6(OH,F)$. $H = 5–5.5$. Dark brown, reddish-brown to black octahedral crystals, or irregular masses. Vitreous or resinous lustre. Light brown to yellowish-brown streak. Distinguished from perovskite by its lustre and streak, from titanite by its crystal form. Ore of niobium.

Pyrochroite. $Mn(OH)_2$. Colourless, yellow, light green, or blue, altering to dark brown and black on exposure to air. Associated with manganese minerals.

Pyroclastic rock. A rock composed of fragments of volcanic rocks.

Pyrolusite. MnO_2. $H = 6–6.5$ (crystals), 2–6 (massive). Light to dark grey, metallic, with bluish tint. Columnar, fibrous, or divergent masses; reniform, concretionary, granular to powdery and dendritic. Soils fingers easily and marks paper. Ore of manganese.

Pyromorphite. $Pb_5(PO_4)_3Cl$. $H = 3.5–4$. Green, yellow to brown prismatic crystals; also rounded barrel-shaped or spindle-shaped forms, subparallel crystal (prismatic) aggregates; globular, reniform, or granular. Resinous to subadamantine lustre. Crystal form, lustre, and high specific gravity (7.04) are distinguishing features. Soluble in acids. Secondary mineral formed in oxidized galena deposits.

Pyrope. $Mg_3Al_2(SiO_4)_3$. H = 7–7.5. Red transparent dodecahedral or trapezohedral crystals; grains. Vitreous lustre. Occurs in serpentinite, peridotite, and kimberlite. Used as a gemstone. Garnet group.

Pyrophanite. $MnTiO_3$. H = 5. Dark red or reddish-brown thin tabular crystals or fine flakes. Metallic to adamantine lustre. Conchoidal fracture. Ilmenite group.

Pyrophyllite. $Al_2Si_4O_{10}(OH)_2$. H = 1–2. White, grey, green, or yellow foliated, lamellar, fibrous, or granular compact masses. Pearly, greasy, or dull lustre. Resembles talc, but has slightly superior hardness. Used for carved ornamental objects, in the manufacture of ceramics and insecticides, and for refractories.

Pyroxene. A mineral group consisting of Mg, Fe, Ca, and Na silicates related structurally. Diopside, augite, aegirine, jadeite, spodumene, enstatite, and hyperstene are members of the group. Common rock-forming mineral.

Pyroxenite. An igneous rock composed mainly of pyroxene with little or no feldspar.

Pyrrhotite. $Fe_{1-x}S$. H = 4. Brownish bronze, massive granular. Black streak. Magnetic; this property distinguishes it from pyrite and other bronze sulphides.

Quartz. SiO_2. H = 7. Colourless, yellow, violet, pink, brown, or black six-sided prisms with transverse striations, or massive. Transparent to translucent with vitreous lustre. Lack of cleavage distinguishes it from other colourless and white minerals. Rock-forming mineral. Occurs in veins in ore deposits. Used in glass and electronic industries. Transparent varieties used as gemstones.

Quartzite. A quartz-rich rock formed by metamorphism of sandstone. Used as a building stone, a monument stone, and an ornamental stone; high-purity quartzite is used in the manufacture of glass.

Radioactive minerals. Minerals that give off radiation due to spontaneous disintegration of uranium or thorium atoms. Detected by Geiger counter.

Raite. $Na_4Mn_3Si_8(O,OH)_{24}\bullet9H_2O$ (?). H = 3. Gold to brown acicular crystals. Occurs in alkalic igneous rocks.

Rammelsbergite. $NiAs_2$. H = 5.5–6. Light grey, metallic, tinged with red; massive with granular texture or prismatic, radial fibrous structure. Occurs in vein deposits with nickel and cobalt minerals such as smaltite, nickeline.

Ramsayite. $Na_2Ti_2Si_2O_9$. H = 6. Colourless fine acicular crystals. Vitreous lustre. Occurs in nepheline syenite. Rare mineral. Not readily identifiable in the hand specimen. Not a valid mineral name; renamed lorenzenite.

Ramsdellite. MnO_2. H = 3. Black massive or platy crystal aggregates. Metallic lustre and black streak. Associated with other manganese minerals in manganese deposits.

Rancieite. $(Ca,Mn)Mn_4O_9\bullet3H_2O$. Black, dark brown, grey metallic, massive; also lamellar. Associated with manganese minerals.

Rare-earth elements. A series of elements from atomic number 57 (lanthanum) to 71 (lutetium) and yttrium that were originally believed to be of rare occurrence.

Realgar. AsS. H = 1.5–2. Orange-red to orange-yellow, granular to compact massive; also striated, short, prismatic crystals. Resinous to greasy lustre. Transparent on freshly broken surface. Alters to light yellow to reddish-yellow powder (consisting of orpiment and arsenolite) on exposure to light. Occurs with orpiment and other arsenic minerals and with ores of antimony, lead, silver, and gold. Decomposed by HNO_3 and aqua regia.

Retgersite. $NiSO_4 \bullet 6H_2O$. H = 2. Dark green to blue-green fibrous encrustations and veinlets; crystals (prismatic) rare. Vitreous lustre. Greenish-white streak. Alteration product of nickeline.

Rhabdophane. $(Ce,La)PO_4 \bullet H_2O$. H = 3.5. Pinkish, yellowish-white, or brown stalactitic or botryoidal encrustations with radial structure. Translucent; waxy lustre. Occurs in pegmatite.

Rhodochrosite. $MnCO_3$. H = 4. Pink to rose, less commonly yellowish to brown, massive granular to compact; also columnar, globular, botryoidal; crystals (rhombohedral) uncommon. Vitreous lustre, transparent. Soluble in warm HCl. Distinguished from rhodonite by its inferior hardness. Ore of manganese.

Rhodonite. $MnSiO_3$. H = 6. Pink to rose red, massive, commonly veined with black manganese minerals. Conchoidal fracture, very tough. Resembles rhodochrosite from which it is distinguished by its superior hardness and lack of effervescence in HCl. Associated with manganese ores. Used as a gemstone and an ornamental stone.

Rhyolite. A fine-grained volcanic rock with composition similar to granite.

Richterite. $Na_2Ca(Mg,Fe)_5Si_8O_{22}(OH)_2$. H = 5–6. Green, brown to brownish-red, yellow, rose-red long prismatic crystals. Transparent to translucent; vitreous. Monoclinic member of amphibole.

Rickardite. Cu_7Te_5. H = 3.5. Purplish-red, metallic; massive. Soluble in HNO_3. Associated with other tellurides from which it is distinguished by its colour resembling tarnished bornite.

Rinkite. $(Na,Ca,Ce)_3Ti(Si_2O_7)_2OF_3$. H = 5. Yellow, yellowish-green to brown tabular or prismatic crystals, and massive. Vitreous to greasy lustre. Rare mineral occurring in nepheline syenite. Not easily identified in the hand specimen.

Rock wool. Felted or matted fibres produced by blowing or spinning molten self-fluxing siliceous and argillaceous dolomitic limestone. Used as insulating material and for acoustic tiles. Now replaced by fibreglass for insulation.

Roemerite. $Fe_3(SO_4)_4 \bullet 14H_2O$. H = 3–3.5. Yellow to rust- or violet-brown, pink, powdery, granular, crystalline (tabular) encrustations; also stalactitic. Oily to vitreous; translucent. Saline, astringent taste. Formed from oxidation of pyrite. Not easily distinguished in the hand specimen from other iron sulphates.

Romeite. $(Ca,Fe,Mn,Na)_2(Sb,Ti)_2O_6(O,OH,F)$. H = 5.5–6.5. Yellow to brown small octahedral crystals; massive. Vitreous, greasy, or subadamantine lustre. White to light yellow streak. Occurs with rhodonite and other manganese minerals.

Roquesite. $CuInS_2$. H = 3.5–4. Grey, metallic, with bluish tint. Microscopic grains associated with copper ore minerals.

Roscoelite. $K(V,Al,Mg)_2(AlSi_3)O_{10}(OH)_2$. H = 2.5. Reddish-brown to greenish-brown scaly aggregates. Pearly lustre. Occurs in gold and vanadium deposits. Mica group.

Rose quartz. Pink to rose variety of quartz; used as an ornamental stone.

Routhierite. $TlHgAsS_3$. Reddish-black metallic grains and veinlets associated with stibnite, sphalerite, pyrite, realgar, and orpiment.

Roxbyite. Cu_9S_5. $H = 2–3$. Bluish-black metallic grains; bronze flakes. Occurs with other copper sulphides.

Rozenite. $FeSO_4 \bullet 4H_2O$. White or greenish-white, finely granular, botryoidal, or globular encrustations. Metallic astringent taste. Difficult to distinguish in the hand specimen from other iron sulphates with which it is associated.

Ruby silver. The silver minerals, pyrargyrite and proustite, are known as ruby silver because of their colour.

Ruitenbergite. $Ca_9B_{26}O_{34}(OH)_{24}Cl_4 \bullet 13H_2O$. Monoclinic polymorph of pringleite with which it is associated and identical in appearance. Originally described from the Penobsquis potash mine, Sussex, New Brunswick, and named in honour of Arie A. Ruitenberg of the New Brunswick Geological Survey.

Rutile. TiO_2. $H = 6–6.5$. Brownish-red to black striated prismatic or acicular crystals; massive. Crystals are often twinned, forming elbow shapes. Adamantine lustre. Resembles cassiterite, but not as heavy and has light brown streak (cassiterite has white streak). Ore of titanium.

Sabinaite. $Na_4Zr_2TiO_4(CO_3)_4$. White powdery coatings, compact, finely flaky aggregates. Silky to pearly lustre. Effervesces in warm HCl. Commonly coated with white powdery gibbsite-like mineral that fluoresces strongly in ultraviolet light. Associated with weloganite, dawsonite, quartz, calcite, and dresserite in igneous sills at the Francon quarry, Montréal, the type locality. Named in honour of Ann P. Sabina, Geological Survey of Canada.

Safflorite. $(Co,Fe)As_2$. $H = 4.5–5$. Light grey, metallic, massive, with radiating fibrous structure; prismatic crystals resembling arsenopyrite. May form cruciform or six-ray star twins. Occurs with cobalt and nickel minerals and with native silver in vein deposits.

Samarskite. $(Y,Er,Ce,U,Ca,Fe,Pb,Th)(Nb,Ta,Ti,Sn)_2O_6$. $H = 5–6$. Black, brownish-black prismatic or tabular crystals, massive. Vitreous, resinous, or splendent lustre. Radioactive. Exposed surfaces alter to brown or yellowish-brown. Conchoidal fracture. Dark brown to reddish or yellowish-brown streak. Occurs in granite pegmatite.

Samsonite. $Ag_4MnSb_2S_6$. $H = 2.5$. Dark grey to black metallic striated prisms. Associated with silver and manganese minerals.

Sanidine. Colourless glassy monoclinic variety of potash feldspar.

Sandstone. A sedimentary rock composed of sand-sized particles, mostly quartz.

Sapphirine. $Mg_{15}Al_{12}Si_2O_{27}$. $H = 7.5$. Light to dark blue, greenish-blue grains; also tabular crystals. Vitreous lustre. Uncommon mineral. Difficult to identify except by X-ray methods.

Scapolite. $Na_4Al_3Si_9O_{24}Cl - Ca_4Al_6Si_6O_{24}(CO_3,SO_4)$. H = 6. White, grey, or less commonly pink, yellow, blue, or green prismatic and pyramidal crystals; also massive granular with splintery, woody appearance. Vitreous, pearly to resinous lustre. Distinguished from feldspar by its square prismatic form, its prismatic cleavage, its splintery appearance on cleavage surfaces. May fluoresce under ultraviolet rays. Clear varieties may exhibit chatoyancy (cat's-eye effect) when cut in the cabochon style. Mineral group including marialite, meionite.

Schapbachite. High-temperature form of matildite, $AgBiS_2$. Not a valid mineral name.

Scheelite. $CaWO_4$. H = 4.5–5. White, yellow, brownish, transparent to translucent; massive. Also dipyramidal crystals. High specific gravity (about 6). Generally fluoresces bright bluish white under short ultraviolet rays; this property is used in prospecting for this tungsten ore mineral.

Schiller. Internal near-surface reflection of light, producing a display of spectral colours, or iridescence, as in feldspar (peristerite).

Schist. A metamorphic rock composed mainly of flaky minerals such as mica and chlorite.

Scolecite. $CaAl_2Si_3O_{10} \bullet 3H_2O$. H = 5. Colourless to white prismatic crystals (generally twinned); also radiating acicular to fibrous aggregates. Vitreous lustre. Occurs in cavities in basalt. Zeolite group.

Scorodite. $FeAsO_4 \bullet 2H_2O$. H = 3.5–4. Green, greyish-green to brown crusts composed of tabular or prismatic crystals; also massive, earthy, porous, or sinter-like. Vitreous to subresinous or subadamantine lustre. Soluble in acids. Secondary mineral formed by oxidation of arsenopyrite.

Selenite. Colourless, transparent variety of gypsum.

Selenium. Se. H = 2. Grey, metallic, acicular, tube-like crystals; aggregates of crystals forming sheets. Red streak. Associated with pyrite deposits.

Seligmannite. $PbCuAsS_3$. H = 3. Dark grey to black, metallic; short prismatic to tabular crystals. Brown to purplish-black streak. Associated with sulphide and sulphosalt minerals.

Senarmontite. Sb_2O_3. H = 2–2.5. Colourless to greyish white, transparent; octahedral crystals or granular, massive. Forms crusts. Resinous to subadamantine lustre. Soluble in HCl. Secondary mineral formed by oxidation of antimony minerals. Minor ore of antimony.

Sepiolite. $Mg_4Si_6O_{15}(OH)_2 \bullet 6H_2O$. H = 2–2.5. White, greyish, yellowish, fibrous, scaly, earthy, clay-like, or compact nodular; silky, waxy, or dull lustre. Secondary mineral formed from serpentine, magnesite. Massive variety is referred to as meerschaum and was used for making tobacco pipes.

Serandite. $Na_6(Ca,Mn)_{15}Si_{20}O_{58} \bullet 2H_2O$. Pink to reddish prismatic crystal aggregates. Vitreous lustre. Occurs with analcime, aegirine in nepheline syenite. Distinguished by its colour and crystal form.

Sericite. Fine scaly or fibrous muscovite; an important constituent of some schist and gneiss.

Serpentine. $(Mg,Fe)_3Si_2O_5(OH)_4$. H = 2–5. White, yellow, green, blue, red, brown, black massive; may be mottled, banded, or veined. Waxy lustre. Translucent to opaque. Asbestos (chrysotile) and picrolite are fibrous varieties. Formed by alteration of olivine, pyroxene, amphibole, or other magnesium silicates. Found in metamorphic and igneous rocks. Used as an ornamental building stone (verde antique) and for ornamental objects.

Serpentinite. A metamorphic rock consisting almost entirely of serpentine.

Serpierite. $Ca(Cu,Zn)_4(SO_4)_2(OH)_6\bullet 3H_2O$. Light blue, minute, elongated, lath-like crystals; also tufts, crusts of flattened fibres. Transparent with vitreous to pearly lustre. Secondary mineral associated with other sulphate minerals in copper deposits.

Shale. A fine-grained sedimentary rock composed of clay minerals and having a laminated structure.

Shear zone. A region in which lateral movement along rock planes has produced crushed or brecciated rocks.

Siderite. $FeCO_3$. H = 3.5–4. Brown rhombohedral crystals, cleavable masses, earthy, botryoidal. Soluble in HCl. Distinguished from calcite and dolomite by its colour and higher specific gravity, from sphalerite by its cleavage. Ore of iron.

Siderotil. $FeSO_4\bullet 5H_2O$. White, light green to bluish fibrous crusts, needle-like crystals, or finely granular encrustations. Vitreous lustre. Metallic, astringent taste. Not distinguishable in the hand specimen from other iron sulphates.

Siegenite. $(Ni,Co)_3S_4$. H = 4.5–5.5. Grey, metallic, tarnishing to copper-red. Octahedral crystals or massive granular. Uncommon mineral occurring with copper, nickel, or iron sulphides in vein deposits.

Silex. An obsolete term for flint. Used in the Gaspé region, Quebec, for grey to brown chalcedony pebbles found in the area.

Siliceous sinter. H = 7. White porous quartz. Occurs in cavities in basalt.

Sill. A long narrow body of igneous rock that parallels the structure of the rock it intrudes.

Sillimanite. Al_2SiO_5. H = 7. White, colourless, fibrous, or prismatic masses. Vitreous or silky lustre. Distinguished from wollastonite and tremolite by its superior hardness. Occurs in schist and gneiss.

Siltstone. A very fine-grained sedimentary rock with composition between sandstone and shale, lacking the fissility of shale.

Silver. Ag. H = 2.5–3. Grey, metallic, arborescent, wiry, leaf, platy, or scaly forms; crystals (cubic, octahedral, dodecahedral) rare. Tarnishes to dark grey or black. Hackly fracture. Ductile, malleable. Colour, form, and sectility are identifying characteristics.

Sinhalite. $MgAl(BO_4)$. H = 6.5–7. Colourless, yellow, pink, greenish to pinkish-brown, or dark brown transparent vitreous grains, or massive. Occurs in skarn zones, in marble, and in crystalline limestone. Transparent varieties used as a gemstone.

Sjogrenite. $Mg_6Fe_2(CO_3)(OH)_{16}\bullet 4H_2O$. H = 2.5. Transparent tiny thin flexible hexagonal plates; colourless to yellowish- or brownish-white. Glistening, vitreous, or pearly lustre. Rare mineral associated with pyroaurite.

Skarn. An altered rock zone in limestone and dolomite in which calcium silicates (garnet, pyroxene, epidote, etc.) have formed.

Sklodowskite. $(H_3O)_2Mg(UO_2)_2(SiO_4)•2H_2O$. H = 2–3. Light yellow to greenish-yellow small acicular crystals or fibres forming rosettes, radial tufts; also powdery to earthy. Silky, vitreous to dull lustre. Secondary mineral formed from uranium minerals.

Skutterudite. $CoAs_{2-3}$. H = 5.5–6. Grey, metallic, cubic, cubo-octahedral, or pyritohedral crystals; massive, colloform. Resembles arsenopyrite, but is distinguished by its crystal form. Associated with other cobalt and nickel minerals in vein deposits.

Slate. A fine-grained compact metamorphic rock characterized by a susceptibility to split into thin sheets.

Smaltite. $(Co,Ni)As_{3-x}$. An arsenic-deficient variety of skutterudite. Not a valid mineral name.

Smithsonite. $ZnCO_3$. H = 4–4.5. Greyish-white to grey, greenish or bluish; also yellow to brown. Generally botryoidal, reniform, stalactitic, granular, porous masses; also indistinct rhombohedral crystalline aggregates. Vitreous lustre. Has high specific gravity (4.4). Effervesces in acids. May fluoresce bluish white under ultraviolet rays. Associated with zinc deposits.

Smythite. Fe_3S_4. Bronze to brownish-black metallic plates or flakes. Magnetic. Resembles pyrrhotite from which it is distinguished by X-ray diffraction. Occurs with other sulphides such as pyrrhotite, pyrite, chalcopyrite, marcasite.

Soapstone. A metamorphic rock composed chiefly of talc; massive fibrous texture and unctuous feel. Used as a carving medium, for refractory bricks, as marking crayons for metal-workers, and as heat-resistant pads and plates.

Sodalite. $Na_8Al_6Si_6O_{24}Cl_2$. H = 6. Royal blue to purplish-blue granular masses, dodecahedral crystals. Vitreous lustre. Resembles lazurite, but is harder; also distinguished by its association: sodalite in nepheline rocks, lazurite in crystalline limestone.

Soddyite. $(UO_2)_2SiO_4•2H_2O$. H = 3.5. Yellow, amber-yellow to yellowish-green small bipyramidal or tabular crystals or radial fibrous aggregates; powdery to earthy masses and crusts. Vitreous, resinous to dull lustre. Secondary mineral formed from uraninite.

Spangolite. $Cu_6Al(SO_4)(OH)_{12}Cl•3H_2O$. H = 3. Green tabular or prismatic crystals. Transparent with vitreous lustre. Secondary mineral occurring in copper deposits.

Specularite. Black variety of hematite having a brilliant lustre.

Sperrylite. $PtAs_2$. H = 6–7. Light grey, metallic, cubic or cubo-octahedral crystals. Associated with pyrrhotite-pentlandite-chalcopyrite ores.

Spertiniite. $Cu(OH)_2$. Blue to blue-green transparent vitreous lath-like crystals forming microscopic botryoidal aggregates. Soluble in acids and decomposes in hot water. Associated with native copper, chalcocite, atacamite. Named in honour of Dr. Francis Spertini, geologist at the Jeffrey mine, Asbestos, Quebec, the type locality.

Spessartine. $Mn_3Al_2(SiO_4)_3$. H = 7–7.5. Orange to orange-red and brown transparent dodecahedral or trapezohedral crystals; grains. Vitreous lustre. Occurs in granite pegmatite. Used as a gemstone. Garnet group.

Sphalerite. ZnS. H = 3.5–4. Yellow, brown, or black, granular to cleavable massive; also botryoidal. Resinous to submetallic. Light yellow streak. Soluble in HCl, giving off H_2S. Ore of zinc.

Sphene. Synonym for titanite.

Spinel. $MgAl_2O_4$. H = 7.5–8. Dark green, brown, black, dark blue, pink, or red grains or octahedral crystals; also massive. Conchoidal fracture. Vitreous lustre. Distinguished from magnetite and chromite by its superior hardness and lack of magnetic property. Transparent varieties used as gemstones.

Spionkopite. $Cu_{39}S_{28}$. Grey to black, metallic, with green, violet iridescence; microscopic flakes forming aggregates. Generally intergrown with other copper sulphides. Originally described from sandstone and quartzite copper deposits in the Yarrow Creek and Spionkop Creek areas, southwestern Alberta; named for the locality.

Spodumene. $LiAlSi_2O_6$. H = 6.5. White, grey, pink, violet, green long prismatic crystals or platy masses. Perfect cleavage. Vitreous lustre. Distinguished by its form and cleavage. Occurs in granite pegmatite. Ore of lithium. Used in ceramics. Transparent pink (kunzite), green (hiddenite), and yellow varieties are used as gemstone.

Stannite. Cu_2FeSnS_4. H = 4. Grey to greyish-black, metallic; granular massive or disseminated grains. Bluish tarnish. Black streak. Occurs in tin-bearing veins associated with chalcopyrite, sphalerite, tetrahedrite, pyrite, and cassiterite.

Starkeyite. $MgSO_4 \bullet 4H_2O$. Dull white encrustations. Bitter, metallic taste. Difficult to distinguish visually from other sulphates. Formerly known as leonhardtite.

Staurolite. $(Fe,Mg,Zn)_2Al_9(Si,Al)_4O_{22}(OH)_2$. H = 7. Brownish-yellow to brown prismatic crystals commonly twinned forming cruciform shapes. Vitreous to resinous lustre. Colour and habit are diagnostic. Occurs in schist and gneiss.

Steenstrupine. $(Ce,La,Na,Mn)_6(Si,P)_6O_{18}(OH)$. H = 5. Reddish-brown to black rhombohedral crystals or massive. Opaque. Occurs in nepheline syenite.

Stephanite. Ag_3SbS_4. H = 2–2.5. Black, metallic, striated prismatic or tabular crystals, or massive. Decomposed by HNO_3. Occurs in veins in silver deposits.

Stibarsen. SbAs. H = 3–4. Tin-white, reddish-grey, metallic; fibrous, lamellar, reniform, mammillary, or finely granular masses. Tarnishes to grey or brownish black. Perfect cleavage in one direction. Fuses to a metallic globule. Occurs in veins with other arsenic and antimony minerals, and in pegmatite containing lithium minerals.

Stibiconite. $Sb_3O_6(OH)$. H = 4.5–5. Yellow, vitreous, granular to powdery encrustations; also radiating fibrous aggregates (pseudomorphs after stibnite), botryoidal, or concentric. Secondary mineral formed by oxidation of stibnite and other antimony minerals. Yellow colour distinguishes it from other secondary antimony oxides. Minor ore of antimony.

Stibnite. Sb_2S_3. H = 2. Lead-grey, metallic (bluish iridescent tarnish), striated prismatic crystals; also acicular crystal aggregates, radiating columnar or bladed masses, and granular. Soluble in HCl. Most important ore of antimony.

Stichtite. $Mg_6Cr_2(CO_3)(OH)_{16} \bullet 4H_2O$. Light violet scaly micaceous masses associated with serpentine. Also occurs as blebs and veinlets in serpentine.

Stilbite. $NaCa_2Al_5Si_{13}O_{36} \cdot 14H_2O$. H = 4. Colourless, pink, or white platy crystals commonly forming sheaf-like aggregates. Vitreous, pearly lustre. Transparent. Sheaf-like form distinguishes it from other zeolites with which it is associated in volcanic rocks. Also occurs in metamorphic and granitic rocks.

Stillwellite. $(Ce,La,Ca)BSiO_5$. Grey, pink, brownish-yellow, brownish-red to brown translucent to opaque, hexagonal tabular or rhombohedral crystals; also massive, compact, porcelain-like. Waxy to resinous lustre. Occurs with other rare-element minerals in marble.

Stilpnomelane. $K(Fe,Al)_{10}Si_{12}O_{30}(OH)_{12}$. H = 4. Black, dark green, golden to reddish-brown foliated plates, fibrous aggregates. Associated with magnetite, hematite, goethite in iron deposits, and with chlorite and epidote in schist.

Stromeyerite. $CuAgS$. H = 2.5–3. Dark grey, metallic, with blue tarnish. Prismatic crystals or massive. Soluble in HNO_3. Distinguished from arsenopyrite by its darker colour and inferior hardness.

Strontiodresserite. $(Sr,Ca)(Al_2CO_3)_2(OH)_4 \cdot H_2O$. White silky flakes forming coatings; white spheres (1 mm in diameter). Effervesces in HCl. Associated with weloganite, strontianite, quartz in igneous sill rock, Francon quarry, Montréal, the type locality. Named for its chemical relationship to dresserite.

Strüverite. Black. Tantalum-rich variety of rutile.

Sudburyite. $(Pd,Ni)Sb$. Microscopic metallic grains occurring in cobaltite and maucherite. Identified by microscopic examination of polished section of ore minerals. Originally described from the Copper Cliff South and Frood mines, Sudbury, Ontario, and named for the locality.

Sulphur. S. H = 1.5–2.5. Yellow, reddish, greenish tabular, bipyramidal crystals; massive. Transparent; greasy to resinous lustre. Black when admixed with pyrite from which it alters.

Sunstone. A feldspar (orthoclase or oligoclase) containing flaky inclusions of goethite or hematite that cause bright copper-coloured reflections. Used as a gemstone.

Syenite. An igneous rock composed mainly of feldspar with little or no quartz. Used as a building stone.

Sylvanite. $(Au,Ag)Te_2$. H = 1.5–2. Light grey to dark grey, metallic; prismatic or tabular crystals, bladed aggregates, granular. Associated with native gold and tellurides in vein deposits. Distinguished from other gold tellurides by its inferior hardness.

Sylvite. KCl. H = 2.5. Colourless, white, orange-red cubic crystals, or granular massive. Vitreous lustre. Sectile. Bitter taste. Soluble in water. Occurs with halite and gypsum. Used in fertilizers.

Synchisite. $(Ce,La)Ca(CO_3)_2F$. H = 4.5. Yellow to brown tabular or platy aggregates. Greasy, vitreous, or subadamantine lustre. Translucent. Soluble in acids. Associated with other rare-element minerals in pegmatite. Not easily distinguished in the hand specimen.

Synchisite-Y. $(Y,Ce)Ca(CO_3)_2F$. H = 6–7. Small pink to reddish-brown prisms; massive granular. Associated with yttrium minerals. Also known as doverite.

Szaibelyite. $(Mg,Mn)(BO_2)(OH)$. $H = 3–3.5$. White, fine, fibrous or platy matted or hair-like aggregates. Silky lustre. Soluble in acids. Uncommon mineral not readily identified in the hand specimen.

Szmikite. $MnSO_4H_2O$. $H = 1.5$. White to pink, reddish stalactitic, botryoidal masses. Earthy. Secondary mineral found with manganese minerals.

Szomolnokite. $FeSO_4 \bullet H_2O$. $H = 2.5$. White to pinkish-white, fine, hair-like aggregates or finely granular encrustations; also botryoidal, globular crusts. Vitreous lustre. Metallic taste. Associated with pyrite and other iron sulphates from which it is not readily distinguishable in the hand specimen.

Talc. $Mg_3Si_4O_{10}(OH)_2$. $H = 1$. Grey, white, green, finely granular or foliated. Translucent with greasy feel. Massive impure varieties are known as steatite and soapstone, and because of their suitability for carving are used for ornamental purposes. Formed by alteration of magnesium silicates (olivine, pyroxene, amphibole, etc.) in igneous and metamorphic rocks. Used in cosmetics, ceramics, paint, plastic, rubber, chemical, roofing, and paper industries.

Tancoite. $HNa_2LiAl(PO_4)_2(OH)$. $H = 4–4.5$. Colourless to pink equant or tabular crystals, often elongated and commonly in parallel multiple growth. Transparent with vitreous lustre. Conchoidal fracture and two cleavages. Associated with lithiophosphate and apatite in spodumene-bearing pegmatite. Soluble in dilute HNO_3 and in HCl. Originally described from the Bernic Lake (Tanco) mine, Bernic Lake, Manitoba, for which it is named.

Tapiolite. $Fe(Ta,Nb)_2O_6$. $H = 6–6.5$. Black, short, prismatic or equant crystals with submetallic to subadamantine lustre. Rusty or greyish-brown to brownish-black streak. Occurs in granite pegmatite.

Tellurantimony. Sb_2Te_3. Pink, metallic, lath-like microscopic grains associated with altaite. Originally found in the Mattagami Lake mine, Mattagami, Quebec. Named for its composition.

Tellurobismuthite. Bi_2Te_3. $H = 1.5–2$. Dark grey, metallic, platy, foliated aggregates. Laminae flexible; sectile. Triangular striations on cleavage surfaces. Occurs in auriferous quartz veins. Accepted name is tellurobismuthite.

Temiskamite. Name was given to a bronze-coloured material with radiating structure occurring in the Elk Lake-Gowganda (Ontario) silver-cobalt deposits. Synonym for maucherite. Not a valid mineral name.

Tengerite. $CaY_3(CO_3)_4(OH)_3 \bullet 3H_2O$. Dull white, powdery, fibrous coating, or encrustations; associated with yttrium minerals from which it alters.

Tennantite. $(Cu,Fe)_{12}As_4S_{13}$. $H = 3–4.5$. Dark grey to greyish-black, metallic, tetrahedral crystals; compact to granular massive. Black, brown to red streak. Occurs in hydrothermal veins with copper, lead, zinc, and silver minerals. Forms a series with tetrahedrite, but is much less abundant.

Tenorite. CuO. $H = 3.5$. Steel-grey to black, metallic, platy, lath-like, scaly aggregates; also black, submetallic, earthy, or compact masses with conchoidal fracture. Associated with other copper minerals; melaconite occurs in the oxidized portion of copper deposits. Ore of copper.

Tetradymite. Bi_2Te_2S. H = 1.5–2. Light grey, metallic, indistinct pyramidal crystals; also bladed, foliated, or granular aggregates. Blades are flexible, inelastic. Tarnishes to dull or iridescent surfaces. Soils paper as does graphite. Occurs with telluride and sulphide minerals in gold-quartz veins formed at moderate to high temperatures, and in contact metamorphic deposits.

Tetrahedrite. $(Cu,Fe)_{12}Sb_4S_{13}$. H = 3–4.5. Dark grey to greyish-black, metallic, tetrahedral crystals; granular to compact massive. Black to brown streak. Ore of copper; silver-rich variety may be important ore of silver. Occurs with chalcopyrite, galena, pyrite, sphalerite, bornite, and argentite in hydrothermal veins. Forms a series with tennantite.

Tetranatrolite. $Na_2Al_2Si_3O_{10} \bullet 2H_2O$. White prismatic crystals and fibrous aggregates; earthy. Translucent to opaque; vitreous to dull lustre. Transparent in specimens freshly broken from the rock, becoming white, opaque, friable on exposure to air. Associated with natrolite, analcime, microcline in nepheline syenite at Mount Saint-Hilaire, Quebec. Named for its structure, tetragonal natrolite. Zeolite group.

Thaumasite. $Ca_3Si(OH)_6(CO_3)(SO_4) \bullet 12H_2O$. H = 3.5. Colourless to white, acicular or massive. Transparent to translucent; vitreous, silky lustre to greasy. Occurs with calcium silicate and sulphate minerals.

Thenardite. Na_2SO_4. H = 2.5–3. Colourless, white, greyish, reddish, yellowish, brownish, powdery; tabular, dipyramidal crystals. Dull to vitreous lustre. Formed from evaporation of salt lakes.

Thomsonite. $NaCa_2Al_5Si_5O_{20} \bullet 6H_2O$. H = 5–5.5. White, pinkish-white to reddish, light green radiating columnar or fibrous masses; also compact. Vitreous to pearly lustre. Transparent to translucent. Associated with other zeolites. Massive variety used as a gemstone.

Thorbastnaesite. $Th(Ca,Ce)(CO_3)_2F_2 \bullet H_2O$. White silky fibres forming spheres less than 1 mm in diameter; coatings. Associated with baddeleyite, zircon (cyrtolite) at the Francon quarry, Montréal.

Thorianite. ThO_2. H = 6.5. Dark grey to black cubic crystals or rounded grains. Dull to submetallic lustre. Grey streak. Radioactive. Soluble in HNO_3 and H_2SO_4. Occurs in pegmatite, crystalline limestone, stream gravels.

Thorite. $ThSiO_4$. H = 5. Black to reddish-brown tetragonal prisms with pyramidal terminations; also massive. Resinous to submetallic lustre. Conchoidal fracture. Radioactive. Distinguished by its crystal form, radioactivity. Source of thorium. Occurs in pegmatite, crystalline limestone, and hydrothermal veins.

Thorogummite. $Th(SiO_4)_{1-x}(OH)_{4x}$. Grey, light brown, yellowish brown to dark brown, earthy, nodular, massive; encrustation or replacement of thorite or thorium minerals. Secondary mineral formed from thorium minerals.

Thucholite. Hydrocarbon containing U, Th, rare earth elements, and silica. H = 3.5–4. Jet black with brilliant lustre and conchoidal fracture. Occurs in pegmatite. Not a valid mineral species.

Titanite (sphene). $CaTiSiO_5$. H = 6. Brown wedge-shaped crystals; also massive granular. May form cruciform twins. Adamantine lustre. White streak. Distinguished from other dark silicates by its crystal form, lustre, and colour.

Tochilinite. $6Fe_{0.9}S•5(Mg,Fe)(OH)_2$. Black, finely fibrous, acicular, flaky, or platy aggregates; bronze lustre. Occurs in serpentine and in serpentine-bearing marble. Distinguished from graphite by its bronze lustre. Alteration product of pyrrhotite.

Tomichite. $(V,Fe)_4Ti_3AsO_{13}(OH)$. Minute, black, opaque, tabular crystals. Black streak. Associated with vanadian muscovite and quartz.

Tonalite. A quartz-rich diorite containing hornblende and biotite as the chief dark minerals.

Topaz. $Al_2SiO_4(F,OH)_2$. Colourless, white, light blue, yellow, brown, grey, or green prismatic crystals with perfect basal cleavage; also massive granular. Vitreous lustre, transparent. Distinguished by its crystal habit, cleavage, and hardness. Used as a gemstone.

Tourmaline. $Na(Mg, Fe)_3Al_6(BO_3)_3Si_6O_{18}(O,OH,F)_4$. $H = 7.5$. Black, dark green, blue, pink, brown, or yellow prismatic crystals; also columnar, granular. Prism faces are vertically striated. Vitreous lustre. Conchoidal fracture. Distinguished by its triangular cross-section in prisms and by its striations. Used in the manufacture of pressure gauges; transparent varieties are used as gemstones. Mineral group consisting of several species including dravite, schorl, elbaite, and uvite.

Trachyte. A light-coloured lava composed essentially of orthoclase with minor biotite, amphibole, and/or pyroxene.

Trap rock. Dark-coloured, fine-grained dyke rock.

Trembathite. $(Mg,Fe)_3B_7O_{13}Cl$. $H = 6–8$. Colourless to light blue transparent rhombohedral crystals. Vitreous lustre. Occurs with hilgardite and halite. Originally described from the Salt Springs potash deposit, Sussex, New Brunswick, and named in honour of Professor Lowell T. Trembath, University of New Brunswick.

Tremolite. $Ca_2(Mg,Fe)_5Si_8O_{22}(OH)_2$. $H = 5–6$. White, grey, striated prismatic crystals, bladed crystal aggregates, or fibrous; perfect cleavage. Usually occurs in metamorphic rocks. Fibrous variety is used for asbestos. Monoclinic member of amphibole.

Triphylite. $LiFePO_4$. $H = 4–5$. Greenish to bluish grey, cleavable to compact massive; prismatic crystals rare. Transparent to translucent with vitreous to subresinous lustre. Occurs with lithium and phosphate minerals in granite pegmatite.

Troctolite. A gabbro with olivine as the dominant ferromagnesian component.

Trondhjemite. A light-coloured igneous rock composed mainly of Na-plagioclase with quartz and biotite.

Tuff. A rock formed from volcanic ash.

Tundrite. $Na_2Ce_2(Ti,Nb)SiO_8•4H_2O$. $H = 3$. Brownish or greenish-yellow acicular crystals occurring individually or forming spheres. Occurs in nepheline syenite.

Tungstenite. WS_2. $H = 2.5$. Dark grey, metallic, massive, or fine scaly aggregates. Associated with scheelite, wolframite, and sulphide minerals.

Tungstite. $WO_3•H_2O$. $H = 2.5$. Yellow to yellowish-green aggregates of microscopic plates, or powdery to earthy masses. Resinous or pearly lustre. Oxidation product of tungsten minerals.

Tungusite. $Ca_4Fe_2Si_6O_{15}(OH)_6$. H ~ 2. Green to yellow-green platy aggregates resembling chlorite. Pearly lustre. Associated with analcime and other zeolites in lava.

Tvalchrelidzeite. $Hg_{12}(Sb,As)_8S_{15}$. Dark grey, metallic, granular aggregates with dark reddish tint. Adamantine lustre. Associated with cinnabar and realgar.

Twinnite. $Pb(Sb,As)_2S_4$. Black, metallic, minute grains. Streak is black with brownish tint. Rare mineral associated with other sulphosalts. Originally described from a prospect pit near Madoc, Ontario.

Type locality. Locality from which a mineral species was originally described.

Ulexite. $NaCaB_5O_6(OH)_6•5H_2O$. H = 1. White with silky lustre. Occurs as nodules composed of fine fibres and as compact fibrous veins. Source of borax. Occurs in gypsum deposits in Nova Scotia and New Brunswick.

Ullmannite. $NiSbS$. H = 5–5.5. Silver-white to grey, metallic, cubic, octahedral, or pyritohedral crystals with striations on cube faces. Greyish-black streak. Perfect cleavage. Occurs with nickeline and other nickel minerals in vein deposits. Distinguished from pyrite by its colour.

Umangite. Cu_3Se_2. H = 3. Bluish-black grains or massive granular. Metallic lustre. Associated with copper sulphide and selenide minerals such as chalcocite, chalcomenite, and chalcopyrite.

Unakite. A rock consisting of pink to orange-red feldspar, epidote, and some quartz. Used as an ornamental stone.

Uraconite. Probably a uranium sulphate. Yellow to green, earthy, nodular, scaly, or botryoidal crust. Not a valid mineral species.

Uraninite. UO_2. H = 5–6. Black, brownish-black cubic or octahedral crystals; also massive, botryoidal. Submetallic, pitchy to dull lustre. Uneven to conchoidal fracture. Radioactive. Distinguished by its high specific gravity (10.3 to 10.9), crystal form, and radioactivity.

Uranophane. $(H_3O)_2Ca(UO_2)_2(SiO_4)_2•3H_2O$. H = 2–3. Yellow fibrous, radiating aggregates; massive. Occurs with uraninite from which it alters.

Uranothorite. $(Th,U)SiO_4$. H = 4.5–5. Black prismatic crystals, grains. Pitchy lustre. May have orange-coloured sunburst effect on enclosing rock. Radioactive. Occurs in granitic and pegmatitic rocks. Granular variety distinguished from thorite and uraninite by X-ray methods. Variety of thorite containing uranium. Not a valid mineral name.

Uranpyrochlore. $(U,Ca,Ce)_2(Nb,Ta)_2O_6(OH,F)$. H = 4.5. Yellowish-brown to black octahedral crystals, or massive. Resinous to adamantine lustre. Occurs in granite pegmatite. Pyrochlore group.

Valentinite. Sb_2O_3. H = 2.5–3. Colourless, white to greyish prismatic or tabular striated crystal aggregates; also massive with granular or fibrous structure. Adamantine to pearly lustre. Transparent. Associated with stibnite and secondary antimony oxides resulting from oxidation of metallic antimony minerals.

Valleriite. $4(Fe,Cu)S•3(Mg,Al)(OH)_2$. Very soft, sooty. Bronze-black, platy, massive with perfect cleavage. Occurs in high-temperature copper deposits.

Veatchite. $Sr_2B_{11}O_{15}(OH)_5 \bullet H_2O$. H = 2. Colourless, transparent, platy or prismatic crystals; white fibrous masses with silky lustre. Occurs with howlite, colemanite, and other borate minerals.

Vermiculite. $Mg_3Si_4O_{10}(OH)_2 \bullet xH_2O$. H = 1.5. Silvery-amber or light brown, flaky, sheet-like aggregates. Pearly lustre. Expands or exfoliates on heating, which distinguishes it from mica. Formed by alteration of phlogopite and biotite. Used as an insulator in the construction industry, for concrete and plaster, as a lubricant, and as a soil conditioner.

Vesuvianite. $Ca_{10}Mg_2Al_4(SiO_4)_5(Si_2O_7)_2(OH)_4$. H = 7. Yellow, brown, green, violet transparent, prismatic, or pyramidal crystals with vitreous lustre; also massive, granular, compact, or pulverulent. Distinguished from other silicates by its tetragonal crystal form; massive variety is distinguished by its ready fusibility and intumescence in a blowpipe flame. Also known as idocrase. Transparent varieties are used as a gemstone.

Villiaumite. NaF. H = 2–2.5. Dark red, pink, orange, finely crystalline or massive. Transparent; vitreous. Occurs in nepheline syenite.

Vinogradovite. $(Na,Ca,K)_4Ti_4AlSi_6O_{23} \bullet 2H_2O$. H = 4. Colourless to white fibrous and spherical aggregates; prismatic crystals less common. Transparent; vitreous. Occurs in nepheline syenite.

Violarite. $FeNi_2S_4$. H = 4.5–5.5. Light grey, brilliant metallic; tarnishes to violet-grey. Massive. Distinguished by its violet tarnish. Associated with copper, nickel, and iron sulphides in vein deposits. Rare mineral.

Vivianite. $Fe_3(PO_4)_2 \bullet 8H_2O$. H = 1.5–2. Colourless transparent on fresh surfaces, becoming blue, greenish-blue to dark blue translucent due to oxidation. Vitreous to dull lustre. Prismatic crystals; bladed, globular, fibrous, powdery to earthy aggregates. Streak is colourless to bluish white, quickly altering to dark blue or brown. Soluble in acids. Darkens in H_2O_2. Occurs as a secondary mineral in metallic ore deposits and as a weathering product of iron-manganese phosphates in pegmatite.

Vlasovite. $Na_2ZrSi_4O_{11}$. Colourless to light brown crystals and grains. Vitreous, pearly, or greasy lustre. Excellent cleavage. Occurs in alkalic rocks.

Voggite. $Na_2Zr(PO_4)(CO_3)(OH) \bullet 2H_2O$. Colourless, transparent, acicular, microscopic crystals; white matted fibres. Occurs in centimetric cavities in an amygdaloidal basalt dyke cutting a weloganite-bearing sill at the Francon quarry, Montréal, the type locality. Resembles dawsonite. Name in honour of its discoverer, mineral collector Adolf Vogg of Arnprior, Ontario.

Volkovskite. $KCa_4[B_9O_8(OH)_4]_4[B(OH)_3]_2Cl \bullet 4H_2O$. H = 2.5. Colourless to pink thin platy crystals. Transparent with vitreous lustre. Occurs with other borate minerals in potash deposits.

Voltaite. $K_2Fe_9(SO_4)_{12} \bullet 18H_2O$. H = 3. Greenish-black to black, dark green cubic or octahedral crystals; also massive granular. Resinous lustre. Greyish-green streak and conchoidal fracture. Decomposed by water, leaving a yellow precipitate. Soluble in acids. Associated with other iron sulphate minerals.

Wacke. A sandstone consisting of generally unsorted angular mineral and rock fragments in a clay-silt matrix.

Wad. A field term used for substances consisting mainly of manganese oxides.

Wakefieldite. YVO_4. H = 5. Amber, yellow, brownish, white, grey, pulverulent; coatings. Dull lustre. Occurs in pegmatite with rare-element minerals. Named for Wakefield Lake, Quebec, which is near the Evans-Lou mine, the type locality.

Wallrock. Rock forming the walls of a vein, dyke, or other ore deposit.

Warwickite. $(Mg,Ti,Fe,Al)_2(BO_3)O$. H = 3.5–4. Black opaque prismatic crystals without terminations, rounded grains, granular aggregates. Adamantine to submetallic, dull, or pearly lustre. May have coppery-red tarnish on the surface. Occurs with spinel, chondrodite, serpentine in crystalline limestone.

Waterlime. A clayey limestone containing alumina, silica, and lime in the proper proportions to produce cement by the addition of water. Also known as 'cement rock'.

Wehrlite. Mixture of hessite (Ag_2Te) and pilsenite (Bi_4Te). Not a valid mineral species.

Weloganite. $Sr_3Na_2Zr(CO_3)_6 \bullet 3H_2O$. H = 3.5. Transparent yellow to orange-yellow, colourless prismatic crystals terminated by pyramids; also massive. Conchoidal fracture. Vitreous lustre. Effervesces in HCl. Originally found at the Francon quarry, Montréal, and named for Sir William E. Logan, first director of the Geological Survey of Canada.

Whitlockite. $Ca_9(Mg,Fe)H(PO_4)_7$. H = 5. Colourless to white, grey, or yellowish rhombohedral crystals; granular to earthy massive. Transparent to translucent with vitreous to subresinous lustre. Soluble in dilute acids. Occurs in phosphate rock deposits and in pegmatite.

Willemite. Zn_2SiO_4. H = 5.5. Colourless, yellow, green, white, reddish brown, massive or granular; also prismatic crystals. Vitreous lustre. Soluble in HCl. May fluoresce green. Nonfluorescent variety difficult to identify in hand specimen. Minor ore of zinc.

Wilsonite. An altered scapolite (to muscovite). Pink, rose-red, mauve to violet. Translucent variety used as a gemstone. Named for Dr. James Wilson of Perth, Ontario, where it was originally found. Not a valid mineral name. Pinite is the preferred term for muscovite alteration from scapolite, feldspar, or spodumene.

Witherite. $BaCO_3$. H = 3–3.5. Colourless to white, greyish, yellowish, greenish, or brownish six-sided dipyramids and prisms; also tabular, globular, botryoidal, fibrous, or granular massive. Transparent to translucent with vitreous to resinous lustre. Effervesces in dilute HCl. Occurs with barite and galena in low-temperature hydrothermal veins.

Wittichenite. Cu_3BiS_3. H = 2–3. Grey, metallic, tabular crystals, or columnar, acicular aggregates; massive. Fuses easily. Soluble in HCl and gives off H_2S; decomposed by HNO_3. Alters readily to yellowish-brown, red, blue, and eventually forms covellite.

Wodginite. $(Ta,Nb,Sn,Mn,Fe)_{16}O_{32}$. H ~ 6. Reddish-brown to dark brown and black irregular grains. Submetallic lustre. Occurs in granitic rocks. Ore of tantalum with uses in electrolytic, nuclear reactor, and aircraft industries.

Wöhlerite. $NaCa_2(Zr,Nb)Si_2O_8(O,OH,F)$. H = 5.5–6. Yellow, brown, orange tabular or prismatic crystals. Vitreous lustre. Occurs in nepheline syenite. Rare mineral.

Wolframite. $(Fe,Mn)WO_4$. $H = 4-4.5$. Dark brown to black, short, prismatic striated crystals; lamellar or granular. Submetallic to adamantine lustre. Perfect cleavage in one direction. Distinguishing features are colour, cleavage, and high specific gravity (7.1–7.5). Ore of tungsten.

Wollastonite. $CaSiO_3$. $H = 5$. White to greyish white compact, cleavable, or fibrous masses with splintery or woody structure. Vitreous to silky lustre. May fluoresce in ultraviolet light. Distinguished from tremolite ($H = 6$) and sillimanite ($H = 7$) by its inferior hardness and by its solubility in HCl. Occurs in crystalline limestone and skarn zones. Used in ceramics and paints.

Woodhouseite. $CaAl_3(PO_4)(SO_4)(OH)_6$. $H = 4.5$. Violet, pink, white, or colourless tiny, pseudocubic striated crystals. Vitreous, transparent. Secondary mineral associated with topaz, lazulite, pyrophyllite.

Wurtzite. $(Zn,Fe)S$. $H = 3.5-4$. Brownish-black resinous crystals (pyramidal, prismatic, tabular) or fibrous, columnar, concentrically banded crusts. Like sphalerite, but has darker colour and brown streak. Occurs with sulphide minerals.

Wulfenite. $PbMoO_4$. $H = 3.5-4$. Orange to yellow, orange-brown, tan, brown transparent to translucent square to thin tabular, octahedral, or prismatic crystals; massive, granular. Resinous. Secondary mineral in oxidation zone associated with vanadinite, mimetite, pyromorphite, galena, cerussite.

Xanthoconite. Ag_3AsS_3. $H = 2-3$. Dark red to orange or brown tabular or lath-shaped crystals. Adamantine lustre. Orange-yellow streak. Fuses readily. Associated with ruby silver; at LaRose mine and at Keeley mine, Cobalt, Ontario.

Xenotime. YPO_4. $H = 4.5$. Reddish or yellowish-brown, grey prismatic crystals similar to zircon. Vitreous to resinous lustre. Distinguished from zircon by its inferior hardness. Occurs in pegmatite and alkalic igneous rocks.

Xonotlite. $Ca_6Si_6O_{17}(OH)_2$. $H = 6.5$. Pink to white, microscopic to fine, compact fibrous masses. Vitreous to waxy lustre. Very tough. Weathered surface is chalk white. Pink variety is used as a gemstone.

Yarrowite. Cu_9S_8. Dark grey to black, metallic, flaky or platy (microscopic) aggregates with green-violet iridescence. Associated with chalcopyrite, bornite, and other copper minerals from which it alters. Indistinguishable in the hand specimen from spionkopite. Originally described from the sandstone and quartzite copper deposits in the Yarrow and Spionkop Creeks area, southwestern Alberta; named for the locality.

Yofortierite. $Mn_5Si_8O_{20}(OH)_2(OH_2)_4 \bullet 8-9H_2O$. $H = 2.5$. Pink to violet radiating fibres. Associated with analcime, serandite, eudialyte, polylithionite, aegirine, microcline, and albite in pegmatite veins cutting nepheline syenite at Mount Saint-Hilaire, Quebec, the type locality. Named in honour of Dr. Y.O. Fortier, Arctic geologist and director (1964–1973) of the Geological Survey of Canada.

Yttrofluorite. Yttrian fluorite with yttrium substituting for Ca. Yellow, brown, violet, or blue, granular massive. Density and hardness are somewhat greater than in fluorite. Not a valid mineral name.

Yttrotantalite. $(Y,U,Fe)(Ta,Nb)O_4$. $H = 5–5.5$. Black to dark brown prismatic or tabular crystals; irregular grains, massive. Submetallic, vitreous to greasy lustre and conchoidal fracture. Grey streak. Occurs in pegmatite.

"Yukon diamond". A term used in the North for concentrically banded black, dark brown, or tan cassiterite pebbles found in placers in the Yukon Territory. Also known as 'wood tin'. Used as a gemstone.

Yukonite. $Ca_3Fe_3(AsO_4)_4OH•12H_2O$. $H = 2–3$. Black to dark brown irregular masses. Decrepitates at low heat and when immersed in water. Easily fusible. Found originally at Tagish Lake, Yukon Territory. Named for the locality.

Zavaritskite. $BiOF$. Yellow to grey, granular to powdery, with greasy to submetallic lustre. Associated with bismutite, bismuthinite, bismuth.

Zeolites. A group of hydrous silicates of related composition, but differing crystallization; water is given off continuously when heated, but can be taken up again. Heulandite, chabazite, stilbite, natrolite, analcime belong to this group. Formed from magmatic or hydrothermal solutions, or by alteration of feldspar minerals. Used as water softeners, as gas and impurity absorbents, and in heat reservoirs.

Zinc. Zn. $H = 2$. Light grey, metallic crystals, grains, scales. Brittle. Perfect cleavage. Formed from oxidation of sphalerite.

Zinkenite. $Pb_9Sb_{22}S_{42}$. $H = 3–3.5$. Grey, metallic, columnar to radial fibrous aggregates, massive; indistinct slender striated prisms. Tarnishes to iridescent surfaces. Occurs with stibnite, jamesonite, and other sulphosalts, and galena, pyrite, and sphalerite in veins formed at low to moderate temperatures.

Zircon. $ZrSiO_4$. $H = 7.5$. Pink, reddish to greyish-brown tetragonal prisms terminated by pyramids; also colourless, green, violet, or grey. May form knee-shaped twins. Adamantine lustre. May be radioactive. Distinguished by its crystal form, hardness. Ore of zirconium and hafnium. Used in moulding sand, ceramics, and refractory industries; transparent varieties are used as gemstones.

Zoisite. $Ca_2Al_3(SiO_4)_3(OH)$. $H = 6.5$. Grey to brownish-grey, yellowish-brown, violet-pink, green aggregates of long prismatic crystals (striated); also compact fibrous to columnar masses. Vitreous to pearly lustre. Transparent to translucent. Massive variety distinguished from amphibole by its perfect cleavage. Transparent varieties used as gemstones; pink variety known as 'thulite', transparent blue variety, as 'tanzanite'.

References: 14; 16; 26; 49; 136; 139; 140; 141; 158.

CHEMICAL SYMBOLS FOR SELECTED ELEMENTS

Ag - silver
Al - aluminium
As - arsenic
Au -gold
B - boron
Ba - barium
Be - beryllium
Bi - bismuth
Br - bromine
C - carbon
Ca - calcium
Cd - cadmium
Ce - cerium
Cl - chlorine

Co - cobalt
Cr - chromium
Cs - cesium
Cu - copper
Dy - dysprosium
Er - erbium
F - fluorine
Fe - iron
Ga - gallium
Gd - gadolinium
Ge - germanium
H - hydrogen
Hf - hafnium
Hg - mercury
I - iodine
In - indium
Ir - iridium
K - potassium
La - lanthanum
Li - lithium
Mg - magnesium

Mn - manganese
Mo - molybdenum
N - nitrogen
Na - sodium
Nb - niobium
Nd - neodymium
Ni - nickel
O - oxygen
P - phosphorus
Pb - lead
Pd - palladium
Pt - platinum
Rb - rubidium
Re - rhenium
Rh - rhodium
Ru - ruthenium
S - sulphur
Sb - antimony
Sc - scandium
Se - selenium
Si - silicon
Sm - samarium
Sn - tin
Sr - strontium
Ta - tantalum
Te - tellurium
Th - thorium
Ti - titanium
Tl - thallium
U - uranium
V - vanadium
W - tungsten
Y - yttrium
Yb - ytterbium
Zn - zinc
Zr - zirconium

INDEX OF MINERALS, ROCKS, AND FOSSILS

INDEX OF MINES AND OCCURRENCES

Contents
This CD-ROM contains the full contents of Miscellaneous Report 48 in .pdf format, including any maps or oversized figures.

System requirements
PC with 486 or greater processor, or Mac® with OS® X v. 10.2.2 or later; Adobe® Reader® v. 6.0 (included for both PC and Mac) or later; video resolution of 1280 x 1024.

Quick start
This is a Windows®-based autoplay disk. Should the autoplay fail, navigate to the root of your CD-ROM drive and double-click on the autoplay.exe file. Mac® users must use this method to begin.

****

Contenu
Ce CD-ROM renferme le contenu intégral du Rapport divers 48 en format .pdf, y compris les figures surdimensionnées ou les cartes, s'il y a lieu.

Configuration requise
PC avec processeur 486 ou plus rapide, ou Mac® avec OS® X v. 10.2.2 ou ultérieure; Reader® v. 6 d'Adobe® (fourni pour PC et Mac) ou version ultérieure; résolution vidéo de 1280 x 1024.

Démarrage rapide
Ceci est un disque à lancement automatique pour les systèmes d'exploitation Windows®. Si le lancement automatique ne fonctionne pas, allez au répertoire principal du CD-ROM et faites un double clic sur le fichier autoplay.exe. Les utilisateurs de systèmes Mac® doivent procéder de cette façon pour débuter la consultation.